International Boundary
Provincial Boundary
Aimak Boundary . . . .
Railways ++++++++
Roads
Great Wall

P9-ASN-489

RUSSIAN FEDERATION

BURYAT
MONGOL
REPUBLIC

Baikal

Ulan Ude

Chita

khbator

R Onon

R Amur

KHINGGAN MTS

MANCHURIA

Mt Burhan Kaldon

Choibalsan

Ulan-Bator

HENTEI AIMAK

R Kerulen

Underhan

Harbin

Ulan Hot

Xilinhot

JILIN

Erenhot

INNER MONGOLIA

AUTONOMOUS REGION

Changchun

GOBI

Bayan Obo

Ulanhad

ESERT

LIAONING

HAN MTS

Baotou

Hohhot

Zhangjiakou

Chengde

Ejin Horo Qi

Datong

Peking

ORDOS

Yellow River

Tianjin

HEBEI

nchuan

SHANXI

YELLOW SEA

SHAANXI

Xian

THE LOST COUNTRY

THE LOST COUNTRY

Mongolia Revealed

JASPER BECKER

Hodder & Stoughton
LONDON SYDNEY AUCKLAND

Extracts from MARCO POLO: THE TRAVELS
translated by Ronald Latham (Penguin Classics, 1986),
Copyright © Ronald Latham, 1958 are reproduced by permission of
Penguin Books Ltd.

British Library Cataloguing in Publication Data

Becker, Jasper
  Lost Country: Mongolia Revealed
  I. Title
  951.7

ISBN 0-340-55665-X

Published by Hodder and Stoughton,
a division of Hodder and Stoughton Ltd,
Mill Road, Dunton Green, Sevenoaks, Kent TN13 2YA
Editorial Office: 47 Bedford Square, London WC1B 3DP

Photoset in Ehrhardt by SX Composing Ltd, Rayleigh, Essex
Printed in Great Britain by St. Edmundsbury Press, Bury St. Edmunds, Suffolk

Contents

Preface

A Note on the Spelling of Names

The spelling of virtually all the names given in this book has posed a minor problem since they all vary. In addition, the names of the countries, cities and regions have changed, often several times, for political reasons. The Soviet Union no longer exists, the People's Republic of Mongolia is now the Republic of Mongolia, Leningrad is now St Petersburg and so on.

I have chosen to use the name or spelling which was most appropriate in the context of each passage and I make no claim to be consistent. As at the time I went to St Petersburg, it was still referred to as Leningrad, I use the latter name.

Also the spelling of Chinese names varies because there are two different spelling systems – Wade-Giles and Pinyin. For instance Peking can also be written as Beijing. Again I have used the same principle, choosing whichever struck me as the most appropriate.

The Latin spelling of Mongol names also poses a problem as there are no hard and fast rules. Ulan Bator is sometimes written Ulaan Baator, for example, and I make no claims to have followed any scientific principle in my choice but merely used whatever seemed to me to be the most suitable.

It should be noted that Mongols normally just use a single name and it is not impolite to refer to them without using two, as Westerners prefer.

One

Peking

In the heart of Asia lies the enormous and forgotten land of the Mongols. The Great Wall marching westwards defines its southern boundaries, the still waters of Lake Baikal mark the northern limits and in the west the wooded peaks of the Mountains of Heaven and the swampy wilderness of the Saynsk range ring the frontier. Beyond this natural border a sea of grass rolls all the way across Kozukhstan, the Ukraine and over the Carpathian Mountains into Central Europe.

A land of bloody conquerors, of wandering tribes, of prophets, shamans and mystic kings. A country as immense as North America where the wolf still stalks the wild horse across a treeless plain and where the eagle hangs in a blue sky searching the bare mountains for the shy argali sheep that no shepherd has ever tamed.

The first Western travellers to cross those unmapped mountains or to traverse the Gobi's barren wastes since the fall of the Mongol empire had done so only a century ago. They found that the savage warriors whose ferocity had terrified the medieval world had become devout Buddhists ruled by a depraved and syphilitic God-King. The princely descendants of Genghis Khan had been reduced to penurious debtors, disarmed at last by the petty legerdemain of profit and loss.

'Cowardice is the most striking trait of his character. Two centuries of Chinese rule and the warlike disposition has been systematically extinguished,' Lt.-Col. Nicholas Prejevalsky, the famous Russian explorer observed in the 1880s.

Then for the last seventy years a blanket of darkness dropped over this vast region as it fell under Communist rule. Since the 1920s few

Westerners had been allowed to enter what became the world's second Communist state. Once more Mongolia became a remote, forgotten hinterland.

Sometimes when I lived in Peking, I would stand on the Great Wall at the top of one of its many towers and look north where the ragged Western Hills dwindle away in deepening shades of purple. Just beyond, the yellow plains of Mongolia begin.

Mongolia is that close and the Wall itself is only an hour or two's drive from Peking. China seemed to me a crowded, regimented and oppressive place and the thought of those grand and empty lands just beyond the Wall slowly took a grip on my imagination.

Somewhere out there lay, half-neglected, half-hidden, the ancient city of Karakorum, the capital of an empire so great that half the world's peoples had lived under its shadow. It would be fine, I thought, to camp beside its ruins. For days on end one would travel, seeing nothing more than the distant flocks of this ancient race of shepherd warriors.

> A tent is my house,
> of felt are my walls:
> Raw flesh my food
> with mare's milk to drink.

So wrote a Chinese princess in a famous poem, homesick after being sent to live among those barbarian tribes. She dreamed of being able to fly home like the yellow stork but I thought I might rather like it there.

But what was it really like now? What had happened to the Mongols since the 1920s?

In Peking I had once met some Mongols at a wedding party in a bare flat in a soulless tower block with concrete floors. They seemed no more real to me than if I had met an ancient Egyptian on a street in London. They looked so ordinary in their white cotton shirts and standard grey trousers yet I stared at them, seeing the enigmatic survivors of a vanished world.

This book begins in Peking where I worked as a journalist for many years and first became interested in Mongolia. It is not about a single unbroken journey although it does traverse the continent from China, through Mongolia and the Soviet Union.

Inner Mongolia was, as it happened, the first part of Central Asia to become accessible to the outside world when China began to open its doors in 1980. So I went there first in 1988 although much of it was and remains closed to foreigners, and the Communist Party still keeps a tight grip on its people.

It was a couple of years later that I was able to visit Outer Mongolia and was then lucky enough to witness its transformation from deepest Stalinism. From 1990 onwards, it embraced democracy and private ownership but more interesting than that, the Mongols began to rediscover themselves. In the countryside, the old ways of living and thinking resurfaced for the first time in generations.

With the collapse of central authority in the USSR, it was also, much to my own surprise, easy to wander through those republics or regions inhabited by Mongol tribes.

By chance rather than intention I found myself unravelling a history which until now has been hidden or at least obscured beyond all recognition. The history of all the Mongols since 1917 began to see the light of day along with a new pan-Mongolian political movement. A new nationalism was gripping peoples in all parts of the Soviet empire and, in many ways, it seemed that by describing the Mongols, I was recording changes which were taking place all over the region.

Perhaps it is odd, reversing the usual direction of travel books by going from East to West, but Peking is not altogether a foolish place to start.

Peking was after all the capital of the greatest Mongol emperor of them all, Kublai Khan. After conquering China, he decided to move from Karakorum and he chose Peking as the site of his new capital for a particular reason.

It is a halfway house, a borderpost, where the great crowded river valleys of China and their countless rice paddies meet the boundless steppe. Here Kublai Khan could keep an eye on both halves of his empire.

Living there nowadays one almost forgot just how close to the Gobi desert it is. The camels which used to amble through the streets delivering coal thirty or forty years ago have now vanished. It was only in the spring that I would be reminded when strong winds blow a fine dust through the streets. The dust would invade through the doors and windowframes and in the morning I would find it deposited in small drifts as if the desert had laid claim to my floor.

The Mongolians have never forgiven Kublai Khan for moving the capital, preferring to remember his grandfather Genghis Khan, but he is perhaps the Mongol we know best.

Marco Polo worked for Kublai Khan as a senior official for many years and left us a lavish account of the magnificence of his court. It inspired Samuel Taylor Coleridge's poem *Kubla Khan* in which the Khan listens to 'ancestral voices prophesying war' in Xanadu, his

3

pleasure palace.

Marco Polo wrote that Kublai Khan 'was the mightiest man, whether in respect of his subjects or of territory or of treasure who is in the world today or who have ever been, from Adam our first parent down to the present moment'.

Marco Polo, biased though he is, is probably correct in this. When Kublai Khan ruled in the thirteenth century, his personal empire included Mongolia, all of China, Tibet, Korea, Burma, Indo-China, and his brothers or cousins ruled over what was the Soviet Union, as well as Iran and Iraq.

More than that, he sent his navies to Japan, Sri Lanka and Java. Even in 1638, Christian missionaries found people on Java still speaking Mongolian.

In some ways his conquests gave shape to the modern world as we know it. The Japanese developed a new sense of self-confidence after defeating his seaborne invasions for which they thanked a divine wind, the Kamikaze. Thailand emerged as a separate state only after Kublai Khan's armies defeated the ruler of Burma and emptied the temple city of Pagan. China's claims on Tibet stem from his conquests.

Despite all this nothing at all remains in Peking to commemorate him. The visitor can walk around the Forbidden City and of all his vast riches only a large jar of green jade used to store pickles is left to see. And yet it was his architects who designed the Forbidden City, and its exterior walls still follow his plans. His slaves excavated the chain of lakes which grace its interior, among them the Zhongnanhai which lends its name to the compound from which today's Communist leaders rule their empire.

Indeed for a long time, it never really dawned on me that for 150 years Peking had been a Mongolian city. You have to look very hard indeed to find any trace of their occupation. It is as if the English had decided to pretend the Norman Conquest had never taken place.

Yet set beside Kublai Khan, William the Conqueror is a petty chieftain and for the Chinese, the Mongol invasions were not so much an occupation as a holocaust.

'The bones of the slaughtered rose mountain high, the earth was thick with human fat and the rotting corpses gave rise to a human plague,' ran one contemporary report of the conquest of northern China.

Kublai Khan was born on September 23rd, 1215, the year in which Genghis Khan seized Peking, then the capital of the Jin dynasty of Jurchen tribesmen.

It is said that Genghis Khan was only narrowly dissuaded from massacring the entire population of northern China, some 45 million people.

'They are of no use to us. It would be better to exterminate them entirely and let the grass grow so that we can have grazing land for our horses,' Chinese historians quote him saying.

Kublai Khan conquered southern China which was ruled by the Sung Dynasty and which considered itself to be the true guardian of Chinese culture.

Taking the two parts of China together, the Mongol conquests brought the deaths of 18 million and by the end of Mongol rule, which the Chinese refer to as the Yuan Dynasty, the population of 100 million had been reduced by some 30 million.

Estimates vary and scholars dispute whether Mongol cruelty alone was to blame. Floods, earthquakes and the Black Death also took their toll.

The lasting damage was of a different nature. One French historian has written that 'it was as if during the Mongol domination a spring had been broken in the Chinese soul ... the Chinese organism had suffered such an intense shock, had been so fatigued that as soon as the storm was over, it recoiled tightly and timorously within itself.'

Although so few physical reminders of the Mongol occupation are visible in Peking, some features of life in twentieth-century Peking bear more than a passing resemblance to the city Marco Polo described.

He said Kublai Khan so feared an insurrection by the citizens of Peking that he destroyed the original city with its narrow streets and built a new one. He selected only the most politically trustworthy as its inhabitants.

By some odd quirk of history, streets in Peking are still known by a corruption of a Mongol word and called *Hutongs*, especially the narrow alleyways in the part known before 1949 as the Tartar quarter.

Nowadays if you stand looking down the Avenue of Eternal Peace (Changan Dajie), the huge boulevard which cuts the city from east to west, it looks just like the description Marco Polo has left of the city.

'I assure you the streets are so broad and straight that from the tip of the wall above one gate you can see along the whole length of the road to the gate opposite,' he wrote, implying that this design was to enable security forces to keep close watch on the city.

The Italian also details a system of police control much like that in Peking after the Tiananmen insurrection.

Once the town bell has rung the hour 'no one ventures abroad in the city except in case of childbirth or illness: and those who are called out by such emergencies are obliged to carry lights. Every night there are guards riding about the city in troops of thirty or forty. If anyone is found they are promptly arrested and clapped into prison.'

The police state the Mongols established has merely been modernised. Some scholars describe the Mongol's surveillance apparatus as one of the institutional marvels of Chinese history. It enabled no more than 200,000 Mongols to control 100 million subjects.

Every householder had to hang outside his door a list of the inhabitants and inns had to report the arrival of all guests, specifying the day and hour.

The Mongols also categorised the population according to their political reliability. In the first grade came the Mongols themselves, then foreigners such as Marco Polo, northern Chinese and in the last most suspect class, the southern Chinese.

The Mongols preferred to rule from behind a screen. High administrative positions were often held by Chinese or the likes of Marco Polo but they were shadowed by Mongols who wielded real power.

All this bears a close resemblance to the way the Communist Party rules China. Such a system is perhaps the only manner whereby a small minority of outsiders can maintain control over such a large mass.

How then did the Mongols lose power?

It is something of a mystery. Most historians simply assume that in time the soft luxuries of Chinese civilisation sapped their willpower and cooled their military ardour.

In fact this is not borne out by the evidence. The grandchildren of Kublai Khan were frequently fighting amongst themselves. Before the last Yuan Dynasty emperor, Toghon Timur, was expelled in 1368 he was warned of the unrest brewing among the Chinese. His chief minister proposed liquidating everyone in China named Wang, Liu, Li or Chao, which just happens to include the great majority of the population.

It suggests that Mongol ferocity had scarcely abated.

Peking tradition records how the rebellion was organised. At the autumn moon festival the Pekingese eat small round cakes containing little pieces of paper on which the signal for the revolt was supposedly given, just as the Viennese began baking croissants to celebrate Christendom's victory over the Turks. After the Chinese Communist victory the tradition was forgotten in the interests of inter-racial harmony although the cakes are still eaten.

The downfall of the Mongol Yuan Dynasty seems related to two things, curious in themselves, which continued to crop up throughout my journey. One was a preoccupation with mysticism and the other was a recurrence of millenarian movments.

It almost seemed as if history was a maze of mirrors where the same images appeared whichever way you turned. The belief that a new age, a golden era was imminent always seemed to be connected with outbreaks of violence.

Marco Polo recorded Kublai Khan's taste for the miraculous and magical. He enjoyed having representatives of each religion competing for his favour – shamans, Taoists, Muslims, Christians, Buddhists and Confucians all took part in debates and demonstrations of their powers.

Marco Polo said he was so obsessed by augury that he would do nothing without first consulting his astrologers of whom he employed 5,000 in Peking alone.

The Tibetan lamas impressed him the most and in one display of their supernatural powers they supposedly caused his winecup to rise unaided to his lips. A close link between the royal court and Tibetan lamaism was established.

By the time his grandchildren were in power, the imperial palace seems to have been gripped by a peculiar Tantric and Buddhist cult.

Contemporary Chinese accounts suggest that Toghon Timur and his entourage practised black magic rites including sexual orgies under the instructions of Tibetan lamas in a part of the Forbidden City called the 'Palace of Deep Clarity'.

'In front of the emperor, naked men and women had sexual intercourse together. Sometimes princes and their subjects lay under one blanket together, even the underage royal princes took part,' one scandalised contemporary reported, adding that hundreds of girls were selected and brought to the court from around the country.

'The emperor and his friends wore the clothes of Buddhist priests,' the account continues, 'with golden emblems of the Buddha and rosaries in their hands. The sixteen harem girls were also dressed in the gold and red of the Buddhist order with ivory crowns and they performed the dance of the wild geese.'

This account is rather vague and on first sight seems to support the contention that the Mongols had become so decadent they were incapable of firm rule. However, later on the journey I found out more about these strange rites and that they have continued in Mongolia right down to this century.

Another cause of the Yuan Dynasty's downfall was a millenarian movement led by an army which became known as the Red Turbans after the distinctive headdress of its members. By an odd coincidence they were also known as Red Guards or the Red Army.

They proclaimed that a new age of universal happiness was dawning, and the army was led by a man who claimed to be a reincarnation of the Maitreya, or future Buddha. The Maitreya is the messiah or saviour of Buddhism and so the arrival of his reincarnation corresponds to the Second Coming.

A succession of rebellions was organised by secret societies espousing these beliefs. Secret societies are the traditional means throughout Chinese history of organising an insurgency since only in this way can the participants evade the police surveillance system.

One of these was the White Lotus Society which began in Canton and espoused a mixture of Manichean and Buddhist ideas. They believed that a great battle between the forces of light and dark was coming in which the King of Light (also the Maitreya) would triumph.

As it turned out their victory brought a reign of terror that equalled if not exceeded that under the Mongols. The new dynasty was called the Ming, meaning brightness, and it is written using a Chinese character composed of the Manichean symbols of the moon and sun.

The first emperor was a former mendicant Buddhist priest who gave himself the name, Huang Wu, and called his reign 'Vast Military Power'. He is considered by some to have been the worst tyrant in Chinese history – despite the considerable competition for the title – and earned the nickname 'The Pig'.

He invented a horrible method of execution known as 'death by a thousand cuts'. The condemned would die after 3,357 careful strokes of the knife. After a few slices, the executioner paused to give the victim time to recover so that he should remain aware of the next ten strokes.

Huang Wu became increasingly paranoid as he grew older. He constantly saw plots and conspiracies around him and reacted by ordering massive purges, each with ten or fifteen thousand victims. He had his closest companion in arms arrested and accused of plotting to stage a coup backed by the Japanese and Mongols.

Gradually all his former associates were sliced up. Then he destroyed the new state's bureaucratic system – all the ministries and his 'grand secretariat'. Court officials before they set out to the court each morning would bid farewell to their wives and children in case they never saw them again.

As the paranoia mounted and the purges multiplied, the emperor expanded his secret police, which were known by the quaint name of 'guards with brocade uniforms'.

His reign was also marked by profound xenophobia. Every reminder of Mongol rule from the palaces in Peking to Coleridge's Xanadu was destroyed. No foreigners were allowed in to the country and no Chinese was permitted to go abroad. The Great Wall was rebuilt and the emperor dreamed of returning China to the days of the Tang Dynasty.

It is a story which in all its elements is remarkably similar to the history of China under Chairman Mao, as I discovered in Inner Mongolia.

When one autumn afternoon I boarded the train to the Inner Mongolian Autonomous Region as it is officially called, I had little idea of the tragedy Mao's madness had inflicted on its inhabitants. I knew them only from the colour photographs of Chinese propaganda magazines. There, they are always happy smiling herdsmen living the free life on the open steppes, grateful for the benevolence of their elder brothers, the Chinese, who are invariably pictured bringing the benefits of a higher civilisation.

The train leaves Peking's large and dirty railway station and then heads west, winding up wooded hills, past the ancestral burial grounds of the Ming emperors and then through a series of tunnels to the Wall itself.

The train itself was dirty and uncomfortable. I had not been able to get a first class ticket, a soft seat as it is called, and sat grumpily by the aisle straining to catch a glimpse of the countryside through the window. The train was unheated and crowded and like everyone else I was wrapped in a big green army coat thickly padded with cotton.

Soon the cigarette smoke and the body heat created a dense atmosphere thickened by the loud staccato chatter of my Chinese companions. After answering the usual questions about my origin, I lapsed into silence. The more I travelled in China, the more it irritated me and the more I thought with longing of the wide open solitude of Mongolia.

The train breaches the Wall, which the Ming Dynasty had so carefully rebuilt, a few hours later at the city of Kalgan. The name is a corruption of 'Halga', the word for gate in Mongolian and this, as the name suggests, is the real frontier between China and Mongolia.

A Scottish traveller in the 1870s, the missionary James Gilmour, describes the scene well in his account of his travels.

'Standing on the pass above Kalgan, the nearest landscape presents only one feature – the long extended edge of a high table land in the process of being eaten away by the action of water. The view from this part of the road is grand and embraces a vast panorama of mountains and dry torrent beds, with one permanently flowing river, gleaming far off in the west.'

Kalgan was once much better known than now and it is worth explaining why. It was a centre of the international tea trade and Russian merchants lived there, purchasing the tea grown in southern China and then shipping it by camel caravan across the Gobi desert to Irkutsk or Ulan Ude in the Lake Baikal region. From there it would go on to Moscow or St Petersburg.

Kalgan was four days by road from Peking, a fortnight by horse to Ulan Bator, capital of Outer Mongolia, and another fourteen to the Russian border. Another enterprising Scot called Grant established a scheme to bridge the gap between the telegraph services of China and Russia by using the ancient horse-relay system of the Mongol empire. A telegram from London would reach Khiatkha on the Russian border and was then carried by a horserider to Kalgan from where the message could be wired to Peking, Shanghai or Tianjin.

Kalgan was also noted as the headquarters of missionaries from 1865 onwards who came from America, Sweden, Holland and Belgium. My favourite and the earliest of these was the Abbé Regus Huc who together with his companion the Père Gabet and their faithful servant Samdadchiemba travelled by camel dressed as Tibetan lamas in order to 'study the character and manners of the Tartars'.

They started north of Kalgan in what is now Manchuria and two years later arrived in Lhasa. The Abbé Huc wrote an account of their journey: *Souvenirs d'un voyage dans la Tarterie, le Thibet, et la Chine pendant les années 1844-6.*

It was popular enough in Britain to be in print even in the early part of the century and is still an excellent travel book full of acute observation and amusing anecdote. The French missionaries followed much the same route I was taking on this trip, westwards to Hohehote, the present capital of Inner Mongolia, along the Yellow River to Baotou and then to Yinchuan in Ningxia Province.

The Frenchmen found the Mongols so open and naïve they were continually 'undone by the cleverness of the Chinese'. Exasperated by the way the Chinese seem determined to fleece the Mongols – and the Frenchmen – at every turn the Abbé Huc opined that 'the commercial intercourse between the Tartars and the Chinese is revoltingly iniquitous on the part of the latter.'

The Mongols, on the other hand, irritated them, with their extraordinary filthiness, the 'insupportably disgusting' odour of mutton grease and the abominable plague of lice which infested their dwellings.

'Hunger and thirst, fierce winds and piercing cold, wild beasts, robbers, avalanches, menaced death and actual discomfort, all had been as nothing compared with the incessant misery occasioned by these dreadful vermin,' complains the Abbé Huc with no little feeling.

The lamas refused to kill their lice on religious grounds and the two Frenchmen are just as bewilderred by the rest of the Mongols' religious practices. The Frenchmen are frequently petitioned (as they are dressed up as wandering lamas) to employ their divinitory powers to find lost animals.

One famous passage describes a ceremony where a lama removes his own entrails and replaces them before an awestruck audience.

The holy man, after working himself up to frenzied convulsions, 'suddenly throws aside the scarf which envelops him, unfastens his girdle, and seizing the sacred knife, slits open his stomach in one long cut . . . while the blood flows in every direction, the multitude prostrate themselves before the terrible spectacle, and the enthusiast is interrogated about all sorts of things, as to future events, as to the destiny of certain personages.'

Afterwards, apparently none the worse for wear, he stuffed his entrails back and closed himself up.

My journey through the region was neither plagued by lice nor enlivened by such supernatural encounters. In fact it was impossible to get off the train at Kalgan since, like most of Inner Mongolia, it is off limits to foreigners perhaps because it is an important military base.

Worse than this I have to confess that at the time I entirely failed to realise that I was passing through Kalgan at all. It now has a Chinese name, Zhangjiakou, which means the hole or gap in the wall of the Zhang family.

The name was changed after the victory of the Chinese Communist Party in 1949 because the town played a central role in Inner Mongolians' struggle for independence. Kalgan was for a few years the capital of an independent kingdom ruled by a direct descendant of Genghis Khan who was to end his last days, broken and defeated, as an assistant librarian.

His sad story struck a chord in my imagination because his cause seemed both quixotic and tragic. Prince De Wang's life was tragic not just because it ended in defeat, but because it seemed doomed to failure almost from the outset. Yet he had no choice but to try to fulfil his mission.

The events are not well known and it took me some time to piece them together since the story has been obliterated from the history of Outer Mongolia and entirely obfuscated in China. Yet it is essential to describe them or the rest of the journey will be hard to understand.

The division of Mongolia into two parts dates back to the Manchu conquest of China in the seventeenth century. The Inner Mongolian princes were junior partners in the conquest of China by the Manchu tribes and afterwards enjoyed a special relationship with the emperor in Peking.

The western and northern Mongol tribes were rivals and remained a military threat for many years until they were brutally crushed and subjected.

When the Manchu Dynasty was overthrown in 1911, the Outer Mongolians – the Khalkhas – declared themselves independent with the support of imperial Russia. The tsar forced the Chinese to recognise Outer Mongolia's quasi-independence but agreed that Inner Mongolia would remain in the new Chinese republic. The Khiatka Conference of 1913–14 established the legal basis for the division of Mongolia into two separate zones.

In 1917 the old imperial order was crumbling all over the world. After the Russian Revolution and the defeat of the Austro-Hungarian and Turkish empires, many nations emerged and the Buryiat Mongols in Russia led a pan-Mongol movement aiming to unite all the Mongols in one state. Similar pan-Slavic, pan-German or pan-Turkish movements also existed at the time.

About half of the 6 million Mongols in the world now live inside China, more than the total population of the People's Republic of Mongolia.

Although the division of Mongolia is recent and artificial, even when the Abbé Huc travelled through the region, he could already observe the damaging impact of Chinese settlement.

The Frenchman blamed the dreadful droughts and inundations they experienced in the region on the environmental changes wrought by the first influx of Chinese agricultural settlers.

'From that time forth the aspect of the country became entirely changed. All the trees were grubbed up, the forests disappeared from the hills, the prairies were cleared by means of fire, and the new cultivators set busily to work in exhausting the fecundity of the soil.'

It was the very railroad on which I was travelling which brought a fresh flood of Chinese immigrants just as the railways had opened up the American West to development. In the last decades of the Manchu empire, the Empress Dowager Cixi sought ways of alleviating the mounting famine and hunger for land because the corresponding unrest threatened political stability. Although until then Chinese were forbidden to settle and to farm the pasture lands of the Mongols, step by step an official colonisation policy was extended over more and more of the territory on which the Mongols had grazed their flocks.

It was worse after 1911 when the new Chinese Republic declared that all Mongol lands belonged to China and all land titles were invalid unless ratified by the local Chinese authorities.

Sun Yatsen, founder of the new republic, thought that China's various nationalities should be assimilated into one nationality.

'We must facilitate the dying out of all the names of the individual peoples inhabiting China,' he declared.

When in 1924 the railway line was extended from Kalgan to Hoherhote and Baotou, land-hungry Chinese were arriving at a rate of a million a year.

After Sun Yatsen's death, his successor, Chiang Kai-shek, proclaimed the rather unscientific belief that all the inhabitants of China shared a common ancestry and hence there was no justification for any of them demanding independence or even autonomy.

His government's attitude was typified by the President of the Examination Yuan, Mr Tai Ch'uan-Hsien, who declared that: 'The power of any people is derived from their culture. Chinese culture is superior to that of the Mongols and is the foundation upon which the Chinese state had been erected. Hence, from now on, the Chinese should exert every effort to confer their culture on the Mongols, who should strive to receive it.'

Nowadays some 18 million Chinese live in Inner Mongolia swamping the 3 million or so ethnic Mongols. The tide of impoverished Chinese peasant farmers forced the scattered Mongols out of their rich grazing pastures and they responded with small scale attacks and rebellions. The general anger stimulated demands either for independence or unification with Outer Mongolia which at least had independence although it was obviously becoming no more than a Soviet satellite.

Some of this anger led to violence but it took a political form after 1924 when the Inner Mongolian People's Revolutionary Party was formed. It was created under the patronage of the Nationalist and Communist Parties, themselves formed several years earlier, which were then co-operating throughout China. Four years later the Chinese warlord Feng Yuxiang abolished it when the Nationalist Party turned on the Communists throughout China, massacring them in large numbers.

The Nationalists continued to refuse all demands for autonomy. In the late 1920s and early 1930s, several Mongolian delegations visited Chiang Kai-shek requesting his support and an end to immigration, but he rejected their demands. Instead he encouraged further immigration and split Inner Mongolia into four provinces – Chahar, Ningxia, Jehol and Suiyan.

After Chiang Kai-shek had destroyed the Communists' power base in the cities, its members retreated into the countryside and adopted an overtly conciliatory tone towards the minorities in whose territory they were forced to operate.

Shortly after the Communist Party was founded it issued a manifesto which foresaw an autonomous state in Inner Mongolia. By 1930 the Party had enshrined the right of minority areas to secede from the state in article 14 of its new constitution.

Naturally this made the Communists more attractive than the Nationalists and several Mongols joined up and were sent to Moscow for training. One of these was Yun Tse, the son of an Inner Mongolian prince whose family had been raised to the nobility by the Manchus. Yun Tse was raised in Chinese culture to the extent that he spoke no Mongolian at all but in Moscow he adopted the pseudonym, Ulanhu (also written Ulan Fu), which means 'red sun' in Mongolian. Later he would regret this as there could be only one red sun in China – Mao.

By the end of 1935 Mao, who considered retreating with his guerilla forces to Outer Mongolia and establishing supply links with the Soviet Union, was even more anxious to win the loyalty of the Mongols. He issued an appeal promising to help them to 'preserve the glory of the epoch of Genghis Khan, prevent the extermination of their nation and embark on the path of national revival and obtain their independence enjoyed by such people as those of Turkey, Poland, the Ukraine and Caucasus.'

It is a statement that was absurd even at the time since Stalin had just ensured that millions of Ukrainians had starved to death partly in order to crush the last breath of Ukrainian nationalism. Mao did however acknowledge the very real threat of 'extermination' facing the Mongol nation.

Many Western travellers, before the Communist curtain had descended on the region, were equally convinced with all the certainty of Darwinian social science that as a race the Mongols were doomed.

In 1920 the Peking correspondent of *The Times*, David Fraser, thought the Mongol's laziness and practical incompetence qualified him for extinction. He was 'not fitted to compete with the outside world. Therefore, he has become the sport of other peoples and the destiny of his land is being decided by foreigners.'

One of those foreign powers taking an interest in the fate of the Mongols was Japan. The imperial Japanese army had already turned

Manchuria into a puppet state, Manchukuo, led by the pathetic figure of the 'last emperor' of China, Henry Pu Yi.

The Japanese told the Lytton Commission sent by the League of Nations to investigate the situation in Manchuria, 'it is our mission to help the Mongol race free itself from Chinese oppression.'

According to the Tanaka memorandum of 1924 which defined Japan's strategic aims, Japan had to absorb Manchuria and Mongolia before grabbing the much greater prize of China.

Japan set aside part of Manchukuo, Hsingan, as purely Mongol territory where Chinese immigration was outlawed, schools using the Mongol language were established and where the Japanese did their best to raise the lamentable standards of public health observed by the French priests.

As the Japanese army extended its control southwards into China, it set up another independent Mongolian region, called Mengchiang, which the Japanese promised would, together with Hsingan, eventually form the basis of a greater Mongolian state.

Its capital was at Kalgan and had I managed to wander through its steets the grandiose palace and administrative buildings of the Japanese occupation would probably still be recognisable. The ones in Manchuria are built in the style best described as nineteenth-century town hall and are still magnificent.

De Wang, the hereditary prince of the Xilingol region, who claimed to be the thirty-third direct descendant of Genhis Khan, was appointed to rule this kingdom. His full name is Prince Demchukdongrob and he is generally known by his Chinese name, De Wang. Wang means king and the De is just the first syllable of his name.

The Japanese never fulfilled their promise of establishing a new greater Mongolian state nor did they even unite Mengchiang and Hsingan. The project was taken so seriously though, that all official documents were dated by referring to Genghis Khan's year of birth.

Japan's ambitions played an unacknowledged but crucial role in world history. In 1939 the Japanese launched an invasion of Outer Mongolia and their subsequent defeat at the hands of the Soviet forces persuaded Tokyo to tackle America first. The road to Pearl Harbor, one might claim, led through Mongolia. At the battle of Halkingol, the Japanese lost 15,000 men, and subsequently thirty generals were dismissed. During the campaign, which lasted all summer, the Japanese tried out their best equipment, including biological weapons developed by the notorious Unit 731 based in Harbin, Manchuria.

The Japanese had expected to find a Soviet Army weakened by Stalin's purges and incapable of resistance. Subsequently the Japanese

High Command decided to defer further conflict with Moscow and only in 1945, when Japan was on the point of total defeat at the hands of the Americans, did the Soviet Union declare war against Japan. In fact, Soviet troops formally accepted the Japanese surrender in Kalgan.

The Japanese defeat in 1939 fatally weakened their image among the Mongols. Relations deteriorated as the Japanese commandeered ever greater number of livestock to sustain their war effort. Yet in contrast with either the Chinese or Russian Communists who were to emerge the victors, the Japanese made determined efforts to preserve Mongolian culture. They built 1,000 elementary schools in eastern Mongolia, set up hospitals and experimental livestock farms run by the Zen Ren Kyohai or Good Neighbourhood Association – a sort of Japanese VSO.

The best Mongolian students were sent to Japan for further education, as were Buddhist lamas. Even today there are thousands of middle-class Mongolians living in Japan although some returned to Inner Mongolia where they were given high posts until the Cultural Revolution.

De Wang was far less of a puppet than the pathetic Pu Yi and the Japanese found it difficult to persuade him even to see their point of view. Although they lost interest in their initial aim of unifying Mongolia, De Wang was still determined to establish an internationally recognised Mongolian state and refused to cut off his pigtail, the mark of a Manchu subject, until he had succeeded.

As the war ended, the possibility of unification on Soviet terms was good. Victorious Outer Mongolian troops arrived with the Soviet army, intending to claim Inner Mongolia as their war booty. On Stalin's orders they brought De Wang's son and two daughters to Ulan Bator for indoctrination.

At Yalta Stalin reneged on this plan, allowing his ally Chiang Kai-shek to keep Inner Mongolia, but the Chinese leader did agree to recognise Outer Mongolia's independence after a token referendum. In 1946 De Wang celebrated China's diplomatic recognition of Outer Mongolia by cutting off his hair.

His own position was made no easier. Inner Mongolia was divided into different administrations all claiming various degrees of autonomy and each with their own currencies and armies. Some Inner Mongolians looked to the Chinese Communists, others to the Russians, a few to the Chinese Nationalists and a still smaller number belatedly attempted to engage American interest in their fate.

As the civil war between the Communists and Nationalists developed in China, Chiang Kai-shek kept De Wang under house arrest in Peking for two years hoping he would abandon his demand for independence for Inner Mongolia.

In the meantime the Chinese Communists moved into Inner Mongolia and in 1947 set up an Inner Mongolian Autonomous Area under Ulanhu. At the time Mao, rather oddly, paid tribute to the patriotism of the Mongolians and their anti-Japanese resistance.

In 1949 De Wang was able to escape when the KMT commander of the region around Peking surrendered to the Communist forces without a fight. De Wang tried to set up an anti-Communist state in the Alashan region of Inner Mongolia but it was a hopeless last stand.

The Communist forces absorbed each fragment of Inner Mongolia in turn using threats and bribes, and finally De Wang was forced to flee to Ulan Bator with his remaining followers, preferring, he said, the oppression of his countrymen to that of the Chinese.

Even in this, he failed. His countrymen betrayed him. In 1950 a Chinese delegation from the newly established regime in Peking arrived in Ulan Bator with a list of collaborators and military criminals for extradition. De Wang's name was at the top and the Mongolians, anxious to be on good terms with their fellow Communists, handed him over.

He was imprisoned in Fushun Prison, Manchuria, together with Pu Yi, and subjected to re-education. He was forced to write and rewrite endless self-confessions repenting his actions. Along with Pu Yi, he was formally pardoned in 1963 and given the humble post of deputy librarian in Hohehote. He died, ostensibly of natural causes, in 1966 at the beginning of the Cultural Revolution.

His cause, even if he had succeeded in outmanoeuvring the big powers around him, had already been rendered hopeless by the sheer number of Chinese already living in the national homeland. The Mongolians, then outnumbered three to one, would have had to expel these impoverished settlers by force. The Chinese would have to have been segregated and ejected, something no government in Peking would tolerate.

With the arrest of De Wang died the last chance, it seems, of uniting the two Mongolias.

From Kalgan, a branch of the old railway line takes one to Datong, a big sprawling industrial city on the frontier with Inner Mongolia. It is as unattractive as any other post-1949 Chinese city except that about ten miles outside it lie some of the most remarkable stone carvings in Asia.

Colossal statues of the Buddha, sixty, seventy feet high, have been chiselled out of the living rock and peer down on the visitor with placid smiles. An almost forgotten people called the Tobas or Tubas, who ruled an empire in northern China 1,500 years ago, built them in a sudden outburst of religious passion.

I went to see them, hiring a small taxi – an already clapped-out Lada driven by a swarthy former peasant with a sullen face and thick lips – at the station. The countryside around was poor with the yellow leached soil supporting little more than sparse fields of desiccated sorghum or corn.

According to legend a million captives laboured for a hundred years to carve the images. Along the cliff face there were not just the giant images with nine-foot-long pendulous ears but thousands of diminutive Buddhas, each seated within their own little grotto so that the rock seemed from a distance as regular and fragile as a honeycomb.

At the bottom of the cliffs, I was joined by a handful of Chinese tourists noisily sucking ice lollies despite the cold sharpened by a stiff breeze from the west.

The Tobas were a Turki-speaking nomadic tribe who arrived, like so many other peoples, out of that great blank emptiness of Central Asia in the fourth century AD. By the middle of the fifth century they had conquered all of northern China and for a while the capital had been here at Datong. One of their emperors ordered the construction of the caves in a fit of remorse. Later the Tobas moved further south and established another capital on the banks of the Yellow River and some time in the seventh century they vanish as a people from the history books.

The Chinese refer to them as the Northern Wei Dynasty, giving them a Chinese name, although they were anything but Chinese, drawing their religion and art from the Indo-European Gandharan culture of northern India. From the Chinese, they borrowed their system of administration and invented their own script using characters loosely based on Chinese.

For many centuries the site had been ignored, honoured neither as a shrine nor a monument to the former rulers. The Tobas had seemingly disappeared without a trace but there is a legend which explains how during an archery competition the wily Chinese had persuaded the nomads to leave.

When the day of the competition arrived, the Chinese champion fired an arrow which flew so far that no one could follow its course. When riders were sent out to find it, they discovered the arrow embedded in the ground at the foot of the mountains.

The Chinese had placed it there beforehand but the nomads, astonished by their defeat, took this to be an omen. They retreated into the mountains and steppes of Mongolia, leaving the rich farmlands of the south to the Chinese.

It was much later on, after I had left Outer Mongolia and was in the Soviet Union, that I came across a Turki-speaking people, the Tuvans, who might well be the descendants of the Tobas but that story will have to wait for later.

The next morning the train brought me the short distance to Hohehote, the offical capital of the Inner Mongolian Autonomous Region. It was formerly called Guihua which means 'turning towards civilisation', the name given to it after it had been conquered by the Chinese. Following the Communist victory, it was given a new and Mongolian name which means 'blue city' as a gesture to Mongolian feelings. The naming of things is always laded with some political significance in China and so many names had been changed in this century that it is only with difficulty that one can study contemporary maps and retrace the routes of earlier travellers.

The Abbé Huc certainly came here though, stayed at the 'Tavern of Eternal Equity' and remarked that Guihua was a garrison town with 'a beautiful noble appearance' surrounded by high defensive walls. Guihua, it seems, was then as much a frontier post as Fort Laramie in the heyday of the Wild West. These days, though, it presented the usual dismal vista of shabby concrete apartment blocks, grubby shops and empty boulevards. All that was missing was a giant statue of Chairman Mao visible with outstretched arm at the end of one of the boulevards. Perhaps I would see it later.

At the station I was met by some Mongolian friends of friends who arrived on horseback, their shaggy mounts making a delightful contrast to the customary collection of battered Ladas and olive-green jeeps on the forecourt. It was such a theatrical gesture that I immediately warmed to them, the first 'real' Mongolians I had come across.

One was a big sombre man with broad shoulders, in a policeman's uniform; the other dressed with more panache in cavalry twills and high boots and a leather jacket flung over his shoulders. Their faces were broader than most Chinese and the epicanthic fold more pronounced giving them a more menacing aspect until they relaxed in big smiles.

A Chinese friend had arranged for a group of about ten of us to meet in Hohehote for a trip to the grasslands. The two Mongolians took us to a big new Western-style hotel, leading their horses, hoofs clattering on the road surface and attracting a few curious glances from other pedestrians.

The hotel had a wood-panelled dining-room and we met the rest of the group for a breakfast of eggs, ham, coffee and rolls laid out on a sparkling-white tablecloth. It was all an unexpected pleasure, especially as outside the window I could see the horses with their long straggly manes, champing at their bits. There were horses everywhere, on the tablecloths, napkins, plates, saucers and just about everywhere in the hotel where you could stick an emblem.

Afterwards we went off to the racecourse, which the former Governor of Inner Mongolia, Ulanhu, had had built. The two Mongolians had borrowed some horses from the local team and we all tried them out, cantering nervously around the track. The horses were small but too lively for me.

The bigger of the two Mongolians, Darga, then took us to a shooting range. He seemed to have a sort of obsession with guns. In his house, where we later went for tea and steamed dumplings, he had a big oil painting of himself with a revolver in one hand, a skull in the other. Even in the portrait he was dressed in his uniform with a pair of handcuffs hanging from his belt.

'I painted it myself,' he said gravely. I looked at him with new interest and wondered what sort of man would see himself like this, an arbiter of life and death. He showed us the rest of his paintings but by comparison they were dull and conventional efforts.

Darga was in his late thirties and like most of the rest belonged to the Cultural Revolution generation. The events of those tragic years took centre stage in all his conversations. Even when we set off in a minibus to the grasslands, he and the others in the group sang the songs of the Cultural Revolution which they had learned in their youth. It surprised me. The subject is almost taboo among most Chinese and if they do mention it, they talk of it with horror and not a kind of maudlin affection.

'Of course, we remember the songs of our youth,' Dulao, the livelier of the two said with a laugh.

As we drove past the factories and workshops, there were still slogans from Chairman Mao's Little Red Book visible on the redbrick walls which surrounded them. Darga pointed out one compound with dismal rows of deserted brick huts.

'The Red Guards lived in those huts,' he said. They were in fact built by former Red Guards, the educated youth sent in their tens of thousands from the coastal cities to be re-educated in the countryside after the failure of the Cultural Revolution.

The youths were forced to construct their own camps and plant their own food in the uncultivated grasslands. Often they destroyed the environment, exhausted the underground water supplies, cutting down any trees and stripping away the precious topsoil.

Our bus was soon heading along a two-lane tarmacked road through the countryside. I had expected to find a flat savannah with waving grasses but instead it was quite hilly. A few scattered sheep cropped the grass short and from time to time we saw a low mud hut, with pig pen at the back, which belonged to some Chinese peasant.

Gradually, though, the landscape flattened out and the signs of human habitation became fewer and fewer. It was not quite the sea of tall grass stretching from horizon to horizon and bent by each breeze that I had imagined and instead it had a bare, well-worn feel about it.

The Abbé Huc found that while it did not inspire the awe and terror of a truly Romantic scenery, he experienced 'a sentiment of gentle religious melancholy which gradually elevates the soul without wholly excluding from its contemplation the things of the world.'

I was looking forward to my first glimpse of the white beehive-like tents the Mongols are famous for, but few of the Inner Mongolians still live in their yurts other than in the summer when the herds are taken to fresh pastures.

My companions said that the traditional ways were slowly being revived after the collectives were broken up after 1980. The herdsmen became quite prosperous as, under private ownership, the herds grew in size.

Then as Chinese officials began to complain of overgrazing and the threat of desertification (a fashionable problem all over the world from the late 1970s), a huge reafforestation project was launched the length of Inner Mongolia, called the Great Green Wall. Hearing this, I was reminded of the first Ming emperor, Huang Wu. He too began a vast reafforestation project in northern China, planting the stupenduous total of one billion trees, mostly mulberries which the silkworm thrives on. The Great Green Wall was largely a failure though, since many of the trees died from neglect.

At any rate, we saw no trees until we arrived at a collection of white yurts set in the middle of a pleasant grassy bowl. I immediately began to think of this, the tourist camp, as Yurtsville. It consisted of five rows of white yurts, each erected in a little apron of concrete with a tin shack for a bathroom stuck on the back and a row of street lanterns by the entrance.

Inside, the standard Chinese hotel room had been duplicated: two comfy armchairs with a table in between on which two mugs and a vacuum flask awaited the occupant.

The whole idea of the authorities replacing the labour camps of the past with tourist camps struck me as distasteful but I put this aside when dinner turned out to be a surprisingly cheerful affair. There was mutton soup, boiled mutton, roast mutton followed by cold mutton. Each course was chased down with toasts of a white spirit, Baijiu, and according to Mongolian custom everyone had in turn to propose a toast and sing a song or recite some verses before drinking. On the neighbouring tables some locals were feasting too and several started dancing.

During the meal I sat next to Dulao who said he worked as a policeman and the two friends had met when they served as border guards. Now he spent most of his time making television films.

'I should be there now,' he said with his usual careless laugh and pretended to wind a camera. He both wrote and directed television dramas for the Inner Mongolian Television Station.

His latest project was a drama called *Desert Song*, about a young nomad who is in love with a beautiful girl. A nobleman asks a lama to help his barren wife produce an heir, and in return for his help, the lama demands a gift: the tibia of a young girl, to turn into a trumpet blown during temple prayers.

The nobleman kills the girl and has her tibia covered with silver. Her lover swears revenge, kills the nobleman, but is captured and left to die in the desert wrapped in a cowskin. As it shrinks in the sun, he dies a slow death.

'A true story from the feudal past,' Dulao laughed, and I was not sure whether he was joking or serious.

Afterwards we went out to dance in the clear night air. The girls Dulao had brought with him set up a cassette player under one of the suburban steet lanterns and put on a Beatles tape. It felt too odd to hear those Liverpudlian voices on the steppes of Mongolia and I left after a while.

Away from the artificial light, the sky was a brilliant blaze of stars. The Milky Way curved in a broad band from horizon to horizon and I lay down on the grass counting the shooting stars.

There was an old Buddhist temple not far from the tourist camp, which we went to see in the morning. It was in the Chinese style with floating eyes and it rose out of the grassy plain like a galleon trapped in ice.

Like most temples in China it had been reopened but only as a museum so we had to buy tickets at a counter. Inside we found ourselves in a ruined bulk. Mildewed silk banners hung from a ceiling from which old paint was peeling like the skin of an old scab. A smell of burning rancid butter and sweet incense mingled in the darkness.

Two old men shuffled forward, each wrapped in a red cloak that left a skinny shoulder bare. They had wrinkled and shaven heads and were obviously lamas, and not caretakers as they told us. They said the temple had just been reopened but when I asked when and why it was closed, they seemed taken aback.

'What happened here?' The shorter of the two lamas repeated my question, wheezing heavily. He seemed dazed, even traumatised, and searched through his memory.

'Red Guards come smash temple,' he at length breathed out in broken Chinese.

'Closed long time,' he added and gestured vaguely around the darkness. Before the Cultural Revolution hundreds of monks had been living here as it was not so much a temple as a monastery. He said all the lamas had been taken away and put in labour camps and he had worked as a shepherd until the Chinese had told them to reopen the temple for the tourists from the camp.

I tried to find out from the caretakers whether their religion had been fully restored in Inner Mongolia but they moved off and after a while we left, depositing a handful of money on the altar.

Although the dissolution of the monasteries in Tibet is widely known, the destruction of the large lamaist religion in Inner Mongolia is rarely, if ever, mentioned.

The Mongolians had been converted in the sixteenth century when the most powerful Khan conferred the title of Dalai Lama, meaning Ocean of Wisdom, on the head of the Gelugpa or Yellow Hat sect in Tibet.

After the Manchus had established their rule over China, they had actively sponsored the spread of Tibetan Buddhism as a way of pacifying the Mongolian tribes and channelling their warlike tendencies into religion.

As the Abbé Huc observed:

It is certain that the Government of Peking, while it leaves to poverty and want the Chinese bonzes [priests], honours and favours lamaism in a special degree. The secret intention of the Government in augmenting the number of lamas, who are bound to celibacy, is to arrest by this means the progress of the population in Tartary.

The recollection of the former power of the Mongols ever fills its mind; it knows they were formerly masters of the empire - and in the fear of a new invasion it seeks to enfeeble them by all the means in its power.

The policy was so successful that like the Tibetans, every Mongolian family sent one son to be educated in a monastery.

The Reverend James Gilmour was openly astonished and envious of the lama's success.

'It would be difficult to find another instance in which any religion has grasped a country so universally and completely as Buddhism has Mongolia. Not only does his religion insist on moulding his soul and colouring his whole spiritual existence, but it determines from him the colour and cut of his coat,' the Scottish missionary wrote in his book *Among the Mongols*.

In fifteen years he managed to make only one convert but his book became a bestseller which the *Spectator* compared to *Robinson Crusoe*.

Although Lhasa was the spiritual centre of lamaism, the Manchus built up the importance of the Yonghegong temple in Peking. It became the residence of the most important Mongolian reincarnation or living Buddha and housed a golden urn called the Altan Bomba which was used to select which of a number of possible infants was a genuine reincarnation.

Previously this had taken place in Lhasa but from the late eighteenth century onwards the selection was made by an official in charge of the Ministry for the Dependent Territories, a sort of colonial office for Mongolia and Tibet.

The Manchus already steadily increased the number of living Buddhas in Inner Mongolia until there were 250, all selected, appointed and financed in Peking.

The Yonghegong is now known as the Lama Temple and is a major tourist attraction in Peking. A peculiarity of the complex is a series of paintings, which the authorities have prudishly covered with a curtain, showing various deities in erotic poses.

The temple was also famous for its miracles. Chinese monks, jealous of lamas, once tried to play a trick on them. Sacred Buddhist texts were placed under the seat of the temple's chief lama before a visit of the Emperor Kangxi. When in the presence of the emperor the lama was asked if he felt superior to the scriptures, he denied it but attendants were sent to pull out the holy volumes. To their amazement, the pages were all found to be blank.

In the afternoon a performance of wrestling and horse riding was scheduled. Six buses drew up on the grass and a crowd of Chinese officials, dressed alike in dark blue or grey Mao suits, descended. They stood around, excited by the unfamiliar wide spaces around them, taking pictures of one another.

The locals had brought out a camel and a ladder so you could climb on to the beast and strike a pose. Eventually some Mongolians drove up on their motorbikes and changed out of their jeans into silk costumes.

As we waited, I fell into conversation with one of the officials. He said they were all attending a national meeting in Hohehote.

'This conference is about administrative reform,' he explained with satisfaction. He pushed his sunglasses back on his nose. Next year it would be held at a famous beauty spot in the south, he said.

He peered owlishly at the half-dozen Mongolians who had set off for a brief horse race and said he preferred being in China.

'Cultural levels are still very low out here,' he said and gestured at the Mongols who were demonstrating some wrestling. He had struck the stance high cadres like to adopt, his hands drawn behind his back pushing his small paunch forward.

The Chinese drove off and in the evening we were again the only visitors staying in the camp. We attended a performance of Mongolian singing and dancing staged in a big tent. A few locals scattered around the empty benches joined us to watch the painfully contrived show. At the most ludicrous point a man dressed in a black tutu did a solo dance pretending to be an eagle.

Afterwards we went out to drink some more colourless Baijiu in one of the tents. The two policemen explained why relations with the Chinese are so poor and to talk of the Cultural Revolution again.

A story emerged of a bloodbath, a pogrom really, which in its scale dwarfed anything else in China. Nearly 800,000 people were imprisoned and tortured, between 23,000 and 50,000 were killed and 120,000 left permanently maimed. Yet the events have never been fully reported either in or outside of China until now.

'All the records are still at the police headquarters. The cases are all on file,' Darga said and described what had happened.

'They sent work teams from Peking made up of inspectors and interrogators. The victims were starved, then beaten and imprisoned. People said there were seventy-two types of torture listed but the worst were committed by our own people,' he went on. He talked in a low monotone with an almost morbid fascination for the horrible details.

'They burned people with pokers and cigarettes. They put the pokers up the vaginas of women and even used dynamite against a woman pregnant with a "traitor",' he said.

'Some people were kept in holes in the ground, handcuffed so tightly that their wrists became inflamed and paralysed. Many people had their legs broken. Almost anyone would be arrested, however poor and ignorant they were,' he explained.

The events that led up to this holocaust are part of the complex and confusing history of the Cultural Revolution, but the blame falls squarely on Mao's shoulders. He claimed that tens of thousands of Mongolians belonged to an underground party which was plotting unification with Outer Mongolia. This party was called in Chinese the Neirendang or the Inner Mongolian People's Revolutionary Party, the one that had briefly existed in 1924.

'Because Mao said it existed everyone had to confess to being a member. The interrogators promised that if you confessed you would be freed. Of course no one confessed voluntarily to belonging to something which no longer existed and, if you did confess, then you had to reveal the names of other members and they were arrested in turn,' Darga said. All the confessions were recorded with meticulous bureaucratic detail.

The Neirendang plot was invented by Mao's secret police chief, Kang Sheng. As vindictive, cruel and paranoid as the first Ming emperor, Huang Wu, Mao was determined to get rid of his former comrades. They had turned against him, blaming him for the Great Leap Forward, his insane attempt at mass industrialisation and collectivisation which cost the lives of 20 to 30 million people.

His chief target was the then president of China, Liu Shaoqi, with whom he had worked since they had been at college together. Another earmarked victim was Ulanhu, who had studied with Liu Shaoqi in Moscow.

Like other provincial governors, Ulanhu had wielded the power of a vice regent since the Communist victory. He was head of everything – first secretary of the Party, governor, university president and political commissar of the regional military forces and so on. Ulanhu was also the most senior Party official from any ethnic minority with an alternate seat in the politburo.

He was opposed to the Cultural Revolution from the start. He resisted the Red Guards Peking had despatched to all the provincial centres to wrest power from the established Party leaders.

Then in 1966 Red Guards effectively staged a *putsch* in Hohehote by occupying the telegraph office, railway station, the main newspaper offices, the radio station and other government buildings.

They said Ulanhu was the 'ruler of an independent kingdom' who had forced the masses to study Mongolian instead of the works of Chairman Mao, and dragged out the acting mayor whom they charged with 'frenziedly promoting revisionism and national splittism'.

Ulanhu sent in troops loyal to him with machine-guns, rockets and even artillery, who surrounded the buildings occupied by the Red Guards and forced them to surrender.

The Guards responded by demonstrating on the streets until Ulanhu ordered his troops to open fire on the massed ranks of chanting students.

This sparked off further unrest. Like other provincial leaders, Ulanhu countered it by creating his own group of Red Guards so that the Inner Mongolia East Shines Red Revolutionary Rebels fought with the Third Headquarters of the Revolutionary Rebels of Hohehote in pitched battles. Hundreds died.

Chinese Premier Zhou Enlai invited representatives from all the factions to meet him in Peking but Ulanhu, suspecting a plot, refused to attend. He sent a delegation instead which agreed on a temporary truce.

This lasted only two weeks and then Ulanhu rearrested all the radical students. He went on to ignore other instructions from Peking until Mao responded by sending in the deputy commander of the Peking garrison, General Deng Haiqing, leading detachments from the 21st Army Corps in neighbouring Shaanxi Province. By April 1967 troops loyal to Mao had occupied Hohehote, declared martial law and imposed a curfew. The civil war was over, Ulanhu had lost.

He was arrested and publically accused of calling for 'Mongolia for the Mongols', of eulogising Genghis Khan and of planning to break away from China. Mongols were removed from all levels of government and replaced by Chinese brought in from outside the province.

Younger Mongolians formed an underground resistance and called themselves the Genghis Khan Combat Corps. Many were arrested, shot and imprisoned. None of the Mongols present that night nor anyone I later asked could say how many had died in this orgy of violence but worse was to come.

With Ulanhu out of the way, the persecution of the Mongols could begin in earnest and the massive campaign to unearth the members of the fictional Neirendang was launched.

There were other consequences. The Inner Mongolian Autonomous Region was broken up and the parts incorporated into neighbouring provinces. It effectively became a crime to speak Mongolian, wear Mongolian clothes, use the Mongolian script or indeed employ any form of Mongolian identity. From primary school upwards, instruction in Chinese was compulsory.

Millions of extra Chinese were settled on Mongolian land. Some were political prisoners in so-called Production and Construction Corps, others were the ex-Red Guards forced out of the cities into the countryside.

When it was all over and Mao was dead, Ulanhu was restored to power, his sons promoted and the region was restored to its original shape.

Yet few efforts have ever been made to bring to justice any of those responsible for these atrocities. General Deng Haiqing was allowed to retire with honour although 10,000 signed a petition – a rare event in China – demanding that he be brought to trial.

Few of those persecuted were rehabilitated and still fewer compensated for their material losses. Worse still, none of the Chinese settled on Mongolian land were returned. Population figures in China are unreliable but the number of Chinese in Mongolia increased from 5 to 18 million between 1949 and 1980.

The sheer weight of these numbers now makes any prospect of realising De Wang's dreams of reunification or independence so remote as to be impossible. Even if China were to become a democracy, the Mongolians would have little hope of escaping the grip of the Chinese state.

Darga and Dulao seemed at the time to accept the situation with weary resignation. Life now was better than before but the sense of injustice festered beneath the surface. They expressed too a feeling of resentment against the outside world that had ignored their plight.

Perhaps the lingering fear that everyone in China lives with, kept them from telling me more. Later on, though, I heard that some secret pro-independence societies do exist in Inner Mongolia and anti-Chinese opposition has continued.

In 1981 students in Hohehote led three months of protests and were joined in the streets by thousands of others. The events, which were never reported inside or outside China, were sparked by a secret Party document proposing to settle an extra 400,000 Chinese from Tibet and other parts of China, in Inner Mongolia.

The students wanted an end to all immigration, the return of all pastureland and the restitution of all the wrongs committed during the Cultural Revolution. The Party sent in troops armed only with fire-hoses and carefully avoided the outright use of force. Student leaders were eventually allowed to send a delegation to meet Hu Yaobang, the diminutive and relatively liberal-minded Party leader. At first he agreed to their demands but later had them all arrested and imprisoned.

Their demands were quietly forgotten. The authorities have continued to crack down on all attempts to organise resistance to Chinese rule. More demonstrations and arrests followed in 1989, 1990 and 1991 as hopes were inflamed by the collapse of Communist rule in the Soviet Union and Outer Mongolia.

The ancestral home of De Wang continued to be a hotbed of resistance and in 1987 the Party secretary of Xilingol Aimek fled to Outer Mongolia hoping to find support, but Ulan Bator felt pressured into handing him back and he was given a ten-year jail sentence.

Long after I had left my friends in Yurtsville, their stories lingered on in my mind. It was the thought that nearly a million people could be persecuted and tens of thousands murdered a short train ride away from the diplomats and journalists in Peking without anyone hearing about it. It was hard to accept that it could simply remain unreported.

I suppose one reason is that it was all simply too unbelievable. It was not until I saw secret Party documents which confirmed the figures that the two policeman had given me, that even I really believed them.

Inner Mongolia had been a showpiece for the Chinese Communist Party during the 1950s. It served both to demonstrate the Party's enlightened minority policies at work and to woo Outer Mongolia away from its Soviet patron.

A great effort was made to show how Mongolian culture was being better respected in China than across the border. The Chinese Communists even patronised the Genghis Khan cult, while in Outer Mongolia even Genghis Khan's name was taboo. Under Soviet rule the traditional Mongolian script was outlawed and Russian ways substituted for Mongolian traditions.

Why then was Mao so determined to crush the Mongolians? In the 1930s when Mao was a struggling guerilla leader, he was promising the Mongolians full autonomy and the right to secede. Then thirty years later, his policies were almost genocidal.

There was in fact a gradual shift. The closer the Chinese Communist Party came to power and the less it needed to depend on the support of minorities as the fighting moved out of their areas, the smaller the promises became.

By 1941 the right to secede was quietly dropped from the Party's programme. After victory in 1949 even to make such demands was officially labelled 'reactionary' and 'counter-revolutionary'. Anyone found guilty of being a 'counter-revolutionary' could (and still can) be sentenced to death since it is not only a political but a legal term.

The reasons for the change are partly inherent in Communist thinking.

Lenin said that during the revolutionary stage, the proletariat could form an alliance with bourgeois nationalist forces in order to seize power. At this stage nationalism was to be encouraged but later, under Communism, only the economic relations between citizens would matter.

'The fusion of nations will be completed when the state withers away,' Lenin predicted.

According to Marxist theory, national consciousness is merely a manifestation of the bourgeois state of society. Marx said nationalism was 'a tool' which the bourgeoisie employs to perpetuate its rule. Therefore, once the proletariat of any state had won power, nationality problems would simply disappear.

In the Soviet Union Stalin was happy to grant his minorities minor concessions in such relatively trivial matters as language, in the belief that these were just a temporary expedient.

In a Socialist state, economic relations between its members would be more important than nationality. Further down the road towards Communism, members of small minorities would voluntarily reject their own language once they realised the economic benefits of speaking Russian. In reality Soviet policies barely differed from the outright assimilation policies of Tsarist Russia.

As Stalin said: 'The national problem can be solved only by drawing the backward nations and peoples into the common stream of a higher culture.'

Mao seems to have followed this line in the first years after the Communist victory. Yet the tolerance towards minority cultures was already weakening by the end of the 1950s. During one political campaign in 1958 some Mongolian intellectuals were arrested, charged with nothing more than promoting 'nationalism'.

Mao had even less patience with minorities who resisted progress towards Communism when a year later he tried to force march China down the road to full Communism with the Great Leap Forward.

He antagonised his own colleagues with this disastrous experiment which led to up to 30 million deaths, and Mao was forced out of real power for a few years.

Mao believed – and this was quite orthodox thinking – that when all class differences disappeared, national and ethnic distinctions would also vanish, leaving a homogenous proletarian culture.

It was also an axiom of Mao Zedong thought that 'what has been called nationality struggle is in reality a question of class struggle.'

In 1965 Mao launched himself back into power with the Cultural Revolution, determined to sweep away his opponents and to put his theories into practice.

He had now inverted orthodox thinking to mean that while national and ethnic differences remained, class differences could not disappear. While Stalinism assumed that minorities would voluntarily abandon their separate language and culture and assimilate into the mainstream, Maoism demanded that they should be forcibly eradicated.

Thus any member of a minority race was automatically liable to be classified as a class enemy, and to become a class enemy was to be stripped of all legal and civic rights.

The concept of class struggle was at the root of the horrible violence of those years. While in 1956 Mao had said that class struggle 'was basically over' in China, he reversed himself ten years later. Mao was now urging the Party to emphasise 'class struggle every day, every month and ever year'.

Mao explained his sudden discovery of the unresolved class struggle in two ways. Firstly he paraphrased Stalin by claiming that 'the deeper the Socialist revolution, the greater the resistance and the more . . . anti-Party and anti-Socialist inclinations are exposed.'

Then in the same year, 1965, he accused Stalin of having misunderstood the Marxist-Hegelian theory of dialectics. While Stalin had distinguished four underlying principles, Mao declared there is only one law, the law of contradiction.

This was summed up in the mysterious slogan, 'One divides into two' daubed on walls all over China and applied to every facet of life from nuclear physics to cooking. It meant that even after the synthesis of thesis and antithesis, it is still possible to find a 'contradiction'.

This perverted logic boiled down to the idea that anything or any situation can be divided into two opposing parts. Just as a person is made up of good and bad parts, Mao said that even in a Socialist country like China where the class question had basically been resolved, contradictions remained.

National minorities inevitably belonged to the bad parts if they insisted on retaining their distinct identity. This is why in Peking, with a population of 8 million, there were 10,000 deaths during the Cultural Revolution. Yet in Inner Mongolia which, after it had been dismembered had the same population, the official death toll was over twice as high and concentrated among the small minority who were Mongols.

Even now the ideology of class struggle has not changed in China. Mongolian Nationalists arrested in 1991 were accused of presenting class struggle as a nationalist issue.

An internal Chinese Party document explains that these illegal organisations had:

blurred class alignments, ignored class issues by distorting the conflict between the reactionary ruling class and working peoples of various
nationalities and presenting it as the cultural antagonism and conflict between one nation and another to show that the estrangement between
Mongolian and Han [Chinese] people is of long standing.

Still, I wondered whether this absurd philosophical justification
whether it really explains anything at all. I never met anyone in China
who now took Maoist thought seriously or even remembered what it
meant.

Why then were so many Chinese willing to torture tens of thousands
of innocent people into confessing membership of a non-existent party?

It was all surely just a pretext. The conspiracy Mao and his hench-
men had invented was believable only because it struck a buried chord
of racial hatred among his followers. Mao with his Red Guards had revived the furious rampages of the Ming Dynasty's Red Army.

The small province of Ningxia lies south-west of Hohehote and the
train ride is one of the best in China. After the great iron and steel
town of Baotou, the track follows the Yellow River as it winds in a
great loop through the sand dunes and wild bare mountains of the
Ordos desert.

After Baotou my carriage was half empty and with the windows
open, a fresh breeze blew in from the desert. Even this far from the
coast, the Yellow River was already broad and laden with the brown
mud which gives its colour.

Baotou, an ugly sprawling Chinese city of one million, was one of
the great success stories of China's early modernisation. It was started
in the heyday of Sino-Soviet co-operation and the Chinese completed
it after the Russian experts went home.

It was built to take advantage of the rich coal seams and the iron ore
mine at Bayan Obo. The mountain was a religious site as the 'obo' part
of its name signifies. The Inner Mongolian writer Malqinhu described
in a short story how Mongolians attacked those trying to mine it, cutting off the ears of their victims and hanging on them a banner which
said 'This is the fate of anyone who follows the Chinese Communists.'

The border with Outer Mongolia is only a few hundred miles away
and before the train reaches Yinchuan, the capital of Ningxia, it once
more passes through the Great Wall.

It is a good place to end a journey through Inner Mongolia because
somewhere in this region Genghis Khan met his death in rather
mysterious circumstances.

The area was once ruled by the now forgotten Xia people who are remembered by little else but the name of the province. Ningxia means the extermination of the Xia. They created a civilisation here which flourished between the tenth and twelfth centuries.

Chinese historians called them the Western Xia Dynasty, borrowing the name of an ancient Chinese dynasty, but they were probably a Tibetan people who called themselves Tanguts, or so Marco Polo referred to them.

Like the Tobas they were devout Buddhists although only a few of their statues and grottoes have survived in remote valleys far from the Yellow River.

Energetic and inventive, they created a successful agriculture by diverting the Yellow River into a network of canals. They grew rich too on the trade along the silk route which went westwards from Yinchuan to Dunhuang and the other oasis towns towards the Tianshan Mountains and the passes into Hither Asia.

The region is now called the Ordos and when the Abbé Huc arrived here he found the remaining Mongols wretched and poor.

'Wherever you turn, you find only a bare soil without verdure; rocky ravines, marly hills, and plains covered with a fine, moving sand, blown by the impetuous wind in every direction; for pasture you will find a few thorny bushes and poor fern, dusty and fetid.'

The defeat of the Western Xia Dynasty was Genghis Khan's first act of foreign conquest and the first successful onslaught by his nomad tribes on the fortified cities of a settled culture.

Genghis Khan set out in 1207 with 12,000 men on the first of three campaigns. The Mongols easily defeated the Tangut troops but were unable to take the cities.

At one city they hit upon an ingenious idea. They agreed to abandon the seige if the inhabitants handed over all their cats and birds. The defenders agreed and the Mongols then attached cotton to the tails of the animals which they lit and then the released animals returned to their old homes setting the city in flames. At another city, possibly on the site of present-day Yinchuan, they attempted to dam an arm of the Yellow River and ended up flooding their own camp.

The Tanguts become the Mongols' first vassals. Genghis Khan returned here fifteen years later when his armies' conquests stretched from the Black to the Yellow Sea. Although already in his seventies, Genghis Khan was preparing to mount a fresh invasion of China. The Tangut emperor had refused to obey his overlord's request to furnish him with troops and Genghis Khan arrived to punish him for this disobedience.

According to some histories, Genghis was already sick after a bad fall while out hunting, but he routed one Tangut army and then began to lay siege to the fortified cities. The Yellow River had flooded and on a plain covered by a sheet of ice another battle took place. The Mongols bound their horses' hoofs with cloth to prevent them slipping, and massacred the Tangut forces.

Genghis then left part of his army to continue the seige of the capital while he moved around the kingdom in an orgy of destruction. The Tanguts decided to sue for peace and a mission arrived bearing gifts, 'dazzling images of Buddha, gold and silver cups and bowls, young boys and girls, and horses and camels all in multiples of nine.'

Genghis Khan may have been dead by the time the mission arrived because according to one account his last instructions to his followers were: 'Do not let my death be known, do not weep or lament in any way, so that the enemy shall know nothing about it. But when the King of the Tanguts and the population leave the city at the appointed time, annihilate them!"

According to Chinese historians, 'not one hundredth part of the population survived and the countryside was covered with human bones.'

A western Mongolian account of the seventeenth century alleges that Genghis Khan lusted after Korbelin, the wife of the Tangut king, and took her into his tent.

She was determined to avenge the defeat of her people. The chronicle explains that the beautiful Korbelin 'inserted inside her vagina a small pair of pincers and, having injured the sovereign's member, she took flight and threw herself into the Yellow River.'

The story sounds more Freudian than factual but no satisfactory account of his death exists. Chinese sources claim he died further south in what is now Gansu Province on the upper reaches of the Wei River; others claim he was buried at Ejin Hor Qi, halfway between Yinchuan and Baotou. A mausoleum has been built there which supposedly contains some of his possessions which hereditary guardians living in white tents preserved down the centuries.

Whatever the truth of the matter, his followers obeyed his command so thoroughly that little remains of the Tanguts as a race or a civilisation.

Yinchuan is off the tourist trail and these days has a large Muslim population. The Hui people are the mixed descendants of Chinese and Middle Eastern traders, with hooked noses and beardless Chinese features. In 1860 they launched a rebellion which lasted twenty years and was led by an imam revered as an incarnation of the Holy Spirit. It was finally supressed by the Manchus with great bloodshed.

Most of the city bears the customary stamp of Chinese urban planning but there is a handsome white mosque built of marble with Saudi Arabian money. The main hotel has an Arabian feel to it with a pleasant garden set inside a courtyard.

Next morning I took a car out to the imperial tombs of the nine Xia emperors. They lie about ten miles outside the town across a stony plain which still bears traces of former irrigation canals. The setting is true Ozymandias country. Red mountains rise abruptly from the desolate plain and at their feet are scattered about seventy tombs over an area of fifteen square miles.

The largest constructions are the nine imperial mausoleums but traces of a palace built by the dynasty's founder Li Yuan-hao which covered twenty-five hectares have been found.

The architectural style of the mausoleums is now impossible to identify and possibly unique. The wood has long since rotted away leaving pyramid shapes, about thirty feet high, of weathered mud bricks. Around their base I found fragments of blue and yellow tiles and further out, remnants of some mudbrick walls which had once enclosed the tombs.

The tombs are said to resemble nothing else in China.

Almost nothing is known of how the Tanguts dressed, their music, laws, architecture or origins. We do not even know what they looked like. The only clues are manuscripts discovered in 1907 by the great explorer of Central Asia, Sir Auriel Stein. He found documents written in a hitherto unknown script in Dunhuang where they had probably been hidden from the Mongols.

The script is composed of characters rather than an alphabet, as if it were based on Chinese. It has still to be decoded although work began in Japan during the 1930s.

Next day I went back to wander among the deserted ruins, drawn by the mystery and finality to which they bore such poignant witness. The Tobas had left us the caves and huge statues of Buddha but of the Tanguts only these piles of eroding bricks remained. The people who had constructed these mausoleums are so forgotten that even their existence is now preserved only in a name which commemorates the Mongol victory.

After their defeat the surviving Tanguts had been assimilated just as Mao had tried and nearly succeeded in extinguishing every trace of the Mongols. Well before Mao, Western travellers to Mongolia had found a race so degenerate and backward that they believed it was fated to disappear.

'The Mongols have become the serfs of their rulers, downtrodden, overtaxed and bereft of that energy, fearlessness, and warlike spirit with which they had once astonished the world,' wrote the English explorer Douglas Carruthers in 1913.

As I walked slowly across the silent plain from tomb to tomb, I wondered what explained the rise and fall of the Mongols. Central Asia seems littered with the remains of such half-forgotten peoples – the Scythians, the Huns, the Vandals, the Mongols – who seem to emerge with regularity from the obscurity of the steppes to build powerful empires and then fade into insignificance.

Was there some pattern or force which ran through the shared destinies of these peoples?

The question continued to haunt me as I travelled westwards across Central Asia. It was only on the last stop, in Leningrad, at the other end of this great continent, that I came across someone who had, explanation of the mysterious rhythms of Central Asian history.

As I left the tombs to return to Peking, I bent down and picked up a fragment of a broken clay tile. It still bore faint traces of blue glaze and I slipped it into my pocket as a small keepsake.

Two

Ulan Bator, May 1989

It took two years to get a visa to Outer Mongolia. Mr Tornon, the press attaché at the Mongolian Embassy in Peking, was apologetic each time I came to ask what was holding things up.

'Ulan Bator, no reply, I keep trying and trying,' he would say, and since we were becoming friends would describe the beauty of the prairies and the mountains. What a pity it was that I was not there now, he would say, just when the spring flowers carpeted the ground, or if autumn was passing by, that I was not on the steppes drinking the fermented milk of wild mares. His eyes would mist up at the thought.

'Yes, yes, I must help you. We must be optimistic,' he would conclude each meeting and send off another telex to his obdurate masters in Ulan Bator.

Before Mongolia's glasnost, 'il tod' as it was called, no Westerners were allowed into Mongolia. With the relaxation of controls, about one foreign journalist a year was being allowed in. My opportunity came in May 1989 just before Mikhail Gorbachev was due to visit China and when, as part of the general easing of regional tensions, the withdrawal of Soviet troops from Mongolia was underway.

So one day, with the precious visa in hand, I arrived at Peking airport with two companions. The flight to Ulan Bator was not announced or listed anywhere but out on the tarmac we spotted a small plane with a horse painted on the side. This was Mongol Air.

A weekly flight to Ulan Bator had just started up after thirty years of cold war between Mongolia and China but the airport authorities were obviously still reluctant to make the flight public.

We waited in the May sunshine for a late passenger. He turned out to be the minister of television on one of the first ministerial visits to China and he had collapsed at a banquet with liver failure. It was his corpse which joined the flight and this was our first hint of conditions in Mongolia.

The plane took off and travelled northwards for an hour over a desolate green and yellow plain. We descended into a valley, surrounded by green hills sprinkled with fresh snow, but so full of smog it was as if there were a giant kettle somewhere pumping out steam. Ulan Bator's airport was almost as big and far cleaner than Peking's and there a Mr Erdenbileg from the Foreign Ministry greeted us with a noiseless laugh and whisked us off in a large black car.

The airport apron was full of Soviet military planes and on the way into town we passed a monument to the Soviet military presence, a large battletank poised to take off a concrete ramp.

The pastoral idyll which Mr Tornon had created in my mind did not match my first impressions of the capital. Ulan Bator had enough factory chimneys belching out smoke to blanket Los Angeles.

The industrial revolution had clearly arrived before us and I feared the coming five days would be spent in a schedule full of model factories and boastful statistics of escalating industrial output.

On the streets everyone was dressed like bankers after the Wall Street crash. They walked about with sedate respectability in black trilby hats, black leather shoes with woolly scarfs tucked into dark grey woollen overcoats.

Could these really be the same people who had once called themselves the 'Scourge of God'? And of whom the Queen of Armenia had said they were as 'hellish of aspect, as voracious as wolves in their hunger for spoils and as brave as lions'?

Ulan Bator was a curiously muffled and sedated city. I found its broad avenues undisturbed by any motor traffic unnervingly quiet. I found it unnervingly quiet. It seemed not so much repressed – there was no visible evidence of controls – as sunk in funereal torpor. The absence of certain things gradually became noticeable – the lack of spontaneity, of people talking together in animation, of any kind of emotion except a grudging patience.

One afternoon, I walked around the city unaccompanied by my Foreign Ministry minder and entered a butcher's shop. The long line of people stood in complete silence waiting to be served. No one was pushing or shoving and everyone pretended to take no notice of the presence of a foreigner until I began to take photographs. Then someone must have called the police; a man in uniform emerged from nowhere and started shouting at me. I moved off but the whole time no one else said a word, as if they were frightened of talking to foreigners.

Nothing was sold on the streets, not even a newspaper. There were no markets, private shops or restaurants either.

Some people lived in modern apartment blocks but most of the population lived in white tents arranged in neat rows behind wooden palisades. They covered the hillsides around the city like a Latin American barrio. Even water was rationed. People queued to use a public pump and paid for it with a ticket.

Most curious of all, there was nothing that recalled the past. Not a trace of Genghis Khan or his great empire; even in the official history museum none of the rooms filled with exhibits and maps mentioned him once. It had never happened as far as this regime was concerned. Inner Mongolia was ignored too and instead a huge poster towered over the city centre with a blood-red picture of Lenin. Underneath he proclaimed: 'The Party is our soul.'

History began with the revolution and its hero was Sukhbator. A statue of him astride a horse sat on a windy concrete field nearby.

People stood in front of him to have their photographs taken. Behind the statue lay his tomb, a bunker of pink and grey granite which bore an uncanny resemblance to Lenin's tomb in Red Square.

Around the square were some attractive baroque buildings in shades of pink and green. There was the Party headquarters fronted by a row of impressive doric columns, the Foreign Ministry, the National Theatre, the Party Museum and so on.

In a nearby museum was a mock-up meeting of the two great men, Lenin and Sukhbator. Next to this little *mise-en-scène* was a white bust of their two heads. In 1920 Sukhbator had requested the help of the Bolshevik revolutionaries by sending a message hidden in the hollowed-out handle of a riding crop.

Lenin had passed on the revolutionary mantle to Sukhbator at the meeting in Moscow in 1921. Sukhbator, much the younger man, had died in 1923, a year before him.

The tomb also contained the remains of Marshal Choibalsan, the Mongolian counterpart to Stalin, who ruled from the beginning of the 1930s until his death in 1952. By a curious coincidence his death preceded Stalin's also by a year. A little way off was a statue of Stalin himself, one of the few left in the world. It seemed that time had stood still in Mongolia since his death and the city was still deep in mourning.

The main street past the square was lined by the embassies of fellow

Socialist countries and each had a little box outside for propaganda photographs. They showed identical scenes: the founder's tomb in a big square or rows of concrete tower blocks so that it was hard to tell if one was looking at Zagreb, Budapest, Bucharest, Pyongyang or Warsaw.

One afternoon, I came back from interviewing an official and went into the hotel restaurant attracted by the beat of aggressive rock music. Inside the large and near deserted dining-hall was a futuristic jukebox with flashing lights. Three Russians, two men and a raven-haired girl in a clinging black dress, were dancing to its music.

'I am from the Caucasus; show me how to dance disco,' the girl demanded without further ado. We all shuffled around until I realised she was hopelessly drunk and so were her friends.

The next morning I came down to breakfast and met the silver-haired deputy director of the Institute of Planning whom I had interviewed the day before. A small neat man in a black suit, he had insisted that central planning was so successful in Mongolia that any economic reforms were out of the question.

He was still dressed in the same suit at breakfast and calling for another round.

'More champagne!' he shouted waving an empty vodka bottle at a waiter. North Korean champagne arrived pink and sweet and then Mr Central Planning tried first to kiss me, then my neighbour and finally the waiter.

It dawned on me that practically everyone I met was either drunk or trying to get drunk.

The Mongolian hordes were noted for their tendency to overindulge and even Genghis Khan, while condemning it, took a fairly moderate line.

'No one should get drunk more than three times a month and twice would be better still. Once would be even more praiseworthy. Never to get drunk would be best at all – but where should we find anyone so strict as this?' he is recorded as saying.

Now seemed a more serious problem. Perhaps it was a palliative for boredom that too rigid an adherence to central planning inspires or just a clinical symptom of profound unhappiness.

The hotel bar had erratic opening hours but it was always full of both drink and drinkers, especially Russians with hard currency in their wallets.

'Whisky? You want whisky!' Arslan, the barman shouted. 'But please, I have six kinds! Which one you want?'

The bar also had a jukebox, and Charles Aznavour was crooning

'Lili Marlene' in German. The Russians were mostly military officers from the large Soviet garrison who sat in the smoky darkness too catatonic to notice even this disturbing musical aberration.

Although I had expected the troop withdrawal to make Mr Gorbachev popular in Ulan Bator, people spoke of him with deep suspicion. They disliked the rationing of vodka which three days a week led to hundreds lining up in queues.

Over lunch at the British Embassy I tackled the resident experts on the alcohol consumption problem.

'Oh, no, I don't think they drink much, do they, John?' the deputy chargé d'affaires said to her husband over a lunch of roast beef, boiled carrots and peas.

Britain was then the only European country to maintain an embassy in Mongolia. The British diplomats said they liked the life there. It was true that in the winter they could hear wolves howling in the hills around the city but they had a tennis court at the back, the golf was good and they grew fresh vegetables in the summer when the ground unfroze for a few weeks.

If they seemed a touch defensive, it was, I assumed, only natural since every visitor probably asked himself what terrible gaffe had they committed to be posted to Outer Mongolia.

To be fair, the British Embassy may have been unaware of the country's main preoccupation but the Soviet expatriates were practising a robust form of apartheid.

The Russians lived in separate apartment blocks, attended separate schools and hospitals, shopped at special shops, drank in special bars and rode to and from work in their own buses. Mongolians were being physically evicted when they tried to enter shops reserved for the Soviets. The community, numbered at least 100,000 troops, experts and their families, was enormous in a country with a total population of only 2 million.

Despite decades of official friendship, relations had deteriorated to the point where few Russians dared venture out alone at night. On a later visit a group of drunken Mongol youths with sticks surrounded me one night and were about to set to when they realised I was not a Russian.

Even in the daytime it was rare to see a Russian in the purely Mongolian parts of town. Officials took little trouble to disguise their desire to see the Russians leave.

The Soviets took equally little effort to hide their contempt for their hosts. When we visited the Soviet Embassy I asked one of the diplomats if he could imagine a greater Mongolia one day but he misunderstood the question to be whether Mongolia would ever be a great country again.

'What do you think?' the Russian replied with a nasty sneer.

The Soviets ran Mongolia as a colony, the 16th republic, as they called it in private. The only official outlet for Mongolian nationalism seemed to be philatelic. Tourists stopping off the Trans-Siberian train, enthralled by the colour and size of the stamps, bought them by the page. They showed spaceships, astronauts, factories, flowers, trees, trains, aeroplanes, costumes, mountains, birds, bears, camels and tanks all in bold bright designs. They were so big and exuberant, they seemed to proclaim 'Look, Mongolia really does exist.' You needed to stick so many on a postcard to England, there was no room left to write anything except 'Guess where I am?'

Outside the post office, the only colour even in May was to be found at the last monastery left in Mongolia. In Ganden monastery, bright primeval colours glowed in a gloomy chapel from the candles burning before the silk drapes and paintings of strange deities.

Aged monks administered to a few equally aged worshippers who shuffled about touching the man-size prayer wheels outside or prostrated themselves full length on prayerboards. The monks were vague or surly when questioned.

Another temple, the Choijin Temple, was purely a museum and inside one of the chapels the walls were covered by extraordinary visions of hell where monstrous devils decapitated, raped or boiled in oil a host of sinners.

One afternoon, I took a taxi to see the cemetery on the outskirts of the city. It was a curious sort of place. There were thousands of graves all over a hillside, some quite elaborate with headstones and iron railings around them and a little tin house for the spirit on top. Relatives had also taken the fan wheels from old engines and now they spun around like prayer wheels. Many of the deaths seemed to be bunched together in the same years, hinting at some secret tragedy, although what I did not then discover. When the wind gusted, there was an unnatural movement all over the cemetery as the blades twinkled silently in the fading light.

The only other site of historic interest was the palace of the Bogd Khan, who had been Mongolia's God-King, the equivalent of the Dalai Lama.

The floating eaves and the golden roofs of the temple and palace seemed like discarded film props beside the drab proletarian blocks of concrete apartments around them.

One evening we met the foreign students living in Ulan Bator for a drink. There were only a few including an Indian with a doctorate on the Law of the Sea who was now inexplicably engaged in an ethnographical study of Buddhism among the Mongols and a French girl studying the legal system of Genghis Khan. In his day, she said, the penalty for urinating into a fire was death.

They warned us not to be deceived by appearances. Below the surface things were changing in Mongolia, revolt was in the air. Someone had thrown red paint over Stalin and black paint over Marshal Choibalsan. Support for a green movement was brewing, the old people were praying more openly and although the secret police were still powerful, dissent was brewing.

We had to hurry back to Peking to cover Gorbachev's arrival in Peking and took a train full of Soviet soldiers returning to their barracks. Some of them would get out when the train stopped at a few buildings in the middle of nowhere.

I wondered what on earth they did to fill their time there. From the train, I could see nothing but herds of grazing horses and then camels' as the scenery changed from green hilly pastures to the flat and sandy scrub of the Gobi desert.

We shared a compartment with some Mongols and with the intimacy that train journeys bring, we slowly fell into conversation with them. We began to realise how little of Mongolia we had grasped.

There was a young man with a bright yellow shirt and natty black leather tie with his wife, who had studied in Dresden and spoke German. Her black hair was spikey and punkish and she wanted to know about Suzi Quatro.

'What happened to her? We haven't heard her songs for a long time,' she said. I was so taken aback that it took me a while to catch on that she was talking about the British rock star.

Her husband said British rock was better than American.

'We prefer groups like Pink Floyd or Deep Purple to Michael Jackson or Madonna,' he said and seemed to mean it. The couple lived on a collective farm and he played lead guitar in a local band.

The other couple in the carriage were much older. The husband was Chinese by origin although he had forgotten his mother tongue and was married to a Mongolian.

All four were on their way to visit relatives in Inner Mongolia, on the other side of the border.

'We haven't been able to cross the border since the 1950s,' the Chinese man said. 'Who can tell if anyone I once knew there is still alive?'

The young couple said that last year they had received a letter from an uncle for the first time. For thirty years no contact at all was allowed and now they were taking the first chance to cross the frontier.

'Mongolia is just like Germany, a country divided by the super-powers,' the Suzi Quatro fan said.

Six months later the East German News Agency correspondent reported the first pro-democracy demonstrations in Ulan Bator. By late March 1990 the government resigned and the first elections in Mongolian history were scheduled.

The country began to change with absurd speed.

The democratic movement started in September when a handful of intellectuals held a secret gathering and decided that something must be done to galvanise the country's sluggish pace of change.

In the past any kind of dissent was impossible. One man who had pasted up a public protest was arrested after the police tracked him down by identifying the number of the typewriter he had used. There were so few typewriters that any machine could be identified.

At first the police detained the activists and confiscated their leaflets but then as, one after another, Communist regimes in Eastern Europe collapsed, the activists became bolder and the police more reluctant to intervene.

The Mongolian Democratic Association (MDA) was formally launched on December 10th, 1989 at a rally ostensibly honouring UN Human Rights Day. A mere 200 people attended holding aloft their banners which said 'Destroy Bureaucratic Oppression' and 'Support Perestroika and Glasnost'.

As in all the best revolutions, the rebels had the good songs. A band called Honk, meaning 'bells', played 'The time has come to wake up.'

The first big rally took place in 1990 on Sukhbator Square on Lenin's birthday, January 21st, when everyone pretended to be honouring the great Russian saviour. It was −30° and although few attended, more rallies took place on the following weekends and the numbers rose. By the fourth rally, the crowd filled Sukhbator Square shouting the ancient battle cry, 'Mongols! To your horses!'

Arriving in mid March the first thing I noticed, driving from the airport, was that someone had changed the huge slogan carved on a hill overlooking the city. By changing a few letters it now read 'Long live Meat' instead of 'Long Live the Mongolian People's Revolutionary Party'.

In the city centre the statue of Stalin was missing, removed one night from its pedestal in front of the Academy of Sciences by a nervous government.

Faced by unprecedented opposition, President Batmonkh, who had been in power since 1984, seemed poised to follow the example of his Chinese comrades and shoot the young protestors.

In a replay of the events at Tiananmen in Peking, the Mongolian Democratic Association decided to hold a hunger strike on the square. The participants vowed to fast to the death unless the entire politburo resigned and a provisional parliament was chosen to organise free and fair elections.

In fact so little foreign news reached Mongolia that China was not the inspiration. The hunger strike was inspired by Dr Charles Hilder, an American whose ninety-day hunger strike in front of the White House against the Vietnam War was given enormous publicity in the Soviet Bloc. The Mongolians knew from Dr Hilder's book how to prepare themselves by drinking litres of salted water to clear out their digestive systems.

When they started at 2 p.m. on March 4th, the temperature was −15°. An ambulance from the Mongolian Red Cross waited nearby while the ten hunger strikers dressed up in traditional Mongol clothes positioned themselves in front of Sukhbator's statue. At night they slept outdoors and allowed themselves water mixed with glucose.

More hunger strikers joined them and the spectators in the square increased in number. Monks from Ganden Monastery arrived to give their blessing and the new Indian ambassador, a senior lama from Ladakh, blessed cotton threads which they tied around their necks.

Many Mongolians found the whole idea of a hunger strike quite astonishing.

'Why are they going hungry? Whatever happened in the past there has always been enough to eat in Mongolia,' people said.

The government counter-attacked but often in a ludicrous fashion. Newspapers printed pages of letters supposedly written by indignant citizens decrying the hunger strike. Schoolteachers explained to their classes that the leader of the MDA, a twenty-eight-year-old philosophy student called Zorig, was a certified schizophrenic.

By the second day of the strike, the army was standing by ready to crush the protest. To provide an excuse for a crackdown, groups of drunken youths armed with stones and sticks appeared on the square.

The politburo met in permanent session inside the large grey government building at one end of the square. When the politburo despatched two of its members to plead for an end to the strike they were jostled and insulted by an angry crowd.

By Thursday night the atmosphere was turning nasty. Thousands gathered outside the government building or marched around it shouting for the Party to resign.

Other people commandeered buses and taxis and drove to the Soviet Embassy and President Batmonkh's private residence. Fights and scuffles broke out in which at least seventy were injured and one man was stabbed to death.

The politburo sat late into the night debating what to do. Initially all except the President were in favour of using force to suppress the challenge to their rule. Yet by 7 p.m. on Friday, President Batmonkh, the sixty-three-year-old former university rector, issued a statement announcing the politburo's decision to resign *en masse*. On the following Monday a three-day-long meeting of the Party Central Committee elected a new politburo and organised an extraordinary meeting of the Great People's Hural.

The struggle was far from over and there would be more hunger strikes and protests but the Party's seventy-year-long monopoly on power had been breached.

It had been a calm and bloodless affair compared to the fall of equally hardline regimes in Romania, Albania or Bulgaria. Moscow had probably refused to condone the use of force but I had the feeling that everyone, even some of the Party leaders, was simply too sick of the system to want to continue with it.

The first open session of the parliamentary body, the Grand People's Hural, was broadcast live on television. Top of the agenda was the removal of Article 82 of the constitution which guaranteed the Party's monopoly on power.

Compared to the drama on the streets this was a comic opera affair. The deputies were mostly bowlegged men from the countryside attired in the traditional Mongol *del*, a silk gown of bright red or blue tied at the waist with a broad orange sash which hung down to big black leather riding boots.

They all had big earnest faces burnished by the sun to mahogany brown and despite the gravity of the occasion could not help but digress into local problems of yak breeding.

Most of them found it hard to grasp what was going on. They were Party nominees unanimously 'elected' under the old system and found it hard to imagine that democracy could consist of anything else. They were stunned when the MDA said that since they had been appointed rather than genuinely elected they had no right to pass new laws.

One burly herdsman in a *del* edged with gold filigree countered with an especially arresting attack. In a basso profundo voice, he expressed his deep indignation that the hunger strikers had chosen to make their protest on International Women's Day when, as the world was aware, this was an occasion sacred to the memory of one's mother.

Not only would Mother not like it but it should not be done in front of the children. One delegate, a middle-aged teacher, complained that the MDA's unreasonable behaviour had set a bad example to her pupils. Now, she puffed, children the length and breadth of the land were going on hunger strikes if their demands were not instantly met.

Many speakers were less ingenious and simply decried the opposition's 'extremist' demands and there was loud stage laughter after someone proposed nominating the young bespectacled Zorig as the country's next vice president.

The debate went on for a week. The majority were clearly reluctant to prepare for the first multi-party democratic elections in Mongolia's history and what would indeed be the first in any Asian Communist state.

Outside the Hural meeting, it was as if a great dam had burst. A society which the previous May had appeared forever lost in a Stalinist timewarp exploded into such furious and bewildering activity that it was just like watching an ants' nest which had been poked by a stick.

It was impossible to keep up with the variety of people who suddenly emerged in public waving pieces of paper with their ideas and plans.

The Great Hural was flooded by 30,000 letters, petitions and proposals just on how to revise the election law. All sorts of unlikely-sounding organisations sprang up.

The Union of Young Lamas wanted the constitution changed to guarantee religious freedom. The Union of Mongolian Believers (in Buddhism) demanded the introduction of compulsory religious education. A delegate from the Railway Workers' Union wanted to bring back the old writing script. And when a Mongolian Green Party wanted to register there were loud gasps of surprise in the whole hall.

A delegate from the Union of Wrestlers proposed dropping the voting age to sixteen because half the population was under twenty-five. Someone else countered with the suggestion that in future all MPs should be at least fifty-five.

The suggestions became crazier and crazier. A herdswoman got up to say what the herdsmen needed was more television sets in order to 'lift the quality of their spiritual life' and awaken the forces of perestroika.

Several men in military uniforms protested vehemently when the Opposition suggested abolishing the army to pay off the national debt. This, said the army men, was a disgusting and unpatriotic idea.

However, the chief of the secret police said he wanted to apologise for the past activities of his organisation. It was now, he freely confessed, a discredited organisation in need of rapid 'democratic changes'.

Everyone laughed, though, when a man in a grey suit said the trouble with this country was that there were always 'too many talkers and too few producers'.

As the debate went on, the heady freedom of free discussion was accompanied by an upsurge of suppressed nationalism. On the following Sunday, the by now customary rally was held on the square. Speakers from the Green Party, the Social Democratic Party, the Mongolian Believers Association, the Free Trade Unions and even the tentatively named Association of Non-Affiliated Citizens held forth from the top of an old truck.

The crowd of six or seven thousand, carrying banners which said 'Arms are Democracy' and 'May religion flourish for centuries to come' listened to everyone patiently. The most enthusiastic applause was reserved for a Mr Dojodorje who announced that he had just founded an Association for Remembering and Respecting Genghis Khan.

Although the link between democracy and this bloodthirsty conqueror escaped me for the moment, Dojodorje, who worked as a television journalist, was determined to glorify his spirit.

He proposed building monuments in his honour, re-creating his palace, or rather his royal tent, and duplicating his style of government with a council of advisers. These and other projects he proposed were to be financed by donations from all the nations which owed the Mongols a cultural debt. These included, according to Dojodorje, everyone from the Finns to the Red Indians in America and the Indians in India. Loud cheers of approval greeted this optimistic plan.

Genghis Khan had, of course, been labelled a 'reactionary' by the Communist Party doubtless because Moscow was sensitive about the 200 years of Russian subjection to the 'Tartar yoke'.

From being a 'non-person' in Mongolia, he was now becoming a cult figure and I began to notice more and more people proudly wearing little gold lapel badges with his whiskered face on them.

One evening I went to see a popular Mongolian rock band called Soyol Erdene and the climax of the concert came at the end when the lights dimmed. A huge portrait of Genghis Khan descended on to the darkened stage and as a spotlight illuminated the twelfth-century leader's face, the audience clapped rhythmically as the pop group sang 'Can you forgive us, Genghis Khan?'

The new Genghis Khan cult was accompanied by a fresh upsurge in violent outbursts of anti-Russian feelings. There were several stabbings of Russian soldiers and similar incidents although none was reported by the press. A German film crew's car was stoned by youths who mistook them for Russians.

It was easier now to find out just how badly the Soviets had ruled Mongolia. One day I met a factory worker at the MDA's headquarters who insisted on taking me to his animal-hide-processing factory.

The walls and corridors were covered by exhortatory slogans in red and photographs of model workers. Vast and mysterious vats bubbled away in the workshops. It was the biggest in Mongolia and although it was built in the 1960s, it was already dangerously obsolete. My guide said workers at the factory had died prematurely from inhaling chemical fumes and their children were born deformed.

'They told us we lived in a Socialist paradise,' the worker said bitterly. 'But the Soviets dumped their obsolete equipment on us, and every one of them lorded it over us as experts – even the Russian truck drivers were experts – who got paid three times more.'

Then someone spotted me and raised the alarm. My guide disappeared round a corner and I fled together with my interpreter.

At the MDA's headquarters, which were just a couple of untidy rooms in a university building, I ran into a former secret policeman who was more concerned about the spiritual legacy of the Soviet occupation.

'Everyone in Mongolia has become slave,' Enktushin said bluntly. He was a small man in a suit who had studied criminal law in the Soviet Union and then worked for twelve years in Mongolia's Ministry for Internal Security, the official name of the secret police.

People's way of thinking had been twisted, he said, by living in a climate of spying and secrecy where mail was routinely opened and telephones tapped.

Many citizens had worked as paid informers for the police. Now after decades of total subordination to the Soviets, people blamed the Soviets for everything instead of examining their own responsibility for this evil system.

In his ministry – and indeed every ministry – the first and second floors were fully occupied by 'Soviet instructors' who took every decision.

'People thought that the Soviet Union was our best and closest friend but every one of our leaders was a Soviet agent,' he said.

Enktushin believed the way out of this spiritual crisis was to hold Nuremberg-style trials in Mongolia not merely to punish those responsible but to show exactly how the system was run and by whom.

He wanted the former president Yumzhadyn Tsedenbal, who ruled from the 1950s to 1984, extradited from the Soviet Union and put on trial for human rights abuses.

'We must ensure that these crimes never happen again in Mongolia,' Enktushin said.

He was quite serious about the need to hold such trials and it began to be openly discussed although everyone realised that a precondition was an Opposition victory at the polls.

The political negotiations over the forthcoming elections continued. Most of the politicians on either side had only the haziest ideas about the mechanics of democracy.

'What on earth is proportional representation?' the chief government spokesman said, exasperated after meeting Western journalists who had made him aware of the confusing variety of options available.

The ruling party was clear enough about its ultimate aim – to hold the elections in such a way that it would stay in power.

The date was set for July and the Communist Party cleverly managed to gerrymander the constituency boundaries. In the country-side where the Party was strongest, constituencies often had as few as 1,000 voters but those in urban areas where it was weakest had 10,000 voters.

The Opposition split into a number of parties such as the National Progressive Party which took Thatcherism as its ideology or the Social Democratic Party which looked towards Austria or Sweden and talked about social justice.

A leading member of the National Progressive Party was a grandson of Sukhbator. He worked for the state bank, spoke fluent English and explained to me that Mongolia should embrace radical capitalism with a fullscale privatisation programme including shares and stock markets.

Most foreigners shook their heads in disbelief when they heard these plans. The nearest thing to a free market which had existed in Mongolia for the past fifty years was a sort of jumble sale held on Sunday mornings on a hillside beyond the yurt suburbs. The government had felt so ashamed of it that foreigners were kept in ignorance of its existence until the demonstrations.

You had to buy a ticket to get in and once inside, nobody seemed to have anything worth selling. People stood around opening their coats to pull out a pair of shoes, a shirt or an old bra as you went past. A few stood behind stalls which offered bits of broken television sets and radios. Transactions were quick and furtive.

The Mongolians have always been described as diffident about trade or entirely lacking in any commercial nous. Ogadei, one of Genghis Khan's sons, happily paid visiting merchants whatever price they demanded and seemed to find money a confounded nuisance.

On being informed that his storeroom contained 20,000 gold ingots, he supposedly retorted, 'What profit do we derive from storing all this, since it has to be constantly guarded?'

Communism had hardly fostered trading expertise. Mongolian ministries acted merely as the local offices of ministries in Moscow and ninety-five per cent of trade was with the USSR.

Moscow manipulated the Mongolian economy to its own advantage, buying its minerals cheap and delivering them for a profit on the world market and by selling oil to Mongolia at above world-market prices.

Sukhbator thought Mongolia could quickly create a ranch-style economy once the state-owned livestock was sold off. The country would become part of the Asia–Pacific Region and be linked to development of Siberia and Manchuria with the help of Japan, the United States, South Korea and Taiwan. The country would negotiate with the Chinese to open up a new railway route to the port of Tianjin on the Chinese coast.

He thought foreign investment would pour in. Western oil companies would come in to develop the Gobi's huge oil deposits which the Russians had neglected.

The currency, the tugrik, could easily be made convertible since the country exported internationally traded commodities. Mongolia is one of the world's top producers of gold, copper and uranium. On top of this there would be exports of sheep, goats, cashmere wool, camels and horses. Mongolia could be like Australia, he said, a lucky country.

At first it was disappointing to return at the end of the year to see so few visible signs of change. Nobody on the street looked any better off. On the contrary the shops had never been emptier. People waited silently against one another waiting to buy a few old potatoes, shrivelled cabbages and bottles of 'Grill Sauce'.

As expected the Communist Party had won the elections in July but its members were now divided amongst themselves on how to proceed with economic reforms.

Yet however small the material change, the mental furniture of the Mongols had undergone a wholesale refurbishment.

The newspaper vendors on the street caught my attention first – there were simply so many of them. Where once there was only the Party newspaper *Unen* (Truth) and that was sold by compulsory sub-scription, now there were dozens of people lined up one after another selling dozens of newspapers, magazines and books too, by previously outlawed authors. Some said there were now forty newspapers, real broadsheets with cartoons, jokes, translations from foreign publications, offering an intellectual feast.

As I walked along buying each of them, forcing my freezing fingers to count out a few coins each time, it seemed as if everyone in Mongolia was either busy writing a newspaper or reading his neighbour's.

If this was not true, everyone was at least changing jobs, and often changing more than just their employment.

One afternoon I ran into an old acquaintance, Enkhbat, a hulking man in his early thirties drinking vodka in the hotel restaurant.

'Drink!' he commanded and then a broad smile creased his large and rumpled features.

'I have divorced my wife,' he announced triumphantly and poured me another glass.

'This is democracy, this is freedom,' he said savouring the words. In the past, he explained, a divorce was forbidden but now everything was possible. Enkhbat had not only abandoned his ill-tempered wife but also his job as an English teacher.

'I hated teaching those awful rude students,' he said.

'So what are you going to do now?'

'Oh, I am going into business. I am going to make money,' he boasted. He poured himself another slug and leaned over confidentially. The plan was this: he would use his savings of worthless tugriks to buy small Japanese generators from some herdsmen who had each been given one as part of some aid package.

The shepherds, who had done without electricity the rest of their lives, would gladly part with them, and then he would go to Hungary. There he could resell them at ten times the original price. Cash in hand he would then go to Czechoslovakia where he had heard Russian cars were going cheap.

In Prague he would put the car on a train to Ulan Bator where he could either sell it making a 300 per cent profit or work as a taxi driver. It sounded impressive, entrepreneurial but risky, I said. He shrugged this off.

'The fact is,' he concluded, 'nobody can tell me what to do any more. It's my life now.'

At lunch the next day I sat across the table from a young man with an even more innovative idea. Suchsharghal had studied computer programming in Germany and was telling me about the youth opportunities programme he was employed to administer when he suddenly asked if I wanted to buy some dinosaur eggs.

'I have a friend who found them in the Gobi,' he said, as if they had just fallen off the back of a lorry.

'What kind of dinosaur eggs?' I asked foolishly, as if only the free range kind would do.

'Oh so-oo big,' he said, outlining with his hands the shape of a small artillery shell. 'And very heavy, made of stone.'

'Your friend, did he, er, find them himself?' I continued, suspecting that finding and selling secondhand dinosaur eggs must be an unusual if not illegal activity.

'Oh, no, you can find them everywhere in the Gobi, just by walking around,' he replied airily.

'Surely, it must be against the law to sell them to foreigners?' I said, still unconvinced.

Suchsharghal looked bashful.

'Now we have market relations, it is time to learn how to buy and sell,' he said.

Across the social spectrum, everyone was busy taking the initiative. The lamas at Ganden Monastery had voted out their head lama, calling him a government stooge.

Sexual liberation was in the air despite a great shortage of condoms and there was a campaign to lift the laws forbidding abortion. The youth theatre put on a play with frontal nudity. A beauty contest was organised and a nightclub with go-go girls in sequins had opened briefly.

The most moving example of the new determination of people to take control of their lives was found just outside the hotel, where a strike by the Association of Mongolian Invalids was in progress. The Association was set up immediately after the politburo's resignation but now the members were dissatisfied by the subsequent efforts of the government and their chairman to improve their living standards.

The protest began with fourteen invalids, some in wheelchairs or lacking several limbs, who camped out in the corridors of the Palace of Sports.

Gradually more and more joined in until after five days the government gave in to their demands. These included better welfare benefits, action on the UN Decade of Invalids, special television and radio programmes for the deaf and blind, proper premises for invalids to gather, and some offices for their pressure group.

I found the new chairman sitting in their offices in the Palace of Sports, smoking cheap cigarettes with long paper filters and looking drawn.

Mr Algaa was not handicapped although his sister was. He had been a senior Party official before leaving his job in March to join a private company.

'I took this job on because, well, I suppose I felt guilty,' he explained, puffing slowly on a cigarette.

'We didn't do enough in the past to help the handicapped so people like me have to show our remorse,' he said. 'In the past' was the phrase which kept on coming up to describe the previous seventy years.

The country's 40,000 invalids had been neglected, he went on to explain, and were even forbidden to form an association. No department except the Mongolian Red Cross took any responsibility for their wellbeing.

He suggested I come back to meet one of the strikers, a fireman who lost three limbs, if I wanted to know more.

When I returned, Algaa showed me a video called *Power of the Soul* which told an extraordinary story. It presented the ex-fireman lifting 170 kilos of weights, rotating on a trapeze, cycling along a lake, cooking at home with his wife and daughter. Then it showed him learning to write with great physical effort, holding a pen with an arm severed below the shoulder as he studied for a university degree.

Eight years earlier he was putting out a fire when his ladder fell on to an electricity pylon carrying 6,000 volts. His colleague died but they rescued him by amputating a leg and two arms. After eight operations he had survived.

When Bayarmagnai walked into the room there seemed, astonishingly enough, to be nothing unusual about him except for the black gloves over his artificial hands.

He talked slowly and bitterly about 'the past'.

'For years and years we were kept in darkness about the possibilities, the new technologies, the potential to make our life more bearable. All we did was slavishly follow one country, and one system,' he said.

'The worst thing was not the lack of proper equipment, wheelchairs and so on, it was just so hard to do anything. Nobody would let you help yourself because they didn't want to take any responsibility, nobody did. Invalids like to work, they don't like to sponge off the state but there was no room for initiative in such a bureaucratic system,' he said.

The authorities refused to allow him to go to university so he taught himself to ride a bicycle. Cycling is not a popular sport so he managed to beat fifteen others in a race which convinced the authorites to allow him to attend university.

Yet it still took three years for a doctor to give him permission to go on a cycling tour around the country. No doctor was willing to take the responsibility.

'So much time was wasted, such unnecessary waste,' he sighed.

When the senior prison officer, a pink-faced young man in a fierce
Soviet-style hat, said he had joined Amnesty International it was
evident we were going to visit a very different sort of Mongolian labour
camp to the one I had imagined. Attitudes to crime and punishment
were not what they were.

Deputy Colonel Survalzmlagch smiled happily at my astonishment.
Major Batbataar, the other officer in the jeep, revealed that he was not
a brutal guard either but editor of *Repentance*, a new magazine aimed at
convicts.

I had the honour, he said, of being the first Westerner to visit a
Mongolian jail and he was there to record it. The last recorded visit
was in 1913 by Mrs Beatrix Bulstrode, an English lady living in Peking
who took off to indulge, she wrote, her 'fascination for the unknown,
deep love of the picturesque and inherent desire to revert to the
primitive'.

Outside Ulan Bator she found a little wooden stockade with heavily
bolted doors. Her description still makes horrifying reading.

> As we entered, the gaolers, who struck us as being a most unholy-looking
> couple who literally gloated over the misery of the prisoners in their power,
> met us and called our attention, quite unnecessarily, to a trio of pale-faced
> Mongols sitting on the ground just inside the gates. Their hands and feet
> were heavily chained together, and they fell on their knees when they saw
> us.

Then, when her party entered one of the prisons she found a heavy
wooden chest, some 4 to 4½ feet long by 2½ feet deep, locked by two
strong padlocks.

> To our horror we discovered that it contained a man – one might have
> imagined that a wild beast to be sent by train was temporarily imprisoned
> therein! But a man! The hole in the side was of sufficient size to enable the
> prisoner to thrust out his manacled hands. This also provided the sole
> means of ventilation. But this unfortunate creature was well off compared
> with the others we saw subsequently. At least he was breathing in the open
> air.

The dungeons were so full that this prisoner had to remain outside.

> While we were discussing his pitiable lot, clank, clank, went the great bars
> and bolts, and the gaoler had opened the double doors leading to the first

dungeon. There must have been from twenty to thirty coffins in this, some piling on top of the others, and the atmosphere was absolutely putrid.

The two Mongol officials, ostentatiously holding their long sleeves over their noses, told her that never under any circumstances whatsoever were the prisoners allowed to come out except for execution or – rarely – to be set free. The majority were in for life sentences.

One's eyes growing accustomed to the darkness – the only light that penetrates it is from the doors when they are opened – one became gradually aware of wild shaggy heads poking through the round holes in the coffin's sides. I was standing, quite unconsciously, close to a coffin, when, glancing down, I saw a terrible face, nothing more, almost touching the skirt of my riding coat. Beside one coffin was a pool of blood which told its own tale. Within it there was a poor devil coughing his lungs up.

A Russian officer who had accompanied them spoke a few words in Mongolian to one of them but they were too dazed to understand.

'Their minds, like their limbs quickly atrophy in this close confinement,' she said.

In a second dungeon they found a similar number of Chinese in the coffins.

It struck as infinitely sad to find these gentle, highly civilised Chinese here, Shansi merchants most of them, friends and neighbours no doubt of the men with whom we had drunk tea in their charming guild rooms adjoining the little temple on Mai-mai-Ch'eng. There they were, shut up for the remainder of their lives in heavy iron-bound coffins, out of which they could never under any conditions or for any purpose move. They could not lie down flat, they could not sit upright, they were not only manacled but chained to the coffins. They saw the daylight but for a few minutes, when their food was thrust into their coffins through a hole four or five inches in diameter, twice daily.

In one way only did they score over their Mongolian fellow-sufferers. Their narrower Chinese skulls enable them, painfully and with difficulty to protrude their heads through the hole on the coffin wall. The Mongol cranium is too wide to do so at all.'

Major Batbataar said the box prisons were an invention of the cruel Manchus.

'This is not Mongolian justice. We are going back to our old ways now, to the laws of Genghis Khan, which are more humane,' he said enthusiastically.

The Mongolian branch of Amnesty International had opened two months earlier and they now wanted their prisons judged according to international standards.

Half an hour later we arrived at Salhit high security prison. It was a beautiful site. Behind a river the setting sun stained a backdrop of snowy mountains a modest pink and in front by the prison entrance the guards had built themselves little wooden holiday chalets.

The prison housed about 300 convicts serving terms from five to fifteen years for serious crimes such as rape or murder.

Security was feeble – just a fence and a couple of unmanned wooden watchtowers. My hosts said it was even laxer elsewhere and the least dangerous criminals did time in a uniquely Mongolian invention – 'nomad labour camps' – which moved from place to place.

The chief of political education, Lt.-Col. Gechr Aradna, welcomed us stiffly and we went into his office. He wore the dark sunglasses which policemen seem to find an essential accoutrement even in Mongolia. His office was comfortably furnished with a Japanese television set and he explained that the labour camps were run as highly profitable and productive enterprises. He was planning to start up a new business, raising foxes and sables for fur export.

The only profitable part of the entire Mongolian economy seemed to be the prison system.

Like all the other senior officers he had been educated in the Soviet Union. In fact the whole prison system was entirely copied from the Soviets and run according to Marxist-Leninist theories of re-education.

As he explained it, the idea was that the prisoners were reformed, becoming new men after listening to his daily lectures on dialectical materialism and the Socialist system.

'All these lectures were a complete failure,' he confessed gravely and he removed his shades as if they were no longer needed.

'Now, we are putting our trust in religion. Buddhism is the new moral force in our society,' he said. One of his deputies came round and offered me a bowl of sticky sweets while I considered this last remark, stunned into silence.

Democracy, he went on, had brought other changes. The prison system had passed from the control of the Ministry of Internal Security to the Ministry of Justice two months before. This meant that the secrecy which had surrounded the prisons was lifted and prisoners now received letters, parcels and family visits.

'Soon we shall open a public pay phone to allow prisoners to call home every day if they wish to,' he said. 'We want to make it easier for them to integrate back into society when they leave here.'

News of the pro-democracy hunger strikes in Ulan Bator had raised even greater hopes among the prison population. Many prisons had their own hunger strikes, with convicts demanding a general amnesty and representation in parliament. Officials from the Supreme Court and General Procurator's office had to go and placate the prisoners with promises. About ninety were freed although there was no general amnesty.

Under the old system the people's courts handed out sentences for the most minor crimes. People were jailed for two or three years for selling religious paintings or for losing a few animals. It was almost impossible to prevent animals dying during Mongolia's severe winters but shepherds were found guilty of the destruction of state property.

'This will no longer apply as we are privatising all livestock,' Lt.-Col. Survalzmlagch said humorously. Then we went on a tour of the prison.

The entrance to the prisoners' quarters was through gates hammered together from tin cans.

'Soviet colleagues who came here were astonished by the lack of security. In the Soviet Union it would require many guards with guns and dogs to stop prisoners escaping,' Lt.-Col. Aradna said with satisfaction.

Inside was a quadrangle with a couple of basketball nets. The head prisoner appeared and led us to a large new prayer wheel by a notice board put up by the Mongolian Buddhist Association.

At the back of the canteen, a small room had been turned into a chapel. Incense burned in the dimly lit room where a man dressed in saffron robes greeted us. The prisoners had painted pictures of Yama, the god of Hell, which hung on the walls. In the centre of the room stood a large statue of Tsong-Kapa, the founder of the Yellow Hat sect of Tibetan Buddhism.

The caretaker of the shrine said he had shot and killed a friend but now he was trying to atone for his sins. The rest of the inmates were outside digging the foundations of the new fur farm. They looked in good condition and gathered round to talk.

'Hello, how are you?' one of them said in English. He had been teaching himself English for five years and waiting, with unwarranted optimism, for his first chance to practise it.

The prison wardens invited me to ask questions of the prisoners. I handed round some cigarettes and was wondering how to begin when a big man pushed himself forward.

'I want to be free,' he said bluntly. 'I am only here because of the corruption and nepotism of Socialist justice. Many others are innocent too.'

A shifty-looking man in a black woolly hat protested angrily that the president had promised a general amnesty but nothing had happened. 'There is no justice under Socialism,' he declared.

The big man said he had been imprisoned for murdering a man in a drunken brawl eleven years ago. He alone was arrested and those responsible had escaped because they had better political connections. Perhaps, I thought, the big man was telling the truth and many of the prisoners should not be here at all.

'Why don't you escape?' I asked. 'It would be so easy.'

'Where could we go? There is nowhere to go,' the man wearing the black woolly hat said despairingly. At first I thought he meant that the countryside was so desolate, it offered no sanctuary. Then shrugging his shoulders, he added: 'We are Mongols and our conscience would never allow us to escape.'

Even after we left I was not quite sure what he meant. Was this the slave mentality Enktushin talked about? Or did the prisoner mean that as a Buddhist he sought real absolution?

My interpreter Amarjargal liked to quote G. K. Chesterton: 'When people stop believing in something they will believe in anything.'

Amarjargal dressed in Paris fashions and detested the Communists. He was prodigiously well read and said his favourite author was Iris Murdoch.

He claimed the Communists had made the people believe so many lies in the past they were able to believe anything now.

Everyone was talking about flying saucers and people with 'special powers'. A book had come out with drawings and descriptions of various aliens visiting Mongolia and everyone seemed to know someone who had seen one.

The most sensational tale, reported in an extensive television programme, detailed the grave threat to the country posed by a shepherd who had lost a magic chalice entrusted to him by some visiting aliens.

The enraged aliens had beaten him and warned that if the chalice was not recovered in six months death and destruction would follow.

Astrologers said it had been found and was being sold by an antique dealer in Hong Kong or London. The programme was produced by the television journalist Dojodorje of the Genghis Khan Remembrance Society. He told me that he believed the shepherd's account and was planning to place an advertisement in *The Times* to recover the chalice before it was too late.

Amarjargal was sceptical about this story and others but even he thought strange things did happen in Mongolia. There was reincarnation, for example. When his elder brother had suddenly died a few years ago, his mother had drawn a flower on his back with red ink as it was the custom to leave a mark on the corpse. Two years later, his sister had given birth to a girl and on the baby's back was the very same flower in red ink.

We went along to see the most famous authority on such matters. Dr Bor was a respected professor of pedagogy at the State University who had devoted years to studying the paranormal in his spare time.

Dr Bor was a very serious man whose natural gravitas was emphasised by his large head with thick greying hair and portentous manner. A grey overcoat and black hat from the Gromyko era hung next to his desk on which he had piled the eighteen books and thirty papers which were the fruit of his research.

His fascination with the subject had begun as a child, he explained. Three of his uncles had been lamas and one of them was a famous astrologer.

All three were shot during the purges in 1937. Ever since the secret police had waged a brutal campaign against all religious and superstitious practices. He recalled that in the 1940s, the family of a young boy of Hubsogol Province famous for his ability to see far into the distance had been executed for spreading superstitious beliefs.

Dr Bor's research was fraught with danger but he had begun in the 1960s when he was teaching in the countryside by investigating a girl with similar telekinetic powers.

'At that time people's attitude was very different from now. They would put you in prison for that kind of thing,' he said.

'Naturally many people were reluctant to talk about their special abilities,' he added with regret.

Then in 1972 he set about removing the prejudice against such research and published his first book on parapsychology.

'Many people thought it was in the non-scientific sphere and a sign of backwardness and said faith-healers were cheating the people,' he said regretfully.

'Now there is a boom in this field,' he said with grave satisfaction. Reports of Mongolians claiming to possess extraordinary powers were flooding in.

'For example, there is a woman in Budar who can see things happening up to eighty-six kilometres away,' he said. 'She closes her eyes and can see what her mother is doing in her *ger*.'

This was not a bad range although the champion, he said, was a Dutchman whose powers extended to 111 kilometers.

'There are also four people in the Ulziijargal district who can tell just by looking at you what illness afflicts you or if you have committed a crime. Then there is a girl who can set objects on fire just by thinking about them,' he said enthusiastically.

Mongolia has a long tradition in faith-healing, he continued. The best can even perform brain surgery with their bare hands. His own daughter had been cured in this fashion after slipping on ice and badly fracturing her skull.

'Afterwards, the skull was X-rayed and there was no trace of the damage,' he said.

The latest marvel was a sixteen-year-old milkmaid who had encountered a group of extraterrestrials the previous October and was now recounting her experiences in the media and to audiences in a big circus tent outside Ulan Bator.

The aliens had very narrow faces with a white complexion, wore gowns which radiated light, and offered her a kind of berry to eat. They invited her for a trip on their flying saucer.

As they whizzed over Ulan Bator and other industrial centres, the conversation in the spaceship went like this.

'Why are you in Mongolia?' she asked.

'We have travelled over many countries,' the aliens replied.

'And what do you think of it?'

'We find this is a most backward place, especially economically. Mongolia must change its old ways and speed up the reforms,' advised the aliens, giving extraterrestrial backing to the Mongolian Democratic Association.

Leaving Dr Bor's office we ran into another television producer with a great interest in the paranormal who hosted a weekly science programme. He knew the girl who could set things on fire and promised to set up an interview.

We met a few days later to go to her home and on the way he explained that he was hot on another great story. A man had been found who could divine the existence of gold or uranium deposits and even the secret burial place of Genghis Khan. The man was so vital to state security, the producer claimed, that on the orders of the president, he was being guarded in a secret location.

The girl lived in a new apartment block and when we arrived, we found the father in a three piece suit sitting on the sofa with his daughter, a former cook.

She was a plump moonfaced creature and leaving her father to do the talking, carefully studied her fingernails, painted a bright pink. It had all began on April 8th, days after the hunger strike had forced the government to abandon Marxist-Leninism.

She had been clearing out a wooden box in the family yurt that day when at precisely eleven o'clock, she smelt something burning. When she rushed out, she found the felt lining of the *ger* on fire and summoned the fire brigade.

At first her son was investigated as he was suspected of being a re-incarnation of a living Buddha. Over the next two months there were seventy-one separate incidents and it was established beyond reasonable doubt that she was the cause of this spontaneous combustion.

When she was curious or afraid then in some inexplicable way something would start burning. For instance if she realised that she had forgotten to bring in the washing, then whoosh, it would all go up in flames.

'It is very hard to keep nice new clothes. When I think of them, they are ruined,' she confessed shyly.

The government quickly reacted by establishing a commission of eleven leading scientists to study the phenomenon under a five-year programme. The President gave her father a new job and this new apartment. The prime minister ordered the School for Traditional Medicine to give her a place and to shorten the course from six to four years to ensure that her mental energies were not dissipated on 'useless subjects'.

Unfortunately the scientists found she was incapable of ignition on request.

'It is involuntary,' the father gravely explained. All the scientists have found so far were unusually high levels of bio-energy. In the meantime she discovered that she also possessed telepathic powers.

'I can foretell what will happen to my family or if someone is talking about them,' she said modestly. Her grandfather had good intuition too and could foresee the future with sixty to seventy per cent accuracy.

Amarjargal was suspicious and suspected the whole business was just a ruse to jump ahead on the housing list.

She rejected such suggestions with an air of martyrdom.

'I just want to be an ordinary woman. I don't want to have any extra-ordinary powers, it makes me afraid,' she demurred.

At last I could bear no more hedging around and asked to see a demonstration of her powers.

'Many people wish to see her but we allow very few people to come and see her,' her father said sternly.

'So what are you thinking about now? Perhaps we could find a bit of clothing to set fire to?' I said, looking around the room for something suitable.

There was an uneasy silence. Her father was apologetic. It would not be possible. She could not perform on request. She could control it but at best stop herself from involuntarily setting something on fire. Perhaps when I came next time, or next year.

Six months later when I returned to Mongolia, the girl and her father were in prison charged with fraud. Dojodorje had also been forced to admit on television that the whole affair of the chalice and the extraterrestrials had all been made up by the shepherd.

Yet there was a sense of ancient mystery in Mongolia's vastness that was hard to dismiss as a reaction to decades of sterile regimentation. One Sunday morning I hired a car to visit a place in the countryside called the Shrine of the Holy Mother Rock.

The taxi's tyres were worn to a smooth finish and despite the road's icy conditions the driver set off with great confidence. Within a few miles of leaving the airport road, the asphalt gave way to a grass track that wandered through unmarked featureless spaces.

A few months earlier, it would have been impossible to just take off like this. Without a special pass stamped by at least four separate departments we would have been turned back at a police checkpoint on the outskirts of the city.

That Sunday morning no one stopped us and indeed the whole morning we saw no other vehicle, just an old man plodding along and tugging his disdainful camel behind.

We stopped and I photographed the camel which looked in the snow as dissonant as a horse in a swimming pool. When we asked the old man where he was going, he gestured over the distant horizon and said 'over there' with an affability I found foolhardy.

Everything shrank to a mere speck in this landscape. The low and gently curving hills, ground to mere crests by the passing millennia, confused my eye. Big flocks of sheep or cows that in England would have crowded a hillside, dwindled into distant dots.

A few hours later when the sun was sparkling brightly through a gentle mist, the driver stopped the car and turned it in the direction of a snow-covered ridge.

'It is here somewhere,' he muttered to himself as the car bounced in and out of snow drifts. Sometimes he got out to see if we were still following a trail buried under the snow.

Since liberalisation, the Shrine of the Holy Mother Rock had become the most popular cult for people in Ulan Bator. The driver claimed to have taken many visitors in the summer and I had imagined a sort of Lourdes, with busloads converging noisily at a gaudy shrine in the expectation of miracles. This, on the other hand, was turning out to be an altogether more uncertain venture.

After three or four false starts we seemed to hit on a track and the car headed for a gap in the hills. It was harder uphill and we were often stuck in snowdrifts. It took an hour of digging and pushing to get over the brow of the next hill but on the other side we skidded down, zigzagging crazily.

We found a small frozen spring in a little valley dotted with boulders. The holy rock was surrounded by a wall of turf about waist high and decked with a collection of coloured rags. It was not much of a sight.

Next to it a small and official-looking blue sign had been planted which said, 'Recognised and Protected by the Association of Mongolian Believers'.

On closer inspection, the wall was not made of turf but of thousands of individual bricks of tea. The bricks were stamped 'Hunan, China' and little sparrows hopped about pecking at the tea. It was so quiet and windless, I could hear the sound of their wings beating the air.

The rock was garlanded with old scarves, pullovers, office ties, several socks and a pair of baby shoes. There were also coins, banknotes, a child's exercise book, a Czechoslovakian labour medal embossed with Stalin's head and a piece of paper signed by six members of one family. It said, 'Please help us Holy Mother to be happy and live for a long time.'

In front of the stone was a small altar made of an upturned crate on which bowls of milk or sweets and bottles of Chinese Maotai and Mongolian vodka had been left. Other bowls lay on the ground in a pile like a heap of dirty washing.

All round the frozen springhead were smaller rocks, each with its own little pile of votive altars and offerings. One was topped by a broken speedometer and the frame of an old radio. Spanners, sparking plugs, screwdrivers, screws, nuts, bolts and several car keys lay scattered in the snow. Next to this repository of spare parts was an empty bottle of Beefeater's London gin.

The driver recounted the story of the Holy Mother with grim satisfaction. In the 1970s President Tsedenbal had launched one of the periodic anti-religious campaigns to reassert the value of 'true scientific knowledge'. The local Party secretary ordered the rock destroyed but only managed to lop off the head and two stony arms.

When attempts to blast it with dynamite failed, the Party secretary decided to use a tractor and drag it away. The driver attached ropes to the rock and pulled and pulled until darkness fell. Then he spent the night in a nearby *ger*, determined to continue in the morning. When he awoke, his tractor had burnt to ashes. Shortly afterwards the Party secretary died suddenly, his children fell ill and the other officials involved were dogged by similar bad luck.

It proved as hard to move the rock as to root out the locals' faith in their deity. Seventy years of Communism had failed to block up the ancient wellsprings of beliefs which populated the land with good and bad spirits. And despite the new sign planted by the Mongolian Buddhist Association, this place had nothing to do with Siddhartha's message.

According to legend, a good kind shepherdess had tended her flock of lambs here in ancient times. When she died, she became a spirit. She and her animals turned to stone. Now, those who are unhappy or ill come and seek her help, bringing small gifts.

'If you have nothing bad in your heart,' the driver said, 'then she will help. If you only come once and disappear, then it is no use.'

The message of the gifts was a curious one in a Socialist society. The libations of wine or milk I understood, but the Mother Rock was also a mutual benevolent society. People in need could borrow the money – hundreds of tugrik in soggy notes lay there – and return it later. Drivers left the spares not just as a spiritual insurance policy, but as a help for others. Somehow the shapeless rock inspired more generosity than the slogans from a hundred Party congresses.

As we spoke, two girls on ponies appeared over the brow of the hill. With their ruddy wind-chaffed cheeks and braided hair, they looked hardy and free. They dismounted and perambulated around the edge of the wall of tea as tradition dictates. From time to time they stopped to kiss the wall of tea.

Then they bowed in front of the stone, knocking their heads against the ground. After praying silently and with scarcely a look in our direction, they rode off singing, leaving us with the silence.

When I came back to Mongolia in May 1991, I rented out a flat, as the hotel was full of evangelists, religious and economic. I preferred the flat. It was looked after by Tunga, the chirpy wife of an MP, and in the morning she brought a big tray of breakfast and, with her sister Ariuna who was learning English, liked to sit and talk.

Although there was still snow on top of the nearby mountains, the May sunshine was warm enough to leave the windows open. The building was near the barracks and I was usually woken early by squads of recruits chorusing a marching song as they set off for their duties.

Tunga, delighted with the novelty of my presence, brought too much

food – sausage, cream, eggs, cucumber – bought from who knows what
secret supply.

'I shall grow fat in Mongolia,' I said. Tunga and Ariuna laughed.

'Oh Mister Becker, no one can get fat in Mongolia,' Ariuna assured
me.

The missionaries in the hotel had begun arriving immediately after
the first pro-democracy rallies almost eighteen months ago. American
Indians from Baptist groups arrived first and after them came Roman
Catholics, Lutherans, Pentecostalists as well as Mormons, Ba'athists
and Scientologists. Some Muslim imams for the Kazakh minority had
turned up too.

I began to recognise them sitting at lunch in the hotel restaurant and
eyeing each other mistrustfully. At one end were teams from the World
Bank or similar organisations, and at the other were the various
missionaries, recognisable either by their youth or sometimes by their
accompanying children.

A friend urged me to attend a Sunday morning meeting of these
new converts to Christianity.

'Tell the world that Christ has come to Mongolia,' he said.

The handful of Christians were already deeply divided into different
and competing fellowships. At the centre of their dispute was the correct translation of the Bible.

Christian missionaries are nothing new in Mongolian history. It is
only by the narrowest of chances that the Mongols had failed to
become Christians in the eleventh century when some scholars reckon
that up to three quarters of the tribes were converts to Nestorian
missionaries. Several had Christian names like Markus.

After Genghis Khan's death, one European missionary, William
Rubruk, arrived at the royal camp near Karakorum and joined a congregation of Christians celebrating Easter. Marco Polo reported a
Christian-led revolt against Kublai Khan and also found Christians in
many cities during his travels around China.

The Nestorians are a now almost forgotten branch of the Church,
whose followers are still found in Iraq or Eastern Turkey and call
themselves the Chaldean or Assyrian Church.

The split in the Church stemmed from the Council of Ephesus in
AD 431 summoned by the Byzantine Emperor, Theodosius II, to settle
disputes which were partly political and partly a theological dis-
agreement over the nature of the Holy Trinity.

Afterwards, the followers of a Patriarch Nestor renounced all connection with the Church of the Roman Empire and styled themselves
the 'Children of the East'. For ten centuries they struggled to spread

the gospel in the East, reaching China in AD 635 and achieving considerable success.

The presence of Christians among the Mongol armies attacking the Muslims from the East may be the origin of the legend of a mighty king, Prester John, said to rule a great kingdom in the Far East.

Marco Polo has a confusing chapter describing how Genghis Khan defeated Prester John and although scholars do not take this as historical fact, it does suggest that if Prester John's kingdom existed anywhere, it was in Mongolia.

I found about thirty people of different ages already seated in the classroom of a teacher-training college when I arrived, far more than I had imagined. There was a broad range of people of different age and sex. A few had converted while studying in Moscow or Leipzig or Budapest.

Such fellowship meetings had been regular events for several months and more converts were being baptised every month in the Tolla river.

Some of the new converts said they wanted to establish a national Church which reflected the Mongolian style of doing things. That was why, one explained to me, there was no proper service and no foreigners conducting the meeting.

'We will be like the early Christians, meeting to study the Bible and learn about Jesus,' a young man who had studied in Leipzig said.

The atmosphere was quiet and studious. Psalms were written up and translated on the blackboard, then the congregation was invited to stand up and talk of their progress.

An old man of sixty-nine said that since he was a child he had wanted to know who had made the world and all things in it. A schoolboy got up and asked what language God had spoken.

Later everyone was handed a little slip of yellow paper with a question on it. The recipients were asked either who had written the Old Testament or who Christ was.

One boy, asked to explain the Holy Trinity, said God had three names just as a man could at the same time be a son, father and husband.

Before the service ended, the former student from Leipzig said he wanted to play some music he heard while studying in Germany. It had affected him very deeply, he said and then he put on a cassette tape of a Bach organ fugue.

I had the feeling no one else there had ever heard Bach before and as the rich harmonies filled the room, the Mongols sat motionless.

A stock exchange was the last thing I had ever expected to find in Mongolia. Walking through Sukhbator Square I came across some Austrian workmen busily converting an old cinema. So far there was nothing but dust inside but I felt a twinge of regret for the era about to vanish as I looked around this absurd, ugly architecture with its walls painted deep red and its high white pillars.

This was the wedding-cake style Stalin had made famous. Until then I had only been dimly aware of how readily I had traded an image of a land filled with silk-clad princes, mountainbound mystics and warriors on horseback, for a forbidden, secret country immersed in the cruel conventions of Marxist-Leninism. The one kind of mystery seemed as engaging as another.

Some other Austrian contractors were finishing the modernisation of the State Bank of Mongolia. A television monitor watched the visitor entering polished wooden doors into a hall where the soft hum of computers had replaced the clickety-click of wooden abacuses.

It had a nice smell of sawdust and perfume and a secretary in a smart leather skirt and high heels ushered me into a meeting-room. Gustav Klimt prints hung on the wall above the fresh coffee bubbling away in a percolator.

Next door several young men in pinstripe suits sat in the dealing-room watching the computer trading screens flashing up green figures.

'The exchange rates in Tokyo and London,' a girl from Hong Kong explained helpfully. She was helping to induct about 200 Mongols into the ABC of stockbroking.

Zholzhargal was the head of the stock exchange, and its inspiration. He was only twenty-six and seemed to have walked straight off Wall Street. Under a blue blazer, he wore red braces and the sort of stripey cotton shirt bankers like to wear.

Zholzhargal's father was an ex-trade minister, his mother a former finance minister and his brother was the governor of the central bank. He had developed an enthusiasm for capitalism while studying in Hungary where his parents had been posted for a while.

His thesis was on 'The Efficiency of Mongolia's Foreign Trade'.

'The last seventy years have just been a terrible mistake, an awful waste. Central planning was a complete failure,' Zholzhargal said, lighting up a Marlboro.

'If it were not for Communism Mongolia would have become as wealthy as New Zealand or Texas,' he maintained.

'What about greed? Social equality?' I said.

'Why do you Westerners come and tell us about social equality? Look what equality we have here now!' he said, becoming extremely irritated. A Danish economist had recently been and warned him of the perils of excessive liberalisation. Zholzhargal had taken him to the front of the Ulan Bator Hotel and shown him the plainclothes policeman who kept the Mongols from entering without written permits.

'This is how things really worked under Socialism, even now the secret police control us!' he had told the Dane.

Zholzhargal was still angry at the incident.

'I just want to live in a normal country where you don't spend your life queuing or living in fear,' he said.

In 1989 Zholzhargal worked in the central bank and then spent six months in America studying its economic system on a UN scholarship.

In the autumn following the elections, he produced a plan on how to privatise most of the economy in a year. It took two weeks to write, locked in a room with seven friends and a PC.

The public response was a storm of protest. Older economists scoffed that this was 'small children playing games with the market economy' but the worsening economic crisis strengthened the case for drastic remedies.

The plan was simple. You tot up the total value of the economy, divide it by the population and give everyone a ticket to buy whatever they wanted in a grand everything-must-go boot sale of state assets.

A few things like the post office or power stations might remain in state hands but the rest, schools and hospitals included, would go.

It worked out that every Mongolian could claim a share worth 10,000 tugrik or about 100 US dollars.

All the necessary legislation on company law, bankruptcy, tax, customs and private ownership was being pushed through parliament.

In the first stage everyone would get a pink coupon (with a picture of Genghis Khan on it) to bid for livestock, small shops and other small enterprises. Later a blue voucher would entitle them to buy shares in industrial enterprises.

The new stock market would facilitate this redistribution process rather than to establish a rival to Hong Kong or Tokyo. Foreigners would, though, be free to buy shares and the balance sheets of the various enterprises on offer would be made public.

Zholzhargal argued that this 'big bang' reform strategy was better than gradual piecemeal change.

'We must destroy the power base of the state bureaucracy in one blow and change the passive Mongolian mentality,' he said. Slower change would lead to corruption because it allowed the Party élite to exchange political for commercial power as had happened in China.

Mongolia's conditions made this approach particularly feasible. It had no foreign debt, nor a large industrial sector dependent on subsidies and no one had any savings or capital of their own to invest.

For several years nobody would have to pay tax, allowing people to accumulate capital and provide the state with time to set a tax collection system. While government revenues dwindled to nothing, Mongolia would borrow from Western governments or institutions like the International Monetary Fund.

Of course it was inevitable, he said, that some would prosper more than others. Zholzhargal took the Darwinian view on this.

'In any society ten per cent of the population has real drive and energy. They will do well; the trick is to give them the freedom to use their abilities and they will carry the others along with them.'

It seemed that if Zholzhargal was right an economic experiment in near-laboratory conditions was about to take place in Mongolia. The Mongolians were about to jump in one bound from 100 per cent state ownership into unbridled capitalism.

Some of the international economists staying in the hotel, they were dazzled by the prospect. One of them shook his head with delight and amazement at the wonderful purity of these plans.

'Can this be true? Ever since I arrived, it felt like I was in some imaginary country,' he said.

Three

The Mad Baron

It would be quite wrong to leave out the story of the Mad Baron simply because no one is left alive who still remembers his brief but horrible reign. Without His Excellency the Khan of Mongolia and the God of War incarnate, the People's Republic of Mongolia might never have come into existence. In addition his life and death, a tale of destruction and divination, empires and visions, seemed to me as Mongolian as buttered tea.

I did try and find some trace, any trace, of Maj.-Gen. Baron Roman Fyodorovich von Ungern-Sternberg's stay in Ulan Bator but there is almost nothing.

Someone once pointed out a wall on what was now a hospital where the Baron had strung up his victims on meat hooks, but beyond that, even in history museums, he is given no more than a few cursory references.

That was all. Indeed it was hard to find much in the city which predates the 1921 revolution which brought the Mongolian Communists to power after the Baron's defeat.

A couple of old buildings – Ganden Monastery, the Choijin oracle temple – remain, but too little to evoke the vast expanse of gleaming golden roofs, of temples cluttered with bejewelled statues and shrines thronged with ragged, penitent pilgrims and of lamas in rich silk brocades wreathed in incense, that once was Ulan Bator.

I looked in vain for the great square where early travellers saw the Tsam religious dances performed by monks dressed in elaborate costumes with huge masks representing the most terrifying demons. It is now Sukhbator Square where each year tanks chew up the concrete in the annual military parade. The temples which once surrounded it were demolished and in their place a cinema, an opera house and the Party headquarters were built by thousands of Japanese prisoners of war.

Old accounts mention a holy mountain, the Bogda Ola, which lies across the Tolla River and on whose peak twice-yearly ceremonies were held to honour the spirit of Genghis Khan. Its wooded slopes were once a game reserve where wild elk, roebuck and boars roamed freely, protected by two thousand lamas who patrolled its boundaries.

Now the mountain honours friendship with the Soviet Union and its secluded valleys serve to shelter the presidential palace, the Party's school for Marxist-Leninism and holiday homes for the politburo.

The city's name now means 'Red Hero' but it was then called Da Kure or Great Monastery and with a population of 60,000 lamas, it rivalled Lhasa. The Bogd Khan, its ruler, styled himself the Champion of God and Supporter of Civilisation. His subjects adored him as a God-King and the seventh reincarnation of the Bogdo Jebstun Damba Khutukhtu.

He ranked third in the lamaist heirarchy after the Dalai Lama and the Panchen Lama and was born in Tibet, the son of one of the Dalai Lama's officials.

Before the revolution Ulan Bator, or Urga as the foreigners called it, presented a rich and revolting mixture of splendour and squalor. Before considering the Baron's contribution more fully, it is worth lingering over the setting and this curious prelate.

The Russian explorer Prejevalsky who arrived in Urga in the last century held up his haughty nose at the smell of it.

'All the filth is thrown into the street and the habits of the people are loathsome. To add to this, crowds of starving beggars assemble in the marketplace; some of them, mostly poor old women, make it their last resting place. Packs of dogs roam the streets ... No sooner is a fresh corpse thrown into the street than wild dogs tear it to pieces and in a couple of hours nothing remains of the dead man,' he wrote.

Amidst this squalor the Bogd Khan lived a life of medieval splendour enriched by religious taxes, benefices, the sale of potions and blessings and the income from the large herds owned by his monasteries. His collection of rare objects – books, paintings and jewels – was so impressive that one visitor, the Polish geologist Dr Ferdinand Ossendowski devoted several pages of his book *Men, Beasts and Gods* to listing his treasures.

His palace is still there although it is now a museum. It looks like the

Dalai Lama's summer palace in Lhasa, a European building with several storeys and a green tin roof. The walls are painted yellow, a sign that the Dalai Lama had stayed there, which indeed he did when the British invaded Tibet in 1904 and he sought refuge in Mongolia.

The Bogd Khan's most eccentric collection was his zoo and the museum still preserves the lifeless remnants – a stuffed giraffe, a polar bear with glassy eyes, a shiny-shelled giant turtle, a sloth, a boa constrictor and several seals.

Unfortunately the Bogd Khan's elephants, who must somehow have survived Mongolia's bitter winters, disappeared after his death. At the museum which was usually closed, a charming and polyglot caretaker tried to explain what had happened. Unfortunately she could manage no more than the same three phrases in any of the six languages she attempted. Finally she brought me to admire his tent, a magnificent affair made from leopard skins and we stood before it in multilingual admiration.

The Living Buddha collected everything and once went on a shopping spree to Shanghai returning with the country's first gramophone and motorcar.

The American explorer Roy Chapman Andrews related that the motorcar's chief use was to electrify those who came to ask his blessing. He had wires connected to the batteries, attached to a long red rope which was thrown over the wall of his palace that pilgrims used to kiss on bended knees.

From the window he would watch and roar with laughter when the worshippers jumped with the shock. Afterwards his subjects rode away, silent with awe at having so clearly received divine emanations from the living god.

In 1919 Mrs Bulstrode described him as bloated, dissipated and cruel. When Dr Ossendowski met him a few years later he found a 'stout old man with a heavy shaven face resembling those of the Cardinals of Rome' with 'wide-open blind eyes'.

The 'personality of the Living Buddha was double, just as everything in lamaism is double. Clever, penetrating, energetic, he at the same time indulges in the drunkenness which brought on blindness,' the Polish geologist said.

A Russian resident in Urga reported that the Bogd Khan, who was also head of government, was often intoxicated by early afternoon and his 'cabinet meetings' usually ended in drunken brawls.

Either this intemperance or perhaps the syphilis which was then widespread in Mongolia caused him to go blind and led to his death in 1924. The Communists certainly portrayed him as a sexual libertine who not only married but consorted with young girls.

The Mongolian scholar, Academician Rintchen wrote a novel in which the high lama is described raping a twelve-year-old girl and then ordering a servant to throw the unconscious girl, tied in a sack loaded with stones, into the Tulla River. Two years later he supposedly went back to the spot and, overcome with guilt, carved the Buddhist mantra, *om mani padme hum*, on a rock which was still to be found until 1968.

In his lifetime the Bogd Khan was not only feared as a divine and debauched monster but revered as a nationalist.

Although he was by origin a Tibetan he supported an uprising against Peking when the Manchus were overthrown in 1911. More than that he backed all pan-Mongolist strivings and tried to intervene militarily in Inner Mongolia.

To celebrate Mongolia's independence he ordered the construction of a ninety-foot-high statue of the deity Ahamokitesheara which was covered with gold leaf and studded with jewels.

The tower built to house it now stands empty in Ganden monastery because in 1939 the statue was shipped to the Soviet Union as a gift to Stalin. Mongolians are demanding its return as a symbol of their regained independence and a search has begun to find it. Records show that until 1958 it was stored in pieces somewhere in Leningrad.

The Communist Party later belittled the importance of the 1911 revolution in preference for the 1921 'revolution' which brought it to power. It spread the story, widely believed, that the statue was an offering to stop the Bogd Khan's increasing blindness.

For over twenty years the Bogd Khan sought to enlist the protection of the Tsar in Moscow and it was Russian support which enabled him to declare independence.

With the First World War and then revolution at home, Russian influence had waned to the point where a Chinese warlord felt strong enough to invade.

In 1919 General Hsu Shu-Tseng occupied Ulan Bator and imprisoned the Bogd Khan. General Hsu then demanded the back-payment of all taxes since 1911, reducing much of the population to beggary.

It was at this low point in Mongolia's fortunes that the Baron appeared on what he claimed was a divinely sanctioned mission to re-establish the empire of Genghis Khan and rid the world of Bolsheviks.

The Baron was a White Russian general escaping from the civil war raging across the border in Russia, with a motley crew of Tsarist officers and brigands.

He claimed to be the scion of a long line of Baltic warriors and mystics descended from Attila the Hun. He said that his grandfather was a pirate who had converted to Buddhism while attacking English merchant ships off the coast of India, and had introduced it to the Baltic.

The Baron had served as a cadet in the Imperial Russian Navy but later joined the Transbaikal Cossacks. It is likely that he first arrived in Urga during the 1911 revolution to protect the Manchu governor or Amban from rioting Mongols. Quite probably he himself became a Buddhist at this stage.

Afterwards he fought against the Germans and then when Russia dropped out of the First World War, he joined the White Army commanded by the notorious Hetman Semenov which operated in the Far East.

According to one account, 'He had not the slightest rudiments of common decency or military discipline ... Only his reckless courage prevented his being cashiered by various commanding officers under whom he had served ... When Ungern-Sternberg entered a café, other occupants retired, for he was an expert with his gun. In his drinking bouts he slew many of his own officers.'

Dr Ossendowski, who was himself fleeing from the Bolsheviks, described him thus: 'A small head on wide shoulders: blond hair in disorder, a reddish bristling moustache, a skinny exhausted face like those on old Byzantine ikons. Then everything else faded from view save a big protruding forehead overhanging steely sharp eyes. These eyes were fixed on me like those of an animal from a cave.'

Another eyewitness wrote that 'he was tall and slim, with the lean white face of an ascetic. His watery blue eyes were steady and piercing. He possessed the dangerous power of reading people's thoughts ... His broad forehead bore a terrible sword cut which pulsed with red veins. His white lips were closed tightly, and the long blond whiskers hung in disorder over his narrow chin. One eye was a little above the other.'

The Baron recruited an army from former Polish and Austro-Hungarian POWs, Imperial Cavalry officers, freebooters, Cossacks and Mongols, to which he added seventy soldiers sent by the Dalai Lama, and a Mongolian princess, his new bride.

A former White officer Dimitri Alioshin described in his book *Asian Odyssey* how, whip in hand and wearing a cherry-red Chinese jacket and blue Imperial Russian Army breeches, the Baron inspected a new batch of recruits.

He would stop at each man separately, look straight into his face, hold that gaze for a few moments, and then bark: 'to the army', 'back to the cattle' or 'liquidate'. All men with physical defects were shot, until only the able-bodied remained. He killed all Jews, regardless of age, sex or ability. Hundreds of innocent people were liquidated by the time the inspection was closed ... His Buddhist teachers taught him about reincarnation, and he firmly believed that in killing feeble people he only did them good, as they would be stronger beings in their next life.

Ivan Maisky, who later became the Soviet ambassador to London, made a secret visit to Mongolia and established contact with a small group of revolutionaries in Ulan Bator, thought the Baron had 6,000 troops including 4,000 White Russians.

The Baron was also thought to have the backing of the Japanese, and at least a dozen Japanese officers were seconded to him.

Many of his troops tried deserting when they realised how mad the Baron was. On one occasion fierce Chahar Mongols were sent off in pursuit of the deserters and returned with a sack full of ears.

Alioshin described the pitiful state of his Russian troops.

'The former Russian officers were dressed in rags, with pieces of leather tied to the soles of their feet. Unshaven and dirty, cynical and cunningly cruel, they were lost to the world. Death was always welcome to them, and they fought like devils. Although utterly neglected, they were the cementing force that united the whole army.'

His adjutant was a huge man called Burdukovski with small clear blue eyes who had a habit of whistling tunelessly. He was known as the Teapot and Dr Ossendowski reported the macabre reason for his nickname. Should the Baron, in the course of an interview, request a teapot, Burdukovski would seize the visitor from behind and strangle him to death.

Then there was Colonel Sepailov, 'always nervously jerking and wriggling his body and talking ceaselessly, making most unattractive sounds in his throat and sputtering with saliva all over his lips.' Even the Baron realised he was insane – the Bolsheviks had tortured and murdered his family – and he twice ordered a commission of surgeons to examine him. Yet the Colonel saved himself from execution by discovering a shaman who declared that if Sepailov died, the Baron's death would soon follow.

The Baron was obsessively superstitious. His first attack on Urga took place on October 26th, 1920, a day which the soothsayers considered propitious. The Chinese, who numbered at least 12,000, drove them back under a withering crossfire.

The Baron, convinced that his mission was part of a divine plan, consulted the oracle bones once more and then waited five days in a severe snowstorm before trying again on October 21st. This failed too and so did two other attempts.

His army retreated and he recruited more men. A few who deserted were caught and roasted alive by being lowered from a tree over a fire.

On January 21st he advanced again, stopping at places chosen according to instructions his clairvoyants gleaned from gazing at the cracks on mutton shoulder bones – the traditional Mongolian method of divination. Meanwhile two carloads of fleeing Jews were caught and 'lynched with great gaiety', as the Baron considered Jews and Bolsheviks one and the same thing.

January 31st was considered propitious and the Baron ordered fires lit on the hills around the city creating the impression that there were at least 100,000 attackers.

The attack went well, the Bogd Khan was released from his palace and 2,000 Chinese troops took to their heels. The rest barricaded themselves in the centre of Urga, especially in the barracks, the Russian Consulate and offices of the Russian Goldmining Company.

Since final victory was not prophesied until February 4th, the Baron ordered a ceasefire but by mistake someone launched a mortar during the night. Alioshin wrote that 'immediately the Chinese opened unsystematic and mad shooting. Machine-guns began their dreadful clattering. The temptation was too great and, contrary to orders, we dashed forwards into battle. The Baron was carried away by the mad impulse also, as we saw him galloping on his white horse in front of our lines, directing us towards the enemy's barbed wire.'

Huge fires burned in the Chinese quarter of the town. The Russians reached the walls of the barracks and blew open the main gates with grenades and then poured in, bayoneting and shooting.

Mad with revenge and hatred, the conquerors began plundering the city. Drunken horsemen galloped along the streets shooting and killing at their fancy, breaking into houses, dragging property outside into the dirty streets, dressing themselves in the rich silks found in the shops. In front of the Chinese banks, lines were formed, where each man was given the right to plunge his bloody hand inside the strong boxes and get what his luck would bring him. Some were fortunate enough to drag out gold coins and bullion. Some were less fortunate and got silver, while many found only paper currency and bank notes, which they immediately threw into the street as worthless, Alioshin wrote.

The Jews were killed under the directions of the chief medical officer, a Dr Klingenberg. Women offered themselves up for rape to save their husbands but were cheated. In a drunken stupor one officer began shooting his own comrades; another, a cadet called Smirnov, indulged his fetish for strangling old women – he enjoyed seeing them quiver under the grip of his fingers as he broke their necks. A Dane called Olsen who protested at this havoc was dragged through the streets by a wild horse until he died.

For three days 'innumerable men, women and children of all ages, races and creeds were hacked to bits and bayoneted and shot and strangled and hanged and crucified and burnt alive.'

The Baron continued the reign of terror by feeding prisoners to his private pack of wolves although his favourite and most used penalty was lashing people to death.

The delighted Bogd Khan bestowed on the Baron the exalted title of 'Khan' and in return the Baron proclaimed him 'Emperor of All Mongolia'.

In the midst of all this the Baron also found time to arrange a bus service and electricity supplies, ordered the first ever cleaning of Ulan Bator, constructed several bridges, published a newspaper and set up a veterinary laboratory.

While this was going on, the Chinese tried sending reinforcements who were all caught and massacred. Dr Ossendowski came across their corpses *en route* to Urga: 'The killed men showed terrible sword wounds; everywhere equipment and other debris were scattered about. The Mongols, with their herds, moved away from the neighbourhood and their place was taken by the wolves which hid behind every stone and in every ditch we passed.'

The Baron's own plans to 'exterminate commissars, Communists and Jews with their families' and to erect 'an avenue of gallows' all the way to Moscow proceeded apace. On May 27th, 1921 he declared Grand Duke Michael 'Emperor of all Russia' and hired 7,000 lamas to invoke divine intervention on his behalf at a cost of 20,000 Mexican dollars.

The Baron took a liking to Ossendowski and together they drove around Urga in a large Fiat at a furious pace. One night he accompanied the Baron on a visit to the Choijin Temple to consult the oracle and discovered why the Baron acted as if he were driven by the furies.

He describes the scene in his book: '"Cast the dice for the number of my days," the Baron demanded of an old priest who brought two bowls with many dice inside. The dice are rolled. The Baron looked and reckoned with them the sum before he spoke, "One hundred and thirty! Again one hundred and thirty!"'

On another night they visited the blind Living Buddha who blessed the Baron and told him: 'You will not die but you will be reincarnated in the highest form of being. Remember that, incarnated God of War, Khan of grateful Mongolia!'

Then finally, on the eve of Ossendowski's departure for China and when the Baron was about to begin his divine mission to save Russia, he summoned yet another soothsayer. A middle-aged woman appeared and Ossendowski wrote that:

She drew a small bag very slowly from her girdle, took from it some small bird bones and a handful of dry grass . . . She began whispering at intervals unintelligible words and as she threw occasional handfuls of grass into the fire . . . I felt a distinct palpitation of my heart, she placed the bird bones on the charcoal, turned them over again and again with a small pair of black pincers, as the bones blacked she examined them . . . contracted with convulsions and began snapping out short, sharp phrases.

'I see . . . I see the God of War . . . His life runs out . . . horribly . . . After it a shadow . . . black like the night . . . Shadow . . . One hundred and thirty steps remain . . . Beyond darkness . . . Nothing . . . I see nothing . . . The God of War has disappeared . . .'

Baron Ungern dropped his head. The woman fell over on her back with her arms stretched out . . .

Baron Ungern finally got up and began to walk around the brazier, whispering to himself.

'I shall die! I shall die! . . . but no matter, no matter . . . The cause has been launched and will not die . . . The tribes of Jenghiz Khan's successors are awakened. Nobody shall extinguish the fire in the heart of the Mongols. In Asia there will be a great State from the Pacific and Indian Oceans to the shore of the Volga. The wise religion of the Buddha shall run to the North and the West. A conqueror shall appear stronger and more stalwart than Jenghiz Khan . . . and he will keep power in his hands until the happy day when, from his subterranean capital, shall emerge the King of the World.

'Why, why shall I not be in the first ranks of the warriors of Buddhism? Why has karma decided so? But so it must be! And Russia must first wash itself from the insult of revolution, purifying herself with blood and death: and all people accepting Communism must perish with their families . . .'

The Baron raised his hand above his head and shook it, as though he were giving his orders and bequests to some invisible person.

Day was dawning.

'My time has come!' said the General. 'In a little while I shall leave Urga.'

He quickly and firmly shook hands with us and said: 'Good-bye for all time! I shall die a horrible death but the world has never seen such a terror

79

and such a sea of blood as it shall now see.'

The doors of the yurta slammed shut and he was gone. I never saw him again.

Dr Ossendowski set off for Peking and the Baron, convinced that he had only 130 days left, began his crusade to liberate Russia. Intending to link up with Hetman Semenov and other surviving Tsarist generals, he moved his troops across the border into what had become the Soviet Union.

His plans provided the pretext for the Red Army's invasion of Mongolia. Ten thousand troops marched into Urga in July 1921 accompanied by 700 Mongols, invited by the Mongolian Revolutionary Party founded less than a year earlier at a conference across the border in Khiatkha.

The Bogd Khan was made head of state and constitutional monarch and a few months later Sukhbator supposedly met Lenin in the Hotel Metropol in Moscow although the meeting was only reported in 1934 and posthumously added to Volume 44 of Lenin's collected works.

Moscow's decision to annex Mongolia seems to have been prompted to pre-empt an invasion by a pro-Japanese warlord in China, Chang Tso-Lin.

Later the entire events were recast as a popular people's revolution although nothing of the kind occurred. The original charter of the Mongolian Revolutionary Party was nationalistic rather than revolutionary. Clause 2 of its charter stated that 'our People's Party strives for the ultimate goal of the union of all Mongolian tribes in a single autonomous state.'

Within a year of the Red Army's invasion, fifteen members of the first Mongolian revolutionary group had been shot, including the several prime ministers. Sukhbator died two years later in mysterious circumstances, perhaps poisoned by Soviet doctors. His body was later exhumed and taken back to the Soviet Union for a post mortem but the results were never revealed.

In the meantime, the Baron Ungern-Sternberg won the first skirmishes but then his advance guard of Chahar Mongols was heavily defeated in an engagement with the Red Army. Arriving at the scene the Baron was so enraged he seized Dr Klingenberg and 'threw him to the ground and beat him with his bamboo until the doctor's legs were broken and he was a complete wreck.'

When one of his deputies, Prince Puntzak, expressed doubts about the wisdom of tackling the well-equipped Russian force head on, the Baron had him buried alive.

Next his small army was trapped in an ambush. Alioshin described the scene: 'We were in the middle of a forest when the Reds opened deadly fire. Our men were swept from their feet like grass before a scythe. Men and horses were piled together in bloody heaps.'

They regrouped again near Khiatkha but were surprised by an early dawn attack. 'The Whites threw away their heavy ammunition, artillerymen cut loose their horses from the gins, the hospital personnel abandoned their wounded, men in charge of our transport left ammunition and food, and all dashed madly into the hills.'

Later he wrote that when the force had reassembled and the Baron had recovered his self-confidence again, he hanged a Colonel Arhipov and burned alive a Dr Engelgard-Eserski. At Erden Zu Monastery, the Baron regrouped his forces and made an offering by throwing his silver to the bottom of the Orkhon River.

In the next attack, the Baron's forces were more successful and wiped out an entire Red division. Another victory followed against the 35th Bolshevik Cavalry Division.

Alioshin describes the scene again. 'The prisoners were forced to dig large communal graves at which they were subsequently lined up. Machine-gun fire was directed upon them, and they fell into the fresh grave. The lucky ones were killed instantly, but those who were only wounded were buried alive when we filled the grave with earth.'

And he adds: 'The Red nurses were given to soldiers hungry for women's bodies. All died during the endless humiliation.'

The Bolsheviks then brought up heavy reinforcements including aircraft. These cavalry regiments closed in on him from the north and another three from the east. The battle lasted for two days and two nights and in the end the Baron was utterly defeated. Semenov and two other Tsarist generals failed to come to his support.

Since Urga was already occupied by the Red Army the Baron decided to head towards Chinese Turkestan while Semenov retreated to Manchuria where he later died at the hands of the Red Army after World War II.

'The Baron rode silently with bowed head in front of the column. The Baron had lost his hat and most of his clothes. On his naked chest numerous Mongolian talismans and charms hung on a bright yellow cord. He looked like the reincarnation of a prehistoric ape man. People were afraid to look at him,' Alioshin wrote.

One night his men decided they had had enough and agreed to kill him. They fired a machine-gun at his tent, pointblank. The Baron jumped out on to his horse, disappeared and then suddenly returned covered in blood. His men stood petrified until a captain named

Makeev drew his revolver and shot him. He missed and the Baron wheeled away and disappeared.

Finally, bleeding, exhausted and helpless, the Baron slid from his saddle and fell to the ground unconscious.

There he remained tortured by ants until some of his Mongol troops discovered him. They were uncertain what to do at first since they still feared him as the incarnate God of War. At length they decided to tie him up with rope and leave him.

The next day he was found by a Red Army patrol, trying to shake off the ants.

'Who are you, stranger?' the soldiers asked. 'I am,' he screamed in his high-pitched voice, 'Baron von Ungern-Sternberg.'

The Baron was then taken before the Supreme Soviet Court at Novosibirsk where amongst other charges he was accused of plotting to restore the monarchy.

He reportedly told his accusers: 'For a thousand years the Ungers have given other people orders. We have never taken orders from anyone, I refuse to accept the authority of the working class.'

He was executed by firing squad on September 15th, 1921. His 130 days over just as the fortune tellers of Urga had predicted.

Four

Choibalsan and the Years of Terror

Marshal Choibalsan is the twentieth century's most obscure dictator. His name is unknown in the West but during his rule around 100,000 innocent people were executed in Mongolia. Somewhere on the outskirts of Ulan Bator thousands and thousands of skeletons lie in mass graves each with a neat bullethole in the back of the skull. There are similar graves all over the country.

Travelling in the countryside I would hear rumours of these execution grounds and burial sites, from a hunter who had found scattered bleached skulls lying in a distant wood near an old monastery, or from a tractor driver who had in some field unearthed a harvest of bones.

It seemed incredible that an event as large and as dreadful as this could remain virtually unknown for so long. Most of the killings took place during the 1930s when no foreigners were allowed into Mongolia and afterwards Mongolia kept its secret.

Even now no one knows for sure how many died. Some estimate that perhaps one in seven members of the country's population perished but I never managed to arrive at an accurate statistic. Certainly no official figure has ever been given for the whole period. A correct figure would have to include the deaths during collectivisation, the ensuing civil war, the numerous political prisoners who died in camps throughout the whole period of Choibalsan's reign, the deaths during purges in the late 1930s, and the execution of most of the country's priesthood.

It was almost an accident that I first became aware of the scale of the death toll when during a lunch in March 1990 someone casually mentioned the estimate of 100,000 deaths. My report, a mere half century late, seemed to be the first account of the event.

A few Westerners did spend time in Mongolia after Marshal Choibalsan's death in 1952, such as Ivor Montagu or Professor Owen Lattimore from Britain, but the deaths are barely mentioned in their books; a few words about purges in the top ranks and that is all.

Professor Lattimore of Leeds University was the most eminent Western authority on Mongolia and must shoulder some of the blame. He was an influential adviser to the American government on its China policy during World War II but Robert Conquest condemns him as 'a noted apologist for Stalin and similar regimes' in his book *The Great Terror: A Reassessment*. He points out that Lattimore called the Moscow show trials a 'triumph for democracy' and after touring Siberia's Gulag camps in 1944 with American Vice President Henry Wallace, he compared them 'to a combination of the Hudson Bay Company and the Tennessee Valley Authority'.

In Mongolia the subject remained closed until the pro-democracy demonstrations although the Marshal had by then been dead for forty years. His statue – a small white plaster affair of a man in an overcoat – remains even now on its plinth in front of the state university and his corpse continues to share the red marble tomb with Sukhbator in front of the Party headquarters on Sukhbator Square.

It is a replica of Lenin's tomb in front of the Kremlin on Red Square but while Nikita Khrushchev eventually had Stalin's body removed, Choibalsan's is still there.

The reason was obvious – Choibalsan's successor, President Tsedenbal, had no desire to expose these terrible crimes because he himself was a party to them. Even after the elections in July 1990 the new government formed by the Communist Party did little to investigate this holocaust or bring to justice any of those responsible.

Yet the records are still there, rows of yellowing paper files, preserved in backrooms of the Ministry of Internal Security. Just as in Inner Mongolia, each folder details the tortures, investigations and sentences with bureaucratic self-righteousness.

The more I heard about what had happened under Marshal Choibalsan and the scale of it, the creepier and the more macabre Mongolia became in my eyes. Everyone around me must have had some member of their family executed or betrayed during the purges. Unless, of course, they or their relatives were responsible for the executions. Yet nobody talked about it or had ever talked about it in public.

The country's population doubled after Marshal Choibalsan's death and since over half are under thirty, they would have grown up largely ignorant of the full extent of the horror. It began to seem to me that it was as if the Nazis were still the ruling party in Germany and everyone was either frightened or too guilty to mention what had happened and why. Instead the population of a whole country was pretending to act as if the purges had never happened.

That was the most terrifying aspect of a totalitarian regime – its power to obliterate the past and instil such fear in its victims that even later the truth is hard to uncover.

Once I was given the telephone number of a commission set up in the late 1950s to examine the cases of erroneous convictions during the Great Terror (as the period is now termed in the Soviet Union). When Khrushchev denounced Stalin's crimes and opened up the labour camps in 1956, he had a similar commission set up in the Soviet Union.

The Mongolians' commission was created with much less enthusiasm. In theory it was still operating but although I rang its office telephone number day after day, no one ever answered.

I managed to meet a spokesman from the Ministry of State Security who said that in ten years the commission had managed to examine the cases of 1,500 people. The official was a dumpy, cautious-looking man in a grey suit and steel spectacles who sat in a deep armchair at the Ministry of Foreign Affairs. The latter had arranged the interview after lengthy negotiations.

He was careful to stress his ministry's great support for the democracy movement but reluctant to talk about the past. He finally became embarrassed at trying so obviously to avoid providing any answers.

'According to our statistics, 30,000 fell victim to the repressions,' he said, 'and between 1936 and 1940 20,000 were executed.

'Of course,' he went on glibly, shifting the blame on to another department, 'our ministry is only responsible for external security, that is for spies, you will have to contact the Ministry of Public Security for comprehensive statistics.'

As, after an hour, we prepared to end the discussion, the official became positively confiding. Was I aware that every organisation in Mongolia was now trying to establish contacts and exchanges with their counterparts in the West? Perhaps I could help?

'We want to get in touch with the British secret service, you see, or the CIA,' he said, shaking my hand and holding on to it just a bit too long. 'We could co-operate, now that we are all friends.'

It was rare for me to meet anyone who still remembered Choibalsan's days although later on when I began travelling in the countryside, I met some of the old lamas who described how their monasteries were destroyed and the monks were quietly led to their deaths.

One November evening, however, one of the young leaders of the democracy movement invited me to a party and I met his sister. When she heard of my interest in the 1930s, she said she was herself trying to discover the fate of her grandfather.

A few days later I came to see her in the evening. I found a Russian woman slightly drunk on the sofa talking to a man who, although he was middle aged, wore what was left of his hair down to his shoulders.

The girl's mother liked speaking Chinese and had been brought up by a mixed Chinese and Mongolian family, after her Russian father disappeared in the 1930s. Her husband, a Buryiat Mongol, had studied in Peking until the Sino-Soviet split when he returned and tens of thousands of ethnic Chinese were thrown out of Mongolia.

'I remember when Marshal Choibalsan died in 1952. We thought, how are we all going to live now? And for days crowds gathered around his grave. And when Stalin died, I was just seventeen years old and still in school. Everyone cried when we heard the news,' she said. Both Stalin and Choibalsan were worshipped as great leaders, almost as gods, she said.

Her daughter wanted to talk about her grandfather, the Russian who had disappeared in the 1930s, and began pulling out some books and old documents. One was a Soviet propaganda book which showed a picture of a tall, smiling European wearing a *del* and carrying a gun. His name was Simukov.

'That was my grandfather,' she said. 'They say he spoke Mongolian well and knew the old script. He could even slaughter a sheep the Mongolian way by squeezing its heart.'

Her mother was not listening and followed her own train of thought.

'At that time, you know, we were ignorant of his crimes. Ordinary people didn't know. Nobody knew. It was like the Middle Ages. When people were in prison we were told they were counter-revolutionaries.'

She was rapidly emptying the bottle of vodka I had brought. She carried on talking but it was hard to tell whether she always drank, or it was recalling the past that made her want to drink.

'People were very afraid of the secret police. We knew there were informers and agents everywhere but we did not know who was one. We were also very afraid to talk to each other. Every tenth person was an informer and for half a typed page of information they paid fifty tugriks. Fifty tugriks,' she said and laughed.

Her daughter continued looking through the pile of papers – scientific studies, cartographic plans and sketches. 'Grandfather wrote many articles in many journals,' she said. 'For eight years he travelled all over Mongolia. He produced the first proper map of Mongolia.

'He took part in the Koslov expedition in 1923 and fell in love with Mongolia. He stayed here until 1938 and was about to publish his most important work when he was arrested,' the daughter continued, almost oblivious of her mother.

'My grandfather just disappeared,' the daughter said. 'It appears that he was arrested in the autumn of 1939. At first he was taken to Ulan Ude and from there to Novosibirsk where he was given a seven-year sentence.'

The NKVD (the forerunner of the KGB) never built many prison camps in Mongolia itself but many Russians and Mongols were sent to the camps in Siberia.

'The last letter came from Arkhansk. He wrote that he would send the exact address later. On the 15th of December 1942, the authorities sent a letter saying that he died in prison of a heart attack,' the girl continued.

'Then a Russian writer, called Boris Poleyvoy, was travelling in Arhanghai Province in 1974 and was astonished when all the old people there recognised him. They thought he was my grandfather because he was also tall and blond. Boris became interested and in Moscow searched out my grandfather's widow. Boris could write nothing until a few years ago when they finally rehabilitated my grandfather. My mother was two when he disappeared and until the 1970s she had no idea of the existence of a family in Moscow,' the daughter said.

Her mother was not really listening though and was now fairly drunk.

'Before my husband died in 1981, I accompanied him to Moscow in search of treatment,' the old woman said and then fell silent.

'Then two months ago, his daughter from Moscow came to Ulan Bator to see if his works are in the archives and it is possible to publish his works. We went to the Mongolian Ministry of State Security but they said they knew nothing about him since it was an entirely Soviet affair,' the daughter said.

I said Simukov seemed to be the only Russian whom people spoke well of. The other man, who had remained silent, then joined in the conversation. Tsolmon was a lecturer at the Institute of Geography, a specialist in glaciology, and had just written and published a little book about Simukov.

'We have to separate the people from the government and from the political system,' he said. Tsolmon who had studied in the USSR was against the rising tide of anti-Russian feeling. By now the old lady was embarrassingly drunk ('these Russians are always like animals with drink,' my companion, Amarjargal had whispered in my ear with unsuppressed hatred) and I decided to leave. Tsolmon came with us.

It was bitterly cold outside and the ice crackled under our feet. Even though it was only nine p.m. nothing was open in Ulan Bator and there was nowhere to go and talk. At one hotel, the Bayngol, they would let me as a foreigner in but not Tsolmon or Amarjargal since they did not have their identity papers with them. At the Ulan Bator Hotel the bar was closed so we sat in a reception room.

'My grandfather was one of the first teachers of geography in Mongolia and taught at the Party school. When he was arrested, one of his sisters took all his notebooks and hid them,' Tsolmon said. 'When she died I was tidying up her flat and found them. They were all that was left from his life and I read them carefully.

'He was a very educated person but what surprised me most was how many pictures of Stalin he had kept. He seems to have worshipped Stalin. He admired Stalin and Stalin had him killed. That was his tragedy.'

After his father's death Tsolmon was brought up by an elderly couple. At the end of the 1930s his guardian, who was an army officer, was arrested and imprisoned. He spent five years in prison and considered himself very lucky because he survived at all. The conditions in prison were brutal. Most of the women prisoners were raped and the men beaten and starved.

'During the holidays, he would ask us to leave the room when he was drinking,' Tsolmon said in his slow and hesitating way. 'You see, he was terrified that we might hear what he said when his tongue was loosened by drink. And then we might betray him at some future time.'

People were frightened of their own children. That, I thought, must be the ultimate goal of any dictatorship when any kind of trust, except faith in the great leader, had been destroyed.

'Even now fifty years on we still preserve an atmosphere of shock and fear from that time,' Tsolmon continued in the empty room. 'Many of those responsible for these murders are still alive and living among us.'

Many people, he explained, were executed in the purges on the basis of false confessions or tip-offs. A person could denounce another just by saying they did not consider them loyal to the state or Party. Many disappeared after such unsubstantiated allegations were made or simply overheard by an informer.

'I know some of them personally. I have a very bad and strange feeling when I meet such people,' he said and then fell silent.

At first I tried to interview some of Choibalsan's former assistants, old retired Party officials now in their seventies or older, but even though Choibalsan had been dead for forty years, it was hard to discover any fresh details.

Sometimes I went to their homes and drank tea in their comfortably furnished apartments; or I would invite them for lunch in the hotel restaurant but it was difficult to believe that these old gentlemen, polite and invariably dressed in an old black suit, were in any way responsible for such ghastly crimes. Evil in the shape of a mad, superstitious Baltic baron was easier to grasp than this suburban gentility.

They appeared willing to help but – alas, it was so long ago and they were so junior . . . Or I would sit there somehow feeling it was impolite to interrupt while they evaded my questions and digressed into long rambling monologues until it was time to go.

Finally I lost patience and bluntly asked one of them how it was that so many Mongols were taken to their deaths without protest. He looked at me silently for a moment and then smiled.

'You know we are a very humble people, used to obeying the authority of the state without question,' he said simply. 'I just believed the Party could not be wrong.'

One afternoon I met a writer who was now a prominent member of the new Parliamentary Committee on Human Rights and who had thoroughly researched the history of Choibalsan.

Byamya was an energetic middle-aged man with grey hair that stood up as if he had just been electrocuted.

'What d'ja want? You want whisky from Schotlant?' He greeted me loudly in English in his crowded office at the back of an exhibition hall. We drank coffee instead while Byamya tried to analyse his own lack of comprehension.

As a small boy he had hero-worshipped Choibalsan. When his body was brought back from Moscow, he went to pay his respects as it lay in state.

'I went nine times! Nine times!' Byamya shouted, holding up as many fingers. 'You see. I supported his personality cult.

'At the time,' he continued in a quieter voice, 'all of us were cheated and deceived but I have to admit I was anxious to accept the lie as the truth.'

'But surely it was odd for a Buddhist people brought up with strong notions of good and evil to worship such a man?' I asked.

'But then look how it happened with Stalin, Hitler or Mao?' he said.

Marshal Choibalsan was hailed in his lifetime as Stalin's 'closest pupil' and to understand his rise to power, Byamya said, one must look at Stalin's career and how his ideas affected Mongolia.

In 1928 Stalin was winning undisputed power for himself in Moscow and overturning the looser New Economic Policy which had been in place since Lenin's death. The Soviet Union began the first five-year plan in the same year, starting a mad dash towards collectivisation and channelling all resources into industrialisation.

Mongolia had to march in step. There was a Party purge, the confiscation of the nobility's private property, the rapid establishment of collective farms and a campaign against all 'feudal culture'. The latter included the traditional Mongolian script which was replaced by the Latin alphabet.

The permanent settlement of nomads in the Soviet Union began in September 1930 and a year later Mongolia was ordered to do the same by the resident representative of the Communist International.

The Comintern directed the activities of parties outside the USSR and in Mongolia Party leaders who ignored its instructions were quickly arrested. Hundreds of Russian 'advisers' arrived to help implement the collectivisation and divide the herdsmen into three political classes: rich, middle and poor.

A rich herdsman or a kulak in Russian (which means fist and was translated as *nodargan*) was anyone with over 200 sheep, while a poor man had less than 200 sheep. The nomads were called together for meetings and kept in tents for four days without food or drink until they agreed to hand over their animals to the state and to join a commune.

The livestock of the 'rich' were then taken away and given to the poor and in desperation, tens of thousands of herdsmen fled to China or Manchuria.

'The poor were usually the lazy or incompetent herdsmen so they just sat in their *gers* eating meat,' Byamya said. Between 1928 and early 1932 the Mongols lost a third of their total livestock, some 8 million animals.

The herdsmen were promised that a Communist utopia of equal shares and happiness for everyone was about to be realised. It was something they readily accepted at first because it was part of Buddhist folklore that after a terrible time of famine and war, a new age of universal happiness would dawn.

Stalin's onslaught against 'feudalism' also took the form of an anti-religious campaign. An Anti-Buddhist League was set up, modelled on the Soviet Union's League of Militant Godless, whose members went around putting out the eyes of Buddhist statues.

The lamas who at the time were still very numerous and powerful fought back and countered with their own prophecies. A millenarian movement sprang up in the Tugsbuyant Monastery in the north-west.

Hundreds of lamas armed with sticks and wearing prayer amulets around their necks – which they believed would render them invulnerable against bullets – began a revolt. The monks were opposed to the confiscation of property, especially monastic property, but were mown down by troops with machine-guns.

A far larger revolt in the same area began in 1932 which spread like wildfire until the country was in a state of civil war. The rebel side was swollen by thousands of Buryiat Mongols fleeing collectivisation in the Soviet Union.

The rebel leaders, often lamas or nobles, wrote letters to the Panchen Lama whom they hoped would come to lead the mysterious armies of Shambala, the never-never land of Buddhism, and bring victory.

It was a brutal and violent war in which no quarter was given. Party members were hanged from trees, flayed alive and had swastikas or red stars carved on their foreheads. If the rebels caught a woman with short hair, it was enough to condemn her as a revolutionary. The rebels tore the beating hearts out of captives, sucked the blood out and hung them on their banners just as in the time of Genghis Khan.

The Soviet Union sent in special troops from the NKVD equipped with tanks and planes. Those who took refuge in the mountains were bombed and despite the overwhelming force which the government side commanded, the revolt continued until December.

Moscow finally ordered the Mongols to abandon collectivisation and disband the communes although the same policies were not reversed in the Soviet Union.

By comparison with the Kazakhs in the Soviet Union, who were also nomadic herdsmen, the Mongols escaped relatively lightly. Of the four million Kazakhs, one million died and eighty per cent of their livestock was lost.

Stalin had other plans for the Mongols. He began to demand that the Mongols should 'liquidate' their lamas. Only if they did so, Stalin said, could they recover the strength that was theirs in the age of Genghis Khan.

Yet no Mongolian leader was prepared to obey his command if only because it would mean killing some 90,000 innocent people. Nearly every family in Mongolia had a son who as a child had been sent to become a lama in one of the many monasteries. Only a few ended up as scholars, the rest performed manual tasks or herded livestock.

In December 1935 the then prime minister, Genden, led a delegation to Moscow to ask Stalin to provide more help against the growing threat of a Japanese invasion.

On at least three occasions, Genden had already refused to obey Stalin's instructions but in a face-to-face interview, Stalin once again ordered him to liquidate the lamas. Stalin insisted that unless Genden destroyed the monasteries, the Soviet Union would withhold further assistance.

'Genden angrily refused and told Stalin what he thought of him. He accused the Soviet Union of practising "Red Imperialism",' Byamya said. 'It was a very brave thing to do.'

In fact it sealed Genden's fate. Ministers who had accompanied Genden were ordered to return to Ulan Bator and quickly organise a Party plenum at which, under Comintern instructions, Genden was attacked for criticising Stalin and deposed.

Genden was kept in the Soviet Union and it was announced that he was 'going on holiday'. He spent a year in exile by the Black Sea before being taken back to Moscow and shot.

In 1936 Stalin brought his successor, Amor, to Moscow and again told him it was his 'duty' to destroy the lamas.

'Stalin was obsessed by the liquidation of the lamas but even Amor refused,' said Byamya who had found hitherto secret records of these meetings.

'If you want, we can organise the campaign and provide the proper methods and equipment,' Stalin had promised the Mongolian prime minister.

'Stalin understood then that unless he liquidated all the intellectuals in Mongolia, he could not carry out his policies,' Byamya asserted, but I wondered if he was right. Stalin had already shown he could carry out whatever policies he wanted in Mongolia.

Stalin's insistence that the lamas should be liquidated had surely little to do with rational politics. What on earth could it possibly matter to Stalin what happened to the lamas? He had never visited Mongolia, which lies about as far from Moscow as Ethiopia is from London and of no more importance to his country's interests.

Perhaps, like the destruction of the monasteries and the imprisonment of the lamas in Tibet and Inner Mongolia thirty years later, Stalin like Mao saw it as a matter of ideological necessity.

Even if this is correct, it does not make what actually happened any more comprehensible. The final solution of the lamas was a carefully planned operation in which all those over about twenty were executed by death squads fulfilling weekly quotas.

It could have been motivated by an atavistic hatred of the Mongols who had ruled the Russians for two and a half centuries; or perhaps Stalin, who had been educated in a seminary, simply loathed all priests.

At any rate he chose as his instrument a Mongolian who had also been educated in a monastery and was willing to ensure their complete destruction.

Choibalsan was one of the original 1920 revolutionaries and alone among them spoke Russian. He first went to Moscow at the head of a military delegation in 1922 but generally played secondary roles until he was arrested and taken to Moscow in 1934.

After Stalin's political victories in 1928, everything that happened in Moscow had to be duplicated in Ulan Bator. Just as Stalin removed enemies on the 'right' and on the 'left', the Mongolian Party too discovered it had 'rightists' and 'leftists'.

There were show trials too just like in Moscow and the details of the conspiracies exposed during these trials were invented at the NKVD headquarters in Moscow.

The 'Lhunbo Conspiracy' of 1934 was one and Choibalsan was implicated and brought to Moscow for further interrogation. According to Byamya's research, it was at this moment, while he was being held at Boutyrsk Prison, that the NKVD selected him as their tool.

As an alcoholic with a weak character he was suitably malleable material and Choibalsan must have only been too aware that only the most complete co-operation would save his life.

He was treated for alcohol abuse and sent back to Mongolia where he was appointed Minister of Animal Husbandry. Soon he was promoted to the post of Deputy Chairman of the Council of Ministers, one step below the prime minister. Stalin then ordered an existing Department of the Interior expanded into a fullblown Ministry of Internal Affairs, and Choibalsan was put in charge.

The popular defence minister, Demid, was the next major obstacle in Choibalsan's progress to the top so the NKVD arranged his murder. The details are curious because instead of just shooting him in Moscow, the NKVD took elaborate steps to disguise what was happening.

Why Stalin should bother to do this is also unfathomable but Demid was invited to spend his leave in the Soviet Union. In 1937 he set off by train with his wife and when they arrived in Irkutsk, a telegram summoning him back to Ulan Bator on urgent business was waiting. Yet on his return to Ulan Bator nobody admitted sending it.

The defence minister set out again and as the train was travelling across Siberia two members of the NKVD boarded the train at Jago station, entered his compartment and asked him to come out with them. After they had killed him, the NKVD men sent a telegram to Moscow informing his wife of his sudden death.

It was announced that food poisoning from a can of spoilt meat was the cause of death and while Demid's corpse was still on its train, Choibalsan was appointed the new defence minister.

He now controlled both the military and the secret police and when the prime minister, Amor, objected to having so much power concentrated in the hands of one man, the Soviets replied that it was just a temporary measure.

Within days of Demid's burial, Choibalsan launched the first round of repression. He arrested all the top Ministry of Defence officials and dozens of other prominent citizens and within a month had put them on trial. Choibalsan then revealed a counter-revolutionary Demid-Genden plot to seize power with the help of the lamas and army.

The whole affair was organised by the Deputy NKVD Chief Frinovsky who had arrived with a delegation just before Demid left for Moscow and who returned in time for the trials. He made a banquet toast urging the Mongolian Party to support Choibalsan in his struggle to crush the lamas and counter-revolutionaries.

Frinovsky, together with his boss Nikolai Yezhov, the People's Commissar in charge of State Security and Stalin's chief instrument, was to be executed in 1940.

Between September 1937 and July 1939, every Mongolian state and Party leader of any significance was arrested and taken to the Soviet Union. Choibalsan made sure that of the seven surviving founders of the Mongolian Revolutionary Party, only he remained, and had men executed with whom he had worked for twenty years.

Anyone with any education was liquidated so that by 1940 when Tsedenbal was appointed General Secretary of the Communist Party at the age of twenty-five, only five people were left in the entire country with more than high-school education.

Education had in any case become completely politicised and schoolchildren devoted their lessons to chanting slogans like 'Down with the British Empire' and 'Down with American Imperialism'.

Choibalsan then despatched death squads around the country led by Russian NKVD officers. They executed over 20,000 monks on the spot and destroyed over 700 temples in addition to many other shrines and chapels. The Russians melted down the gold and silver statues and shipped the booty back to the USSR. I met one eyewitness of this truction who remembered on one day seeing sixty trucks full of silver heading for the border.

Byamya said he had been unable to discover the names of those, especially the Russians, who organised and carried out the tortures and collected the 'confessions'.

The only reference I discovered was in a book by Georg Vassel, a German who was working in western China trying to set up a trans-Asian airline before the war. Called *My Russian Jailers in China*, it describes how he was arrested and imprisoned in Chinese Turkestan when the Soviets were invited in by the local Chinese warlord to help crush a rebellion led by Hui, the Chinese Mohammedans. In prison he also witnessed the beatings and murders of Kazakhs fleeing to China to escape collectivisation in the USSR.

> I was escorted by an officer and two soldiers to a little room where I was confronted by W—, the tyrannical oppressor of Outer Mongolia. He presided over the 'Police Department' – the title under which the GPU [former name of the NKVD] paraded.
>
> If ever anybody in the world had an evil reputation it was this same W—. A favourite simile used by the Chinese to symbolise his treachery was that he was like a poisonous spider that lurked noiselessly until its victim had got well entangled in its web and then slowly tortured it to death.

W—, who was apparently half Chinese, is described as a 'dwarfish creature – a blobular mannikin, who looked more like a caricature of humanity than a human being.'

Byamya showed me an article written by Damdinsuren who was the editor of the Party newspaper when he was arrested in 1939. Damdinsuren said that every official from the Mongolian Ministry of the Interior had an adviser from the NKVD.

He was charged with being a Japanese intelligence officer but survived beatings, hunger, cold and nocturnal interrogations without confessing. He escaped execution but spent six years in labour camps.

The charges which the Russians invented were absurdly implausible. Damdinsuren, who was kept in prison without trial for twenty-six months, wrote that he shared a cell with one lama accused of setting fire to a telegraph office, another who confessed to riding to Japan on horseback to obtain his instructions and a third accused of flying his own aeroplane to a secret hilltop rendezvous with Nazi agents.

Byamya said Choibalsan would personally supervise the torture of many of those brought to the Ministry of the Interior although he was often drunk at the time. He had a little bell which he would ring after signing his name to the list of victims to be shot.

Later I saw an exhibition devoted to the purges which exhibited both the bell and a letter from Choibalsan to Genrikh Yagoda (Yezhov's successor) expressing his gratitude for the generous help given in finding and punishing these criminals.

There were lists of victims by nationality and by profession together with pictures illustrating the tortures employed. People were forced to sit for days on end perched on stools which were so high that their feet never touched the ground.

According to Damdinsuren, Choibalsan was virtually illiterate and had difficulty reading a typewritten letter or signing his own name.

To reward his loyalty, Stalin gave Choibalsan a total of twenty-four cars as presents including a Buick in which he would proudly ride to the countryside to shoot wolves and return with the skins flying from the sides of the car.

His office was furnished simply with a big ebony desk, carpets and a portrait of Stalin hanging on the wall. It was guarded by his personal bodyguards and even his closest officials needed a special pass to enter it.

One of these bodyguards had the special responsibility to seek out and bring him the most attractive women in Mongolia.

The NKVD officers did not leave Mongolia until the end of the 1940s and the country was kept in a state of constant fear. The midnight arrests and executions went on right until Choibalsan's death.

Fictitious plots continued to be invented such as the 'Port Arthur case' of 1947 when 300 were arrested, including the head of the Mongolian Revolutionary Youth League, accused of collaborating with the Japanese and executed.

I found it hard to imagine a more evil person than Choibalsan. The most curious part of meeting Byamya and many other Mongolians was that they now considered him a patriot who deserved far more respect than his successor, Tsedenbal.

It seems that towards the end of his reign, Choibalsan began to feel remorse for his deeds. He even began to stand up to Stalin and refused to heed his Soviet adviser's instructions.

In the last week of the Second World War when up to 80,000 Mongolian troops joined the Red Army in attacking Japanese troops in China, Choibalsan hoped to absorb Inner Mongolia as his share of the victory spoils.

'Stalin was furious when he heard Mongolian troops had crossed the Great Wall and demanded that they withdraw. Choibalsan had to agree but he was very angry,' Byamya said.

It is likely that Stalin intended to make Outer Mongolia join the

Soviet Union and had Stalin lived a few years longer, Tsedenbal would have acceded to his wishes.

In 1944 Tannu Tuva, another Soviet satellite, even smaller than Mongolia, which had been nominally independent since 1922, had voluntarily joined the Soviet Union. Tannu Tuva lies between Mongolia and the USSR and claimed to be the world's third-oldest Communist state.

Like a Russian doll which opens to reveal ever smaller copies inside, Tannu Tuva had its own little Stalin called Salchack Toka who like Choibalsan had orchestrated the same purges and repression.

During a visit to Ulan Bator, Toka urged Choibalsan to follow his example and join the Soviet Union but Choibalsan slapped him in the face. Mongolia angrily rejected Stalin's demand and in 1949 Choibalsan pointedly refused to attend the huge celebrations marking Stalin's seventieth birthday although leaders from every other Socialist country were present.

'Choibalsan loved his country so we still respect him,' Byamya said with a conviction in his voice which baffled me.

In 1952 Choibalsan died of cancer in Moscow where he had been taken for treatment. It is highly probable that Stalin had him murdered.

Five

A Form of Lobotomy

Every two years they all used to meet for their summer holidays at a resort on the Black Sea. The Brezhnevs, the Zhivkovs, the Honeckers, the Ceauşescus and the Tsedenbals. The other couples achieved fame or notoriety but not the Tsedenbals.

It is quite hard to imagine that one can rule a country for about forty-four years and remain unknown. For most of this period few people in the West were aware of Mongolia's existence as an inter-nationally recognised independent country and member of the United Nations.

Yet President Tsedenbal managed it, spending nearly half a century at the helm of his country, first as general secretary and deputy to Marshal Choibalsan, and then as president. It is a record which even when set beside those other hardy perennials in the fraternity of Com-munist leaders, deserves a special place.

Indeed, to have ruled so long and so obscurely marks the only genuine outstanding act of the Tsedenbals. It is a curious thing to do – to strive to be greyer than any of one's peers – and thus survive the longest. It is especially so when as every schoolboy knows, the very name Outer Mongolia has a special call on the imagination. If Mongolia is distant and exotic, how much more so must Outer Mongolia be? And to rule for so long, so wild a nation of people as the horsebound descendants of Genghis Khan that must, surely, demand as savage a whiphand as anyone in these desolate wastes has ever wielded.

The truth is as always different. In a way disappointing. Tsedenbal was no Tartar chieftain, lolling in his tent and dribbling wine from the gilded skull of his dearest enemy. Instead the successor to the debauched Bogd Khan or the murderous Baron Ungern-Sternberg was a mousy little man in a suit, with a boorish wife, obedient to the wishes of his masters in the Russian embassy next door to his palace. It is said that Tsedenbal even hesitated to answer Washington's request to establish diplomatic relations for fear of incurring Soviet displeasure.

He was an official, a bureaucrat of the new times when a tyrant exercised his allotted share of power not by levelling a city and salting its fields or liquidating whole populations but just by issuing a new set of regulations.

Yet what did happen under his rule is no less tragic and sad. Enforcing a hundred restrictions, each petty law meaningless by itself, can crush as many lives as the violent unreason of some tyrant's diseased mind.

Tsedenbal had little in common with Choibalsan except for their beginnings.

'We have been ruled by two bastards and bastards never make good rulers,' one Mongol said, since both were illegitimate children who spent their earliest years schooled in Buddhist monasteries.

Choibalsan presided over far more deaths than Tsedenbal but he managed to prevent Mongolia from being absorbed into the Soviet Union. Alone among the peoples of Central Asia caught between Russia and China – the Kazakhs, Uighurs, Uzbeks, Kirghiz Tadjik, Tibetans, Samyode – the Mongols emerged and survived with a country to call their own. However limited that independence was, it meant to many people that at least some good came of the terrible years from 1920 to 1950.

Tsedenbal set out to render this precious achievement as meaningless as possible. Under his rule a cultural lobotomy took place. He methodically substituted Russian and Soviet culture for Mongolia's rich heritage.

Gradually everything Mongolian was erased. It was customary for all senior officials to marry Russians. Mongolians were obliged to eat sour bread instead of steamed bread, to use knives and forks instead of chopsticks, to wear suits instead of *dels* and to use Russian in the universities, schools, in the bureaucracy and at all important political events.

The story of the chairman of an agricultural co-operative who was sent to be trained at the Party school is said to be based on fact. He was obliged to spend most of his time learning Russian, and finally exploded with anger: 'What is the point of this, will I have to speak Russian to the cows?' He was expelled from the Party and dismissed.

The nomads were peacefully collectivised after 1959 and under a virgin land scheme copied from Khrushchev, Mongolians were obliged to grow their own grain. With the loss of their land and herds, nomadic pastoralism was no longer profitable or even possible and much of the population drifted to the cities, especially Ulan Bator. By the end of the 1960s, half the population lived in the capital or other urban centres.

There life became increasingly regimented and drab. The Chinese, who numbered nearly 100,000 and ran most of the commerce, were expelled and all the shops, markets, small tradesmen and so on were closed. Economic development stagnated aside from the projects run by Russians or East Europeans.

Thus, economic and social policies went hand in hand with the gradual dismantling of Mongolian tradition.

Tsedenbal was born in an area of Mongolia bordering the Soviet Union, which when he later renegotiated the frontier became part of Soviet territory. The NKVD recruited him in his youth, paid for and controlled his education. At twenty-four he was appointed General Secretary of the Party and one of his earliest acts was to sign a decree authorising the use of torture in the interrogation of prisoners.

The NKVD selected his Russian wife, Filatova, an uneducated peasant woman from Soviet Central Asia whom he married in 1947. His first meeting with her was organised by the Soviet Embassy and it is said that he was kept far away from Mongolians even while he was living in Mongolia and that he was incapable of finding a wife for himself.

The couple grew so tired of the country they ruled that they would go on holiday twice a year and spent most of their time at the Black Sea where they became particular friends of the Zhivkovs of Bulgaria. President Zhivkov was eventually put on trial for corruption after the Bulgarians staged a democratic revolution.

The Tsedenbals grew to dislike Mongolia so much they would spend seven or eight months of the year living abroad. It was during the long sunny holidays by the Black Sea that Filatova learned from the wives of other Communist dictators how to behave. She gradually became more and more assertive and tried to establish for herself a position as mother of the nation. Inspired by visits to either Bulgaria or Romania she began building orphanages and children's parks. She would drive around in a white Mercedes on inspection tours but became so unpopular that children would throw stones at her entourage.

Filatova had left school at sixteen but took charge of education. She often arrived at the university with Central Committee members and Education Ministry officials in tow and exerted her influence by insisting that all lectures be given in Russian. Naturally, speaking Russian was one thing she could do better than any Mongol.

The main thing, it seems, was to know and speak Russian so that people said the Mongolian language became distorted and degraded. Even Tsedenbal's speeches were in Russian and had to be translated into Mongolian because he spoke better Russian than Mongolian.

When in Mongolia, Tsedenbal had a steady routine. He would get up at six a.m., perform some gymnastics, and breakfast on bread, butter and yoghurt. In the office he would read the Soviet papers for thirty minutes and would then go home for an early lunch. He rarely visited factories or ministries although his wife increasingly did. A slow and incurious man, Tsedenbal spent a long time preparing speeches; in the evenings he would drink heavily unless Filatova stopped him.

Tsedenbal was not the only choice as the successor to Marshal Choibalsan after his death in 1952. He was a potential victim of de-Stalinisation purges after 1956 as he bore much personal responsibility for the purges and persecution of the 1940s. Several plots to overthrow him were hatched in 1959 and 1960, supposedly backed by the Chinese as Mao was intent on rebuilding Chinese influence in a territory he felt should be reabsorbed into his empire. Tsedenbal was able to thwart these plots with the help of the NKVD which still maintained an overwhelming control over Mongolian affairs despite the partial withdrawal after Khrushchev came to power.

As Tsedenbal did retain power, only a slight liberalisation took place after 1956 which did not bear comparison with what happened in Eastern Europe. While Stalin's statues were demolished in most of Europe, Stalinism was preserved in Mongolia, Albania and North Korea.

The degree of political control reached bizarre levels. Once I ran into someone who worked in the Central Censorship Bureau. It was a big office which until about 1988 employed over sixty people responsible for supervising the publication of absolutely everything. Every article published, whether it was about theoretical physics or yak breeding had to be checked for its political content before it could go to the printing press.

'Even wedding invitations had to be scrutinised and receive a stamp of approval,' the censor said.

'Once someone wanted to publish some cards for lunar new year which we still tried to celebrate although it was forbidden, and showed a Mongol dressed in thirteenth-century armour. Approval was given but then somehow members of the Party's Central Committee heard about it and declared that the card constituted a plot to revive the cult of Genghis Khan. Everyone connected with the affair was dismissed including all the workers at the printing house.'

The worst thing about life under the Tsedenbals was the boredom. Mind-numbing tedium replaced terror as an instrument of state policy, literally part of the planned economy.

Mr Batjargal, a big bulky middle-aged Buryiat who taught building design at the university, described it for me.

'At the time everyone was obsessed by rules so that if the Party said you had to do it, you did it. You had to know by heart all the slogans.

'The most boring thing was a big book, or rather a diary, in which you had to write what you intended to do in the coming year and how carefully you had studied the Tsedenbals' latest speeches. The diary was always checked by the departmental chief.

'Then this plan had to be written and checked every quarter. After a while this was not enough and we all had to write a plan every month. Then we also had to write plans of what we were going to do every week and finally by the end there had to be a daily plan. Each day the plan had to be drawn up and approved by your boss,' he said. It was an escalation *ad absurdum*.

'Until 1989, we used to spend about an hour and a half each day on these plans and diaries,' he continued. 'Often it was very hard to think up a plan. Nobody had very much to do to begin with so it required a lot of imagination to compose a plan. In fact about seventy per cent of the plans was pure fantasy. Actually it did not really matter what you wrote because no one would check whether you had really done what you had planned to do the week before.

'Only the nomads did not have to draw up plans but everyone else, even cleaners and their supervisors, had to think up plans about what they were going to do. On each page of the diary, there would be two sides. One side for what you planned to do and another for the results. The system still functions in schools. My wife's a teacher and some-times she is up until midnight writing out the plan because of course no one is allowed to use last year's plan.

'There were also initiative plans in which you would plan to put more energy into your job. Or there were plans about how to fulfil the resolutions of the Party's last congress. We also had to study everything the Party said. There would be ideology exams, monthly and quarterly, held by the local branch of the Party.

'There were also ideological training plans. We had to go to ideology meetings twice a week, after work on Wednesday and on Saturday morning. So we would make plans about which books we would study or even which newspapers we planned to read.

'Tsedenbal's idea was that making plans would keep people busy. As long as they were not using their minds, there would be no opportunity for any discontent to ferment. And of course with all this checking going on, there were always easy pretexts to arrest anyone at any time. Usually people were not shot but would be sent to the countryside. Above all it was a kind of thought control.

'Of course,' Batjargal concluded with an ironic smile, 'if all these plans had been fulfilled we would all now be leading a wonderful life.'

The inflation in Tsedenbal's 'years of stagnation' in planned diary output was only equalled by the expansion in medal production. President Tsedenbal liked giving and receiving medals and so did Filatova. She was very proud of her medals and to flatter her she was awarded medals for absolutely everything. She wore medals for best frontiersman, best hunter, best sharpshooter, best archer. In fact every time a medal was handed to someone, she was awarded one too. Brezhnev made her Hero of the Soviet Union several times over.

Since material incentives could not be countenanced under a Socialist economic system, moral exhortation plus medals was the substitute. People were once proud to wear them and celebrated their award by holding banquets. On my first visit to Ulan Bator, I was astonished to see women out shopping wearing as many medals pinned to their *dels* as a Soviet marshal.

Among the highest were the Order of the Red Banner for labour heroes, the Order of Sukhbator Medal, the National Hero of the Mongolian Revolutionary Party Medal, the Order of Pole Star Medal and Best Worker of the Fifth Five Year Plan.

Medals were given out for having children too since it was state policy to increase the population as rapidly as possible. Abortion was illegal and at one stage the average number of children per family was seven. After bearing eight children, a woman received the Mother Hero Medal 1st degree. For four children there was Mother Hero Medal 2nd Degree (and 400 tugriks).

One woman vowed on television that she and her husband would 'work day and night to win the first degree medal' after obtaining the Mother Hero Medal 2nd degree on International Women's Day.

As the number of medals proliferated, their value fell. Most people began to get them in the normal course of attending to their daily duties.

Then there were the state prizes. At first a state commission deliberated on who would get the state prizes on the basis of recommendations of the various enterprises and factories. Eventually it was automatically given after five years of work, and to counter their declining moral value, the monetary element of the prizes was increased.

A state prize was worth 15,000 tugriks, a Sukhbator medal came with an extra fifty tugriks a month and so on. By the end, the money became more important than the medals, defeating the whole purpose of the system.

But not quite. Although it appeared that anyone who did their work would earn a medal in any sphere, some people never got any medals. It was usually only the children of herdsmen and workers who were singled out for the highest rewards. Those whose class or political background was wrong received no rewards and this included the many people persecuted under Choibalsan. It was also hereditary. The children of those who had been marked out as politically unreliable inherited the discrimination and so the purpose of the prizegiving committees was to retain this control.

A favourite topic in films and plays was the historic meeting in Moscow between Sukhbator and Lenin. Actors who played the Mongolian hero were required to look dignified and wise. Those who played Lenin had to be Party members. If they made these parts their speciality they were well rewarded with the title Merited Art Worker, 3,000 tugriks in cash and the payment of half their rent.

'It was a mad paradox,' Nyamgavaa, the director of the youth theatre, said. 'Actors whose profession is to create illusions believed the meeting had really taken place. The historic meeting was of course a fiction which, by acting it over and over again, they turned into reality because people believed it had taken place.'

He paused for the punchline. 'And when these actors died, the Party buried them in the Cemetery for Heroes of the Revolution!' he said with a great shout of laughter.

There is always something comforting about how people in the same professions whether in Outer Mongolia or London or Paris resemble each other. Thespians are no exception; Bohemia imposes its own mysterious tribal laws.

Nyamgavaa, short, roly-poly and dressed in a sleeveless leather jerkin, looked as if he were about to stride on to the stage as a rustic in a Shakespearian comedy.

He talked with expansive theatrical gestures and laughed hugely at his own stories. Slender and attractive girls wandered in and out of his office. When we convened to the theatre bar to drink black coffee, the walls were hung with beaten-copper friezes of naked and full-breasted women.

He was hoping to tour Europe with a Mongolian version of *Romeo and Juliet*. The lovers would belong to rival tribes and there would be fights on horseback, Mongolian wrestling, dances as they erected the yurts . . . of course, he said, the balcony scene might be a bit tricky in a yurt.

Mongolian theatre had its own traditions which were all but destroyed by the 1940s. By the time Nyamgavaa went to study in the USSR, no one there believed his country had had any indigenous theatrical tradition. The Mongols, when they ruled China, were fond of plays and Kublai Khan was a patron of the theatre. Indeed some consider Yuan drama to be the apogee of Chinese theatre.

Imprisoned playwrights, directors and actors began to be released in the 1950s and gradually the theatre revived although under the social realist traditions of Soviet drama.

Filatova took an increasing interest in the country's spiritual life and decided that her contributions to the arts would make her famous.

'We became her experimental rabbits,' Nyamgavaa said.

As she spoke no Mongolian at all, Filatova only patronised those who performed in Russian. She promoted singers who sang Russian folksongs but had no interest in those who played Mongolian music.

When she arrived anywhere, she would ask questions and if the musician or actor was unable to reply in Russian, he was fired immediately.

'Since she considered herself the mother of the nation, clever actors who became her favourites started calling her "Mummy" – as if it were her real name. "Mummy, I want to do this," they said, or "Mummy, I want to do that."

'"Ooh, you are dearer to me than my real mother," they would say and then they would appear on television,' Nyamgavaa said, imitating them in a falsetto voice.

'Filatova was the sort of vulgar uneducated Russian peasant woman you meet on the street. She liked to wear large ear-rings with pearls. Behind her desk hung the drawing of a child – to show her love of Mongolian children and she had a secretary in her office who spoke very bad Mongolian,' Nyamgavaa said.

'One day she arrived here and suddenly became angry with our theatre curtains. They were made from an expensive grey material but she said they were the wrong colour, they should be yellow. So we changed them to yellow but she did not come back to the theatre for another ten years,' he said.

Filatova was especially fond of television and in 1982 ordered Nyamgavaa to come back to Ulan Bator to produce a special programme commemorating the anniversary of the Revolution. He went to her office and suggested interviewing the few surviving revolutionary partisans.

'She flew into a rage,' he said, making his eyes big. 'She said, "Why should we show these old people and spoil the whole programme?" '

Finally when he had finished making the programme, she came to a preview to check the result. After watching the first half – about thirty minutes long – she left in a towering rage dismissing all those responsible. The programme never appeared.

'I couldn't understand why until much later when I heard that one of the actors who was her current favourite complained to her when his role was cut.'

The Tsedenbals were also puritanical. In the early 1970s when flared trousers were all the rage even in Mongolia, specially appointed officials stood at the entrance to parks or theatres to measure everyone's trousers with a ruler. No one with trousers wider than fifty cm was allowed in.

Other Party work teams were despatched to stop Mongolians dancing the Twist or wearing long hair. Offenders were immediately dragged off to the barber's.

In the 1970s Nyamgavaa worked in a provincial theatre and put on a play by a Mongolian dramatist called *It is not me*. The plot takes place in a herdsman's family on the eve of the revolution. One of the revolutionaries falls in love with the herdsman's daughter when Chinese troops arrive.

'Local Party officials become angry and frightened and said the play could have dangerous international repercussions. If Peking heard about the way Chinese were being portrayed in the play, they said it could trigger a Chinese invasion. It was very dangerous to continue because at the very least Mongolia's diplomatic relations with China would be damaged.

'In another play I put on, a woman got dressed behind a screen. The screen was rather small and the audience could see her hips and legs appear. Then they said "What are these half-naked women doing in the play? This is Western decadence." I was again sharply censured for promoting moral decline and bourgeois art. Senior Party workers were instructed to "re-educate" me and make me join the Party.

'But once I had joined, I could be expelled and that meant losing one's job, career, housing and the chance of ever getting them back so

I became a sort of prisoner,' he said.

As the Mongols are a nomadic people, I had always assumed that a recorded literature was unimportant for them. All the writing in Outer Mongolia was written in the vaguely familiar Cyrillic and like most visitors I took it for granted, without giving it much thought, that until the Russians came, the Mongols had not been able to write things down.

When one day a long, straggly and arabic-looking script appeared on a new sign hung at the entrance to the restaurant in the Ulan Bator Hotel, I was so surprised that I asked a waitress what it was.

'Mongol, Mongol,' she said proudly.

'What does it say?'

'Oh, I don't know,' she replied (using one Mongolian phrase I was very familiar with) and traced her finger affectionately along the letters. In fact hardly anybody could read it but I began to notice the script appearing everywhere on shops, on office fronts, on posters and even theatre tickets.

Everyone started learning it in evening classes or by watching lectures on television. Civil servants were given two hours a day to study it and the Hural passed a law making it compulsory in schools and universities after 1994. Schoolchildren who had begun objecting to having compulsory classes in Russian and Marxist-Leninism, were in favour.

Tsedenbal had abolished the script in the early 1950s and people hated him for it. At first I found this hard to understand since he had done so many things which seemed far worse.

When it was consigned to the rubbish dump of feudalism, the Central Committee of the Mongolian Revolutionary Party gave the following reason for substituting the Russian alphabet: 'The further cultural development of the country can only succeed along the path of strengthening of friendly relations with the peoples of the Soviet Union and the acquisition of the extraordinarily rich Russian culture.'

Each time any Mongol wrote in Cyrillic, he must have been reminded of a government which slavishly accepted the inferiority of Mongolia's heritage next to that of Russia's. Only one Mongolian tried to oppose the move, Academician Rintchen, whom the Party condemned as a 'worshipper of feudal language' and an 'admirer of backward phenomena'.

Rintchen was a brilliant scholar who knew seventeen languages, translated the works of twenty authors, wrote four books on Mongolian philosophy and was a particular enemy of Tsedenbal. He was also a noted wit and after Stalin's death countered a suggestion to knock down his statue by proposing to move it to the town abattoir where he said it could remind people of Stalin's contributions to humanity.

Changing the script was all Stalin's idea and he was inspired by Kemal Ataturk's decision to adopt the Latin alphabet in Turkey at the beginning of the century. In 1926 a conference in Baku announced that all the Oriental people of the Soviet Union would adopt the Latin alphabet.

After millions had relearned how to read and write, Stalin then decided this was a mistake, they must adopt Cyrillic, invented in the ninth century to convert the Slavs to the Byzantine Church.

Until the Sino-Soviet split even Mao thought Cyrillic was the right thing for his minorities. Soviet and Chinese experts met and in 1956 agreed that the Mongols in China should also use the Russian alphabet. Four years later when relations between Moscow and Peking had deteriorated, Mao changed his mind and reintroduced Latin. Chinese was compulsory during the Cultural Revolution and the vertical Mongolian script was allowed back in use only after Mao's death.

All this ensured that for the past fifty years the Mongols on either side of the Gobi were never using the same script.

'The Mongolian script is based on our way of life,' Jargal, a Mongolian scholar once told me. He had long hair, a straggly beard and ear-rings and during his secret investigations into the origins of the script, Jargal had come up with some novel ideas. When I went to see him, he kept drawing lots of squiggles for me, to show how this letter looked like a bow, or that resembled the action of milking a cow.

I was not entirely convinced by this explanation but it was an issue which exerted and had always exerted a great fascination in Mongolia. One doorkeeper, I heard, had spent ten years inventing his own script to unite all the peoples of northern Asia and was now teaching it in evening classes.

It was Genghis Khan who had chosen the script after conquering the Uighur peoples living in the oases of what is now the western Chinese province of Xinjiang.

Genghis Khan asked his Uighur adviser, Tatatungo, to adapt the Uighur script for the Mongol language. He introduced a system of letters connected by continuous lines from top to bottom, like the marks cut on a tally stick.

Uighur was written the semitic way from right to left, and is based on Syriac, the language used in South-east Turkey when Edessa was a leading centre of Christianity in the second century AD and which the Nestorian Christians had brought to the East.

Early Syriac belongs to the East Aramaic group of semitic languages and like Hebrew has twenty-two letters. Jesus Christ is held to have spoken a form of Syriac.

Genghis Khan apparently decided to avoid following the Chinese system of writing and when Kublai Khan was ruling in Peking, he also rejected it. Other neighbouring nations like the Japanese, Koreans or Vietnamese which had adopted Chinese characters tended to become prisoners of the Chinese intellectual tradition.

Since Kublai Khan also forbade the Chinese to learn Mongolian, he set about establishing a universal script to transcribe the diverse languages of his empire. He ordered a Tibetan priest and scholar, the Phagspa Lama, to devise an entirely new alphabet.

It is called the Square Script because of the shape of its letters, and while it is written vertically like the Uighur script, it is also based on the forty-one letters of Tibetan.

Tibetan writing is in turn based on Sanskrit and dates from the seventh century. Even now lamaist texts are written on oblong sheaves of paper to imitate the palm leaves on which the Buddhist scriptures were first written down in India. The Buddha Gautama Siddhartha actually spoke Pali but his words were written in the Sanskrit of the fourth century which reproduces the sound of Pali just as the Uighur alphabet is deployed in the service of Mongolian.

Kublai Khan's plan failed. The Square Script was never commonly used and virtually disappeared after the Mongol Yuan Dynasty collapsed. It survives in the seal the Dalai Lama uses today, in a few stone inscriptions in China and one stone jar in the Forbidden City.

However, Tibetan continued to influence Mongolian culture because the Manchus encouraged the use of ancient Tibetan as part of their policy of undermining Mongolian nationalism. Mongolian princes translated and printed the Buddhist scriptures such as the Kanjur at enormous cost to counter this policy but lost the battle. The Manchus ensured that the prayers read by the nation's intellectual élite remained incomprehensible to the laity.

It was almost a miracle that Mongolian had survived as a written language until Stalin came to power if one looks what had happened to similar cultures. That of other nomadic conquerors from Central Asia vanished along with their scripts.

Over the last 1,000 years, northern China was ruled for all but the 276 years of the Ming by nomad dynasties. Like the Tobas and Tanguts before them, the Khitans, Jurchen and Manchus developed their own script after winning power.

The Manchu script, invented in the seventeenth century and loosely based on Mongolian, was the official language of the most populous empire in the world until this century. It is now so forgotten that only a few thousand people can still speak it and fewer still are able to read it.

The same fate awaited Mongolian and had Tsedenbal succeeded in his aims, it would have been too late to rescue it from extinction.

Under Tsedenbal many intellectuals were persecuted for their views but the history professor I met one day was an unusual case. Injustice breeds bitterness but the malicious and absurd nature of the charges which first destroyed his career had now driven him to the edge of rationality.

He found himself in the position of a member of the Ku Klux Klan falsely accused of spying for the ANC.

The professor was a short man in a blue suit who radiated nervous excitability. He seemed driven by a furious energy stoked by the intolerableness and apparent hoplessness of his situation even though so many scores were now being settled.

He sat down, perched on the edge of his seat, clutching a large leather briefcase and then abruptly jumped up again.

'He was not a victim,' the professor shouted in the over-loud voice of the slightly deaf, 'but a persecutor and even now he is abusing the time he has left in life.'

He sat down again, pulled a book from his briefcase and with trembling fingers pointed out a photograph of an eminent Mongolian scholar. At the top of it he had already scribbled, 'The bloodless butcher of Mongolian Artists and Intellectuals' in English, just for my benefit.

I recognised the urbane features of Professor Shirendev, ex-president of the Mongolian Academy of Sciences. Owen Lattimore had once made him an honorary graduate of Leeds University and when I had met Shirendev he had proudly pulled out his crimson gown from a wardrobe to show me.

The book described the fate of Tsedenbal's most famous victims – poets, composers, ballet dancers – and there was a section on the professor's life too.

In November 1956, just after Khrushchev's secret speech denouncing Stalin, Shirendev was a senior politburo member who opened a liberalisation campaign encouraging free speech among the intelligentsia.

The professor thrust himself towards me in his excitement to denounce the perfidy of Shirendev.

'I was very young then, teaching at the State University when one day Shirendev with two others gathered us all together and demanded to hear our views on the current situation in Mongolia,' he started.

'At first we were all so afraid that no one said anything, so Shirendev emphasised that he really wanted to hear what we had to say and he promised us,' here the professor raised his hand in oathtaking, 'we would not be punished.'

Some of the academics believed this promise and opened their mouths to criticise the Party. The prominent writer Damdinsuren was brave enough to attack the leadership directly while others complained about Mongolia's subjection to the Soviet Union.

'I also criticised our backwardness, especially the technological backwardness of Mongolia. For instance, I said the foundry of Ulan Bator was using technology from times unknown,' the professor said, burrowing into his bag again and pulling out old newspaper cuttings.

After the meeting, when Shirendev reported back to the politburo, its members were so shocked by the vehemence of the attacks, they passed a resolution condemning Mongolia's intelligentsia.

It was not merely that Shirendev had taken part in this meeting which enraged the professor but that he was the one who had proposed the resolution.

'What kind of democracy do we have now? Those responsible are still in power and even presenting themselves as victims,' he said. The professor thrust the cuttings at me in case I did not believe him.

All who had spoken out were blacklisted and put under surveillance by the Ministry of Internal Security. One by one, each was dismissed, arrested and then exiled. By the end the Party purged over a hundred teachers at the State University.

'The aim all along was to liquidate all intellectuals and replace them with herdsmen – with a bureaucratic intelligentsia,' the professor said bitterly, and then contemptuously added 'or people of Chinese extraction.'

The mention of China stirred him into another frenzied burst of activity. He dug into his briefcase to pull out thick volumes – *A History of the Mongolian People's Republic* in three parts, the *History of Inner Mongolia* and various others written by Chinese historians.

'China has a very greedy attitude to Mongolia,' he said, breaking into English just in case I should misunderstand this.

'The aim of these works,' he said, holding them up one by one, 'is to demonstrate that Mongolia has always belonged to China.'

He scrabbled in one of them to find a relevant passage: 'And to show that our 1911 revolution was a creation of Tsarist policy and so Mongolia is still a part of China. So in their opinon Mongolia never existed as an independent state.'

He had himself devoted much time to researching the origins of the Mongols and found ample evidence that from earliest times, the two peoples were always quite separate. Although his researches were handicapped by the refusal of the authorities to allow him to travel abroad – since he had been labelled as politically unreliable – he had kept abreast of research abroad by ordering books from, of all places, a bookseller in Sussex.

He pulled out yet another dog-eared book, a school primer of Mongolian history and showed me the opening paragraphs underlined in blue and red ink.

The professor had co-authored the textbook in the early 1970s and in the opening lines refuted the theory of a shared Chinese and Mongol ancestry, citing ancient Chinese sources such as the dynastic histories of almost mythical Shou and Xia emperors.

Then suddenly in 1980 the professor was sacked. All over the country special committees were set up to search out every single copy, in private or public hands, and then they were ceremoniously incinerated before the assembled pupils of every school in the country. The president of the Academy of Sciences lit the first bonfire in person.

'Even in the music academy, the musicians burned my books,' the professor said despairingly.

According to a politburo resolution supposedly based on the findings of three 'scientific committees', the professor had betrayed his country by 'relying' on Chinese sources.

'The politburo accused me, me, of being pro-Chinese,' he said furiously. He still found it hard to believe. For years he had published articles attacking Chinese historians for their racial theories.

This was not just an academic dispute. If the Mongols were ethnic Chinese, then Genghis Khan was a Chinese emperor and Peking could lay claim to both Outer and Inner Mongolia. Even today the legal basis of China's claims to Tibet hinges on Kublai Khan's suzerainty over Tibet in the thirteenth century. And of course if Tibet and Mongolia rightfully belong to China, then so do Korea, Burma and Vietnam (and many territories in the Soviet Union), which all became vassals to the Mongols. In 1939 Mao did in fact describe these states and also Nepal as regions which the imperialist powers had robbed from China.

At local Party branch meetings, the professor's friends and colleagues raised their hands to expel him from the Party. His wife divorced him and he was evicted from his apartment.

At this devasting moment in his career, the Chinese government chose to voice its support and the professor pulled out a copy of the *People's Daily* with an article protesting his dismissal ringed with red.

China had only reluctantly recognised Mongolia's sovereignty and Mao had after all said in 1936 that after the Communist victory 'the Outer Mongolian Republic will automatically become part of the Chinese federation at their own will.'

After Mao's victory, the two Communist giants vied for Mongolia's favour with increasing offers of aid as the Chinese tried to lure Ulan Bator out of Moscow's grasp. Tsedenbal rejected the inducements and in the late 1950s as relations between Khrushchev and Mao deteriorated, he purged his Party of leaders suspected of favouring the Chinese. During the Cultural Revolution as the Chinese held Maoist demonstrations in Ulan Bator and a mob attacked the Mongolian ambassador in Peking, Moscow sent troops into Mongolia to avert a possible invasion.

When in 1979 China invaded Moscow's ally, Vietnam, Moscow rushed more armoured divisions into Mongolia to put pressure on the Chinese. Ulan Bator and Peking engaged in a furious exchange of diplomatic insults which culminated with the Mongolians' eviction of three thousand 'lazy freeloaders' – citizens of Chinese extraction – ordering them out of their homes and dumping them on the border.

This was the background but it was still hard to understand what Tsedenbal was up to. Had Tsedenbal humiliated a man known to hate the Chinese in order to antagonise the Chinese further, by showing that even the professor did not despise them enough? And had the Chinese defended him to return the snub? But what kind of leader forces schoolchildren to burn their textbooks in public bonfires as part of his diplomacy?

It was all so absurd that to seek any rationale in it could only lead to madness. The professor was now so obsessed by his desire to reverse this perversion of justice that he was preparing to appeal to the United Nations and the International Court of Justice unless he was fully rehabilitated.

The blatant contradiction between what had really happened and what everyone in the country from the president to his wife pretended was the truth had driven him to reach a more bizarre conspiracy theory.

He brushed aside any possible connection between his fate and the political tensions between China and the Soviet Union. This, he said impatiently, was too farfetched to be true.

The real truth lay in a conspiracy not just against him but the whole country and only he had detected it. His voice dropped to a con-spiratorial whisper.

'Tsedenbal was controlled by secret Maoists in the politburo and these men are still in power even today,' he declared. I was tempted to laugh until I saw the disappointment in his eyes; he was thinking, was I part of the plot too?

One night an interview with Tsedenbal was to be shown on television. The excitement emptied the streets and in the hotel, the staff crowded around a set in the lounge.

Tsedenbal had not been seen since he was ousted in 1984 while on his customary holiday by the Black Sea. Tanks appeared on the streets of Ulan Bator while the new president, Batmonkh, rector of the State University, was hastily elected. The Mongols heard nothing further of Tsedenbal although there were rumours he was living in Finland or even dead.

Now that a television journalist had tracked him down to his luxu-rious home in Moscow there were growing demands to have him extradited and put on trial. But for what? No one was quite sure; some said it should be for murder, others said for corruption and a few said he was guilty of treason.

A murmur of excitement rose up from the expectant audience of waiters and chambermaids as the programme began. First the camera revealed the familiar figure of the television journalist, Dojodorje, sitting in an apartment heavy with Victorian comfort. The camera showed the chandeliers, the photographs of smiling children in silver frames, the antimacassars draped over solid furniture and the net cur-tains shutting out a grey suburban day. A plate of French pastries stood on a large dining-table covered in white linen next to a coffee pot and two dainty china cups.

On the other side sat Tsedenbal, a small, slight man with silver hair wearing a plain white shirt without a tie. With downcast eyes and hands held under the table out of sight, he looked more like a guilty schoolboy than a dictator.

Around me the audience gasped with surprise. Dojodorje showed little of the respect which had been Tsedenbal's due for so long and conducted the interview as if he were already on trial.

'There is evidence that you sent petitions to Stalin requesting the dissolution of the Mongolian State. What do you say to this?' he demanded with barely suppressed venom. Dojodorje had become popular through his series *Judgement Before History* which exposed past misdoings, but had struck me as a louche character with a bulbous drinker's nose. Now he looked stern and harsh.

'I am not guilty of this,' Tsedenbal retorted in a forceful voice and raised his head slightly.

'You met many top leaders of the Soviet Union, tell us about your relationships with them.'

When Tsedenbal silently fixed his eyes on the table, Dojodorje prompted him aggressively: 'What about Stalin, for instance?'

Tsedenbal's voice began to tremble and slur at the mention of the Russian.

'Stalin was very much older than me,' he said. 'I first saw him at a reception which I attended with Marshal Choibalsan in Moscow, 1939. He was a very helpful man, easy to talk to and joke with. He showed me respect and he addressed me with the polite "*vous*" form. He was very fond of Mongolia.'

Given that his meeting came at the height of the Soviet purges, Tsedenbal must have been very gratified by Stalin's politeness and felt lucky to have escaped alive.

'And what of Brezhnev?' Dojodorje persisted.

'I don't remember much about him. He had a very warm feeling towards Mongolia,' Tsedenbal said insincerely and the coffee cup began to tremble in his hand so badly we could hear it rattling against the saucer.

'Do you know about the changes in Mongolia? Or in the Soviet Union? Do you know that the old system has been abolished, that we have liquidated this brutal apparatus?'

Before Tsedenbal could reply, someone behind the camera began shouting and turning the lights on and off and pounding the table. We could hear a woman shouting angrily in Russian.

'You cannot torture him like this. He is a sick man. Stop! Stop!' she bellowed.

Then indistinct but heated exchanges took place in the darkness before the lights came on again. Filatova was no beauty and it was doubtful if she ever had been. She was a big fat woman and we glimpsed her pale face under a thick bun of blonde hair before she turned round and shoved her huge posterior wrapped in a tightfitting woollen skirt in front of the camera.

The screen went blank for a minute or two and then the interview continued as if nothing had happened.

'The authoritarian system has its good points,' Tsedenbal protested weakly.

'You mean you have no information about the changes?'

'No one has explained them to me,' Tsedenbal replied cautiously.

'Well, perhaps the ambassador could provide you with some Mongolian newspapers and then you could take an interest in your country,' Dojodorje suggested sarcastically.

Filatova, more composed now, produced a newspaper but explained that her husband had a problem with his eyes. Dojodorje asked him again about his reaction to perestroika but Tsedenbal looked dazed as if he had not heard the question.

'Who are you?' he asked as if Dojodorje had just entered the room and then he slurped his coffee contentedly.

'You do read the Soviet newspapers, don't you?' Dojodorje tried again, putting a copy of *Pravda* in front of him.

'And what is your name? Have you been in the Soviet Union long?' the old man inquired amiably. It was hard to tell if he was faking this loss of memory or if he really was ill. There were rumours, after all, that the Russians had replaced him because of his failing memory.

Out of sight Filatova erupted again shouting and pounding the table with her fist. We could hear her complain that the interview was only supposed to last ten minutes but someone who stayed out of sight the whole time managed to calm her down.

The interview resumed once more and Dojodorje began to interrogate Tsedenbal about the fate of all his former colleagues.

'Comrade Namsrai belonged to an anti-Party group. He wanted to establish contacts with China so I had to expel him. The man was guilty of Nationalism,' Tsedenbal said, knocking over his coffee cup. Nationalism was the code word for anti-Sovietism.

'Stop this! Stop! Stop!' Filatova shouted but Dojodorje ignored her.

'Why did you exile Damdin in 1956?'

'His main crime was that he tried to establish contacts with Mao and to make use of Chinese settlers. He was a Nationalist, a Chinese spy who tried to split us from our Soviet brothers,' Tsedenbal replied grimly.

'Maybe he was not a spy but you felt threatened by his growing popularity? And that in reality there never was any such Chinese plot?'

'Please, I do not wish to talk about this matter,' Tsedenbal said in agitation.

'And what about the man who was your best friend? What about Baalhajav, who has just been expelled from the politburo?'

'He is an old man, he cannot give details of his personal relations,' Filatova yelled and began switching the lights on and off and then loomed into sight blocking the view of the interview.

'Please do not show this scene. He is already an old man, please don't torture him,' she pleaded and her voice dropped its bullying tone.

'He had a heart attack recently. Our allowance was cut from 974 to 354 roubles a month. We hardly have enough to live on,' she wheedled pathetically. 'They have taken away our car and the prices keep rising . . .'

Her voice changed again, rising to a new and unexpected note of bitterness and anger just like any Russian housewife. In dollars their monthly income was no more than 150.

'Tsedenbal should not be criticised, he worked for the people all his life. He devoted himself to help them, working twenty hours a day, sitting at his desk and sleeping in his chair. And now . . .' But before she finished, the scene was abruptly cut.

The programme shifted to Dojodorje in his studio. He explained how it had taken him months to persuade the authorities to pressure the Tsedenbals into granting the interview. Filatova had hitherto taken extraordinary measures to stop anyone getting near her husband. Some Mongolian students in Moscow had hung around outside the apartment to attack him and she had even hidden his shoes to stop him leaving the apartment.

'Not every Russian woman is like her but unfortunately our ex-leader chose this kind of Russian woman,' he said and began to list all the other charges against her. Despite being a foreigner she had exerted more and more control over the country through her weak-willed husband. Eventually she had controlled all his contacts within the Party and the country.

She became greedy for wealth and flattery, setting up, like Elena Ceauşescu, a Children's Welfare Fund to help orphans and to which everyone had to contribute. Volunteers collected donations for the Fund, but the children's homes were never built.

Instead Dojodorje said the Tsedenbals used the money to build themselves a dacha in a Moscow suburb called Little Sweden where Brezhnev's grandson and other Party grandees lived. All the furniture and fittings, 239 pieces in all, were imported from Sweden and West Germany.

When they left Mongolia they had embezzled a million roubles in cash and shipped containerloads of personal belongings. Dojodorje went on listing more and more charges.

But was it really true? They did not look particularly rich and Filatova's complaints about rising prices had the ring of uncomfortable truth about them. Dojodorje showed pictures of their dacha but it did not look particularly luxurious to me. Its pine furniture and stone fireplace looked as ordinary as any Swedish accountant's. They were better off than other Mongolians but it looked a poor reward for a lifetime of betrayal.

And what if they had embezzled some roubles? It was pointless to put Tsedenbal on trial as if he were a bank clerk caught fixing the books. Did the money which had bought so little really matter compared to his real crimes?

The programme moved back to the interview in Moscow. Tsedenbal was now speaking lucidly and with more vigour, not about his many years in power but of his childhood.

'When I was small, my brother took me to school. It was a monastery school and the monks agreed to accept me but life was very hard and I was homesick. Twice I ran away to my mother but each time she took me back, scolding me. Then I went to school in Irkutsk in the Soviet Union and I was there with my friend who became the foreign minister.'

Later he had this foreign minister exiled to the remote countryside.

'Life in the Soviet Union was very hard. There was nothing to eat or buy. Even for the young there was nothing. Then they took me to Moscow where I studied and things were better before I was ordered back to Ulan Bator and appointed General Secretary,' he said in a slow quavering voice.

Dojodorje made a final attempt to force Tsedenbal to recognise his guilt or show some remorse. He wanted him to admit that Tsedenbal had betrayed his country because he had never loved it.

'Don't you want to go back to your own country now?' he asked.

'I have dreams. Perhaps I will go back when it is warm, in the spring,' Tsedenbal mumbled, looking away.

'Many people ask that you come back to our country.'

'I will visit Mongolia later,' he said hoarsely.

'Don't you want to visit the place of your birth? Don't you miss your homeland?'

'I would like to go back but, you see, I am sick and can only receive my treatment here,' Tsedenbal faltered, and looked down at his hands again. Out of view Filatova could be heard bellowing at him.

The interview stopped there and Dojodorje closed with a few more words from his studio. He had miscalculated because somewhere along the way, Tsedenbal emerged as a victim. The hotel staff stood up and left feeling sorry for this monster.

'Such a sick old man,' I heard one saying, 'bullied by that woman who will give him no peace until he dies.'

When Tsedenbal did die in Moscow a year later, 20,000 attended his funeral in Ulan Bator.

Six

Buddhism

One evening, the barman in the hotel fell to talking about his grandfather who had been a lama trained in Tibetan medicine. Immediately after the revolution in 1921, his grandfather left his monastery to become a 'wordly person'. He married, and his son became a committed Marxist and Party member.

'When the old man died I was astonished by the number of people who came up to me on the street and asked me where all his money was. I had no idea he owned anything at all worth talking about,' Suchschargal the barman said, leaning his elbows on the counter.

When his grandmother died a few years ago, Suchschargal discovered a big, black box in her room, which no one had been allowed to touch while she was alive.

'You know what was inside it?' he asked, reliving his astonishment. 'There were just plants inside.'

Rows of neatly labelled and rare medicinal plants which his grandfather had used to treat the people who sought him out from all over the country. Some of them cost as much as 1,000 tugriks to buy but his grandfather just gave them away in exchange for patients' gifts.

'Usually they brought a bottle of vodka and my grandfather drank three or four bottles a day. When my father, his son, arrived all the bottles and medicines were quickly hidden and the patient pretended to be making a social call,' he said. 'Everyone was afraid my father would report them to the secret police.'

The barman said his father had been shattered by the collapse of Communism and had stayed at home for months brooding in silence.

'Then you know what happened?' Suchschargal said leaning closer. 'He began going to the monastery, just recently my daughter was sick and he went to pray for her. Now he has faith in Buddhism but the funny thing is he still says he believes in Communism.'

Even after the monasteries were destroyed, the Party failed to root out deep-seated religious beliefs. Even senior Party officials and especially their wives would still consult the old monks. They would send their official black cars to pick them up and, hidden behind the lace curtains, the monks arrived at their homes in secret.

Hypocrisy is one thing but it was hard to understand why people clung to their faith in Buddhism after Marshal Choibalsan had crushed it so brutally and completely. I was puzzled by Suchschargal's story and how his father could reconcile the two faiths, and began to visit some of the older lamas to hear how they explained what had happened and why.

There was a nunnery, really just a single *ger*, on a piece of wasteground outside the entrance to Ganden Monastery and I dropped in one afternoon. The head nun sat serenely in the crowded space amid a circle of other women. They were all dressed in sleeveless dresses of purple silk and sat before a plastic statue of Buddha. Candles burned in front of it exuding the rich and homely smell of butter.

The nun's large eyes looked out calmly from a beautiful pale face. I had thought that such large lidded eyes only existed in the portraits of Buddhist saints.

She had been teaching mathematics and looking after her family until, when the hunger strikers brought down the government, she set up this temple. The last convent in the country had officially closed in 1937.

'Every unfulfilled dream is a kind of suffering,' she said with a smile. 'So when I could, I established the Mongolian Women Believers Association.

'In some sense I am still a teacher, concerned with the morals of young people,' she continued.

'A woman who believes will never sin. The moral climate in this country is linked to the supremacy of religion. My beliefs will lead people to do the right things,' she said.

In their spare time she and the other nuns printed and distributed leaflets with her message of love and repentance. All the nuns came from religious backgrounds. The head nun's grandmother had been a nun and her uncle was also a former monk who had instructed her in the scriptures.

'When a human being is born, he is given only a body but has not yet acquired moral convictions or ideas. During life people begin to acquire a sense of morality themselves,' she said.

'The Communists never paid enough attention to moral issues. That was their mistake, they always assumed the end justified the means,' and here she paused and fixed her luminous eyes on me. 'But one must teach people to be morally good. One must teach human beings to observe the duties which God laid on them. Then they will be rewarded.

'If they do not, they will go to hell. I think many Communists will go to hell. They did so many bad things, committed so many sins, I have no doubt they will rot in hell.' Her voice remained low and musical but the other women nodded and clapped in assent.

'Perhaps the Communists were not human beings or how could they destroy so many temples, kill so many monks? They will surely suffer in hell for this,' she continued.

'There is a cause and effect which connects everything. In my opinion if all people fail to be good, then it is possible that the whole world and all mankind will end up in hell,' she said with the air of a prophetess.

'It is said in the Buddhist teachings that after committing many sins, mankind will go through a terrible period of destruction but will then repent and the Kingdom of Shambala will come ... The armies of Shambala will destroy the enemies of Buddhism. Then a new era of happiness will descend on humanity,' she said slowly and with conviction.

'This time is not far off. We must try to bring this time forward.' At this the other women in the yurt shouted blessings.

People began crowding into the tent to listen to a service and she stopped. She presented me with a blue silk Khada scarf as the nuns began opening their square books of ancient Tibetan preparing to begin the chanting.

I noticed a peculiar painting tacked up to the roof of the tent near the altar. A naked woman had her legs wrapped over the hips of a blue god in an erotic embrace. The detail was so sharp that one could see the god's genitals hanging beneath her round buttocks.

'What is this about?' I asked one of the other nuns before leaving. They all giggled knowingly. 'It's just from a calendar someone gave us,' she said and then they began the chanting.

One evening I went back to Ganden to see the oldest lama in the monastery, a noted philosopher. It was a bitterly cold night and we walked through the frozen snow along empty streets past tall concrete apartment blocks.

Javklan, my guide, had mixed feelings about the lamas, believing them to be corrupt and parasitical. Without the large number of celibate monks, he said, Mongolia would have been a strong country with 40 million people. He continued his tirade until we reached the entrance.

'These monks would be happy if the whole country was covered by nothing but monasteries, everybody spent the whole time praying and all the money in the world ended up in their hands,' he said.

The lama's private quarters were a collection of bungalows hidden behind a gate I had never before noticed. We knocked on a door for several minutes before the lama's brother appeared and after some hesitation ushered us into a small room crowded with religious objects.

Lama Jigme worked and slept here. He lay bundled up with sheepskin rugs in a wooden bed gaudily painted in the Tibetan style. Next to his bed lay a pair of wooden crutches. One wall was completely covered by tankas, chests, altars, burning candles and incense sticks. An extraordinarily large selection of alarm clocks lay scattered about the place, each showing a different time.

Butter burned in small brass cups before several large glass cases containing statues of Tsong Kapa, the fourteenth-century founder of the Yellow Hat sect. Next to them was a postcard showing the Dalai Lama and another of surfers in California.

His red robes exposed one bony shoulder. He wore a gold embroidered silk jacket over the robes and his bare arms stuck out as thin as winter branches.

Lama Jigme was quite happy to talk even though it was late. He said he was seventy-nine years old and first joined a monastery when he was eight. He had a brother in America who had fled exactly sixty years ago, first to Tibet, then to India and finally to New Jersey.

His monastery in the south Gobi had 1,000 monks when it was closed in 1937.

'I was at work studying philosophy and attending prayer meetings when the secret police from the Ministry of Internal Affairs arrived,' he said. 'Lorries took away the shrines and other precious objects and the senior lamas were shot. In the seven days, it was all over,' he said. He spoke slowly in an unexpectedly deep and gravelly voice.

For sixteen years he remained in the countryside and then came to Ganden. Officials constantly lectured them, urging them not to worship God or to tell fortunes.

'We continued praying in secret but it was very difficult. People were asked to spy on each other and each day the Communists and secret policemen were watching and asking questions,' he said. He worked in a small factory, really a labour camp, where sixty or seventy young monks made shoes.

'Suffering is very hard to understand,' he said. In the long, long pause which followed, the clocks tick-tocked in an erratic medley. Then he raised his finger. 'Every day we must ask why we suffer. I can explain this in different ways.

'Tsong Kapa said there was once a big iron bird called Hangar which opened its wings and tried to fly to the moon but it fell down. Its strength gave out because it could never reach the limit of the sky,' he said.

'So Tsong Kapa said this is like wisdom,' he continued after another long pause. 'It is a parable meaning the wisdom of Buddha is like a sky without end. No single being can comprehend what God thinks.

'Perhaps Buddha might have stopped this repression. This was a terrible time but the reason God did not act was not that he is impotent but because people were doing evil,' he said. I was getting confused and the old lama, his head nodding on his chest, paused so long that it was hard to tell if he was sleeping or thinking.

'It is written in the book by Tsong Kapa that God is not responsible for what men do. We are each alone responsible for our deeds,' he resumed, 'and we act according to our karma.

'It was predicted at the start of the last cycle there would be wars and repression. It was all foretold,' he said, meaning the sixty-year cycle Tibetans, Mongolians, Chinese and other Orientals use for astrology and divination.

'A new cycle began in 1988 and we can already see that things are much better for Buddhism and for all mankind,' he said.

'So you see it was predicted that the years from 1928 to 1988 would be bad.' There he stopped and his shaven head sank to his chest. I wanted to reply that the past two years had been very bad in Tibet with shootings and arrests and so the prophecy could not be true but Javklan stopped me.

'I will not mention this to him because it will hurt his feelings and confuse him since he does not know what happened in Tibet,' he whispered to me. Then Jigme woke up again.

'There was another prophecy made a long time ago that there would be a period of unending conflicts and wars when everything would be destroyed. The armies of Shambala would then destroy all the forces of evil and a peace would follow when the world would make a fresh beginning. Different people interpret this in different ways, but the general idea must be true,' Jigme said and then fell silent, exhausted by his long speech.

Then I watched with trepidation as he dragged himself over to one side and fumbled in his box. He extracted two packets of biscuits and gave one to each of us as a parting gift.

Javklan stuffed three American dollars into his hand and we left the lama swaying on his bunk, mumbling and chanting to himself.

Jigme seemed to be saying that Stalin's terrible acts after 1928 had been predicted by the lamas and indeed they had known that when the cycle came to an end in 1988 Communism would collapse.

It struck a bell in my memory. In the autumn of 1987, I was in Lhasa when suddenly the lamas launched an uprising which the Chinese suppressed only with much bloodshed. It was hard to understand the timing of the monks' challenge but several monks had spoken about oracles and prophecies. They must have been referring to the predictions concerning this cycle.

But what were these armies of Shambala that both Jigme and the nun kept talking about? Some sort of millenarian beliefs had also inspired the uprising of the Mongolian lamas who were massacred in 1928. The leaders of the 1932 rebellion had also written to the Panchen Lama asking him to lead the armies of Shambala.

Modern Buddhists argue that Shambala was never meant to be a real place but lies somewhere in the heart, to be reached after spiritual journey.

At the turn of the century the Mongols were gripped by a fervent belief that the Kingdom of Shambala was at hand. Some are reported to have searched for a mythical chalice of the Buddha which would usher in the new age even near the capital of the Kalmyck Mongols on the Volga.

In 1904 the British army despatched an expeditionary force to Lhasa led by Younghusband with the aim of stopping Tsarist Russia from annexing Tibet. Suspicions were aroused by reports filtering out of contacts between Lhasa and St Petersburg.

Sir Charles Bell, Britain's representative in Lhasa, later reported that a confidant of the Dalai Lama, a Russian Buryiat called Dorjiev had spread the story that Shambala really existed and was called Russia. He told the credulous Tibetans that the Tsar was ready to restore this mythical Buddhist kingdom.

In 1922 Dr Ossendowski devoted chapters of his book on his adventures to the tales of Shambala and a kingdom under the earth called Agharti from which the armies of Shambala would issue forth.

A senior lama told him in all seriousness that in 1890 the King of the World had appeared in Urga saying that over the coming fifty years, 'More and more people will forget their souls and care about their bodies. The greatest sin and corruption will reign on the earth . . . people will become as ferocious animals, thirsting for the blood and death of their fellows. The "crescent" will grow dim and its followers will descend into beggary and ceaseless war.

'The forgotten and persecuted shall rise up and hold the attention of the world. There will be fogs and storms . . . bare mountains shall suddenly be covered in forests . . . millions will change the fetters of slavery and humiliation for hunger, disease and death.

'Truth and life shall disappear . . . in the fiftieth year only three great kingdoms will appear, which will exist happily for seventy-one years. Afterwards there will be eighteen years of war and destruction, then the peoples of Agharti will come up from their subterranean caverns to the surface of the earth.'

Ossendowski goes on for pages in this vein. Baron Ungern-Sternberg, on the fateful eve of his departure from Urga, was also convinced of this coming apocalypse and ranted about 'the king of the world' who was about to emerge from his underground capital.

A few years later Russian revolutionaries and their Mongolian allies were spreading the story that Shambala was the Soviet Union and Lenin its king.

Sukhbator composed a marching song for his cavalry:

The war of North Shambala,
We march to the holy war of Shambala,
We will die in the war
To be reborn as warriors of Lord Shambala.

Plans were made in Ulan Bator to erect a temple to Lord Shambala with his statue inside and the land was fenced off. The Mongolian Revolutionary Party's congress of 1925 passed a resolution which linked the Soviet Union with Shambala and announced that it was unnecessary to seek the Bogd Khan's reincarnation in Mongolia because he would be reborn in Shambala as a great general.

As relations between Buddhists and state worsened, the lamas countered such stories with their own. They said Lenin was really the reincarnation of the reviled Tibetan King Langdarma who almost destroyed lamaism in the ninth century. They pushed their own version of a Shambala utopia to counter the Socialist one and this all culminated in the 1932 revolt.

Just beforehand, a curious expedition arrived in Mongolia led by the unusual figure of Nicholas Roerich, the Russian painter and friend of Lenin.

Roerich was considered a genius. He was compared to Leonardo da Vinci, hailed as a prophet and a pioneer. At the Moscow Art Theatre he worked with Stanislavski. Stravinsky dedicated his work the *Sacre du Printemps* (the Rite of Spring) to him and he designed the original *mise-en-scène* for it. He moved to New York, founded a school and left a museum dedicated to his paintings which is still there.

His son George Roerich was a noted Orientalist who had studied in Harvard, Paris and London. He spoke Persian, Sanskrit, Tibetan and Chinese, completed the first dictionary of Mongol dialects in Qinghai Province and discovered an artistic style peculiar to ancient nomadic tribes of Central Asia such as the Scythians and Goths which he christened the 'animal style'.

Together, they undertook a lengthy expedition from India across the Himalayas, the Tibetan plateau and north to Mongolia and published three books on their travels: *Trails to Innermost Asia, Altai-Himalaya* and *Shambala, the Resplendent.*

The last is a very peculiar book written in the overwrought prophetic prose which Nicholas Roerich favoured. He was obsessed by the Shambala myth, believing such a paradise actually existed. Before he left Ulan Bator to continue the search in the Altai Mountains, Roerich painted a big canvas entitled 'Rigden Djapo, the Lord of Shambala' which now hangs in a prominent position in Mongolia's central museum.

His book is filled with ancient lamas expounding the hidden doctrines of Shambala or predicting the Second Coming of the Buddha:

Great Shambala is far beyond the ocean. It is the mighty heavenly domain. It has nothing to do with our earth. How and why do you earthly people take an interest in it? Only in some places in the Far North, can you discern the resplendent rays of Shambala ...

With eyes half concealed by the lids, he [an old lama] examines our faces. And in the evening dusk, he commences his tale: 'Verily, the time is coming when the teaching of the blessed one will once again come from the North to the South. The word of truth which started its great path from Bodhigaya, again shall return to the same sites. We must accept it simply, as it is: the fact that the true teaching shall leave Tibet, and shall again appear in the South. And in all countries, the covenants of Buddha shall be manifested. Really, great things are coming.'

Roerich's book predicts a great calamity will precede the new world:

> It is told in the prophecies how the new era shall manifest itself: 'First will begin an unprecedented war of all nations. Afterwards brother shall rise against brother. Oceans of blood shall flow. And the people shall cease to understand one another.
>
> 'But just then the teachers will appear and in places all over the world shall they bless the true teaching. To this word of truth shall the people be drawn, but, those who are filled with darkness and ignorance shall set obstacles.
>
> 'As a diamond glows the light on the tower of the Lord of Shambala. Even those who by accident help the Teachings of Shambala will receive in return a hundred-fold. Only a few years shall elapse before anyone shall hear the mighty steps of the Lord of the New Era.'

Tibetan Buddhist texts refer to a great battle of Shambala when the enemies of Buddhism, especially Islam, would be defeated, bringing peace and happiness to the whole world. A real King of Shambala, ruler of a kingdom somewhere in Central Asia, is said to have attended the last discourse of the Buddha when he revealed new teachings and announced the coming of the next Buddha, the Maitreya or future Buddha, after 3,304 years.

The Buddha's discourse is known as the Mahapariniruam Sutra after the place in South India where he spoke. Nobody is sure where this is now but Nicholas Roerich went to look for it in India until the British barred him as a suspected Comintern agent.

It may be near Hyderabad and the present Dalai Lama has in recent years made a pilgrimage to the supposed site. Even more obscure is the geographical location of this Kingdom of Shambala.

It was mentioned nearly 200 years ago by the Hungarian Tibetologist Csoma de Koros who described a wonderous mountain valley where the initiation of Buddha supposedly took place. It lay somewhere over a mountain pass by a lofty circular mountain. He said it was a model society without want or fear where people lived for a hundred years, rich, strong and beautiful until their death.

Roerich failed in his search and after he died, his son went back to America. In 1957 George Roerich defected to the Soviet Union after the government promised to honour his father's art. Some 400 paintings were shipped to the USSR but only a few were ever exhibited. George Roerich's own Buddhist researches did not flourish either, although he was promised the use of a Buddhist temple in Leningrad. It remained a laboratory for animal experimentation and George

Roerich died in Moscow three years later.

The Roerichs did leave another and more familiar legacy. In 1933, three years after *Shambala, the Resplendent* was published, James Hilton wrote his book *Lost Horizon*. Hilton, son of a schoolteacher in Walthamstow, became Hollywood's highest-paid scriptwriter for such films as *Goodbye Mr Chips* and above all for creating Hollywood's Shangri-La.

Was Roerich's vision of Shambala his inspiration?

Lost Horizon tells the story of how Conway, a disillusioned and aimless veteran of the First World War, escapes from revolutionary unrest somewhere south of the Himalayas. With him in a small aeroplane are Miss Brinklow, a prim missionary from the Inland China Mission, an annoying youth named Mallinson and Barnard, a Wall Street bankrupt.

Their plane is mysteriously hijacked and flown to a hidden valley in the mountains called Blue Moon overshadowed by a cone-shaped mountain called Karakal. The valley, an enclosed paradise of carefree happiness, flourishes free of contamination from the outside world.

Shangri-La is actually the name of the lamasery. Once inside, Conway's guide, Chang, takes him to the High Lama, one of four eighteenth-century Capuchin friars who, looking for remnants of the Nestorian faith surviving in the hinterlands of Asia, had stumbled into the valley. The High Lama is a Luxembourger, Perrault, who through the study of Buddhism and yoga, has found a way of preserving his life for 200 years.

Perrault, perhaps based on the Abbé Huc, bequeaths everything to Conway and speaks in the same poetic, apocalyptic language as Nicholas Roerich, Dr Ossendowski or even the mad Baron.

'He foresaw a time when men, exultant in their technique of homicide, would rage so hotly over the world that every book and picture and harmony, every treasure garnered through two millenniums, the small, delicate, the defenceless – all would be lost like the lost books of Livy or wrecked as the English wrecked the Summer Palace in Peking.'

An apocalypse is coming and Perrault seems to foresee both the coming world war and the destruction of the monasteries of Mongolia and Tibet.

'The Dark Ages that are to come will cover the whole world in a single pall; there will be neither escape nor sanctuary, save such as are too secret to be found or too humble to be noticed. And Shangri-La may hope to be both of these . . .'

Perrault believes that his monastery alone will preserve the seeds for a future revival.

'You will conserve the fragrance of our history . . .' he tells Conway, 'but I see at a great distance, a new world stirring clumsily but in hopefulness seeking its last and legendary treasures. And it will all be here, my son, hidden behind the mountains in the valley of the Blue Moon, preserved as by miracle for a new renaissance . . .'

The little plane bumped to a halt in the middle of the empty steppe. A whitewashed hut which served as the radio control tower was all that marked out Karakorum Airport. Passengers scrambled in and out of the plane, their *dels* flapping in the wind while the pilot leaned out of his cockpit window watching and smoking a cigarette.

Then the plane rattled off and we were left alone looking around the desolate grasslands. This was it. The centre of the world's largest land empire. The Mongols brought the plunder from twenty kingdoms to Karakorum and even the Pope had sent ambassadors here to this godforsaken place by the Orkhon River on a journey which from Europe could take a year.

We shuffled forward with our bags, under a big blue sky, until a truck took pity on us and drove us to a state farm. Up on a hill was an electricity station, a muddy yard with a petrol pump and a school. Dogs and cows wandered forlornly about the rows of shabby *gers*.

When we got off at the truck depot I at last saw the white stupas of the Erden Zu Monastery. It is the oldest and was once the greatest in Mongolia. It was built from the ruins of the ancient capital after the avenging troops of the Ming Dynasty had pursued the remnants of the imperial Mongol court here and smashed everything.

The Chinese general Chang Yuchun had destroyed Kublai Khan's palace at Xanadu before finishing his task in Karakorum. Now the only witness to its former glory is a solitary stone turtle, symbol of longevity, which lies half buried in the grass outside the monastic walls.

The first Englishman to visit Karakorum since those days was an otherwise little-known Borodaile of the Indian Civil Service who came here in 1895.

Excavations in 1946 led by the Russian archaeologist S. V. Kisilev found traces of triple walls, red, blue and green glazed tiles, four gates and a moat less than six feet deep.

The only Westerner to have visited Karakorum in its heyday and left an account was William Rubruk. Inside the mud walls he found twelve 'idol temples', two mosques and one Christian church as well as a bazaar. He compared it to Paris rather dismissively.

'It is not so fine as the town of St Denis and the monastery of St

Denis is worth ten of the palace,' he wrote.

Erden Zu Monastery looks impressive from the outside. High white walls form a square with 108 stupas. You enter through one of the four elaborate gates built in the Chinese style with floating eaves and, by now, faded paintwork. The monastery which once housed an army of monks was largely destroyed in the 1930s and inside there is little to see; three unrestored Chinese-style temples and a large but newly re-paired temple in the Tibetan style. On the gilded roof two golden fawns – the deer blessed by Buddha – look out towards the mountains.

One of my companions, Javklan, went off to make some arrange-ments and I waited with the other, Amarjargal. Javklan, who had introduced me to the old lama at Ganden, had, I discovered, been con-verted to Christianity by some American Protestant missionaries. He was now filled with religious zeal and determined to spread the faith in Mongolia.

Amarjargal, the interpreter and Iris Murdoch fan, was very in-terested in getting to the West, and eventually disappeared in New York while accompanying the President as interpreter. Unbeknown to me, Javklan had been busy trying to convert Amarjargal, for as we walked around the walls, Amarjargal suddenly made an announcement.

'I think I will become a Christian. A Protestant, in fact. What do you think?' he said.

'Why?' I asked suspiciously.

'It seems a very good religion to me. Perhaps it is time I tried some-thing new,' he said with a nervous laugh.

I thought he was slyly testing to see if I was a missionary too but Amarjargal was serious. The way he saw it, he was now free to believe whatever he wanted. If he wanted to try Christianity, then why not?

William Rubruk, the Franciscan monk, when he arrived here 700 years earlier had found the Mongols in an equally open frame of mind, ready to listen to the arguments of Christians, Jews, Muslims or Buddhists.

The French King, Louis IX, who was later canonised, had sent him off to convert the Mongol Khan in the hope of creating an ally against the Saracens.

The Great Khan was Mongke, a conservative and puritanical man by Mongol standards who ruled an empire stretching from Syria to the China Sea. His brother, Kublai Khan, was at the time engaged with campaigns against the Sung Empire ruling southern China. Mongke was himself to die in China five years later and Kublai Khan then moved the capital of the Mongol empire from Karakorum to Peking.

For the moment the prospects of a concerted attack against the

Muslim world were good. The Middle East had been badly weakened by repeated Mongol invasions and Christendom under the leadership of Louis IX was determined to launch new crusades.

In 1244 the Sultan of Egypt had taken the offensive, sacked Jerusalem, massacring the Christian population, and then defeated the Franks at Gaza.

For the next four years Louis was in Palestine fortifying crusader castles and coastal cities and another war was imminent.

Louis IX fell ill but by 1248 had recovered and was off on another crusade. While *en route* in Cyprus, he had received a Mongol mission led by two Christians from Mosul in Iraq called Da-ud and Markos who proposed a joint Mongol-Christian attack on the Muslims.

Middle Eastern terrorists were out to assassinate Mongke after the Mongols destroyed the Valley of the Assassins, the headquarters of the fanatical Ishmaili sect in northern Iraq. Security at Mongke's court was tight when Rubruk arrived and he mentions that those who entered the imperial *ger* were subject to body searches.

Rubruk's whole account of his journey to Karakorum is fresh and vivid. Beside it Marco Polo's ghost-written travels seem inspired by the preoccupations of a travelling salesman. The travels are full of tedious details about where to buy cheap and sell dear or salacious hints of where the girls are free and easy.

Rubruk's report is couched in a long letter to Louis IX and was only preserved by the efforts of William's friend and fellow Franciscan, Roger Bacon.

St Francis of Assisi died only twenty-seven years before Rubruk's journey. The missionary zeal and vow of poverty still burned strong and Rubruk went barefoot, wearing only a single garment, girt with a cord. He noted in astonishment that even in May it was so cold in Mongolia that the tips of his toes froze every morning and he had to walk about wearing boots.

Rubruk left Constantinople on Palm Sunday, April 13th, 1253 and arrived at Mongke's headquarters (he is also referred to as Khan Mangu) just after Christmas.

It was not until Palm Sunday 1254 that he actually entered Karakorum. After blessing some willow branches – still without buds – he 'entered the city around the ninth hour [three p.m.], raising the cross aloft on its banner and making our way as far as the Church through the Saracen corner, which contained a bazaar and a fair ... The Nestorians came in a procession to meet us.'

Rubruk's task was not as hopeless as it might seem. He was not the first Christian missionary to try and there were already many Nestorian priests and converts in the camp.

The sudden conversion of whole tribes and kingdoms was not an unusual event in the Middle Ages. Several accounts have come down to us suggesting that it was customary for rulers to demand religious debating competitions. After a sort of free-market contest among the various representatives of the faiths on offer, the ruler made a choice and his people followed suit.

There is an eleventh-century Arab account of how the King of the Khazars, who ruled an empire between the Caspian and Black Seas, embraced Judaism which is reported like this:

> So he [the Khagan] sent to the Christians for a Bishop. Now there was with the King a Jew, skilled in argument, who engaged him in disputation. He asked the Bishop: 'What do you say of Moses, the son of Amran, and the Torah which was revealed to him?'
>
> The Bishop replied: 'Moses is a prophet and the Torah speaks the truth.'
>
> Then the Jew said to the King: 'He has already admitted the truth of my creed. Ask him now what *he* believes in.'
>
> So the King asked him and he replied: 'I say that Jesus the Messiah is the son of Mary, he is the Word, and he has revealed the mysteries in the name of God.'
>
> Then said the Jew to the King of the Khazars: 'He preaches a doctrine which I know not while he accepts my propositions.'
>
> But the Bishop was not strong in producing evidence. Then the King asked for a Muslim, and they sent him a scholarly, clever man who was good at arguments. But the Jew hired someone who poisoned him on the journey, and he died. And the Jew succeeded in winning the King to his faith, so that he embraced Judaism.

The Russian Chronicle gives a not too dissimilar account of how the early Russians, the Rus, converted to the Greek Orthodox Church in the tenth century. Prince Vladimir first listens to Muslim clerics who list the joys of paradise but is horrified to learn of the prohibition against pork and wine.

'Drinking is the joy of the Rus. We cannot exist without that pleasure,' he reportedly said. A German delegation from the Latin Church is next, then a mission of Khazar Jews and finally some Byzantine Greeks who win by disparaging their rivals and by inviting a factfinding mission to Constantinople.

Rubruk too is later forced to take part in one of these religious debating competitions.

His mission is first dogged by a number of setbacks. He discovers a competitor in the form of a disreputable Armenian monk of whom he paints a lively picture.

The monk was 'swarthy and lank, wearing a tunic of the roughest hair-cloth, that reached halfway down his shins, over it he had a black silk cloak padded with squirrel fur and beneath the hair-cloth, he was girded with iron.'

The Armenian, he is horrified to learn, has gone about promising that if the Khan converts, Christendom will submit to his leadership. Conversions were always a double matter of convincing theological arguments and presenting the geopolitical benefits that a new alliance would bring to a convert. He thought the Armenian was going too far.

On January 4th, 1254 he is taken to court, meets the Nestorian Christians and is delighted to discover that one of the Khan's wives is a Christian already.

Unfortunately he does not get very far on this occasion or others since his interpreter is always too drunk to be of any use by the time the talk gets around to theology. Help is at hand when he meets another William, a French mastercraftsman from Paris with a brother who runs a shop on the Grandpont in Paris. His son is a much more reliable interpreter.

Drink was even then an abiding interest of the Mongols. At the entrance to the Khan's palace, Master William constructed the most ingenious drinking aids of all time. Rubruk gives us a detailed description. It is designed as a large tree of silver, with four silver lions at the roots, each containing a conduit pipe and 'spewing forth white mare's milk'.

There are four more conduits leading to the top of the tree with their ends curving downwards, and over each lay 'a gilded serpent with its tail entwined around the trunk of the tree'.

The branches, leaves and even the fruit of the tree are made of silver. Out of these pipes come wine, koumiss, boal (a drink from honey) and rice ale.

On top is an angel holding a trumpet which is made to appear to sound by a man with another trumpet hidden in a hole under the tree. With a blast of the trumpet servants come and serve the Khan's guest with a choice of drinks.

Rubruk describes where this mechanical cocktail cabinet is in the palace.

'The palace resembles a church, with a middle nave, and two sides beyond two rows of pillars, and three doors to the south side. The tree stands inside, opposite the middle door, and the Khan sits at the northern end in an elevated position so that he is visible to all. There are two stairways, leading up to him, and the man who brings him his cup goes up one and comes down the other.'

Rubruk stayed with William and his wife, who is also French, and they have a jolly dinner together with someone called Basil, the son of an Englishman, who had been born in Hungary.

Then the day dawns when Mongke decides to hold the religious contest. The rules are clearly laid down. 'No man shall be so bold as to make provocative or insulting remarks to his opponent, and no one is to cause any commotion that might obstruct these proceedings, on pain of death.'

The Khan is not himself present all the time but is informed about the arguments presented. The Christians are only partly united but find allies among the Saracens as they share a belief in the existence of one all-powerful God.

The Buddhists take the Manichean view that 'one half of things is evil and the other half good, or at least there are two principles, and as regards souls, they all believe that they pass from one body to another.'

To support their case the Buddhist team bring along a three-year-old boy from China who, Rubruk reports, is in his third reincarnation, fully capable of rational thought and able to read and write.

The Buddhists throw Rubruk a difficult question asking, 'If your God is as you say, why has he made half of things evil?'

"That is an error," I said. "It is not God who created evil. Everything that exists is good." All the tuins [Buddhists] were amazed at this statement and recorded it in writing as something erroneous and impossible.'

The Buddhists press home their advantage by asking, 'Where, then, does evil come from?'

"Your question is at fault," I said, "you ought first to ask what evil is before asking where it comes from. But go back to the first question, whether you believe that any god is all-powerful; and afterwards I shall give an answer to every question you care to ask."

The Khan's secretaries urge the Buddhists to respond and finally they reply that no god is all-powerful, 'at which the Saracens burst into loud laughter'.

Rubruk then triumphantly asserts that, 'So, then, not one of your gods is capable of rescuing you in every danger, inasmuch as a predicament may be met with where he does not have the power.'

Although Rubruk appears from his account to emerge victorious (since the Saracens admit that the gospel is true), he was forced to confess: 'For all that, no one said, "I believe and wish to become a Christian." '

When it was all over he reports that 'the Nestorians and Saracens alike sang in loud voices, while the tuins remained silent; and after that everybody drank heavily.'

The next day the great Khan himself summons Rubruk for a final audience before he goes home. Mongke puts forward the Mongol view of the world at the start of their meeting which Rubruk reports verbatim:

'We believe that there is only one God, through whom we have life and through whom we die, and toward him we direct our hearts ... But just as God has given the hand several fingers, so he has given mankind several paths. To you God has given the Scriptures and you Christians do not observe them. You do not find in the Scriptures that one man ought to abuse another, do you?'

'No,' I said, 'but I indicated to you from the outset that I had no desire to be at odds with anyone.'

'I am not referring to you,' he declared. 'And likewise you do not find that a man ought to deviate from the oath of justice for financial gain.'

'No, my Lord,' I said. 'And to be sure, neither did I come into these parts in order to make money: on the contrary I have declined such as was offered to me.'

And there was a secretary present who vouched for the fact that I had refused one iascot [a kind of rich cloth] and some silk cloth.

'I am not speaking of him [Rubruk],' the Khan replied.

'So then, God has given you the Scriptures, and you do not observe them; whereas to us he has given soothsayers, and we do as they tell us and live in peace.'

He drank four times, I think, before he finished this speech.

And with this Rubruk's mission ends in failure and Rubruk adds in despair that only 'had I had the power of Moses perhaps I could have convinced him.'

It took him another year to get home. The opportunity for a Mongol-Christian alliance was lost and Christendom's last crusade was to end in defeat when the Franks were swept out of Palestine.

Javklan finally appeared and waved us into the Tibetan temple where about thirty monks aged from five to ninety were holding a service. Apart from their big Mongolian boots curled up at the toes, they were sitting just as Rubruk described them.

'All their priests shave the head and beard completely, dress in saffron colour and observe chastity from the time they shave their heads, living together in communities of 100 or even 200. On the days when they go into temple, they put down two benches and sit opposite one another in facing rows like choirs, holding the books which from time to time they deposit on the benches.

'Wherever they go, they constantly have in their hands a string of 100 or 200 beads, like the rosaries we carry, and keep repeating the words *on mani batam*, which mean "God, you know". This was the translation one of them gave me . . .' Rubruk wrote.

When I arrived the monks had just finished drinking tea and were polishing their wooden alms bowls. Other bowls piled high with bread, biscuits, sugar and cheese stood around them and there was a fragrant smell of burning juniper.

The oldest lama then led a recitation in a basso profundo which the others repeated like a class of schoolchildren conjugating irregular French verbs. A few countrywomen sat on benches at the back, under-standing nothing of the ancient Tibetan. From time to time the monks banged drums, clashed cymbals and blew their conches.

As I found it incomprehensible, I wandered about, taking a close look at the fine silk tapestries and paintings hanging on the walls. Some showed Buddhist saints, floating on little clouds with haloes around their heads. The majority depicted monsters treading on miserable sinners, devils eating the limbs of other sinners and in one a bull was raping a woman. One monster had blue skin, three eyes and rode a beast sidesaddle. Another wore a girdle of human heads with the expressions on their faces picked out with affectionate detail.

The monsters outnumbered the saints and it seemed that evil exerted a greater fascination for the artists than piety.

When the service ended, several geriatric lamas shuffled over, smiling and no more surprised to see a foreigner than a demon with a necklace of skulls.

They invited us to their office which was next door in a new building. We had to go up the steep wooden staircase and the lamas clambered stiffly up, clutching at their robes and cackling away.

The temple had only reopened ten days before and they were still busy restoring it. The office contained nothing more in the way of furniture than a desk with a bright red telephone on it. Once when it rang, it provoked great excitement and solemnity in the lama who answered it.

Denden, the senior lama who was eighty, wore a red and yellow cap with upturned wings which perched over his pixie ears. He did most of the talking and bubbled with irrepressible joy at the changes he had lived long enough to see.

The monastery once had 2,000 monks and thirty chapels. The

monks had not taken part in the revolt of 1932, but in the spring of 1937 he said the secret police came and arrested everyone, group by group, took them away and killed them. First they arrested all the top lamas and then killed them in order of rank.

'We were very young like you are so they didn't pay much attention to us,' Denden said and his face puckered up into a humorous smile.

The secret police had gathered up all the manuscripts and books, thrown them on a pile outside a gate and set fire to them.

'All we saved from the monastery was this,' Denden said pointing to a wooden plank that hung on the wall behind him which I had not noticed before. It was a *Gande* and used for some obscure purpose in religious ceremonies.

'They took us to Arhangai provincial centre and put us in prison,' he continued.

'It was so crowded there was no room inside and even in winter we were kept outside in a fenced compound. Many people froze to death. Every day they would come and take a few away and shoot them near the river bed. Then they covered them up with earth,' he said.

'The campaign lasted several years. I heard of at least two monks who escaped and hid in the mountains. Local people brought them food every day but in the end, as always, someone betrayed them,' he said.

Gombochir, who was seventy-nine and had silently been fingering an ancient snuff bottle, broke in with his story.

'When I was thirty they took me to the provincial centre and I spent forty days in prison. Then I was taken to another prison in Ulan Bator where I worked for eight years, mostly as a carpenter. I was given a ten-year prison sentence but because of my behaviour, I was let out two years early.

'In the first prison, only the young and strong survived. Trucks arrived every night and then the warden called out some names. People got up and were taken to the truck. They never returned so I suppose all of them were executed. If you were young, you had a chance of surviving.

'We never resisted or protested. The older monks just thought it was fate so if this was their karma there was no good objecting. The police just took them to a deserted place, made them dig a grave and then shot them in the back of their heads,' he said.

'All we had to eat was boiled rice once a day so when I was taken to Ulan Bator, I couldn't move. I was so weak someone helped me on to the truck, otherwise I would have died,' Gombochir said.

Another lama, Jiggid, said very senior lamas were tried and shot in

Ulan Bator but the rest executed where they were found. In one local monastery he knew of, the soldiers needed seventy camels to carry off the booty which included much gold and silver.

'All the public security forces had a fixed quota, just like industrial workers. And they competed with one another,' he said.

'If an officer failed to fulfil his production quota he would be arrested and killed. Once a truck was bringing arrested monks to Ulan Bator. They had been many days without food and went into a *ger* to eat. Afterwards one monk didn't hear the order to move and stayed behind. He was terrified and tried to catch up with the others.

'When the guards arrived at the jail, they discovered they had one counter-revolutionary less and so to make up the quota they seized a young herdsman on the street and executed him with all the others,' he said.

Despite the persecution, somehow the lamas continued worshipping. In the more recent times they gathered in a *ger* pretending to have a vodka-drinking session. Even so someone informed on them and in 1982 they were arrested and questioned.

Then it was time to go and we all clattered down the stairs and clambered into a waiting truck.

'Just like the ones that took away the monks!' Denden joked with macabre humour.

The truck dropped off all lamas outside their *ger*s and we got off with Denden who had agreed to put us up for the night. Inside it was warm and a young girl came in with tea. As we sat around the fire chatting, I saw he had a collection of prayer wheels disguised as old tin cans. A little knob at the top turned a prayer written inside. He said the secret police regularly inspected his *ger* and confiscated all religious objects.

As we sat there, Denden's parishioners came in for brief consultations.

First was a large man in a big felt hat and motorcycle goggles. He sat down and offered his snuff box round and then began an absurd conversation.

'Can you tell me where my cow is? I have lost it,' he asked, looking at me expectantly.

'Sorry, no idea,' I replied politely.

'It is a six-year-old cow,' he added helpfully.

'No, really, haven't a clue.'

'I thought that you being a foreigner you would have special powers,' he said accusingly.

'No, er, nothing very special.'

'Ah,' he said stoically. There was a long hiatus in the conversation as the snuff box was passed around once more.

'You see, before Mongolia had democracy,' he resumed, 'you were not allowed to speak to foreigners even to ask them to find a cow.'

'Um,' I hesitated, reluctant to shatter any illusions about the advantages of Western-style democracy. Denden, who was enjoying my discomfort, then rescued me by undertaking to find the errant cow.

He leaned back, closed his eyes, moved his fingers along the beads of his rosary while muttering incantations under his breath. Then he pulled out a book, riffled through the dog-eared folios and declared that: 'Your cow must be in the South. Someone has taken it,' and when he saw the herdsman looking morose, added, 'but he has not yet slaughtered it.'

The man put his goggles on and gratefully took off for the south side of the mountain. Soon another man came to ask for prayers in favour of his son who was serving his army conscription. A third man came in to discuss his new medical practice. He had learned the arts of traditional medicine from his father but was only now allowed to practise.

He demonstrated with my pulse.

'You are an emotional person, your health is normal but you suffer a shortage of blood and in the past you suffered a problem on your left side.'

Javklan had his liver problem correctly diagnosed. Amarjargal had his headaches explained away.

'This is the first time I have felt a foreigner's pulse,' he said, 'which is very interesting because it is lighter – you eat less meat – and thus easier to diagnose.'

One woman came in who wanted to know the right day to cut her three-year-old boy's hair. This was a key ritual in Mongolian life. Denden pulled out his calendar and consulted the stars.

'Hummn, born in November 1988, that is the month of the rabbit, no, the month of the pig, that means the first haircut ought to be in the year of the pig or the horse,' he said.

Another lady came in worried about quarrelling with her husband. She suspected the reason might lie in an astrological mismatch. He was born in the year of the cow but she in the year of the monkey but Denden reassured her that such arguments were normal and nothing to worry about.

A while later an attractive young girl wearing high-heeled white boots came to ask about dreams. Her boyfriend had dreamt that all his teeth were falling out and she had dreamt he was about to die. She asked Denden if they were really destined for each other.

He did his routine with the rosaries and said all would be well. She need only ask the lamas to read some prayers on her behalf.

'I told her to ask for the words of Tsun Diwi which help especially when someone is under an unfavourable star or the years do not co-incide,' he explained afterwards. 'The verses do away with obstacles and bring Buddha's blessing.'

When it was dark we went next door to his daughter's *ger* where a big black cauldron of noodles and meat was bubbling on the stove.

After we had eaten, Denden tried some of my coffee.

'Oh, it makes you feel fresh,' he commented.

He had a down-to-earth attitude to the occult when I asked him about divination and the many stories of lamas who through tantric studies develop magical powers. He did not believe monks could fly through the air and laughed even louder at stories about flying saucers and aliens. As to exorcism, he said there was a special book on how to evict bad spirits but he never used it.

'I don't believe in this kind of thing,' he chuckled. As we drank the coffee an old Russian film about the October Revolution flickered on the black and white television set. Women wailed over corpses scattered on empty streets. A man wandering with an anguished face through a desolate city was seized and tied to a tree.

'I am not an intellectual! I tell you I am a worker,' he shouted desperately before being shot. I thought of the nun's vision of a hell full of Communists.

'Have you read Dostoevsky's *The Devils*?' asked Amarjargal.

'He thought these revolutionaries were possessed by devils,' he went on without waiting for my reply.

'What about hell?' I asked Denden. 'If you don't believe in flying saucers and so on, what are all these pictures of demons and hell in the temple?'

'We Buddhists believe there are eighteen hells. In number eighteen you are boiled alive in a big pot of oil,' he specified.

Hell, he explained, is ruled by Yama who has a head like an ox, a third eye of wisdom in the middle of his head, wild boar's teeth jutting out of his mouth and his left hand grasps a magic club with a human skull at the end.

There are hot hells and cold hells, where victims are immersed in icy glacier water, not to mention 84,000 outer hells. Special sins merited special torments.

'What about your religion?' he inquired. 'I hear that since we have democracy people are propagating your religion in Mongolia.'

'Yes, this is true and in my religion we too believe in hell,' I said, surprised by the old man's acuteness.

'But some people end up in purgatory and have to wait until God decides if they should go up or down,' I said.

'Then perhaps they must wait a long time,' Denden laughed.

'We have more circles of hell, twenty-four, where big devils with horns like a cow and a long tail carry pitchforks to push you into pots of boiling oil,' I said and got up and pretended to be a devil with a pitchfork.

'Oh, now that we have democracy in Mongolia, I see we shall have a competition in hells too!' he laughed.

Next day we cadged a lift to Shang Monastery, another old centre of Buddhism. Some officials took us in their jeep along a track across the grass. On the way we stopped for some lunch and sat inside the jeep carving cold beef off the bone and drinking distilled mare's milk.

The senior official turned out to be responsible for ideology in the province. He was the very man who had oppressed Denden but was quite happy to talk about the past.

'Of course, I believe in Buddhism myself. I could become a monk tomorrow if I wanted,' he said, biting into an onion. 'I just need to change my clothes. I know all the chants.'

'The thing is,' he continued, carving off a big chunk of meat, 'we should not go back to the situation in the 1930s when there were so many monasteries they controlled the economy and society.

'We had to smash the monasteries or we Communists would never have been able to rule properly. People were too obsessed with religion hereabouts.

'Perhaps, we overdid things, made some mistakes,' he said, pausing to swig down some more koumiss. Then he reconsidered.

'No, we made serious mistakes and I must recognise that. We did many bad things.'

We drove off again and I said that people in England had once been obsessed with religion. They sent missionaries all over the world, even here to Karakorum but now few people really believe and most of our churches are empty. Materialism had done the work of the execution squads.

'This religious boom won't last for ever here either,' he said. 'Come back in ten or twenty years, no perhaps fifty years and Mongolia will be a different country.

'Of course,' he added sadly, 'it will also be different from the country we wanted to make.'

Javklan told me how he had seized 30,000 tugriks from a friend of his who secretly painted and sold tankas and then spent the money on building a new bridge.

Gradually the man became drunker and started defending himself more to his conscience than to us.

'I was doing my job. Somebody had to do it. It was a good salary, people respected me and I had a car,' he said.

When I asked him about divination and magical powers, the local ideology chief turned deadly serious.

'There are, of course, people who really possess special magical powers but,' he said with a note of indignation, 'there are others who only pretend to be able to foretell the future in order to exploit the masses.

'Such people do not genuinely help people. I fought against these frauds and shysters. Yes, that is what I did,' he said firmly. We drove the rest of the way in silence and at Shang got out to find a tiny settlement of yurts overlooking a big flat valley.

Shang was once a rival to Erden Zu and one of the holiest shrines in all Mongolia. The old monastery had been down in the valley but the remains are now covered by wheatfields.

All that remained was an enclosure on the brow of a hill which held three crumbling former temples which had been used as barns, a fifteen-foot-high prayer wheel and three *ger*s which now served as temples.

We spent the night in one of them which was cluttered by the usual religious paraphennalia – cymbals, bells, scissors, shrines with a row of little dough figures in front and a pair of long Tibetan trumpets. The nightwatchman said all of it had been kept hidden for fifty years by the local people.

The watchman was about thirty, quite talkative and something of a poet although he had only four years in school. During his army service he wrote verses criticising the star wars programme; now he had composed several on the religious renaissance. Did we want to hear them?

He dug out some scraps of paper from his *del*, cleared his throat and began to declaim:

> The White Horse year is very good
> The Ocean of our faith is being filled
> The good life is coming!
> Blue Mongolia with its blue banner
> Will have a great future.

We all applauded and, heartened by our appreciation, he recited a longer one called 'Confession to the Holiest Saint':

> We are now worshipping the Obo
> We are celebrating the new time,
> Tradition has been reborn
> The shrines of our youth rebuilt
> You have made Mongols swim in the Ocean of Belief
> Before the end there is a new beginning
> The light was nearly out,
> The thread was nearly broken
> Held only by a man aged eighty
> Please make donations for the renovation!
> All good deeds will be rewarded.
> *Om Mani Padme Hum.*

Sunrise was cold and red and when I awoke little boys dressed in crimson robes like lamas were already drifting around collecting dung.

We went to see Dashzeveg, the oldest monk in the village. He was crouched over an old manuscript when we entered his dark and dirty *ger*. He seemed rather grumpy at first but he handed round a small box of menthol snuff from West Germany and told us about his life.

At one time every family was obliged to send one son to the monastery. He was eight and was very homesick when his parents packed him off. All the young monks were eventually obliged to choose a faculty like medicine or astrology and he chose theology. It had 1,500 monks who lived in four quarters, divided according to their place of origin.

The monastery had thirteen scientific faculties and like the others was a replica of Nalanda, the last great Buddhist monastery in India, which flourished on the banks of the Ganges until its destruction by the Turkish Muslim invaders in the seventh century.

Dashzeveg was twenty-four when the repression started. Interior Ministry officials suddenly arrived and seized all the monks and prominent noblemen. They burned all the monastic treasures and even buried the ashes. All the leading monks were shot and buried in mass graves.

A few treasures were rescued and hidden away in mountain caves or under *ger*s.

'As soon as we heard about the demonstrations, we dug up the old books and treasures which were all wrapped in waterproof paper,' he said gleefully.

'This was hidden in a pile of cow dung!' he said holding up the book he had been working on when we arrived.

Dashzeveg then suddenly turned and asked me to explain Christianity. He had heard something about it and was curious to know more.

I briefly explained that Jesus, Son of God, descended to earth 2,000 years ago. The Romans crucified him because they thought he was a political leader but in order to save us and not himself he had died so that we might wash away our sins and avoid going to hell.

I don't know what the translation was like but he listened carefully.

'Christianity has much in common with Buddhism. Buddha is the representative of God on earth,' he concluded.

Over a century ago the Abbé Huc was struck by the same thought during his travels through Mongolia. He found the similarities between the lamaistic rites and those of the Roman Catholic Church positively disturbing.

The lamas, he noted, hold confessional services twice a month and even a kind of eucharist in which the lamas sprinkle holy water and worshippers receive three holy pills and a drop of sacred wine from a skull.

He recorded a tradition that Tsong Kapa had had meetings with a stranger from the West with a long nose and piercing eyes. Huc suggested that this man was a Christian missionary and so influenced Tsong Kapa that he introduced similar rituals as part of his reforms of Tibetan Buddhism.

Shang was built sixty years after Erden Zu in 1647 by the first Bogd Khan, who chose this spot when he was just thirteen. The boy was supposed to be the reincarnation of a Tibetan scholar and historian called Taranatha.

At first there was just a chapel with seven monks and during a religious service the monks rushed out and accidentally crushed a small child to death. Dashzeveg said this was considered a good omen.

The monks were trying to convert the locals, who continued to follow shamanistic practices although there had been a political decision to adopt the Yellow Hat sect of Tibetan Buddhism which Tsong Kapa had created.

The sixteenth-century Altan Khan who adopted the faith was the last to lay claim to the title of Great Khan and brought all the princes together for a grand assembly at Karakorum.

It was a curious affair. The Altan Khan declared that he was Kublai Khan reincarnated while the leader of the Yellow Hat sect said he was the reincarnation of the Phagspa Lama, the inventor of the square script. In the ceremony the Tibetan monk was given the title Dalai

Lama, or Ocean of Wisdom.

At the time the Mongols were still shamanists who stuck to their old customs such as ritually tearing out the living hearts of their prisoners or sacrificing slaves and horses to accompany the dead into the underworld.

'Converting the people was very difficult at first,' Dashzeveg said. There were sort of propaganda teams which went around trying to dissuade people from fighting each other and carrying out their gruesome practices. Tibetan medicine, learnt from the ancient Indians, was used to show the superiority of Buddhist belief over remedies such as placing the foot of a gout sufferer inside a corpse.

A similar process seems to have taken place in Tibet in the seventh century when the Tibetans were probably cannibals. Their shamans were forever seeking to placate the hordes of malignant demons inhabiting the elements and constantly seeking to destroy man.

When the Mongols converted, the lamas simply announced the simultaneous conversion of the demons and all the other spirits of shamanism. They then became honorary defenders of the Yellow faith.

The lamaist pantheon is still the largest in the world. It has Buddhas, Bodhisattvas, tutelary demons, witches, Indian Brahamanical gods and godlings, local country gods and even personal gods.

Dashzeveg began explaining that the tutelary divinities of the temples were brought from Tibet. The word Zu is not a place but the name of the resident divinity in Erden Zu, which was housed in a small chapel at the rear of the temple. The monks had not shown it to me but I saw pictures of a small black statue. Shang had housed another divinity brought from Tibet.

We were straying into the secret realms of tantric belief and our discussion was interrupted by a call to attend the morning service.

Dashzeveg and the other old lamas always delicately steered the conversation away when I asked about these tantric mysteries and strange divinities.

I began to feel that Tantrism is the secret thread running through Mongolian history. The clues crop up everywhere. The pornographic paintings in the Lama Temple in Peking, the Tibetan lama who caused Kublai Khan's wine cup to rise unaided to his lips during an inter-religious competition; the bizarre story of the orgiastic rituals which the grandchildren of Kublai Khan indulged in as their empire collapsed; the dissolute and blind Bogd Khan with his young female victims, and the picture of the god embracing his paramour pinned to the roof of the nuns' *ger* in Ulan Bator. The obsession with grotesque demons in

so many temple paintings, even those in the prison. And the film director in Inner Mongolia with his odd story of the girl's tibia turned into a
trumpet.

The word Tantrism was only coined by scholars in the nineteenth
century from the Sanskrit word *tantra* which means a weave or loom.
What exactly the term denotes is somewhat vague but it used to
describe an intensely private and visionary movement.

It appears to have been well established in Hindu India by at least
AD 600 and some scholars consider Tantrism primarily a Hindu
phenomenon although the oldest datable documents are Chinese and
Buddhist.

About a hundred years later an Indian guru, St Padma-Sambhava,
who was a member of the great Nalanda university, travelled to Tibet,
an area which had been neglected by the great Indian emperor Ashoka
when he had propagated Buddhism in the rest of the region.

St Padma belonged to a branch of Buddhist thinking that had been
heavily influenced by tantric ideas which were popular at the time and
exerted strong influences on contemporary Hindu thought as well.

St Padma founded Buddhism in Tibet and introduced to the
Tibetans a north Indian alphabet then in use. They credit him with
vanquishing all the chief devils of the land by using the Vajra, or
thunderbolts of Vishnu.

He is pictured in temple paintings with a thunderbolt in his right
hand and a skull of blood in his left. The saint is attended by his two
wives, offering him libations of blood and wine in skulls, while before
him are set portions of human corpses as offerings.

Since the Tibetans were probably shamanists and cannibals the
dough figures placed in front of altars are thought to be substitutes for
the living sacrifices.

The branch of tantric Buddhism which St Padma brought to Tibet
is known as Kalacakra Buddhism. One Western scholar writes that it
'is generally considered the furthest removed from traditional Buddhism as it incorporates concepts of messianism and astrology which are
not part of the Buddhist search for liberation.'

The doctrine covers a multiplicity of practices, mental and physical,
in which the rites and yoga are inseparable. It is also remarkable for its
proliferating pantheon, especially the terrifying deities whose role is
partly linked to the adept's use of the lower and baser human
tendencies, such as lust or anger, towards spiritual aims.

Even the extreme dirtiness which early travellers observed among
the Mongols is a kind of spirituality inspired by tantric doctrines which
hold that everything has a divine source, so to wash clothes or utensils

is to lose a divine essence, to throw away part of the universe's cosmic energy.

The fascination with demon possession, clairvoyance and the whole atmosphere of the marvellous in which Mongolians exist each day seemed to have its roots in the tantric philosophy.

Some sources claim that it derives from the treatise known as 'The Journey to Shambala' which teaches the adept how to transcend time and defeat death. The treatise appears in paintings of one Buddhisattva, Manjusri, associated with wisdom, and is also known as 'The Book of Wisdom'. St Padma is said to have left books of this secret lore scattered in hiding-places around Tibet.

Certainly, the Dalai Lama has the power to give a special Kalacakra blessing or initiation, lasting several days, and those who receive it will be reincarnated in the Kingdom of Shambala.

The higher stages which the adept of this doctrine must follow are secret, passed only from master to pupil, but I was fortunate to meet someone prepared to unravel part of the mystery.

The president of the Astrologers' Union, Purensuren, lived in a new complex of highrise concrete flats at the end of a long bus ride. It was after ten p.m. when I arrived but he did not seem surprised to see me. He took me past the living-room where his mother was sitting on the sofa watching a video, to his small bedroom.

It was filled from top to bottom with religious objects but what caught my eye were smooth brown and shiny thigh bones and skulls cut in half. The latter had been turned into drums by stretching – as I learned later – human skin over the top of them.

Purensuren disappeared for a moment to change into his robes. It was hard to tell his age; he was not young but had a strong muscular physique. When we started talking he said he had been paralysed for several years.

From childhood he wanted to learn how to be a lama but it was impossible in those days and he had joined the army and served as an officer. Then he fell ill from a rare disease from which it took him ten years to recover. I could not make out what it was but he said his head and legs swelled up and he became paralysed. The doctors were astounded when he recovered.

During his illness, he had time to pursue his interest in religion and study numerous religious texts and sutras.

'I was very keen to learn the School of Agt but the lamas prohibited me from reading such books,' he said. 'In fact while reading such a sutra, I first fell ill and my teacher said it was because I was reading a forbidden book.'

Yet he persisted and began to think there was a spirit controlling him.

'When I stopped studying someone came and woke me up by pulling away the blanket and calling, "Why did you stop?" Then when I awoke from my dream and looked around, there was nobody there.'

He picked out an old black and white photograph of an elderly lama dressed in full religious regalia. This was not one of his teachers or at least not one of his living teachers. Purensuren was certain though that it was his spirit which was guiding him and driving him on.

'This man was very knowledgeable about the Agt,' he said, 'and he must have selected me as his pupil.'

I wanted to ask him what this Agt School was but he was hesitant and kept looking at me to see whether I knew what he was talking about. It was clearly a secret teaching which should not be discussed with the uninitiated.

For a while we talked about the meaning behind the many tankas and photographs which covered his walls. I was struck by a wonderful picture of the old state oracle dwarfed by his bulky robes and huge heavy crown of iron.

The oracle goes into a trance and is possessed by a spirit which allows him to move with superhuman strength. Questions are put to him and his utterings or rather his ravings are noted down and used to divine correct state policies.

Purensuren said it had strong similarities with shamanistic practices which were absorbed or adapted when the Tibetans converted to Buddhism.

I asked him about the paintings of various female deities. One was a picture of a she-devil clad in human skins and eating human brains and blood from a skull. She is always portrayed riding a white-faced mule with a saddle of her own son's flayed skin. This was Shiva, he said, the Indian goddess who is worshipped by offering a cake made from the fat of a black goat, blood, wine, dough and butter placed in a human skull.

The Mongolians prefer to worship her benevolent opposite, Tara, sometimes called White Tara, who embodies goodness and kindness. He took out a painting of her to show me. She looks Indian but has a white complexion and is still painted wearing the wispy garments of a seventh-century Indian princess.

In Kalacakra Buddhism the already numerous aspects of the god-head divide dialectically in two: good and evil or male and female. Thus there are peaceful and wrathful forms of the same deity. He showed a painting of Avalokita, known as the great compassionate one, and his counterpart Mahakala or Yama, the Lord of Death.

The tantric belief in the duality of all things led to an emphasis on the female half of the godhead, and the importance of female energies which is absent in other forms of Buddhism. That is why the Indian goddess, Shive (or Kali) was worshipped, he said.

By now Purensuren seemed reassured, or perhaps it was because after so many years of keeping his studies secret that he began to open up a little more and talk about the Great Agt.

'It is a path to enlightenment, but no ordinary one,' he said and I leaned foward to hear him better. 'Using the path of Agt is to take a jet plane, while following the other routes is like taking a train.

'One can become a god but only by passing through the Agt,' he continued. In other words, it was like Zen Buddhism: a shortcut to enlightenment which would otherwise take three reincarnations.

'The main reason not many people follow the Agt is because it is very dangerous. One must prepare one's spirit and one's body, train one's patience and humanity,' he went on, lowering his voice still further.

'The mind must control all bodily functions and to be safe one must take many tests along the way. If one fails to learn everything, one can lose control of the internal organs with fatal results. Say in a plane, if something goes wrong, then the plane will crash but in a train when something goes wrong it is not so dangerous,' he said.

'It needs careful preparation. The first step is lots of breathing exercises. The next stage is controlling breathing, the bloodflow and one's internal force,' he continued.

The preparation also involves learning two long sutras by heart. Afterwards the adept should have progressed far enough to demonstrate a little magic such as healing a sick eye by blowing on it, or avoiding drops of rain in a shower.

'Agt means "great surprise", a burst of light,' he said, 'and within the teachings there are different ways of reaching this stage.'

One can have a burst of consciousness which is lower than the Great Arg but to reach the ultimate stage (which he admitted he had yet to reach) further methods are used.

One of these is chanting mantras and meditating on the tankas. Sounds are important because the cosmic energy of the universe is brought into play by inhaling and exhaling air.

The mantras are sacred or ritual formulas such as *Om Mani Padme Hum*. The texts use an elaborate symbolism and conceal a coded language so that *Padme* means 'lotus' but it can also mean 'womb' and indeed the whole phrase – jewel in the heart of the lotus – has or can have a sexual connotation.

Such mantras are used in ritual curing or black magic, he said and the adept can then lick burning iron, open locks by blowing on them. Skilled practitioners can travel long distances through air, which is called 'putting one's soul on the soles of one's feet'.

'When you enter a certain stage, the body becomes weightless as if sleeping,' he said. The adept can check his progress against the signs of growing power mentioned in the tantric texts.

'When I tried to meditate, I had dreams, dreams of friends in heaven, or that I had entered a palace. These are signs of making progress,' he said.

Another technique for inducing an altered state of consciousness was especially popular in Mongolia, he said and picked up one of the polished thigh bones.

Only lamas who had already passed all the novice stages are allowed to perform this but afterwards they are kown as *Dyanci* or paradise lamas. The aspirant must spend 404 days in complete isolation and prayer and the period is divided into four equal periods. The first is by a solitary tree at the edge of a desert; then at a spring; on a mountain; and lastly at a burial ground.

During this time the lama was forbidden to defend himself against anything or to wash himself. Then, exhausted by fasting and prayers, the aspirant experiences terrifying hallucinations and delusions.

'My teacher had strange visions when he was meditating – friends appeared calling him by name, or beautiful women stood before him and even wolves came up to him. He just continued meditating and afterwards realised these were phantasmagoria,' Purensuren said.

'In these 101 days in the graveyard the lama must also feel that his body is taken to pieces and reassembled,' he said.

At this stage the aspirant must make his ritual implements. He must remove the tibia from the corpse of a young girl to make a trumpet, carve a rosary from other bones and use a skull to make a drum.

Purensuren showed me one of his drums which he said was very old. It was made from two crania tied together.

'It is a complex matter to choose a skull so the lama has to study the lines on the skull very carefully. If he chooses one kind, he will be rich, while selecting another kind can prolong his life,' he said.

These macabre tools are later used by such lamas to guide the spirits of the dead during the forty-nine days which a soul spends in purgatory before it is reincarnated into another body.

'He can call back lost spirits or chase away devils,' he said.

Tantric doctrine justifies using all aspects of life to attain illumination. Such repulsive practices also serve to prove that the student is beyond fear or disgust.

At an even higher level of initiation, Purensuren said the lama is required to eat the flesh of a corpse and in particular the brains.

'Of course, it is symbolic but in doing so the adept accumulates power,' he said. 'And this power enables him to prolong his life.'

Purensuren had confessed to this rather reluctantly and had looked at me closely. It seemed only right that we were discussing such monstrous and repugnant practices at well past midnight. I lit a cigarette and said nothing for a while, wondering if Denden or any of the old lamas I had met had ever taken part in such rituals. For a moment, I also thought of Perrault with his mysterious techniques of extending his life for 200 years but this sort of cannibalism was far removed from the innocence of his tranquil valley. It was a philosophy beyond good and evil. One which implies that good and evil are two sides of the same coin and which led one to believe that good can come of degradation, and that evil and suffering brought illumination. It was a philosophy which could reconcile the horrible cruelty of Choibalsan with a conviction that good would triumph.

Purensuren stopped there for a while, thinking as well. It was very late and the room was deadly still. I thought he had finished and would usher us out, when he began talking again.

There was another technique he had not mentioned so far which required a great deal of preparation.

In this the student seeks to bring about the union of male and female within himself and so achieve a new level of consciousness. Tantric philosophy conceives of the universe having two aspects, masculine and feminine, so the sexual union of Shiva and Vishnu symbolises the union of all opposites in the universe and unlocks the secret powers of nature.

The great bliss of sexual union becomes the bliss of enlightenment and the woman a symbol of the emptiness of the universe. Sexuality is placed on the level of the sacred.

He said such sexual rituals were still being performed right up to the 1930s and are supposed to transform the body by a mystical alchemy created out of sex.

'Both parties must reach a certain stage of development to perform this mystic alchemy,' he said. 'In this world it is just sex but really it is two spirits joining together in meditation and yoga.'

The ritual took place in a group and is called the Cakrapuja and is performed by participants arranged in pairs of male and female. Sexual union must be with a woman previously initiated, or with the initiate's wife and supervised by a male and female pair called the 'lords of the circle'.

'In this way each achieves a new perception of reality,' he said matter-of-factly.

In another version which conforms with the doctrine of opposites, the more depraved and debauched a woman is, the more suited she is. This is reserved for higher initiates but the most secret rite, which is reserved for black magic purposes, takes place with a corpse.

At the climax of the ritual, the male must retain his semen at the point of orgasm not just as a sign of profound dispassion but to actualise the non-procreative union of the gods.

The participant's final goal was the simultaneous immobilisation of breath, thought and seminal emission. At that moment the human couple would be transformed into the divine pair and dissolve into the cosmos.

I looked at Purensuren with astonishment. This warrior nation had become a race of mystics searching for an occult path to eternity.

Seven

The Shamans

Great God, I'd rather be
A pagan suckled in a creed outworn
So might I standing on this pleasant lee,
Have glimpses that would make me less forlorn,
Have sight of Proteus rising from the sea,
Or hear old Triton blow his wreathed horn.

William Wordsworth

The shaman is the great specialist in the human soul for he alone is said to see and know its form. Mongols call shamanism 'medicine for the soul' but few of its practitioners are left. In fact when in May I set off to travel to the far North, it was not certain that any remained at all.

For the past half century shamanism had been outlawed and all the shamans persecuted and imprisoned. Even in the 1920s they were still quite common; Ulan Bator had thirty registered shamans in 1929. If any genuine shamans were still left alive, they must now be very old and I wanted to meet one before they vanished.

Friends advised that the best place to look was in a wild and mountainous region close to the Soviet border. It is called Hubsogol after the long deep lake which pokes out of Mongolia like a finger pointing towards Siberia. Usually it is still frozen in May but during the few months of summer, ships ply its blue waters moving coal and timber.

Even the Mongols thought it was a remote region and for that reason, and because it was once a centre of shamanism, I decided to go there.

Shamanism is above all considered a religious phenomenon of Central Asia and the word itself probably comes from the Tungus or Mongol peoples of Siberia, although some scholars suggest a Sanskrit origin.

The true shaman specialises in a trance in which his soul leaves his body and ascends to the sky or descends to the underworld. He is not possessed by spirits but employs them in order to recover the erring soul of the sick or to guide dead souls on their journey to a new birth.

It is certainly mankind's earliest form of religion and as such can be considered the most universal. When a shaman goes into his trance, some claim that he re-establishes a lost time before man's separation from the animal world. Some believe that in prehistoric times, our hunting ancestors considered nearly all animals to be psychopomps – those who accompany the soul into the beyond. At that time all human beings possessed the technique of changing into animals and under-standing their language.

The shaman thus harks back to a period before the mystical solidarity between man and animal was broken.

To do all this, the shaman performs a seance which the best authority on the subject, the Romanian scholar Mirceau Eliade, calls an 'archaic technique of ecstasy'. In contemporary jargon, the shaman attains an altered state of consciousness.

'It is difficult for modern men as we are, to imagine the re-percussions of such a spectacle in a "primitive community",' Eliade writes.

'Every genuinely shamanic seance ends as a spectacle unequalled in the world of daily experience. The fire tricks, the "miracles" of the rope trick, the exhibition of magical feats, reveal another world – the fabulous world of the gods and magicians, the world in which every-thing seems possible, where the dead return to life and the living die only to live again, where one can disappear and reappear in-stantaneously, where the "laws of nature" are abolished, and a certain superhuman "freedom" is exemplified and made dazzlingly present.'

I wanted very much to see such a seance although I knew I would be lucky indeed just to find a shaman. Travel in the region was difficult, I was warned; there was no petrol, and although it might be cold, the thawing ground would turn all tracks into an impassable quagmire.

Although the term shamanism is associated with Central Asia, it exists not just among 'primitives' – aborigines, eskimos, American Indians and so on – but pervades European culture too.

The Old Testament is full of references to 'high places', prophecies and the coloured cloaks of prophets.

The most intriguing element is the connection between poetry, prophecy and shamanism. In ancient Greece the Delphic Oracle entered a trance by inhaling fumes which seeped into her cave below Mount Parnassus. Apollo, the god of poetry, was thought to speak through her convulsive ravings. Her speech was considered to be divinely inspired and the English language preserves the etymological link; 'inspiration' comes from the Latin verb *spirare* – to breathe.

In Central Asia, the shaman summons his spiritual helpers by drumming, speaking a 'secret language' and imitating the cries of beasts and especially the songs of birds.

The climax of a shamanistic seance comes when the shaman falls into a trance and also speaks a secret language of prophecy. He enters into a special state of consciousness which Eliade thought provides the impetus for linguistic creation and the rhythms of lyric poetry.

'The purest poetic act seems to create language from an inner experience that, like the ecstasy or the religious inspiration of "primitives" reveals the essence of things,' he writes.

If poetic language began as a secret language and an act of prophecy, the shaman's trance can also be described as a journey, a spiritual journey. The story of Orpheus, the poet who travels to the underworld to rescue a lost soul has the archetypal structure of a shaman's journey.

In most accounts of Central Asian shamanism, the shaman claims to climb a ladder, a tree or a mountain during his seance in order to contact the world of the spirits.

In the mythology of Central Asia the tree symbolises the Cosmic Tree, and a mountain the Axis of the World, so that the shaman's ecstatic experience is a journey to the Centre of the World.

In other places, a mountain also represents the bridge between heaven and earth. Some claim the seven-layered ziggurats of the Sumerians were constructed as a portrayal of this cosmic mountain. A seven-rung ladder played the same role in the Persian Mithraic cult. In the chief rite, which Roman soldiers brought to Britain, the initiate climbed a ceremonial ladder and at the top rung, the seventh, he supposedly attained the seventh heaven, the realm of pure light and ecstasy. English language still calls this a climax, from *klimax*, the Greek for a ladder.

But how does one become a shaman? Volumes of ethnographical material are devoted to this question describing curious and complex initiation rites and the bestowal of shamanistic powers. The original accounts are by now fifty or a hundred years old but they often suggest that the shaman undergoes a curiously Christian pattern of suffering, dying and resurrection.

None of it is very clear but in one version, the spirits of the shaman's ancestors 'kill' the initiate and then proceed to dismember and cook him. The spirits then count the bones and rebuild the body by fastening the bones together with iron. The iron bars on a shaman's coat are symbols of this. Then the bones are covered with flesh and a new man is born.

Throbbing and shaking, the little Antonov cargo plane creaked into the air. We sat on the pile of bags deposited in the aisle, which threatened at any moment to slide gracefully down to the cargo door and out into the heavens.

I held on anxiously to a box containing a rare collection of non-ethereal spirits. The booze – six bottles of vodka and three of whisky – was undoubtedly the costliest part of the expedition.

It is a matter of fine but important judgement when travelling in Mongolia to properly calculate how many 'presents' are required. Cash has little value. Everything was in such short supply that even armed with dollars there was almost nothing available in Ulan Bator other than strong drink.

Petrol was as scarce as food. To save aviation fuel, a truck had even pulled our plane on to the runway. When we arrived at the provincial centre, Mohron, its petrol supplies had virtually run out leaving the whole region bereft of power. We spent days trying to buy some, shuffling from office to office and clutching a gift hidden in a bag just in case it came in handy.

Hiring a jeep was no easier. The only vehicle in immediate prospect was a battered thing held together by string and affection which we had seen at the airport waiting to pick up passengers.

'It must be even older than you,' I said to the owner who had just started it with a crank.

'Both born sixty-four years ago,' he replied, patting the steering wheel with pride. I was ready to go north with him but with 600 miles over rough country in front of us, my companions protested that a breakdown out there would spell disaster.

While we searched for an alternative vehicle, there was time to enjoy Mohron. As the name suggested its residents lived a life of dull inanity.

For one thing, although the place was rather small, all of it bore the stamp of some strange but redundant compulsion for urban planning.

A city tour revealed a large parade ground complete with viewing stand, a monument to the revolution, a massive statue of a heroic soldier, two office blocks in concrete for Party functionaries, three sparsely stocked shops, a theatre with doric columns, a coffee shop without coffee, a municipal park protected by iron railings and the biggest feature of all was a children's park littered with concrete animals and dead trees.

What I liked best were two new traffic lights, solemnly changing from green to red to amber and regulating nothing whatsoever. Indeed, the whole province only had a mile or two of paved road and even that never carried more than two trucks at a time.

The traffic lights and all the rest of it served no real function other than as symbols representing some other imaginary existence. The traffic lights no more regulated traffic than the shaman's drum made him fly through the air.

Someone had built these parks and monuments but neglected to construct houses for most of the 10,000 or so inhabitants who instead lived in felt tents. What is more no one even wanted the parks. The children, brown and half naked, played on the banks of the river catching tadpoles and all around, like a great promise of freedom, the mountains stretched far and desolate.

Mohron also bred the kind of boredom that made queuing an interesting pastime. One night a crowd of Mohrons (if one can call them thus) pushed and shoved to get into the theatre just for the fun of annoying two policemen standing at the door with batons. The theatre, where a competition of amateur folk singers was on, had plenty of seats but even the policemen seemed to think this a good way to spend some time before the performance began.

Folk culture was experiencing a sudden revival. The acts followed in quick succession. There were long songs, as long and drawn out as the empty steppe; throat songs when the singer sings high and low notes at the same time; songs in praise of mother and songs celebrating nature.

There were recitals too. A thickset man with a round Mongolian hat made a long and sonorous wedding speech. A young girl declaimed in blank verse the sad tale of a young warrior called to war who leaves his betrothed behind. When the soldiers return victorious he is not among them, his saddle is empty.

The audience was moved to loud applause. My favourite was the Dance of the Drunken Darkhats in which a pretty wife drags her swaying, drunken husband home.

But who were these Drunken Darkhats? After the show we emptied a bottle of vodka and a plate of sliced and salted cucumber with

Sigmid, the leading Darkhat poet.

We were now, Sigmid explained, in the ancestral home of the ancient and warlike Darkhat tribe. And casting an appreciative eye at our bottle collection, Sigmid declared it was his duty, as Darkhat and poet, to accompany us. Furthermore, we should know that investigating shamans was a dangerous and delicate matter.

'There are shamans,' he said ominously, 'and there are shamans.'

Sigmid took on the mantle of guide and saviour. He promised to conjure up jeeps and shamans for us.

Sigmid worked as a journalist but his forte was love poetry and he cut a debonair figure around Mohron. He had long hair, a drooping Hunnish moustache, steel-rimmed spectacles and was invariably attired in a grey pinstripe suit and pink shirt.

He appeared to know every woman in town and our journeys from office to office collecting official stamps were always delayed by encounters with past, present or future lovers.

'Oh, what a woman!' he would sigh, fingering the ends of his moustache, as some creature in a bright embroidered silk *del* tripped away.

One day at lunch I discovered the presence of another foreigner trying to leave Mohron. He was a tall, grey-haired, lugubrious Frenchman from Paris and his passion was hunting.

'In the mountains there are wild boar, bear, wolf, wolverine, snow leopard, elk and deer,' he said, listing the possibilities of this hunter's paradise with satisfaction.

He was there to help the Mongolians develop the territory for hunters and on a map showed me large areas of trackless and uninhabited wilderness. Once he had organised his transport, he would stay in the mountains to draw up plans for a time when hunters could land their helicopters, or glide on to the frozen lake in light planes, for a day or two's shooting.

'Out there the animals see humans so rarely they are almost tame,' he said.

Local people had heard him on the radio boasting about his kills – he took a rather melancholy pleasure in detailing his trophies – and it had worried them.

The Frenchman said he worked for the International Foundation for the Conservation of Game, based in the rue de Teheran. Its patron was the brother of the late Shah of Iran.

'*Son majesté est mort, hélas, mais ça ne fait rien,*' he said sadly. '*Ça ne change rien.*'

At last one afternoon when we were ready to leave Mohron, Sigmid arrived in a state of high excitement.

We must reach our destination by ten the next morning, he insisted and we would drive all night. I was very fortunate, he declared, that fate had led me to this spot just at this moment. He had telephoned Tsaghan Nor, the remotest settlement in the north, and heard that for the very first time since 1938, a very powerful shaman would perform sacred rites before the entire community. The ceremony started on top of a mountain at ten sharp.

The shaman was a Tsatang, a member of a rare Turkish-speaking tribe of reindeer breeders. So this was doubly fortunate since the Tsatangs rarely came down from the high taiga.

We left without more ado. Contrary to all predictions, the weather was hot and when six of us – Sigmid, his cousin, my interpreter, the driver and a friend – had crammed ourselves, with gear, spare petrol and food, into a jeep, it was quite stifling.

The Russian-built army jeeps are simple but sturdy. At best they travel eighty kph but mostly they ground their way over rocks or through the mud at little more than walking pace.

As the driver bounced us in and out of the rutted tracks, Sigmid sat in the front brimming over with the highest spirits. He began to declaim his verses in a loud voice. From time to time, he waved his arms around, as if conducting an invisible chorus in front of him.

I had wanted to ask more details of this ceremony we were speeding towards and vaguely imagined some sort of voodoo performance on a mountaintop with lots of chicken blood and bare-breasted women.

I tried to find out more via his young cousin Gambatter, who was sitting quietly with me at the back, but he shushed me.

'You cannot ask Sigmid questions now, just when his heart is over-flowing with tender emotions,' he said reverentially. Gambatter was a dark Latin-looking youth in a green camouflage jacket who was on his way to visit his mother. Sigmid had persuaded us to give him a lift.

'But what on earth is your cousin saying?' I asked irritably. By now we were following a narrow path hemmed in by the cliffs of a gorge and far from any sign of habitation. Nearly an hour had gone by and Sigmid was still in full flood, grandly declaiming verses that had the tiring and emphatic rhythm of Homeric decameters.

'Sigmid is a lyric poet,' Gambatter said as if that justified everything.

'They banned his verses,' he added, after a pause. I looked at the patched pinstripe and its gesticulating owner with new respect. A dissident Darkhat lyric poet, a Byron of the steppes, is something out of the ordinary.

'Now he is talking about his love for a special woman,' Gambatter continued.

'Now, he is saying that he would like to be the King of Womenkind. To love 1,000 women, to sleep with 500 and marry 100 of the most beautiful women in the world. It is very fine.'

Sigmid then stopped, holding his arms aloft in triumph at the acclamation from the empty hillsides before us. Then he turned round and explained.

'No one dared publish my poem "King of the Women". It was forbidden and I was attacked for undermining Socialist morality.

'Communists cannot understand what is love,' he regretfully concluded.

The country now resembled Dartmoor and was dotted with piles of windworn rocks shaped like dolmens.

When Sigmid had run out of verse or at least breath, Gambatter talked about himself. He worked for the forestry ministry and was now helping the French hunter, but sailing was his real calling.

'I am sick of the mountains,' he confessed. 'At night I dream of the sea and the smell of salt.'

It happened like this. When he was finishing school, he was selected to study in the Soviet Union. The local Party chiefs had decided to set up a fish farm on Lake Hubsogol. The lake, the largest in Mongolia, is reputedly Asia's deepest and its fish are famous in the USSR although the Mongols rarely eat them.

The Party sent him to study fish farming. Naturally this required a large volume of paperwork. In the Soviet Union every specialisation has a number and some official wrote the number 1020 on his documents instead of 1013. So to Gambatter's surprise, he found himself on the Caspian Sea not studying fish breeding but ocean navigation.

'Once I was in the Soviet Union nothing could be done about it,' he said.

At first he studied at the naval college and then they sent him out to the Atlantic to develop his navigational expertise.

'Of course, all the sailors made fun of me. They said at least when you are back home in the desert, you can guide your camel by the stars.'

Five years later he returned home, a ranking navigator in the Soviet navy, and further disaster struck. His instruments disappeared when the plane carrying them crashed.

Although he was now the most senior naval officer in Mongolia, the Mongolian navy had no place for him. It does exist but consists of one boat with seven crewmen who spend the summer chugging up and down the lake pulling barges full of coal or oil.

'You see, there's not much call for navigators in Mongolia,' he said unnecessarily. 'Even sailing up the lake, you can see the mountains all the time.'

Had it not been for the October Revolution things might have been different. It was only the fall of Tsar Nicholas II which prevented Mongolia from expanding its navy. In 1908 the State Duma approved proposals to build canals and locks along the Yenisey River which rises near Lake Hubsogol and flows, 7,000 miles later, into the Arctic Ocean.

The Tsar approved the project but when the first buildings in Kizil, the capital of neighbouring Tuva, were finished the Revolution ended the project.

It was well after midnight when we reached a pass in the mountains. It was marked by an obo, a shrine, dedicated to the spirit of the pass and we stopped to leave some offerings of coins and sweets among a row of bunched fir branches housing some bleached horse skulls. They gaped wickedly in the faint starlight.

Past the obo the trail plunged down to a small settlement called Ulan Uyl. We spent the night there among a cluster of wooden cabins and *ger*s and woke an uncomplaining caretaker who lit the stove in a large *ger* reserved for guests.

Next morning the air was fresh and laden with the smell of pines. It felt alpine and when we left just after dawn, freshly fallen snow had clothed the high mountains around us. Sigmid, who had grown up here, said it had once been the site of a big lamasery.

'In the woods you can find the skulls of the executed monks,' he said but there was no time to stop if we were to make the ceremony in time.

We crossed rivers in full flood, swollen with melting snow-water. On the way back, the waters were so high, it was desperate work to ford them. We were forced to wait hours for a tractor to pull us across one torrent whose icy waters poured through the doors.

A track took us through a land of wide glaciated valleys on which clouds cast huge shadows, dappling brown meadows on which the first green shoots of spring were only now appearing. Herds of horses, yaks and sheep grazed peacefully in the distance.

Although I imagined that in this primordial scene the animals were wild, we did pass the homesteads of their shepherds. Sigmid was related to every one of them it seemed and at every second or third *ger*, he insisted on dropping in to say hello.

'They would think it rude of me if I passed without greeting them,' he apologised.

'But Sigmid,' I pleaded, 'you have over a hundred relatives, we will never get there on time at this rate. Even then we still have to climb a mountain to reach the ceremony.'

As Sigmid's visits became ever more perfunctory, he became increasingly agitated by being obliged to be so ill mannered. Then finally just before midday we topped the brow of a hill and there below us lay the glittering expanse of a frozen white lake, Tsaghan Nor. I hoped the ceremony we had come so far to see was not already over.

We headed straight for the Party and government offices. Horses were hitched outside a wooden cabin like in the Wild West but once inside, we found their owners standing about clutching bits of official forms for the Party secretary to sign.

The Party chief was a smooth-shaven man in a dark suit. He sat behind a large wooden desk and scrutinised my business card with careful deliberation. My impatience at an end, I burst out: 'Where is the ceremony? Where are the shamans?'

He raised his eyes towards me and then answered mildly that the ceremony was scheduled for ten a.m. the next day. I glared furiously at Sigmid for getting the day wrong but he looked away totally unconcerned.

'It's nothing to do with shamans,' the Party chief also corrected me.

'We have invited several lamas to bless the spirit of the mountain. It's not a shamanistic ceremony at all,' he said, injecting a tone of disapproval at the mention of shamans.

'You are welcome to attend,' the Party chief continued. 'I am sure you will find it very interesting. It will be the first time we are holding the ceremony for over fifty years.' He offered to provide horses to take us up the mountain.

So much for Sigmid's expertise on shamanism, I thought, and then the Party chief said that the reindeer breeders I had hoped to meet were far away in the taiga. On horseback it would take at least a week to reach them and by jeep it would be impossible. I groaned; we had, it seemed, made the journey for nothing.

Then, seeing my disappointment, he added, 'You could always go and see old Gombuhu. He's a Tsatang and a shaman but I hear he is rather difficult.'

We found old Gombuhu sitting in a forest glade with his granddaughter, doing nothing. The long afternoon rays filtering through the pine trees cast pools of light and shadow. A little way down the track, a few horses tethered to a tree by two white *gers* marked his home.

'It is good to meet visitors on the way. Then one can show good manners and invite them inside,' he said warily. He spoke slowly with a thick accent.

His round eyes peered, a little bloodshot, from a skin stained a mahogany hue darker than any I had seen before. He was about five feet tall, clothed in blue boots, a brown *del* and a grey trilby. He looked more like a forest pigmy than a Mongol.

'No,' I insisted. 'Let's stay here in the forest and talk in the sun.' He seemed pleased by this and agreed.

For a while he sat gently puffing on a long pipe with a silver bell hanging from the stem. Occasionally he put his hand inside the fold of his *del* to pull out an old tobacco pouch and refill it. It felt like interviewing a garden gnome and I wondered how to proceed.

'And how is your health?' I inquired and looked at the white stubble of hair covering his bare head. 'They say you are now very old.'

Gombuhu thought he was either seventy-eight or eighty-seven and in good health apart from a certain stiffness in his knees.

'It is difficult to get on a horse now,' he confided and lifted up a knee to demonstrate.

'Well, we have brought you some presents,' I continued. We gave him some bags of sweets, bars of soap and a litre bottle of Ballantyne's finest.

He distributed sweets to his granddaughter, a dumpy, taciturn creature in a green *del* who sat behind him and regarded us with deep misgiving.

From within his *del* Gombuhu withdrew a silver bowl which he rubbed lovingly and began to fill from the bottle still wrapped in a brown paper bag.

He poured a libation to the spirit of the forest before draining it himself. Then he threw a handful of sweets into the air. We all followed suit. The Mongols dipped their fourth fingers into the bowl, flicked a few drops in the four directions and then smeared some on to their foreheads.

'This is a good spirit. It is nice and strong,' Gombuhu said, beginning to mellow.

'It is important to share with the spirits of the mountains and forests because they provide everything,' he explained.

As he helped himself with evident satisfaction from the bottle clutched on his lap, the talk began to flow more easily. Gombuhu said the rest of the Tsatangs, of whom there were only a hundred or so, were up in the mountains. He now lived here with his daughter who had married a Mongol and herded cattle and sheep.

In 1959 the Tsatangs were forced to hand over all their animals to the state and now looked after them on behalf of the collective farm.

Last autumn they came down from the taiga to celebrate the birth of the one thousandth reindeer.

Their reindeer are rather small, he said, never more than four feet high. He had heard of bigger ones.

'I have seen pictures of that Father Christmas and noticed how big his reindeer are.

'But of course I don't believe they can fly through the sky,' he added in the knowing tone of someone who is not going to fall for tall stories.

He remembered little about the collectivisation but said his people originally came over the mountains to the north from Tuva, in the Soviet Union, where the majority were Tsatangs.

'The spirit of my father is there in my native place,' he said, 'but these days it is very difficult to travel there.

'The spirits of this place are very bad. Very dishonest,' he asserted and complained in particular about the deity which inhabited the peak we could see across the valley. He had been invited to tomorrow's ceremony in its honour but was against going.

'The lamas would not like it,' he said.

The conversation moved on to shamanism but Gombuhu was rather cagey and reluctant to talk openly. As the shadows lengthened, he became incoherent, slurring and spitting out the words.

'I know what you want,' he said suddenly. 'But do you have permission? Have you paid money? I don't mind how much you pay as long as it is settled.'

We all began to be confused. What did he mean? What money? Did we have to pay him to perform a seance? Or bribe the Party secretary? At that stage I was happy enough merely to have found a shaman and did not dare hope to achieve more.

Everyone explained that our visit was officially sanctioned. Everything was squared with the Party secretary and so there was no need to be frightened.

'Many things have changed in Mongolia. Everything is permitted now,' I said and started off about the triumph of democracy, the collapse of Communism, and so on.

Gombuhu looked at me with glassy-eyed scepticism and imbibed deeply from his bowl of Ballantyne's. At length he relented. He would put on his costume tomorrow and we must arrive at one p.m. sharp. We could take photographs but that was all.

His daughter arrived on a horse, leading several calves. A middle-aged woman with a calm smile, she decided it was time to get her father home. We bundled him, with some difficulty, into the jeep and deposited him outside his *ger* still clutching his bottle in a paper bag.

'Don't touch the threshold,' he grumbled. 'And go round the *ger* clockwise.' Then he stumbled inside chanting or swearing to himself.

In the evening, it was still so hot we went swimming in the warm shallows of a little stream.

For dinner someone had given us a long fish like a pike from the lake but the cooks in the guest house refused to touch it.

They were boiling up a big smelly piece of sheep fat for the festival. Mongols consider the back of the sheep where the winter's fat is deposited the prime cut.

'We just don't know how to cook a fish,' admitted the older of the cooks whose full form was wrapped in a bloodstained apron. 'I have never eaten fish.'

Mongols like Tibetans eat neither fish nor fowl. After a death the relatives are anxious to free the soul as quickly as possible from its corporeal frame so that it may find a new body. The fresh corpse is traditionally left to carrion birds or fish to consume. Naturally they fear that by eating such creatures they might be consuming the reincarnation of the departed.

We ignored this proposition and steamed the fish. It tasted good with fried potatoes. Talk at the table came round to the subject of shamans. We all agreed Gombuhu emanated a special force, a strange presence.

'I couldn't look into his eyes, it made me nervous,' confessed the driver who was called Byamsuren, or rather 'Saturday', after the day of his birth. He said he heard of a shaman arrested in the 1930s who slipped out of his handcuffs, broke a hole in the prison wall and escaped. When the soldiers caught up with him, he flew away over the cliffs.

Gambatter said shamans like to fight each other and compete in trials of strength. He knew of a case where a young shamaness challenged a lama who had belittled her abilities to a supernatural duel. Lamas themselves developed special powers such as avoiding raindrops in a thunderstorm or piercing themselves with swords. The shamaness, who was pregnant, took a sharp knife and prepared to remove her baby and then put it back. She sliced open her belly but having overestimated her powers, died soon afterwards.

Sigmid thought one had to be very circumspect with such people because there are black shamans and white shamans. The white shamans use good spirits to cure the sick but black shamans employ spirits from the underworld. They can put a curse on you from a distance.

He did not believe this until one day in the mid 1970s he was staying in a village when a young man, an official, mocked an old shaman, calling him ignorant. The old shaman, who was forbidden to practise, became very angry. At a gathering one night, people were sitting round the fire when the young man suddenly got up, threw off his clothes and crawled around naked, howling like a dog. When he awoke from the shaman's spell he could remember nothing.

'The shaman had shown his power by completely humiliating him in front of the whole community,' Sigmid said.

Gambatter talked about another kind of shaman who controls the weather with magic pebbles called Zad stones. The magicians gather them from falling stars, carefully watching at night to see where they land.

Sigmid started off on a true story which had taken place in Mohron. In 1978 a huge and uncontrollable forest fire raged and desperate officials summoned a local shaman. The Party condemned such superstition but the officials were at their wits' end. They commanded the magician to use his powerful Zad stones and create a rainstorm to put out the fire. The shaman complied and the raging fire was extinguished.

'And then,' Sigmid said, 'the committee arrested the shaman and fined him for indulging in illegal activities.'

Nobody could think of a story to trump that and Sigmid suggested seeing an old woman who lived in the settlement and knew more about shamanism.

When we arrived at her yurt, the old lady was delighted to talk. She offered us salted tea and biscuits and we sat around the stove in the faltering light of a candle.

Her mother had been a shamaness and her father and grandfather shamans. Her uncle had had the most remarkable career of the whole family. He had started as a shaman, then became an officer during the Second World War and ended his life as a lama.

She was not herself properly trained but she had the power.

'I have intuition,' she said and lowered her voice to a whisper so the grandchildren could not hear. 'For instance, I can tell if a day is good or bad for something.

'Or say if someone loses something, like a cow, I usually know where to look,' she said. She was very serious. In the flickering candlelight, her small face as round and wrinkled as a winter apple fixed on me calmly.

'We need shamans because they protect our people from bad spirits and cure them when they are sick. Of course, when a man dies, a shaman cannot bring him back to life.'

'What about his soul?' I asked.

'These candles that we burn are lights to help dead souls find their way from their home to the underworld. Otherwise they will wander about lost.

'Now if we don't bury people properly, the souls will wander in purgatory. But a shaman can go to the underworld and guide the lost soul. You see, only a shaman is free to move between the three worlds,' she said, meaning heaven, earth and hell.

'What does the underworld look like?'

'It is very like our own world with gods and spirits and is ruled by the Erlich Khan. When the shaman goes before the god of the under-world, he must be humble and free of sin, so shamans are good people.

'Now each person's soul is kept in his belt. We tie a knot, preferably three knots to be sure, in the belt before we go to sleep so that no one can steal the soul. When a person dies, his belt is put in his grave,' she said.

'How,' I wondered, 'did you manage during the time when shaman-ism was forbidden?'

'Everything has its own time and place. When the Russians were here shamanism was forbidden but they brought their medicines. Now the world is changing. So we are rebuilding the tombs of the old shamans and this means their spirits can help us once more,' she said. It was all because of an unusual event in July.

'It is difficult to define what, but there was some interaction between the upperworld and earth,' she hinted mysteriously.

'Oh, you mean the democratic elections last year?' I asked, slightly baffled, but she had made her own analysis of international trends.

'Strange things are happening,' she insisted. 'Perhaps a war coming. I think there will be a war between China and the Soviet Union,' she prophesied.

Next morning, the melting ice on the lake crackled and groaned in the bright sunshine. I walked around Tsaghan Nor as everyone was busy preparing for the festival. The settlement had the feel of a pioneer camp and consisted of a collection of wooden cabins with a school and an airfield, on the other side of which were rows of *gers*. The villagers gathered near the school, dressed in their best *dels*, where a truck was ready to take them to the wooded peak which loomed over the lake.

We decided to drive over and remind Gombuhu of our appointment before going on to the festival.

When we arrived at the clearing, he was standing on a tree stump and his granddaughter was about to help him into the saddle. He looked displeased to see us and was rather gruff. He said curtly that he was going to the festival after all but insisted he would be back by one o'clock.

So we sat dozing in the sun with his daughter, Choloun, and waited for him to return.

'He is probably embarrassed about getting so drunk yesterday,' she said. Gombuhu had finished off the whole litre bottle of whisky after we had left and had spent the evening wandering around muttering and chanting to himself.

'He could still walk though,' she said. His drinking had become un-controllable after his wife died four years ago. They had been married for fifty years.

'Now he runs after a drink like a child after candy,' she said sadly.

After a while, when it was obvious that he was not going to return, we set off across the valley to look for him.

We arrived at the foot of the mountain to find that gaily coloured pavilions were being erected in a green meadow dotted with the hardy buds of white edelweiss. A buzz of amateurish commotion that village fêtes or school sports days engender hung over the preparations. Nothing would begin until the ceremony was over. The men were already on their way up and Gombuhu had gone on his horse with them. People told us we might run across him halfway up when the trail became too steep for a horse.

We walked up the mountain through a silent pine forest, panting and sweating in the midday sun. The peak, the Three Beauties, was about 7,000 feet high but the air under the trees was close and oppressive. We hurried on, hoping that even if we failed to find him we would arrive before the ceremony was over. As we climbed we could hear the sound of distant chanting and hearty blasts from a conch shell. At length we emerged out of the forest canopy to find ourselves at the base of a steep rocky pinnacle. Some horses were tethered there, licking patches of snow, but Gombuhu was not in sight. We clambered up to the summit.

About thirty people were ambulating anti-clockwise around a rough pile of stones, chanting a prayer in ragged unison. The cairn was topped by branches festooned with white ribbons and prayer flags. Around it were smaller piles of stones and on a lower outcrop a tall and lonely pine was decked with white ribbons like a Christmas tree.

On one side the land dropped steeply away. Below I could see the wooden cabins, the White Lake, Tsaghan Nor, and beyond its farther shore a range of jagged snow peaks marched northwards. Away to the

West, the land presented a gentler vista of pasture and forest.

Inside the cairn was an altar with enough space for another ambulation. It was littered with bottles of vodka, sour milk, a few coins and piles of crescent-shaped biscuits heaped on a platter.

The worshippers had placed offerings of wooden tablets carved with horses, sheep, cattle, deer and other animals. Coloured cloths printed with images of the same five animals hung from sticks; substitutes, perhaps, for the living creatures which in ancient times would have been sacrificed.

The worshippers gave us some chunks of meat and a few biscuits. An old man with thick glasses held out a bowl of vodka, presenting it ceremoniously with both hands held underneath. I drank it solemnly. The Party secretary, now dressed in thick blue *del*, boots and a grey trilby hat, looked on with an amused smile and then poured a libation on to the rocks.

We had arrived too late to witness more. A lama who had spent hours reciting certain prayers (no one knew what they were) and blowing his conch was no more to be seen. Without the priest, everyone seemed uncertain what to do next.

'Should we go round again?' someone asked. Then the remaining twenty or so men shuffled round the obo again. This last rite completed, they all set off down the mountain and were soon out of sight. We were left alone with the ribbons flapping in a clean cool breeze.

What it all signified, I still do not know; perhaps some sense of power emanated from this high place which the shaman and the lama and the local Communist functionary all recognised. It was not exactly fear which brought them here but respect and I had a sense of obligations, long overdue, being fulfilled.

Ethnographic theory would suggest the mountain represented the cosmic axis of the universe and the ribbons symbolised the ropes used to climb up to heaven. Perhaps, but nothing else suggested such a grand purpose unless you tipped your head up and noticed how big and blue the sky looked.

At any rate Gombuhu was avoiding us and so we plunged back into the trees. The sports were in full swing by the time we had walked back down. Gombuhu was sitting underneath a blue awning with other local worthies drinking tea and continued to ignore us.

Such festivals are called *naidams* and were once held all over Mongolia to honour each local spirit whose presence is marked by an obo. The Communists outlawed the worship of trees or mountains and instead ensured *naidams* honoured the founding of a collective or some other political anniversary. The founding of the Mongolian People's

Republic is celebrated each July with a great national *naidam*. It was always accompanied by parades and speeches, but the competitions in the 'Three Manly Sports' – archery, wrestling and horse-racing – generated the real excitement.

This little *naidam*, with the spectators in bright-coloured silks sitting under the awnings in a meadow, had all the charm of a medieval joust. We sat down in the shade to watch, quenching our thirst with buckets of tea and nibbling some bread and cheese.

The archery contest was the first and the least impressive. The archers used the same light compound bows of wood and horn and gut which their forefathers had used on horseback. The best warriors could fire an arrow 700 paces, further than the English longbows used at Crécy. On this occasion they were lamentably incompetent, barely managing fifty paces. I don't think anyone there had used a bow for years.

We were joined on the grass by two teachers from Tuva who had arrived in Tsaghan Nor the previous autumn. The Tuvans and Tsa-tangs are the same people and speak an ancient turkic tongue. The Tsatang children spent most of the year in a state boarding school while their parents stayed in the taiga with their reindeer and were obliged to speak Mongolian. Now this minority policy was overturned. The border with the Soviet Union, which had been closed since the 1930s, was open again although it had taken the women three days to travel from Kizil, the capital of Tuva.

The teachers made a jolly pair and seemed to find life in Tsaghan Nor quaintly rural. One evening they invited me over for coffee and talked about the theatre in Kizil as if it were second cousin to Drury Lane or Broadway. They had pictures of Tuvans dressed up in powdered wigs playing Tartuffe or wearing tights in a production of *Romeo and Juliet*.

Meanwhile, the horse race was coming to an end. The jockeys, young boys between seven and twelve, rode bareback a distance of fifteen miles. It was early in the racing season and the horses were still thin and bony after the long winter. The winner galloped in, hanging on to the back of a fine white stallion.

Mongolian horses are small, no more than ponies, but astonishingly tough. Their speed and endurance always enabled Mongol troops to take their enemies by surprise. With these horses, Mongols could swiftly travel large distances, crossing deserts in the heat of summer, or waging war in the depths of winter. While other breeds would have died without proper forage, these horses survived on desert bushes or scraped the snow off the grass.

Marco Polo said that in emergencies, Mongol warriors would cut the veins of their mounts and drink the blood to refresh themselves. Even during the Second World War half a million of them were given to the Red Army and pulled artillery at the front.

Next came the wrestling, a very gentlemanly and courtly affair. Traditionally each combatant has a Second, usually an old man, whose duties consist of removing the round tasselled hat at the start of a bout and replacing it at the end. At more formal meetings, the Second is obliged to make a speech praising his champion. The wrestlers dress themselves in boots, trunks and a small waistcoat which allows each to find a firm hold on his opponent. At first the two circle around, pawing at each other's shoulders and struggling to find the best grip. The loser is the first to touch the ground with a knee, elbow or back.

It resembles sumo wrestling with much lumbering around and sudden bursts of aggression. Fat men with short legs and low centres of gravity tend to have an advantage. Not always though. I watched one man, slight and wiry, defeat several much larger opponents by sheer grit and determination before falling to the champion.

After winning a bout the victor performs a short heavy-footed dance, flapping his raised arms while turning around slowly. It is supposed to imitate the flight of the legendary bird, Garuda.

The final pitted a tall slim man with a brown Derby hat against one of the stubby fat types. Stubby got ready for a long bout of endless circling and shoulder-pawing and his opponent played along with this for a while. Then suddenly, in one swift lunge, the Brown Derby shot his right leg between the other man's feet, pulled his left shoulder down while with his right arm he jerked the short man into the air and, thrown off balance, Stubby fell backwards on to the ground. It was a triumph of speed over bulk.

The winner earned himself a big platter of meat and sheep's fat and the two posed for photographs.

The rays of the late afternoon sun slanted through the trees while we sat and watched the final contest unfold. In the general happiness of the occasion, one of the Tuvan teachers composed a little poem. It was hard to get the translation right but a few lines stick in my memory.

I am a girl of the taiga
with ten thousand white reindeer
The green moss is my bed
and the silver stream my tea

Sigmid gallantly felt inspired to counter with verses of his own.

> Keeping ajar the day of spring
> filled with cuckoo's calls
> We will keep shut the door to autumn
> when we must part
> and leave this time
> when the yearling whinnies.
> On the third day after the new moon
> on this lovely summer's day
> I came to the Three Beauties
> and gave gifts to the spirits.
> The girl from the taiga
> shines like the sun off a horse's back
> and the camp of her people flickers
> on the mountain like a star.
> The young fisherman
> shows his strength in the wrestling ring,
> while the men from the White Lake
> are gathered under the mountainside
> like flowers in spring.

The next day we found Gombuhu sitting crosslegged on the grass outside his *ger* and puffing away at his pipe in a very agitated manner.

'I want all things established before we begin. I don't want to be criticised later,' he said testily.

His daughter was tying up a few mooing yak calves and came over to join us. Two tiny lambs with curly black and white wool followed her to share the shade with us.

She explained her father's unease. Some officials had driven up the night before, snooping around to see what Gombuhu was up to.

'Perhaps they were just curious to see a seance,' I said.

'No, no,' she said, embarrassed to reveal the family's shame. 'You see, he is afraid that if they catch him he will go to prison again.'

Ten years ago (Gombuhu thought it much less), local officials launched a political campaign against the Tsatangs, harassing and arresting many of them. A party of officials even went up into the mountains to arrest him for superstitious practices.

He was sentenced to three years' imprisonment and then taken to Mohron. From there he was sent to Ulan Bator for another trial. His sentence was reduced but he spent two years in prison.

'It broke his heart. He couldn't stand being cut off from nature,' she said. 'And the anxiety killed his wife. Now he fears all officials, because he knows what power they have over him.'

Gombuhu could call up the spirits of the dead but was powerless against the terror of state bureaucracy. All at once he was no longer endowed with the mysterious aura of a woodland Merlin but another sad, pathetic victim. The evasive behaviour which I had understood as the jealous guarding of ancient rituals, I now recognised as the familiar secretiveness which fear breeds. A wave of sympathy and then guilt washed over me. It seemed grotesque that the long arm of Marx had stretched across the centuries and a huge continent from the British Museum to this remote spot to hurt this harmless old man.

Perhaps it was wrong to blame Marx but all of the Tsatangs arrested with Gombuhu were innocent of any crimes, yet the state had considered their life on the high taiga too free of Party control. No group, it seems, no matter how small or insignificant was allowed to escape and cherish its own beliefs.

Now that the problem was in the open, we conferred with Sigmid and the daughter. It was agreed they should go off and beg written permission from the Party secretary which would set Gombuhu's heart at ease. An hour later they came back with a typed document, signed and sealed by the Party secretary.

It read:

May 18, 1991

Dear Mr Gombuhu,
There will be no efforts from our side to limit your activities and everything you do depends on your own free will. Our workers only came last night out of curiosity and not to spy on you. It is entirely your concern if you wish to help these people.

Signed

Shlagua,
Chief of local authorities

Gombuhu insisted I add a letter of my own which I did. When the two had been read and translated, Gombuhu folded up the two letters carefully, wrapped them in a handkerchief and tucked them into his *del*. Then he beamed with relief.

He silently pulled out a small leather bag and emptied it out on to his blanket. Little coloured pebbles glinted in the sun. He stared at them intently for a few moments and declared, quite firmly this time, that he would don his shaman's costume at ten p.m. that night.

This business settled, Gombuhu felt free to talk. The stones were for divination, and not Zad stones, he explained. His father had warned him against using Zad stones and angering the spirits of the sky.

I told him that in England people used tea leaves for divination. He listened sympathetically.

'Well, each person has his own method and his own powers,' he pronounced tolerantly.

Shamanism ran in the family. His grandfather and father had both been shamans. Gombuhu was the youngest of six children and his father wanted him to be a lama but he kept running away from the monastery. Then his father decided to teach him about the spirits and ceremonies. It was difficult to learn.

'He explained how people behave when drunk and what lies behind it. He told me what illnesses there are and how best to cure them,' Gombuhu said.

He also instructed him on how to meet a spirit in a dream or in a seance.

'I was quite young and didn't understand everything he taught me,' he said. 'And now I forget many things.'

We began to eat a picnic of bread, cheese and tomatoes. Gombuhu had never seen a tomato before but after eating one cautiously, said he liked it.

Gombuhu was very hazy about his initiation only saying that he was required to perform continuously for several weeks.

As for his costume, his wife made a new one after his imprisonment. 'It is just a tool like a car to carry you to places, or like wearing your best clothes to a festival,' he said.

Only certain days are right to perform seances; it depended on the phases of the moon. He performed when people asked him to help their souls become stronger and overcome sickness. During a seance he would fall into a trance and see hills, mountains and rivers. He would see a certain place and three days after the seance, it would come to him what needed to be done. He would then tell the sick person to visit such and such a place and make an offering.

'It is as if I was really present at that place,' he went on. 'I don't tell people what offerings to give. It is up to them. I don't know if they get better either, I just tell them what to do.'

It was during such a seance that he saw Tsaghan Nor and decided to move here with five other families.

'There were few reindeer people here and nature was good. We heard Mongolia was a good place to go,' he said.

Others said that the Tsatangs had fled Tuva to escape the murderous repressions in the 1930s and which continued after Tuva officially joined the Soviet Union in 1944.

I asked him about the white ribbons which hung on the trees nearby and on the mountain top.

'It is an offering you make to the spirit of the place to bring well-being to the cattle and the people. There is no special ceremony but if we cut down trees for wood, it is to stop the spirits from being angered,' he said and we fell to talking about conservation.

'If you had shamans in England you wouldn't destroy nature,' he said and then a thought occurred to him. 'I guess that is why you came here, to learn something.

'The children don't know these customs either. In those years many unusual things became rare. Many books and precious things were destroyed or disappeared,' he continued.

'But why did these things happen? Were the spirits angry?' I asked.

'Everything has its time and place. Changes occur like the seasons. If we do the proper things, then we will reach the good time,' he said simply.

'At least I have lived on long enough to see the beginning of happy times,' he said. The thought cheered him, the deep folds in his brown skin wrinkling into a deep smile.

Gombuhu had been unwilling to talk much about the initiation process which plays such a big role in anthropological discussions of shaman-ism. A few weeks later I happened to meet a Mongolian professor who had been inducted into shamanism as a young man. He knew Gombuhu, whom he said was a black shaman. His teacher had been a Tsatang too and the professor gave this description of how he was initiated into the mysteries.

'I was twenty-four in 1959 when I met a famous shaman at Ulan Uyl. He took my pulse and said, "You will be a great shaman." So I decided to become a shaman.

'He taught me verses which I had to learn by heart so I wrote them down, memorised them and on the first attempt repeated them accu-rately. The shaman said I was very capable and he would accept me as his pupil.

'The shaman made me a little drum and a stick from the leg of a reindeer. We rode by reindeer for two days until we reached a place called Red Taiga. As shamanism was prohibited, the shaman had kept his equipment in this cave since 1946.

'We had to breathe life into the drumstick, which for a shaman was like a horse, a means of transport. We sat up the whole night heating it by the fire. He began to chant prayers and when the stick was filled with life, the shaman began jumping over the fire even though he was over eighty. His body became lighter and lighter. After a few jumps he fell down, tired and unconscious. I lit the stick, put it into his mouth and he returned to consciousness.

'Afterwards the shaman said I now had a horse but he told me that I would not become a black shaman.

'"I can tell from your features and body that you are not able to fight but only cure people," he said.

'After this I had to learn sixty verses and commit them to memory within three days. I was given no food or water until the task was done. In two days I had finished and was then ordered to keep repeating the verses until the little stick had turned into a she-reindeer.

'I didn't really believe the stick had turned into a reindeer but I thought if I didn't say I had seen a reindeer, I would never get anything to eat. I was hungry so I said I saw a reindeer.

'The shaman then asked me what the deer looked like, so I made up a description. The shaman corrected me and said I should take off my glasses, pointing out that it had one ear erect and the other was creased.

'The shaman then sliced meat into seven little pieces to make a soup. The seven pieces represented the seven stars of the Great Bear. He put the pieces in a row and took away the fourth which he said was my star and told me to keep it. I still have the fourth piece of meat. He said if I was ever close to death, I should take it out and eat part of it but if I showed it to anyone, then within three years I would die.

'The shaman then said I would make a good shaman and he began to breathe life into a magic staff with the help of his tutelary spirit. I also had to learn another 100 verses in two days. The idea was that if I repeated the verses often enough, the staff would materialise into a dog.

'Then the old shaman began complaining that his ribs hurt and said someone had put a spell on him. He ordered me to use the staff to find out who was responsible.

'I repeated the verses for a whole day and night but when I looked at the stick all I saw was the stick and not a dog.

'On the third day I lied and said I saw a white dog. The shaman corrected me and said it was a black dog. Once more I blamed my glasses for my mistake.

'The staff is used to point out the source of any trouble and it suddenly came to me that it was a bear who was responsible for his pain.

'Ah, said the shaman, that is probably true because he had not eaten bear's meat for five years. So if he ate some bear's meat everything would probably be all right.

'On the way back we met a young bear and shot it. We ate the meat for three days and afterwards he said his ribs felt better.

'In this way I passed the lowest stage and became a young shaman. The shaman was then eighty-two and died later aged ninety-nine. Shamans always pray to ninety-nine spirits, fifty-five on the right side and forty-four on the left side. So he lived for ninety-nine years and saw ninety-nine skies. Before he died, he sent me his costume and I then donated it to a museum.'

The light was fading and a fierce wind had blown up when we arrived for the seance. Stars twinkled through the branches of the trees and somewhere a raven croaked loudly.

Loose canvas gripped by the wind was flapping violently against the side of the *ger*. A few neighbours, big silent herdsmen, sat around the stove, perched on small stools, drinking tea. They seemed to share my nervousness.

We brought the two teachers from Tuva with us and Gombuhu was delighted to meet them. The teachers brought Gombuhu a yellow brew made from certain pine cones which grow only in Tuva or so they said. Gombuhu relished talking of his home and he was so overcome with memories that he wept.

At last when the *ger* was lit only by the feeble rays from an oil lamp, Gombuhu pulled aside the curtain behind which his costume hung. Choloun, his daughter, opened a wooden trunk and pulled out his drum, drumstick and head-dress.

She helped him into the coat, which was so heavy that it was hard to lift up. The coat was blue and long multi-coloured ribbons like snakes hung from its back. On the shoulders, collar and arms, big pieces of iron clanked against each other. The coat and boots were made of embroidered reindeer skins.

The hat of bright forest-green was rimmed with yellow. It was crowned with eagle feathers that touched the roof of the *ger*. Long ribbons of white and red hung down in front of his hat, obscuring his face.

Gombuhu took the big drum, which was nearly half his size, in his left arm and then, with the drumstick made from a reindeer leg in the other, he began beating and singing.

The stick had small bells and rattled to a rhythm which gradually increased in tempo. His head, transformed into a huge and monstrous shape by the hat, swayed and shook.

'Ah – yee-ya,' he chanted.

'Dom-dom-dom,' went the drum.

'Ah – yee-ya,' he went on, burying himself in the drum, his coat clanking like a manacled ghost.

Outside the rain began to beat down on the sides of the *ger* with another insistent rhythm.

Watching the old man moving so lightly under his heavy coat to this violent tempo was disturbing, even frightening. Beads of sweat – or were they tears? – gathered on his face, half hidden in the drum's shadow.

'Ah yah, ah yah,' he sang, the intonation rising and falling.

Then he stopped, wheezing heavily, mopped his brow with his stick before speaking in a quiet but hoarse voice.

'Mercy upon us, I am very old now without my strength,' he pleaded, 'but I am still alive, I can still perform. Please spirit come to me. I can still help people.'

He seemed to communicate with the drum itself. He began drumming again and the beat accelerated to a climax when he threw the drumstick inside the drum and listened for a reply.

'Coo-koo,' he said as if the bird itself were now present.

'Coo-koo.'

Then he growled inhumanly, a harsh rasping sound that seemed to emerge strangled from the depths of a great powerful beast. The bear or whatever it was, seemed to be there, with us, inside the *ger* and inside Gombuhu.

He was possessed. The growls became menacing snarls.

My hands became clammy and the camera slipped from my grasp. The hypnotic drumming and the singing when it began again came like a primeval lament wrenched with great pain from inside him.

Then he stopped, breathing heavily from exhaustion. He turned to us, his face still hidden, a transformed being. One by one we knelt down in front of him, spreading out a *del* or skirt on to which he cast the drumstick in a sudden and decisive gesture.

'Toerig,' he said to the first person, who replied, uttered the same word, picked up the stick and handed it back.

'Toerig,' I replied too, and when he received the drumstick, he sniffed it and moved on.

Then it was over.

His daughter removed his hat, heaved off his coat and wrapped a *del* around him. We saw once more nothing but an old man shuffling around on arthritic knees.

Gombuhu eased himself before a small table which he set out like an altar. In the middle he placed a bowl and on one side a bottle of whisky and on the other a bottle of vodka. He lit a candle and mopped the sweat off his brow.

The rest of us began speaking in whispers. Outside a dog barked furiously. The daughter stoked up the stove and a sweet fresh pine smell suffused the *ger*.

Gombuhu poured whisky into the bowl, stood up swaying gently, spoke briefly and intelligibly to some invisible presence, and threw the whisky into the air. He poured a second bowl and tossed it on the stove, filling the shadows of the small place with the comforting familiar smell.

The bowl was passed to each of us in turn and we too made libations.

Gombuhu poured another drink, lifted the bowl above his head and started off on a long speech.

'You came here to learn about shamans and your affairs are now blessed with success. It is not me which wishes you success but my spirit.'

He explained that the seance was shorter than normal because no one present was facing difficulties that required the assistance of either of the two spirits he had summoned. Then he emptied the bowl.

Afterwards when the bottles were empty we went outside and stood in the darkness, chatting like theatregoers after a play. One of the herdsmen had a mournful manner and addressed me, his big hands twisting in uncertainty.

'One day in the forest a bear ate my sister and her children. I saved one little girl and their flock of sheep but they all died later,' he said.

'This terrible thing is hard to understand, especially because I believed very strongly in the spirits and sought their help. You may believe in them but now I don't know . . .' he faltered, looking at me anxiously as if I could explain the meaning of what had taken place.

'Oh that old Gombuhu, he can't drink for nothing,' the old shamaness Soeren said, deftly rolling a cigarette with a page torn out of *Truth*, the Party newspaper.

'We had a contest once to see who could drink more,' she said, lighting up and inhaling deeply, 'and he fell down drunk as a lord but I was as right as rain.'

She wore a daring red pillbox hat stuck over her cropped grey hair and her big feet shod in black boots poked out from her brown *del*.

Soeren took little persuading to perform a seance for us although it was broad daylight. Her only condition was to wait until one o'clock but in the meantime she kept up a stream of explanation about the mysteries of shamanism.

Her home was on the way back to Mohron and Sigmid had suggested we meet her. The *ger* lay behind a small lake on the edge of an enormous plain which was surrounded by mountains on all sides. It seemed we had travelled for hours along the bottom of a giant bowl. Soeren was a Darkhat and this plain had served for generations as a gathering place for the tribe.

The shamaness said she was about seventy-five years old and now lived in a large but sparse *ger* with her daughter's family. It was calving time and in a corner was a little pen with straw where a newborn bundle of skin and bones bleated piteously for its mother whose large head loomed anxiously at the entrance.

Shamanism was in the blood, Soeren said. There were shamans in her family going back ten generations. She had become a shamaness at thirteen when the idea just popped into her head. Her daughter, Bayer, who crouched in the corner, was about to graduate herself as a shamaness in a fortnight's time.

Among the Darkhats, initiation took only a week and during this time the novice met his or her tutelary spirit. For Soeren it was the spirit of her dead aunt.

'It was difficult to get used to at first. Sometimes Auntie visited while I was working at home,' she said, twisting another roll-up.

She became convinced that under these circumstances no one would marry her so she went to a mountaintop and she threw away all her equipment. Then she fell ill and lost so much blood that she almost died so she took it up again.

I asked whether sacred trees or mountains were significant.

'Ah yes,' she said somewhat vaguely. 'There is a special shaman tree in the forest where we go and pray. No one else may touch it or there will be serious spiritual consequences.'

She forgot the reason because when she was eighteen, the government arrested all the shamans and smashed all the tombs of their ancestors. Her training was cut short. Furthermore, she was unable to attend the convocations of top shamans where this ancient lore was passed down to younger members. Once a year shamans from all over Mongolia had gathered in a cave somewhere in this region. From her description, it sounded like the annual meeting of any professional body. Top shamans exchanged notes and tested the powers of novices who, if they passed, were awarded the equivalent of doctorates. At the closing ceremony, a grand seance was held for Tengri, the great spirit of the sky.

Soeren said that in the past few months, her family had started restoring the tombs of the old shamans. They were situated on various remote hills and were sort of spirit houses or burial chambers in which the deceased's possessions were housed exactly as they were when he or she was alive.

I never managed to see one of these places but Soeren explained that their souls became the spirit of the place they were buried. I did not quite understand this (although I would on a later trip) and before I could ask, Soeren digressed into a series of long anecdotes about her family.

In old age, one of them had fallen in love with a young girl riding by. Unable to marry her, he had cursed her and she immediately fell down dead. Later her spirit took revenge and he died. Ever since that event, some time in the seventeenth century, the two families have barely exchanged a civil word.

Then there was another ancestor, a bit of a scrounger, who, when a rich family refused him a handout, caused their bull to die. He removed four of its ribs for his lunch and when the owners opened up the carcass, the ribs were missing.

'Anyway, don't worry, we will probably meet some of these ancestors later,' she said cheerfully. 'In Mongolia the dead are very much alive.'

It sounded rather alarming, cohabiting with dead and living relatives, but she made it seem less supernatural than superdomestic.

On an altar at the back of the tent, the ancestors were present, or re-presented, by a row of metal figures attached to pieces of felt. These were the Onghon, just as William Rubruk had described them on his journey. The proselytising lamas had largely destroyed them when they converted the Mongols, and even before Stalin's time they were a rare sight in Mongolia.

Spirits of a liquid nature were set up on another kind of altar – a bottle of whisky, and another of vodka. By now I was beginning to wonder if the dual meaning of 'spirits' in English was more than fortuitous.

As she readied herself for the seance, Soeren explained her costume which was made by her mother twenty-five years before.

For a shamaness the buckskin drum and coat had to come from a female reindeer. The lumps of fluted and twisted iron tied on to it were, she said, like the armour of knights; they protected her against all dangers during her spiritual flight.

A silent son-in-law helped her into her coat. He hovered anxiously behind her during the seance, ready to catch her if she fell. Even so, she chose to perform sitting on a chest, her feet shuffling to the rhythm of her drum.

As she settled in, she began mumbling and muttering to herself and the rest of us fell silent. Through the *ger*'s skylight, a shaft of light descended like a spotlight in which motes of dust danced.

Bayer, her daughter, crouched in a bright blue silk *del* beneath the bottles, with a wooden pail of milk and a spoon to hand.

The shamaness turned away from me, the knotted ropes dangling over a face creased in concentration or perhaps in ecstasy.

She rocked backwards and forwards.

'*Ye ha kara kye, ka kekara,*' she intoned, her voice rising and falling in a wild and sonorous sound.

First, she called her personal spirit, speaking in a sort of blank verse:

> My father with silver hairs
> My mother with greying locks
> My fate which looks after me.
> My idol which supports me
> Send me thy Onghon [spirit]
> Let it be a good day
> When everything goes right
> Let nine wishes be fulfilled
> And the six parts of the body be joyful
> I call you from far away
> From a place to which no horse can go
> Please be merciful and hear my plea
> As ye listen to the pleas of others
> All men are equal, all horses run alike
> So please show mercy and look kindly on my wishes
> And send me a spirit!
> Saloh! Saloh! Saloh! Saloh!

Sometimes she whistled, barked like a dog or howled like a wolf. At other moments she laughed aloud as if possessed. Three of the spirits she called entered riding on animals – a horse, a deer and a wolf. Two spirits who had been alcoholics in their lifetime, spoke through her, demanding something to drink, and I could detect her voice imitating their speech.

Bayer poured some of the vodka into a bowl and gave it to her mother who drank it down greedily.

'I don't want vodka, I want some of that foreign drink,' one of these spirits said irritably. Bayer hastily opened the Scotch and poured the spirit a generous finger.

Meanwhile Bayer kept tossing spoonfuls of milk on to the altar with the Onghons. She recognised each spirit as it entered and shouted an apology for wasting their time. She explained to the spirits why they were being called:

> My silver-haired grandmother who saves us
> And my grey-haired mother who preserves us
> We are calling thee only
> Because of the wishes of the travellers from afar
> And only for this reason
> Nothing dangerous has happened.
> We who remain here after your death
> We who look after all that ye left behind
> We who were created from thy bones
> We who are just drops of thy blood
> Look and See! Keep and Protect!
> My kindly grey-haired mother please take care of us!
> We who are the farthest ends of thy root.
> Look and See! Keep and Protect!
> Mother of magic, Mother of mystery!
> Take care of us, keep and protect us!

Bayer repeated the invocation to all six spirits which appeared. Soeren was in contact with thirty-two spirits and of those called, four declined to come.

After an hour Soeren went into a fit. Her body twitched and shuddered, her eyes rolled up and she collapsed off the box but her son-in-law caught her before she reached the floor. We fell silent in fear and astonishment and the stillness was broken only by the whimpering of a small child.

Then she woke up and smiled.

She changed out of the coat and stood below the skylight through which the spirits had passed. Then talking fluently as if the spirits were still present, she held up her hands in supplication to the light pouring through the opening.

She once again explained to the spirits why a proper seance was not required. In three days' time she would meet with them again. Then she threw an offering on to the stove.

She explained a while later that she did not actually see the spirits.

'There is just a flash like lightning and the idea or image of the spirit appears before my inner eye,' she said.

Then it was time for fortune telling and we were invited to consult her about the future. She pulled out some worn and ancient coins and spread them out on her palm.

'Your life is happy. Some people will be jealous but you should not listen to them,' she said to me.

It was also time for more drinks. Soeren liked the whisky so much she decided that she was in the mood for a sing-song. Off she started, singing duets with Sigmid with an affectionate arm draped over me. It had passed with none of the frightening intensity of the seance with Gombuhu.

'It was a pity though,' she said as we left, 'that you had nothing of importance to ask the spirits.'

A few hours later as we sat watching a river in full spate, waiting for a chance to cross, Sigmid was once again inspired and scribbling another poem.

By now his declamations and their insistent rhythm irritated me. Soeren was right, I had nothing really to ask the spirits.

Perhaps, as Eliade had written, the hidden springs of lyricism I hoped to glimpse were lost to modern men. They are still there for Sigmid, but Soeren's world with its magic which can transform men into animals or spirits was lost. For me, all that remained was no more than a spectacle.

Eight

In Search of Genghis Khan

> There came into the world a blue-grey wolf
> Whose destiny was Heaven's will.
> His wife was a fallow deer.
> They travelled together across the inland sea
> And camped near the source of the Onon River
> in sight of Mt Burhan Kaldun
>
> The Secret History of the Mongols

Who was Genghis Khan? What prompted him at fifty to set out on the path of world conquest?

No one really knows the answers. We do not even know where he is buried.

Under Genghis Khan the Mongols burst on the civilised world like a storm and in two generations had conquered half the people on earth.

'They annihilate empires as one tears up grass. Why does heaven permit it?' a Chinese historian asked in horror.

The Holy Roman Emperor Frederik II believed they must be the scourge of God.

'One knows not whence this savage race derives the name of Tartar, but it is not without the manifest judgement of God that they have been reserved for these latter times, as a chastisement for the sons of men and, perhaps, for the destruction of Christendom. This ferocious and barbarous nation knows nothing of the laws of humanity,' he wrote, asking Christendom to unite and oppose them.

At the height of their power in Asia and Eastern Europe 'scarcely a dog might bark without Mongol leave'. Yet Genghis Khan left no statues, temples, monuments or tombs. He appeared and vanished like a divine wind leaving nothing in his wake.

This is unique among the great conquerors of history. Until the turn of the century, almost nothing was known about Genghis Khan. He looms out of our history books, a blank cipher for unprovoked destruction.

The papal legate Giovanni Piano Carpini arrived in Mongolia a generation after his death and reported that the Mongols 'vaunted in their songs the loudness of his voice, which sounded like thunder in the mountains, and the strength of his hands like the paws of a bear, which could break a man in two as easily as an arrow.'

Chaucer apparently mentions him in the Squire's tale:

> Cambynskan which in his time was of so great renown,
> That ther was nowher in no region
> So excellent a lord in alle thing.

Aladin Juzjani (1226-83), the Persian historian, provides in his *History of the World Conqueror* an equally unreliable description of him.

> Trustworthy persons have related that Chinghis-Khan, at the time when he came into Khorasan, was sixty-five years old, a man of tall stature, of vigorous build, robust in body, the hair on his face scanty and turned white, with cat's eyes, possessed of great energy, discernment, genius and under-standing, awe-inspiring, a butcher, just, resolute, an overthrower of enemies, intrepid sanguinary and cruel ... He was an adept in magic and deception and some of the devils were his friends.

The only existing portrait was painted many years after his death in the Chinese style by an unknown painter during Marco Polo's lifetime. It hung in the Forbidden City until Chiang Kai-shek took it with him to Taiwan.

Right up to the last century, the Mongols were held to have left no written records or literature. Another historian, Rashid al-Din, the Jewish Vizier to Gazan (1295-1304), the Mongol ruler of Persia, mentions a *Secret History* he was unable to read because it was re-stricted to family members.

Then in the 1860s, a curious document fell into the hands of a Russian priest living in Peking who called himself Palladius and had a penchant for collecting old manuscripts. He was the abbot of the

Russian Orthodox mission to China, which was situated on the vast site of the present Soviet Embassy close to Yonghe Gong Buddhist temple.

It was the find of a lifetime. The manuscript was the chronicle which Rashid was forbidden to see. The text of the *Secret History of the Mongols* was in Chinese characters which gave a phonetic rendering of antique literary Mongolian.

Palladius set about translating it but died in Marseilles in 1878 before he was able to complete the task. A Russian Mongolist, A. Pozdneev, published the first chapter but nothing more until his death.

It was rumoured that Palladius' work was stolen by a student until another student discovered it by chance in a corner of Pozdneev's desk.

In 1899 a Japanese historian found another copy of the *Secret History* and by 1907 it had appeared in print for the first time. A full translation into a European language was not published until 1940 when the German scholar Erich Haenisch printed it in wartime Berlin.

Most of what we know of Genghis Khan derives from the *Secret History* which corroborates and enlarges the accounts of the two Persian histories.

It is the only genuine Mongol text to have survived that period and scholars assume that the Ming Chinese destroyed everything else after the revolt ended Mongol rule in China. A history of each khan once existed but these together with the khans' great seals are now lost.

The *History* was probably written in 1240 only thirteen years after the death of Genghis Khan but as a record it is sometimes confusing.

Composed in rhythmic prose interspersed with epic poetry, it covers the semi-mythical ancestry of Genghis Khan, episodes in his life and ends with the succession of Ogodei, one of his sons.

Many of the places and people described are obscure and the details contradictory. Above all we are left without a clear picture of Genghis Khan. Strangest of all, his death and burial are reported almost perfunctorily.

For more we must look to a seventeenth-century work in Mongolian, *The Golden History* (again a twentieth-century discovery). As the funeral cortège sets off, one of his generals sings a lament:

> While thou didst swoop like falcon:
>   a rumbling wagon now trundles thee off:
> O my king!
> Hast thou in truth then forsaken thy wife

and thy children and the Diet of thy people?
O my king!
Circling in pride like an eagle while
thou didst lead us
O my king!
But now thou has stumbled and fallen,
like an unbroken colt,
O my king!

It is now established that Genghis Khan died aged seventy-two on August 18th, 1227 near Chung-shui, north of the River Wei in the mountains of eastern Gansu in China, after bouts of fever which began with a fall from his horse.

The *Secret History* mentions that he was buried on Mount Burhan-Kaldun beneath a spreading tree. The mountain has not been identified and the site remains hidden or forgotten.

The search for his tomb began in the 1920s as the Mongols, free at last of centuries of Chinese or rather Manchu domination, undertook a national revival.

The efforts stopped after 1929 when Stalin consolidated his position as unchallenged leader in Moscow. Like Genghis Khan, he too was fifty when his full reign of terror began.

Until Stalin's death, all mention of Genghis Khan was forbidden in Mongolia and the areas associated with his name were taboo.

In Ulan Bator I heard that the search had just resumed. A joint Mongolian and Japanese expedition was under way, searching for Mount Burhan-Kaldun. I thought I would visit the area.

I started by inquiring at the headquarters of the Genghis Khan Hearth Society. It had stained glass, white marble stairs and a huge alabaster statue in the foyer which imparted a profoundly religious atmosphere to the building.

The Palace of the Pioneers was formerly a musuem sacred to Lenin not Genghis but the Hearth Society had set up its offices here after the Party decided to rent the place out and capitalise on a now redundant building. It all amounted to as neat and symbolic a reversal as one could wish to find.

The Hearth Society, according to Mr Namchin, one of its officers, was dedicated to restoring Genghis Khan's name and position in world history.

In the near future it hoped to erect monuments, museums, and palaces in his honour. In the imperial residence would be a throne and seats for his nine commanders-at-arms. A Genghis Khan music and dance ensemble would tour the world and if the tomb was discovered, even bigger monuments would be erected.

As Mr Namchin saw it, Genghis Khan was held in loving esteem abroad and foreigners were eager to make contributions to fund these projects.

'We have written to your Queen for a contribution,' he said, holding up a piece of paper. It specified that all funds should urgently be transferred to the Bank of Mongolia, Ulan Bator.

A large contribution from the Queen would ensure her a seat inscribed with gold letters at the Great Council. She would in effect become an honorary adviser to Genghis Khan.

'I am sure Her Majesty would be very interested,' I said politely.

These activities were important, Mr Namchin explained, because there must be no doubt that Genghis Khan was a Mongol. The trouble was, some people said he was born across the border in the Soviet Union. And the Chinese claimed he was a Chinese emperor and is buried on Chinese soil.

If they found the tomb in Mongolian territory all would be well. That was why this expedition was so important.

He provided me with maps and directions. The new season of exploration was just getting under way and in the meantime, I should visit Delun Boldag where he was born, clutching, as the *Secret History* relates, a clot of blood the size of a knucklebone in his tiny fist.

It was rather hard to get there but perhaps a plane could be arranged from the provincial centre, Underhan. I spent the next few days hiring a jeep and making other arrangements in order to drive to Underhan.

As these preparations were being made, I wondered why anyone other than the Mongols should want to claim Genghis Khan for themselves.

Alexander the Great or Napoleon are still revered but Genghis Khan is commonly held up as a symbol for unbridled conquest and destruction. Bram Stoker, after all, chose to make his Count Dracula a direct descendant of Genghis Khan.

He was to provide a model that a succession of rapacious leaders in Asia sought to emulate. After the empire collapsed, his successors vied to claim his mantle and the vast territories that had fallen to his armies.

Membership of the Genghizid line was a crucial qualification. Tamerlaine never proclaimed himself a great khan but appointed as khan a true Genghisite, Syurhatmish, to give his power legitimacy.

Even the great Manchu Emperor Kang Xi, who inflicted a crushing defeat on the Mongols, married a descendant of Genghis and appropriated the imperial seals to give himself authority.

The struggle continued this century as Stalin, Mao and the Japanese fought for control of the vast spaces of Central Asia and offered rival versions of Genghis Khan's historical significance.

The Japanese appointed a descendant of Genghis, De Wang, to rule what they hoped would become a new Mongolian state. So anxious was Emperor Hirohito to promote Mongolian nationalism (and deflate Chinese nationalism) that a huge mausoleum was commissioned to commemorate Genghis Khan.

Chinese claims to his legacy are based on the legend that he was buried on the spot where he died. For centuries a small tribe guarded eight white tents in the Ordos and supposedly preserved his ashes and various relics.

Four times a year they held ceremonies in his honour and people came to present offerings of silk scarves or yak butter. The guardians made animal sacrifices and possessed ritual texts written in an unintelligible jibberish known as the language of the gods.

The shrine survived until the Muslim rebellion of 1862 to 1877 when all the relics are thought to have gone up in flames. The Japanese were anxious to obtain the copies, if that is what they are, to hold a huge celebration for the anniversary of his birth which tens of thousands attended.

In the early 1930s Stalin, who was anxious to dampen down Mongolian nationalism and promote Russian nationalism, commissioned a damning biography by a Polish writer.

The relics were hidden from the Japanese in Qinghai until 1954 when the Chinese Communists brought them back to mark the 727th anniversary of Genghis Khan's death. The Chinese also restored the old sanctuary tents and guardians and subsidised the annual ceremonies.

They even went further and built the mausoleum according to the Japanese designs and on June 16th, 1962, organised huge festivities for the 800th anniversary of his birth (which they considered to have taken place seven years later than the date honoured by Mongolians).

The Mongolians reacted to news of the big celebrations being prepared across the border in China by deciding theirs would have to be bigger and better.

They put up a large stone monument at his birthplace, issued stamps of his portrait and of his war banner and organised a major conference.

Chinese leaders praised his conquests and before a gathering of 30,000 described them as 'a mutual cultural exchange between East and West'.

In Moscow Khrushchev, shaken by the Hungarian uprising and the trouble brewing in Czechoslovakia, was alarmed by this outbreak of nationalism among the Mongols and decided to cancel the celebrations.

Russian scholars published articles attacking Genghis Khan as a symbol of reaction. The stamps were hastily withdrawn and are now collectors' items worth several hundred dollars each. Temurochir, President of the Society for Mongolian-Soviet Friendship and the politburo member responsible for the celebrations disappeared. All others connected with it were arrested and charged with 'Nationalism'.

'Genghis Khan's predatory wars led to a reduction of Mongolia's productive capacity and brought untold misery to the Mongolian people. Any denial or underemphasising of the reactionary nature of Genghis Khan's deeds amounts in essence to deviation from the basic position of the party and to stimulating Nationalism,' *Unen* newspaper said at the time.

Perhaps it all smacked too much of Stalin's personality cult for Khrushchev to tolerate. Genghis Khan like Stalin embodied the idea that individuals not economic forces are the stuff of history.

In China, the mausoleum was shut during the Cultural Revolution and only reopened in 1979.

The first stop after we set off on the journey was the checkpost a few miles outside Ulan Bator to show our papers. Stalin's internal passport system ensured that the nomadic Mongols could not even leave or enter the capital without written permission.

Twenty miles further on, the metalled road petered out into a rough track across the steppes. We headed for Genghis Khan's birthplace in Hentei aimak, famous for its rich countryside.

Herds of horses and sheep grazed on its green pastures which were carpeted with spring flowers – primroses, marigolds and buttercups. Occasionally one glimpsed a solitary shepherd on a horse.

I could never get used to seeing camels in this setting. They were moulting, and in a breeze the winter fur flew off leaving them looking like a fluff-pile carpet which has seen better days. Nothing could change their earnest lugubrious expressions, even the indignity of being reduced to the state of semi-nakedness.

All along the roads, the elegant cranes in grey plumage as sober as a city suit stalked about in stilted courtship dances. When we rattled past they took off vertically, tucking their long legs underneath like wheels retracting into the undercarriage.

Common too were the short tubby marmots. They are intensely curious and they would hop along to the side of the road, stand up, and when the jeep was almost on top of them, would then disappear into their holes, dropping out of sight like a ball down the pocket of a billiard table. Brown eagles with strong white chests perched on the telegraph poles and regarded their antics with humourless calculation.

We saw one eating a young lamb once and when we came close it took off, lifting its prey with a leisurely strength.

The route took us past a small mining town. Barada was just a long street of tall housing blocks down which I saw a nomad on horseback stop at the traffic lights like a film extra in Manhattan.

The driver tried to find a friendly place where we could eat but gave up. All the housing blocks were identical and numberless.

The location of another acquaintance was unmistakable. About 100 tanks and armoured vehicles lay on the steppe like a pile of broken toys, gun barrels poking out in all directions. Pigs snuffled among the rusting hulks which formed a pigpen littered with straw.

The owner lived in an old *ger* nearby and he and his wife greeted us, followed by a shoal of ragged children.

Amargarlam, the tank farmer as I dubbed him, was in fact quite rich and the first real entrepreneur I met in Mongolia. As a pot of meat and potato stew cooked on the stove, he and the driver discussed privatisation and business.

The tank farmer was like an early American settler building a ranch in the wilderness. He was a driver, and his wife a factory machinist until they had quit their jobs last year to rent some land.

Now they were farmers raising chickens, pigs, horses and sheep and planting potatoes and onions. He was collecting bricks to build a proper ranch house and a chicken coop. Eggs are an almost un-heard-of luxury. We had brought some, hardboiled, and gave them to the children as a treat.

The work he and his three brothers did would require thirty people if they were a state enterprise, he boasted. This was only the beginning though, the only obstacle to other money-making ventures came from local officials who thought he was getting too rich.

The driver, a fat friendly man called Ghazan, shuffled uneasily hearing all this. His idea was to use the coupons allocated under the state privatisation scheme to operate a private bus. He was worried about petrol. If the shortages continued where would he be then?

Most people, he thought, were being too hasty and rushing into new ventures. It was better to wait and see, just as it was in the 1950s when they collectivised.

I asked what the tanks were for. The farmer said the departing Soviet troops sold them for a song and he bought them to resell as scrap metal. He predicted a shortage in the future and a good profit.

He had bought petrol too and let us have some.

Further down the road we passed the Soviet army camp, a small city in fact, which housed a tank division. There were still plenty of neglected tanks left inside and an air of neglect, even defeat, pervaded the place.

We stopped and asked a soldier loitering by the gate if there was any food to buy in the camp shop. He shrugged his shoulders and shook his head in resignation.

Conscripts spent two years at such camps going slowly mad with boredom. There was little else to do but train. Around the camp, the steppe had been turned into an exercise ground and it had small shooting ranges with model tanks pulled on rails. It already looked deserted and soon the last Soviet troops would be gone.

That night we slept in a truckdrivers' hostel. The driver stayed in the car so no one could steal the petrol.

The next day we arrived at the provincial capital, Underhan, but the airport was closed. There were planes but no aviation fuel. We would have to continue by jeep or turn back.

At the Party offices we found members of the Genghis Khan Hearth Society planning a similar trip.

Mr Damdinjev, the retired correspondent of *Truth*, invited us to join him. His grandson and two monks were coming along for the trip which was only 300 kilometers. Afterwards they intended to join the expedition in time for Buddha's birthday on May 28th.

I decided against it. The rivers might be impassable and it could take a week to get there. Mr Damdinjev was rather vague about the details and inspired little confidence.

Instead we had lunch, drank vodka and discussed journalism with his colleagues.

'What is journalism like in a capitalist country?' they asked wistfully.

'Here we can now write the truth,' they said. 'Only since there is no paper, no one can print it.'

Mr Ozhgoosh from the state news agency said he could send no more than one story a week.

Instead he wrote poetry in his spare time. He preferred lyrical verse and observed that several poets who had written about Genghis Khan had been imprisoned.

'People don't understand,' he said as the afternoon wore on, 'that journalists don't drink becuse they want to get drunk. We are not relaxing but working. The creative juices are fermenting all the time.'

On the long journey to Mongolmert where the Genghis Khan expedition was based we spent the night at a settlement which had once
been a labour camp where Stalin had sent the troops of General
Vaslov. The general had fought on the German side during the war.

A division had worked a wolfram mine and left behind some pretty
wooden Russian cabins with painted windows in which their guards
had lived.

In the morning the sound of chanting woke me. A splendid-looking
lama appeared, dressed in a thick robe of yellow silk with large blue
cuffs tied by a broad red belt. He wore a red cap on his head and
peered at me through thick spectacles.

He was on his way to a ceremony marking the restoration of the
monastery he had joined as a boy of eight. When he was nineteen, he
enlisted and fought as an officer in the war.

'In all those years I never abandoned my beliefs. I just waited for all
this to pass,' he said simply with a wave towards the huts.

We left the old labour camp and a few hours later we struck a trail
going north up a wide and deserted valley. A brown river flowed calmly
through it and stunted willow trees lined the banks and islands.

This was the River Onon, one of the three rivers which form a
triangle where the Mongol nation was born. The expedition called
itself the Three Rivers Expedition.

The Onon flows east to join the River Amur which empties into the
Sea of Japan. A second river, the Tulla, meanders through Ulan Bator
and then twists north into Lake Baikal.

The third river is the Herlen which drains south into a handful of
lakes in the Gobi desert.

This then was Genghis Khan country and it looked much as it must
have in the twelfth century when he was alive. The untouched valley
was deserted and a grassy steppe spread from either bank wide and
opened to a long ridge of lightly wooded slopes.

It is odd but the *Secret History* omits all reference to the Mongol
tribe in its account of Genghis Khan's beginnings.

Even today Mongols are at a loss to account for their name. Some
believe it comes from 'Mon Gol' meaning the river Mon. Others say it
should be pronounced 'mun gol', interpreting 'mun' as correct, basic,
true; and 'gol' as pivot, centre, essence, and the combination of these
words as true essence.

It is usually pronounced more like 'mo'huls' and when Tamerlaine's
grandson invaded India in 1526, they became known as the Moghuls.

The dynasty lasted until the British dethroned and imprisoned the last Moghul emperor in 1857.

Genghis Khan's father, Yesugei, was the chieftain of a small tribe, the Taijit. He abducted Genghis Khan's mother, Hoelun, from the Buryiat tribe. The ancestral home of the Buryiats (probably a corruption of Borgin, Borjin or Bargin mentioned in the *Secret History*) is possibly near Karakorum. The Buryiats now have their own republic in the Russian Federation which I hoped to visit.

Wife-snatching was common in those days and later Genghis Khan's first wife, Borte, was abducted. Afterwards she gave birth and this is perhaps why his first son was named Joche, meaning guest.

Genghis was born Temujin after a Tatar chieftain his father defeated. His name derives from a turkic word, *temur*, meaning 'iron' and the *jin* is a suffix so that together the name means man of iron or ironsmith. So in fact Genghis Khan's real name can be translated as 'Smith'.

Tamerlaine's name comes from the same route and also means 'of iron' and later Josef Vissarionovich Djugashvili called himself man of steel or Stalin.

While Temujin was still a boy, his father, Yesugei, was poisoned by members of the Tatar tribe. It is a curious irony that the Mongols were to become known abroad as Tatars or Tartars and Central Asia was called Tartary or even High Tartary.

The Tatars were clearly enemies of the Mongols but after Genghis had subdued them, he always placed them in the advance guard of Mongol armies. So anyone asking what people were coming was told – the Tatars.

The transformation of their name to Tartars came, according to the English historian Mathew of Paris from a silly Latin pun by the French king Louis IX who said they were not Tatars but *ex tartarus*, meaning from the region of hell mentioned in classical tales.

After his father's death the family fell on hard times. Temujin by sheer force of his will and personality built up a small force and served the Kin emperor who ruled northern China.

He returned to his homeland and twenty years on declared himself 'lord of all peoples living in felt tents'. In 1194 he was proclaimed a Great Khan. Twelve years later, when he was fifty, he summoned a great tribal gathering, a Khuraltai, which crowned him Genghis Khan.

Even the meaning of this title is unclear.

The word – properly pronounced Chinggis – resembles a turkic word *tengis* denoting sea or ocean so perhaps the title means Oceanic or Universal Khan.

Professor Onon at Cambridge University has proposed in his new translation of the *Secret History* that it should signify Almighty Spirits. Therefore, correctly translated, these years saw his transformation from Smith to Lord of Almighty Spirits.

Only at this point did Genghis Khan begin organising the tribes for world conquest.

What impulse had propelled him to lead his men, who even at his death numbered only 120,000, against the mighty cities and impregnable kingdoms around them we can only speculate. The *Secret History* does not explain.

A vital part of this nation-building reorganisation was the introduction of a common law, the Yasa or Jasagh drawn up only a few years before the Magna Carta. The *Secret History* makes clear the huge significance of this codex.

'When my successors have ruled for 500, 1,000 and 10,000 years and those who take my place will continue to follow the laws and customs prescribed by Genghis Khan and to do so without alteration, heaven will vouchsafe them help and blessing,' Genghis Khan is reported saying.

The Yasa lays down for example that 'the man who is taken with a stolen horse or camel shall return it to the rightful owner and also pay a fine consisting of animals similar to that stolen.

'If unable to pay this fine, he must give his children in place of animals and if he has no children, the criminal shall be slaughtered like a sheep, that is to say his legs shall be bound together, then his belly ripped open and his heart squeezed by the slaughterer's hand until the animal dies.'

The consequence of ignoring Genghis Khan's injunctions is also made clear:

'They will live long and enjoy the pleasures of life. But if they depart from my Yasa, the realm will crumble into dust and rock. Once again they will call for Genghis Khan but they shall not find him.'

By late afternoon, we arrived at Mongolmert, a collective centre consisting of a few huts and *ger*s. The expedition's camp was a little way outside and neatly divided between the small trim Japanese tents and the large shapeless canvas structures of the Mongolians.

A small shack with a smoking chimney was the cookhouse where we announced ourselves.

'It is lucky to come when food is ready to serve,' a large fat woman with a red face declared, producing mugs filled with dumplings boiled in milky tea.

The cook soon endeared herself to me by rushing out of her hut and shouting, 'Banzai!' whenever food was ready.

'Mongols have big stomachs, but foreigners' are very small,' she observed, shaping two meaty fists to convey the narrowness of our gullets. After eating our fill we settled down to hear more about the progress of the search.

The expedition's leader was a Mongolian ethnographer, Professor Badamhatan. A tall lanky man with white hair down to his shoulders, he had once been a rising star in the Communist Youth League and was rumoured to be an illegitimate son of Marshal Choibalsan.

His search for the tomb was a piece of archaeological detective work. He found at least five mountains in Mongolia called Burhan-Kaldun and in addition collected stories about Genghis's tomb all over Asia.

He narrowed the search down to two mountains including one in Hentei aimak.

Professor Badamhatan's research was still illegal but he managed to continue it in the field on the pretext of studying the burial practices of the ancient Mongols. He excavated thirty tombs in this area and discovered that Mongol tombs are normally just a round pile of stones, about two meters across, usually on the eastern side of a mountain. The earliest tombs date back to the tenth century AD.

One day he took me to see an example on a hill near the camp. It was a barely noticeable circle of scattered grey stones covered with green and blue lichen. A small stone, called a pillow, on which offerings were set, stood apart facing the sunrise.

Every tribe had its own burial place and a distinctive feature was the efforts made to hide or disguise them. Mongolia is littered with tombs and burial cairns and those of the Huns are the largest and most prominent.

Professor Badamhatan began to notice that the Mongol tombs were often set close to Hun graves. The Mongols considered themselves to be the descendants of the Huns and indeed heirs to their empire. They modelled their military organisation and tactics on the Huns'.

The Huns were a mixture of turkic- and Mongol-speaking nomadic tribes which shared a pre-historic Altaic language. The term, Altaic, comes from the mountain chain that curves from north to south through the Soviet Union, Mongolia and China.

The Huns were shamanists and believed there were three worlds – heaven, earth, hell – and equipped themselves for the afterlife, taking wives and horses with them.

The first Hun tombs were excavated by a Russian scientist, Koslov, in 1926. They were formed by large piles of granite blocks, eighteen to twenty metres across and sometimes forty-seven metres in diameter. About six metres underground he found a circular log framework covered by a roof. Some seventy or more horse skeletons with riding tackle lay between the logs.

Some tombs were vast – twenty to twenty-five metres deep. Under the cairns were burial chambers, constructed like log cabins, where the deceased lay in a wooden coffin carved from a tree trunk.

The tombs were furnished with ornaments and carpets decorated in a peculiar animal style showing fantastic aquiline griffins, hurtling deer, horse and riders and intertwined struggling animal bodies.

In 1929 Russian archaeologists made even more remarkable discoveries excavating five tombs in Pazyryk Valley in the Altai mountains. Preserved in the tombs dated between the fifth and second centuries BC were numerous objects of wood and skin, wool and silk from China, fine clothes of fur including the oldest shorthair teased carpets in the world.

All the object were also decorated in the animal style. Most astonishing of all, the archaeologists found that embalmed human bodies and horse carcasses had survived perfectly intact.

The corpse of one man was so well preserved it was possible to clearly see a complicated pattern of fantastic animal motifs tattooed all over his chest, back and legs. His skull had been broken in battle and then scalped.

Although the site, 4,000 feet above sea level, was south of the Siberian permafrost line where the ground just below the surface is perpetually frozen to the hardness of rock, the tomb and the bodies had been permanently frozen. Due to the special conditions connected with the barrow's construction and the severe high altitude climate, ice had formed under the cairns.

However in Mongolia the majority of Hun tombs had been robbed and Professor Badamhatan became convinced the Mongols were determined to ensure this would not happen to theirs.

According to a Mongolian saying, 'whoever witnesses the death of a khan becomes a pillow under his head.'

The accounts of Mongol customs by travellers such as Marco Polo bear out the extraordinary lengths taken to preserve the secrecy of the burial:

You should know that all the great lords who are of the lineage of Chinghiz Khan are conveyed for burial to a great mountain called Altai. When one of them dies, even if it be at a distance of a hundred days' journey from this mountain, he must be brought here for burial.

And here is a remarkable fact: when the body of a great Khan is being carried to this mountain – be it forty days' journey or more or less – all those who are encountered along the route by which the body is conveyed are put to the sword by the attendants who are escorting it. 'Go!' they cry, 'and serve your lord in the next world.'

For they truly believe that all those whom they put to death must go and serve the Khan in the next world. And they do the same thing with horses: when the Khan dies, they kill all his best horses, so that he may have them in the next world.

It is a fact that when Mongo Khan died [grandson of Genghis who died of dysentry in 1259 while fighting in China] more than 20,000 men were put to death, having encountered his body on the way to the burial.

The missionary Giovanni Piano Carpini describes how a Mongol grandee was buried sitting in his yurt with a table on which were a dish of meat and a jug of koumiss, and that a mare and foal and a horse with its saddle were buried with him. The skin of another horse, stuffed and impaled on a pole, was set above ground.

Excavation of more recent tombs showed that the attempt was always made to bury a khan exactly as he had lived. Yet until now no tomb of a Mongolian khan has ever been found.

The Ilkhans of Persia or the Khans of the Golden Horde were no longer buried in Mongolia. Many were converted to Islam but there are rumours that during the Second World War the tomb of Joche, who founded the dynasty of the Golden Horde, was discovered in Kazakhstan.

Professor Badamhatan concluded that Genghis Khan was buried sitting upright just as he would have sat in his *ger*. As there are strict rules about the positioning of objects and people in a *ger*, as the host he would be sitting facing the entrance where his weapons and a leather pouch for fermented mare's milk would hang. In most Mongol tombs a man would be buried with his armour and saddle and a woman with her needles and mirror.

It was equally likely that Genghis Khan's body has also been preserved deep frozen. Although the permafrost line was not so far south when he was alive, since then massive logging in Siberia has stripped away the forest cover and the permafrost line has extended to Mongolia.

Just what state his body would have been in by the time it reached the mountain is another question.

After all, Genghis Khan died in the hot weather of August. According to some legends, his followers salted his body; others claim he was encased in horse manure which is noted for its preservative qualities. The lama near Karakorum had also preserved the holy texts in a pile of horse dung.

The official history of the Mongol Yuan Dynasty, the Yuan Shi, mentions that three khans – Genghis, his successor Ogodei and Kublai Khan – were buried in the same place with the former at the top of a mountain and Kublai Khan below.

After studying such documents, Professor Badamhatan concluded that it was probable that the tombs of fourteen khans are on the same mountain. The fourteen range from Genghis Khan down to Toghon Timur, the last to rule in Peking, from 1338 until 1368, and who died four years later.

But where exactly are the tombs?

In 1980 he began by investigating the local legends lodged in the memories of the pre-Communist generation. On the pretext of his ethnographic research, he interviewed all the old people in the Hentei region that he could find.

'They were intensely suspicious and were afraid to talk about Genghis Khan. It was four years before anyone was willing to open up to me,' he said.

Yet nearly every hill and river in the region bore some connection with the life of Genghis Khan. One day he pointed out to me a low hill not far from the camp where locals claim at the age of ten, Genghis Khan first conceived of a plan to build an empire.

He took me to see one of his sources, an eighty-eight-year-old Buryiat who lived down the valley. Damba sat perched on his bed and was happy to tell stories and drink vodka.

'Let us be healthy and live long!' he said heartily with unwarranted optimism. It was hard to keep his attention on the subject of Genghis Khan. His mind wandered too easily back and forward across the centuries. The events in the thirteenth century seemed as fresh to him as those of the 1930s and of equal interest.

Damba's family had fled the Soviet Union in the early 1920s but on Stalin's orders they were subsequently brutally persecuted. His father, secretary of a co-operative farm, was shot as a counter-revolutionary and the family ostracised.

'Everyone could insult me because I was the son of a counter-revolutionary,' he said in his piping voice. 'Then a while ago, they wanted to give me a paper saying that my father was rehabilitated.

'But I said, "If he had done nothing wrong why should he be re-habilitated?"' Then he added, 'Of course, if he was still alive it would make sense.'

Damba said some people had become rich finding treasure from the tombs. He remembered a gigantic cauldron which could hold 200 litres which his brother had found on a mountaintop while hunting wild boar. Then there was the case in 1936 when a man had found a gold sceptre and a golden bowl which he claimed had belonged to Genghis Khan. He tried to hide it but gabbed about it when he was drunk so the secret police came, arrested him and took away his treasures.

He had learned about Genghis Khan as a child listening to hunters telling stories around the campfire. One had killed 300 bears and another 301, he pointed out as evidence of their reliability.

'It happened like this,' he began, 'Genghis Khan's brother brought the body back but it was a Turkish captain who was in charge of the burial. He was determined to bury it so that no one would ever find it again. First he hid four different but identical coffins so that no one would know which was the correct one. One was buried here, one in the west, one in the Altai Mountains and one near the Onon River.

'When he buried him here, the place was surrounded by troops for three months and inside the enclosure, they grazed herds of horses which trampled the ground above the tomb. Then he offered a prize to anyone who could detect where he was buried,' Damba said, 'but no one could.'

Professor Badamhatan warned me not to take these accounts as literal truth. By sifting through the many stories and identifying the common elements which might hold a seed of truth, he discovered the key to the search.

In this region a vast area of land had once been called the *Ich Horig* – the Great Taboo.

He pulled out a Japanese-made satellite map and moved his fingers over the contour lines.

'This taboo covers an area of roughly 240 square kilometers of wilderness. And this is the sacred burial ground of the Mongol khans,' he said.

The Burhan-Kaldun, a wooded mountain massif, rises about 7,000 feet out of a complex network of valleys and mountains. Somewhere on its slopes is a Mongolian Valley of the Khans were one of the greatest warriors in history sits, rigid and frozen in death.

The imperial sanctuary was inaccessible from every direction except the south. Badamhatan had spent many months trekking on horseback over the area trying to identify its precise borders. It is wild and dangerous country. Once he narrowly escaped death from a bear ravenous after the long winter.

The taboo was protected by more than wild beasts. He discovered preserved only in the memories of the old people, the story of a tribe which for 700 years had from generation to generation loyally protected the secret of the sanctuary.

When Genghis Khan died fifty families were appointed the guardians in perpetuity and ordered to ensure that no one else entered it on pain of death.

Only they could graze their herds, and they and their descendants were freed of all tax obligations. They maintained three lines of defence on three small valleys which cut across the Herlen valley, only way into the sanctuary.

The professor said he found evidence for this in the writings of Rashid al-Din, the Persian historian.

The guardians came from a tribe known in Mongolian as the Urianghai, the people of the forests, and are the present-day Tuvans in the Soviet Union. They were conquered by Genghis Khan and given as the fief of his son Tuli, father of Kublai Khan.

Tuli and his troops, which now included the Urianghai, guarded Genghis Khan's war standard or black banner. The holder of the black standard was one of the nine councillors of Genghis Khan and permitted to sit in his presence.

These special praetorian guards became known as Darkhats from the verb *darkblagh* which means to prohibit or forbid. Sigmid the poet was one and their ancestral home is the vast bowl west of Lake Hubsogol.

The Darkhats of the Ordos in China earned their name because they were the custodians of the White Standard used in peacetime and are therefore distinguished from the others by being called White Darkhats.

This standard was patterned on that of the earlier Turkish khans and consisted of a pole surmounted by nine long-haired white (or black) yaks' tails. Its shape so resembled a cross that when the Mongols invaded Georgia, the Georgians thought they must be Christians and followers of Prester John.

After Genghis Khan's death, the White Darkhats remained in the Ordos to guard this banner and his other possessions – sword, spear, arrows, quiver and saddle – and to honour the spot where he died even though the usual custom was not being followed. Genghis Khan was not buried in the Ordos as tradition demanded but brought to this sacred mountain.

In 1912 the Bogd Khan dared move the Black Darkhats from the sanctuary and appointed them to work as servants of his mother-in-law but chose to maintain the taboo by decree.

The Bogd Khan also brought back in 1923 an ancient banner, perhaps the original black banner, but it has since vanished.

The people who now live in this area had preserved the taboo and continue to respect the wishes of Genghis Khan but elsewhere knowledge of the site disappeared.

At first the locals were opposed to the expedition until Professor Badamhatan persuaded them that its purpose was not to open the tomb but to preserve it.

The Japanese had reluctantly agreed that the tomb would not be opened without the express permission of the Mongolian people. This would mean a referendum which would probably reject disturbing his remains. Newspaper articles had already appeared voicing objections.

Everyone was aware of the curse; anyone who dared disturb his tomb would bring disaster on the land.

Professor Badamhatan had studied under Professor Mikhail Gerasimov of Moscow State University, who had dared flout a similar curse regarding the tomb of Tamerlaine the Great in Samarkand.

The warning inscribed on the marble and jasper coffin said: 'He who opens this tomb will bring upon his country an invader more terrible than me.'

Professor Gerasimov opened the tomb in June 1941 and a day later, June 23rd, Hitler's armies stormed across the Soviet border.

The professor thought that it would be easy to verify that it was the tomb of Genghis Khan without opening it. It would certainly be near the summit of the mountain. On the other hand, no objections would be raised against opening up the tombs of the other khans such as Kublai Khan.

I wondered whether the Japanese would be satisfied with leaving the tomb of Genghis Khan undisturbed. One reason for funding the expedition must be to rival the great European archaeological discoveries at Troy or on the Nile.

One night I visited the correspondent of the *Yomiuri Shimbun*, Kazuaki Nagai, whose tent had been turned into an office, humming with fax machines and other electronic equipment that kept him and the expedition in daily contact with Tokyo via a satellite link-up.

The expedition was launched on the initiative of another correspondent of the Japanese daily newspaper as soon as the pro-democracy protests had come to a successful conclusion. The Japanese side was providing the cash and technology including a mysterious device shaped like a torpedo. It was carried aloft by a helicopter and could detect underground structures such as a tomb.

Nagai told me another reason for Japan's interest in the search. Many Japanese believe that Genghis Khan is not really Mongolian but was born in Japan.

The legend concerns Yoshitsune, the greatest and most beloved of all Japanese heroes. The brilliant and celebrated young general was forced to flee from his brother Yoritomo in 1186 although Yoshitsune's victories had made his sibling the most powerful shogun in Japan. Accompanied by his gigantic companion Benkei, he found refuge in a kingdom in northern Japan. Eventually an enemy army of 20,000 trapped him and so, cut off in a palace with only eight followers, he supposedly plunged a dagger into his stomach, committing ritual suicide.

He was only thirty-one when this happened and the story goes that instead of committing hara-kiri, he took a ship and fled incognito resurfacing in Mongolia and beginning a new career as Genghis Khan. The dates do correspond. If Genghis was born in 1155, as some scholars believe, then he was exactly the same age as Yoshitsune.

After I left the Japanese journalist and lay in my sleeping bag trying to get warm, I wondered what would happen if the expedition were to open the tomb and did indeed find a Japanese samurai inside.

The professor had drawn us a map but frankly, he said, our chances of reaching Mount Burhan-Kaldun were poor. He had tried it last year using four Japanese jeeps but they had turned back defeated.

Spring is the worst time to try when the ground above the permafrost melted into a marshy morass which every few yards would trap our vehicles.

Even if we traversed the taiga, we still had to ford the River Herlen which was now in full spate and afterwards we then had to climb the mountain. He suggested we went back to Ulan Bator and waited until the summer dried out the ground.

The local Party chief scratched his head sympathetically when we saw him in his office. Perhaps we could go by helicopter, he suggested. Or on horseback, or we could take a tractor ... He gave it some thought and promised to organise something.

He was keen to go himself since the next day was Buddha's birthday, May 28th, when a ceremony in honour of Genghis Khan was customarily held on the mountain. Genghis Khan was actually born on May 31st but Buddha's birthday is always an auspicious time to do anything.

Last year the locals had conducted the ceremony for the first time since 1937, when on Stalin's orders all religious practices were forbidden. It had been a major gathering and hundreds of people had journeyed to the mountain riding horses, jeeps, trucks and tractors. Enough to guarantee the safety of all concerned.

We left him to think about it and ran into our friends from Underhan. There were five of them, three journalists, two disreputable-looking old men who turned out to be lamas and Mr Damdinjev's grandson who had arrived in a jeep and a battered old van.

Fortunately we had not joined them on their trip to Genghis Khan's birthplace, as it was eventually aborted due to an absence of petrol.

They were impressively nonchalant about the dangers of the journey which had begun to loom in my mind as well-nigh insuperable and we agreed to leave early next morning in the three vehicles available.

During the night a fierce storm broke and by morning the hills around us sparkled with the glitter of freshly fallen snow. The wind kept me awake, shivering with cold. I was up early listening to the big black ravens which hung around the camp uttering strange cries which sounded like water tinkling through a pipe.

A big truck bringing heavy electronic equipment had got stuck in the mud not far from the camp and all the drivers had spent the night dragging it out of one morass after another.

Departure was scheduled for nine a.m. sharp but nobody was ready. I finally found the two lamas, transformed by their bright red gowns into venerable sages, sitting in a small *ger* which had been turned into a temple. A few old folk sat listening to the scriptures being chanted. Afterwards the young novices ate bowls of clotted cream.

By mid-morning a small congregation stood outside the temple and listened to a tall man make a short speech explaining how because of the political changes they could at last openly celebrate this important day.

On such a holy day as the birthday of the enlightened one, he said, a good deed had ten times the spiritual value as a deed performed on any ordinary day.

He invited the assembled congregation to buy paper charms and copies of Buddha's biography for three tugriks.

By the time all this was over, it was lunchtime and everyone went off to the canteen for a meal of rice pudding sprinkled with raisins. I thought it had something to do with the religious festival but it transpired that because of a national meat shortage all official canteens served vegetarian food twice a week.

Then at last our little caravan set off in bright sunshine down the big grassy valley dotted with herds of graceful white and dun-coloured horses.

About twenty miles down the track, we stopped off at a group of *gers* for tea. This was the last habitation before the entrance to the sanctuary. A family of four generations lived here herding horses, from an old couple in their dotage to a raggle-taggle bunch of runny-nosed infants. A young father sat proudly nursing his newborn son.

The old couple, who were eighty-five and eighty-eight, remembered how once, every year ceremonies were held on this date and two others, marking the spring, summer and autumn.

'Many people would come bearing gifts. Special officials sacrificed fifteen sheep and three cows,' the old man mumbled and rubbed his snuff bottle lovingly between his twisted fingers.

'After the revolution the government prohibited the ceremonies but we held them in secret anyway,' he said. He seemed to mean the period between 1923 and 1938.

He was a member of the group responsible for the preparations and would set off a few days beforehand moving all the gear in a cart.

On the eve of the ceremony worshippers spent the night in a little valley below the mountain where they changed into their best clothes and in the morning assembled at a big obo on the summit.

He said they would light big candles and recite poetry in front of it. Two rows of life-sized statues made from stone and attired like warriors stood before the obo. They held swords half drawn from their sheath, or arrows pulled across bows back to the shoulder just as if they were about to fight. He could not remember now who they were or what they represented.

Then, he said, lamas came and filled four huge cauldrons to the brim with gifts of fruit, cheese, bread and sweets. People came from all around and brought white or blue silk scarves.

Afterwards these officials read out a kind of decree. The lamas recited prayers and poured libations of vodka from gold and silver bowls.

After the ceremony there was a little *naidam* with a horse race. That was the only time he dared enter the sanctuary. About the tomb itself he refused to say anything at all.

We set off again and after a few miles came to a big wooden bridge spanning the fast-running waters of the Herlen. This was the entrance to the sanctuary.

The valley narrowed at this point and bushes and tamarind trees grew in thickets along the banks. The hills around were thickly wooded.

Along the way, a short stocky man in a smart grey *del* and matching trilby who was an MP and former Party secretary talked enthusiastically about hunting. Last winter he had shot four wolves in these parts.

'It is difficult to hunt them,' he said, 'wolves are clever with keen eyes and an actute sense of smell.'

They hunted in small packs of three or four and he knew a place where they drove deer over the edge of a cliff. The trick was to observe their habits, then lie in wait while other hunters drove them towards you. You had to be patient and it could take many days to kill one.

'Do you hunt wolves in England?' he asked. I explained that the last wolf in the British Isles was shot around the seventeenth century.

'That's a pity,' he said sympathetically. 'Their stomachs make uncommonly good cures if you have digestion problems.'

He considered the problem for a moment and then he brightened up. 'If you like we could export some wolves to England,' he proposed, 'then you would be all right.'

I explained how given the absence of wolves, people in England liked to hunt foxes but other people objected to this and said it was cruel.

'Oh we have these kind of people here too,' he said. 'They passed some laws to restrict hunting but locals should decide how many animals to kill because they know best how many it is safe to cull.'

He invited me to come back the next winter and together we would go hunting. We would catch wild boar in the woods and roast them. Around here they grew up to 200 kilos and only a year ago he had shot a piglet weighing 100 kilos.

From time to time, when the vehicles became bogged down, he pulled out his binoculars, carefully cleaned the lenses and scoured the hills for wildlife. All I managed to glimpse of the wildlife was a pair of yellow chaffinches which flitted from puddle to puddle ahead of our jeep.

The sanctuary was still the wilderness it was when Genghis Khan's mother, Hoelun, had sought refuge here 800 years earlier after the Tartars poisoned her husband, Yesugei.

A man called Targutai then seized power and Hoelun, fearing for her life and deserted by Yesugei's followers, fled with her sons into the mountains.

'Her hat pulled firmly on and tied tight on her head, she worked from top to bottom the banks of the Onon, plucking wild sorb apples and berries. A juniper branch in hand she prised up edible roots, wild onion and garlic,' the *Secret History* recounts.

Genghis was the oldest son of Hoelun but not the heir to the chieftainship. In the party were two sons by another marriage, Bektair and

Belgutai. One day Genghis and his brother Kasar kill Bektair but it is not entirely clear why, perhaps because Genghis wanted to remove a rival to the leadership or simply in a quarrel over food.

The author of the *Secret History* does not disguise the fact that this is murder. An enraged Hoelun shouts 'You destroyers!' and then complains:

'Apart from our shadows we have no friends,

'Apart from our tails we have no fat.

'At such a time, when the bitterness of the Tayyichi'ut [Taijit] kinsmen knows no limit, when we are asking ourselves who of us will settle this score and "how shall we live?" then you do this to each other.'

In the summer of 1182, Targutai the new chieftain attacked their camp. At night Genghis escaped and hid in a thicket. Nine days later, he emerged weak from hunger and was caught. He was kept a prisoner and forced to wear a *cangue*, a wooden collar.

Yet, miraculously, he escaped and found his mother and family in a place close to where we were driving, close to Mount Burhan-Kaldun. In fact this mountain fastness saved the life of Genghis on two occasions.

'Yes, yes this is where he hid when the chief of the Taijits was chasing him and trying to kill him,' the wolf-hunter explained.

The river was to our left now and visible from time to time through a thick mass of trees and bushes. A wild undergrowth flourished on what, if herds grazed here, would be green pastures.

'There is a cliff somewhere here shaped like a man. Genghis put his belt around it so his pursuers would think it was him. As the stone saved his life, people later always kept a belt around it in remembrance,' he said.

The trail gradually became well-nigh impassable. Water, coloured a reddish brown by the pine trees on hills above, gathered in deep pools on the frozen soil.

The trail was built for logging trucks driven by prisoners from a labour camp near Mongolmert. From a distance the camp looked like a Roman camp with four watchtowers at the corners of the square and walled compound.

The logging has almost stopped and most of the prisoners are freed. When it began early in the 1950s, local residents had appealed fruitlessly to Tsedenbal to stop this sacrilege. The petitioners were then arrested and found themselves in labour camps.

The young Party chief in our jeep, who had exchanged his *del* for a bright-red tracksuit, said when a local monastery was destroyed in

1937, the lamas had hidden in the woods.

'It was once quite a big monastery but there is nothing left of it now. The monks were warned before the secret police arrived and about thirty or forty of them escaped into the forest. They survived there until the early 1950s when they were caught,' he said.

'But there was one lama who escaped from the labour camp they had put him in and went back to the forest. He lived there as a hermit until his death,' he said.

So this wilderness which once sheltered the founder of an empire provided sanctuary for a community of renegade clerics.

It was late afternoon when we passed all three valleys the Darkhats had manned. The Herlen River valley narrowed but on either side smaller valleys led off. There was still no sign of Mount Burhan-Kaldun although I was told it was close by.

Our progress had slowed to a walking pace. One jeep, then the next and finally the van became mired in the black mud. We dug out the wheels and wedged branches and stones underneath them. When one jeep was freed, it pulled the other loose. Both together then pulled the van out of its quagmire. A few yards later the whole performance began again.

So it went on until early evening when the sun cast long shadows across the silent valley. We were still twenty kilometers away from the foot of the mountain.

The landscape was just as the *Secret History* describes it when Merkit tribesmen chased Genghis after abducting his bride, Borte:

> They went round Burhan-Kaldun three times after Temujin but were unable to find him. Here and there they hunted but its sinking mud and thick woods made a dense forest and they were like glutted bears unable to sneak in. Although they followed behind him, they could not find him.

When the Merkits have abandoned the chase, Temujin descended the mountain and beat his breast:

> On the dotted tracks,
> I followed the deer trails.
> I made a yurt of willow.
> I climbed up Burhan,
>
> On Burhan-Kaldun,
> My life like a louse's.
> I was hunted.

My life, the only one, was spared.
With only one horse
I followed the elk trails.
I made a yurt of twigs.
I climbed up on Kaldun,
On Kaldun-Burhan,
My life was like a swallow's,
I was protected.

But Burhan-Kaldun has saved me.
Each morning henceforth, therefore,
Will I honour him with the offerings
Each day address prayers to him:
And after me, my children and grandchildren
Shall remember to do likewise.

Facing the sun, he draped his sash round his neck and hung his hat (by its cord) from his arm. He beat his chest with his hand and, kneeling nine times to the sun, gave offerings and prayers [quoted from two different translations].

Reluctantly, we abandoned the van. The two old lamas, who were both called Jambyn, clambered into our jeep.

The fitter of the two sat behind me bellowing alternative prayers and curses depending on whether the driver chose to charge across a ditch or cautiously edge his way through the murky waters.

This Jambyn had spent most of his life as a miner working the wolfram mine we had passed and had only donned the lamaist robes a year ago. He had been arrested as a young novice.

'Go! Go! Go!' he shouted when the driver hesitated at the edge of a new pool. 'Genghis Khan is waiting for us!' Then at a successful crossing he guffawed with huge delight. Or, when with a grinding of gears, the overladen jeep lapsed slowly into the mire, he intoned a solemn prayer.

At last we abandoned the vehicles and set out on foot to a small pass from which the holy mountain could be seen. Damdinjev, still dressed in suit and tie and still holding the hand of his silent grandson, marched ahead. The older Jambyn stayed behind, his legs too weak to carry him so far.

As we slithered up the slope, a cuckoo called unseen, hidden in the woods where the Herlen swung eastwards.

'Cuck-koo, Cuck-koo,' the bird cried out. From the cliffs came a faint mocking echo deriding this party of dreamers and foolish old men, bumbling in the footsteps of a giant and seeking the memory of a bygone age.

In a way the wilderness had remained a memorial, protecting the lamas over seven centuries after Temujin, his life as worthless as a louse, sought its protection.

The sanctuary was a monument quite distinct from the vainglory of other emperors. Other kings and emperors commissioned from their slaves stone fortresses and marble palaces. The first emperor of China let millions die attempting to reshape nature by erecting a Great Wall. Mao and Stalin left behind them giant statues by the hundred, monuments to their mad self-glorification.

Here the Mongols had destroyed nothing and built nothing. Nor had Genghis Khan or his children constructed vast temples or cathedrals to testify a belief that God had set them aside for a special purpose.

The khans had after all thought they were fulfilling a manifest destiny, subjects of a divine providence but they conceived this to be not a God but nature itself. To honour nature was to leave it untouched.

Genghis Khan and his descendants were buried in tombs which had left no visible trace. Somewhere ahead of me the warrior shepherd slept beneath a forest glade which the wolf glided across at dusk and where swallows flitted in the morning shadows. The Mongols had not sought to conquer nature but to remain a part of it.

As we topped the ridge, we saw another valley where the Herlen reflected the dying rays of the sun sinking behind Mount Burhan-Kaldun. The summit was still hidden from view and as I gazed down into the hidden valley no foreigner had glimpsed before, it seemed to me that the sanctuary had another meaning, as a symbol of a precious hope.

Perhaps its real purpose was to enshrine the longing that somewhere was always a place where a free man could retreat. Where he could lose himself from all pursuit and then refreshed, venture out again and achieve the unbelievable. So that from this forgotten wilderness where all seemed lost, a world of infinite possibilities and opportunities lay within reach.

It was now so late that it was impossible to reach the sacred mountain. Instead it was agreed to hold the ceremony on a hill overlooking the Burhan-Kaldun. We scrambled through the bushes with Jambyn following behind muttering away.

At the top, Perenleg, representing *Truth* and Ozhgoosh from *Montsame* pulled out their notebooks to record the facts while the others lit a small fire.

When all was ready we knelt in a circle around Jambyn, who sat facing the mountain. He fumbled with his dog-eared prayer books and adjusted his spectacles.

He half read, half mumbled a prayer in Tibetan. A stubby finger pointed its way along the ancient Tibetan text, 'Cleaning the World of Bad Spirits', composed a century or more ago by one of the Dalai Lamas.

The recital lasted a considerable time although Jambyn confessed quite unabashed that he had no idea what it meant, or indeed what any of the words signified. He had memorised it as a novice monk but was forced out of the monastery before he learned Tibetan.

The prayer is intended to be read when honouring the spirit of a mountain. A full prayer service should last three hours as it did on Mount Three Beauties in Hubsogol.

'We pray for the sky and the earth to be healthy and harmonious. The earth is our mother and the sky our father,' Jambyn explained later.

'There are ten thousand gods and goddesses but if the father and mother are praised then all the gods will be satisfied,' Jambyn said.

Then he removed a small brass orb from its leather case, took an inlaid flask and with a peacock feather shook a few drops of water on the orb to clean it.

The orb did not represent the world as I first thought but was a round mirror to invoke the spirits of all ten directions.

Then the prayers over, we each took handfuls of food from the tray and flung them over our shoulders in the direction of the mountain.

'We are asking the spirits to be merciful and keep us from evil,' he said. 'We give the spirits presents just like you invite your boss home for dumplings and serve him vodka but, of course, there is no backdoor to heaven,' he added hastily.

'When people no longer show respect to the spirit of the sky, it brings disaster, disease and violence,' he went on.

It began to dawn on me that the service was not really Buddhist or even in honour of Genghis Khan.

It was in honour of the mountain. Genghis Khan had become transformed into the spirit of the mountain. We were not worshipping the spirit of a warrior chieftain but nature.

We opened the bottles of distilled koumiss, and filled a bowl to the brim. Jambyn held it before him and uttered a short speech.

He asked the spirit of Genghis Khan to take care of six worlds – heaven, hell, animals, spirits, human beings and deities.

Finally, before drinking deeply, he made a short plea to Buddha asking that on his birthday he show compassion to all creatures and cleanse the soul of Genghis Khan from the many sins he committed during his life on earth.

The bowl was refilled and passed around, each one of us making a short speech and tossing a few drops of libation. They praised me for respecting Mongol customs by drinking it all in one go. I thanked them for the honour of being present at such a place on such a day.

As the light faded leaving us bathed in shadows from the leaping flames, we consumed several more bottles. Then in darkness the party descended the hill to the jeeps.

Jambyn had so honoured the spirit of the great khan that he could barely walk. Damdinjev held one arm and I the other as we slithered and stumbled through the mud.

'My eyes are dim, I cannot see, I have not brought my specs with me,' I chanted, mantra-like, while Jambyn babbled incoherently beside me.

A hunter's moon had risen behind a raft of cloud by the time we reached the others. We camped by the gently murmuring river and lying before a bright fire drank several more bottles before sliding into gentle oblivion.

Before dawn when the fire had died to a cluster of red embers I woke briefly, my limbs stiff with cold, and heard the distant cry of a wolf.

Nine

Hunting Dinosaurs in the Gobi

'Before us lay Mongolia, a land of painted deserts dancing in mirage; of limitless grassy plains and nameless snow-capped peaks; of untracked forests and roaring streams! Mongolia, land of mystery, of paradox and promise! The hills swept away in the far-flung, graceful lines of panorama so endless that we seemed to have reached the very summit of the earth.

Roy Chapman Andrews

In 1918 the flamboyant American explorer Roy Chapman Andrews drove a Dodge sedan from Kalgan to Urga across the unmapped Gobi desert and became convinced he had found the original Garden of Eden where life began.

In the face of openly expressed scepticism from the scientific world, Andrews returned three times leading the first scientific expeditions to the Gobi in 1922, 1923 and 1925.

Andrews' derring-do tales of camel caravans, battles with bandits, big-game hunting, dangerous swamps and 100 mph sandstorms made him a national hero.

He is undoubtedly the model for Indiana Jones. He looks out of the black and white photographs from the expeditions to Mongolia square-jawed beneath a bush hat, with a Mannlicher rifle and a belt full of cartridges around his waist.

He began his career sweeping the floor of a taxidermist's and ended it as president of the American Natural History Museum in New York. In between, the bushwhacking adventurer hunted everything from whales to tiny shrews, trekked the steaming jungles of Borneo, explored the dense forests of Burma and Yunnan, ventured along the fogbound shores of the Bering Strait, across the wilderness of the Korean hills and reached the summits of Himalayan mountains.

The press dubbed his adventures in Mongolia the "missing link" expeditions. Before he left, Andrews received hundreds of letters from people offering their services. A lady in St Louis telegraphed: 'Regarding search for "missing link", ouija board offers assistance.'

Another lady proposed to go just as a 'woman friend' promising that, 'I could create the "home atmosphere" for you in those dreary wastes.'

Once in Mongolia, he received letters addressed with romantic brevity: 'To R. C. Andrews Esq., anywhere in Mongolia.'

His adventures inspired the relatives of Franklin Roosevelt – Kermit and Theodor – to organise their own hunting expedition to Central Asia which they described in *East of the Sun and West of the Moon*. Afterwards their adventures coloured President Roosevelt's ideas about the East when he entertained Chiang Kai-shek and his advisers on China.

Not only did Andrews find traces of early man but most astonishing of all, he discovered the first genuine dinosaur eggs. Until then, no one was sure if dinosaurs really had laid eggs although as reptiles it was considered likely. At first, even the expedition members found it hard to believe their eyes.

'We realised we were looking at the first dinosaur eggs ever seen by a human being . . . These eggs could not be those of a bird. No birds are known from the Lower Cretaceous, the geological horizon in which the eggs were found, and all the Jurassic and Upper Cretaceous birds were much too small to have laid eggs this size. The elongated shape of the eggs was distinctly reptilian,' he wrote in *On the Trail of Ancient Man*, his account of the expeditions.

'There were more dinosaur eggs – nests of them, single, whole and broken eggs, big ones and little ones, eggs with smooth paper-thin shells, eggs with thick striated shells . . .'

The eggs were found at an obscure site in the Gobi called Ulan Usu which Andrews christened 'Flaming Red Cliffs'.

The scientific community had scoffed at the expedition's chances of finding even a single dinosaur bone but Mongolia turned out to be a palaeontological paradise. The then president of the Natural History Museum, Professor Henry Fairfield Osborn, proposed a theory that Asia was the 'mother of life in Europe and Americas'.

After Stalin won sole power in 1928 American scientists were no longer welcome but in 1990 it was again possible to retrace Andrews' steps. There were still dinosaur eggs left as my friend in the restaurant in Ulan Bator had said.

What could be better than to brush away the dust from eggs of an extinct species still waiting to hatch after 70 million years had turned them into stone? I decided to go egg hunting in the Gobi.

We flew 600 kilometres south from Ulan Bator watching the landscape down below change as the green pastures turned by degrees to a sullen khaki. The land seemed to slowly fall away and rivers, from which the water had long since disappeared, drained into dusty plains. Once I caught a glimpse of the cone of an extinct volcano and a distant lake, a glittering cobalt blue, held out a promise of the marvellous.

When the plane landed at the capital of the South Gobi aimak, Dalan Dzadgad, in the early evening, the desert was glowing pink. It stretched out in every direction to a distant horizon where it curled up like a piece of wrinkled cardboard.

The shifting light came down through the low clouds in strong shafts distorting all sense of my perspective, accustomed to the gentility of the English countryside. The eye strained to judge if those were high mountains at the desert's limits or a low ridge of rocks.

In this enduring setting the small town looked temporary, as if put together with canvas and glue for a Spaghetti Western. Tumbleweed drifted obligingly through the streets, blown by a dry and gentle breeze and doors banged suddenly and noisily.

If it was built for show; it was not intended to conjure up the Wild West but Bloomsbury. The town had a theatre with Greek Ionic columns modelled on the entrance to the British Museum. In the centre was a garden square surrounded by cast iron railings painted black. Several streets, and there were only three or four, had been gentrified with flower beds and grass verges.

The schoolchildren were dressed in costumes copied from some nineteenth-century German high school which had impressed Lenin or some other Russian leader on his travels abroad.

In the hotel restaurant a class of stubby young girls were holding a dance wearing white pinafores over their brown dresses and stockings to celebrate their graduation. Their healthy brown and red faces were pinched with concentration as they carefully manoeuvred each other to Scottish tunes blaring from a giant loudspeaker. Who on earth had introduced 'Marie's Wedding' to the Gobi? Or why?

There was a car park too, quite empty, and a blue sign promised free parking as if the Gobi was Manhattan.

The stern features of Lenin looked out over all this. Next to him was a row of propaganda hoardings showing a cornucopia of consumer goods – washing machines, vacuum cleaners, record players and shopping baskets overflowing with fresh vegetables. Authenticating this consumer abundance, statistics from the last five-year plan marched towards a certain future.

'Let sport be for the whole nation!' proclaimed my favourite and the peeling paint showed a happy couple skiing in the snow. A holiday in St Moritz for every camel breeder.

The South Gobi aimak is as large as England, but a third of its population, about 15,000, lived in this town, mostly in crude huts and *gers*. There was a hotel too, a ramshackle concrete block, and although it was empty, a hard-faced manageress insisted I pay in dollars.

'It's forty for a luxury room,' she snapped. I took a standard room and bargained her down to twenty dollars for two nights. In the room, the light fittings were all broken and the water choked, a reddish trickle, out of one tap. Later she invited me into her office with a furtive gesture and offered to sell a pair of goat horns. One of the horns was deformed into a twisted curl.

'A genetic defect,' she said with a smile.

When Andrews came seventy years earlier, there were no settlements at all in the Gobi and the expedition rarely encountered humankind apart from a few families moving around with their flocks. Even so the revolutionary unrest made life for these isolated people dangerous and uncertain.

In his book Andrews described what it was like:

That day we saw grim evidence once more that for the preceding three years a human life in Mongolia had been worth much less than that of a sheep. At one point Shackleford and I ran over to two yurts to inquire about the road. Three men rode like mad to the hills and we found that only four women were left.

Two were very old, one was about fifty and the fourth was a beautiful girl of eighteen or twenty. They had spread a clean white felt before the yurt and were lined up, trembling and kowtowing.

As we stopped the car a few feet away, the girl ran to get another felt and one of the women rushed inside to bring milk and tea. In a few moments our Mongol explained that we were Americans and would not hurt them. They had never heard of America nor of any white men except Russians. When I gave them a few trinkets, they were pitifully pleased. They clung to one another, crying, and explained that they had expected to be killed instantly.

A short time later we stopped at another yurt, and one of the women had an attack of violent nausea from sheer fright.

A hundred yards or so from the front door of the hotel the town's metalled and potholed road stopped and the desert began.

After several days' discussion and negotiations over a jeep - at first the police chief offered us his, and then the head of the local orchestra found another vehicle – we set off down the gravel track heading north with a tent and a box full of food. The intention was to head for Flaming Red Cliffs but the driver and everyone else was so taciturn, so non-committal that in the end I was not quite sure what had been decided.

For a while I did not care either. It was early June and the annual miracle of spring was just taking place. A few brief showers of rain during the last two evenings were turning the whole plain green. The desert was perfectly level and covered with little stones and the grass shoots poking out among them made the whole place look, for a day or two, like one big abandoned tennis court.

During a whole week of travelling, I never tired of just looking. The landscape changed with every mile, the pure bright light caught, twisted and refracted in an almost theatrical display turning the rocks and lakes a thousand hues. The unchanging vista of rock and stone, of sun and dust that I had imagined was nowhere to be seen. It was bursting with life; birds of all sizes, herds of wild antelope or colonies of rodents scattered in surprise wherever we went.

It was so unexpected. My childhood reading had made the Gobi synonymous with death and desperation. One book I remembered was the story of a Russian prisoner who escaped from a Siberian labour camp and for two years walked south to freedom in India. The Gobi was the hardest part, a death trap of unrelenting size where man and nature alike were cruel.

It is historically the great interlude between East and West across which the weary caravans plodded for months. A great region between the crowded valleys of China and the vineyards and orchards of Hither Asia, between the forests and tundra of Siberia and the hill wall of the Himalayas.

'This desert is reported to be so long that it would take a year to go from end to end; and at the narrowest point it takes a month to cross it. It consists entirely of mountains and sand and valleys. There is nothing at all to eat,' wrote Marco Polo.

In fact the name Gobi is used very loosely. Marco Polo seems to be talking about the Taklamakhan desert in China which he skirted on its southern side. It supposedly means in Uighur, 'those who enter will never leave', and it is a real desert of shifting sand dunes although it does have some rivers. On the northern side it is bounded by the

Tianshan or Mountains of Heaven and beyond is another depression, the Dzungarian basin and the homeland of the western Mongols. North of that are the Altai mountains and only after crossing those, about the distance from London to Casablanca, would one reach Dalan Dzagbhad.

Opinions differ about the origin of the name Gobi. Some claim it derives from a Mongolian word, others that it comes from a general Chinese term for stony ground – *gebi*. Thus Marco Polo or other travellers from the West enquiring about the way ahead would hear they had to cross a region of *gebi* and conclude this was a proper place name.

The true Gobi divides the northern Mongols from the southern Mongols in what is now China. It begins at Kalgan just beyond the Great Wall.

'Below us lay that stupendous relief map of ravines and gorges; in front was a limitless stretch of undulating plan. I knew then that I really stood upon the edge of the greatest plateau in all the world and that it could be only Mongolia,' Andrews wrote.

The plateau forms a shallow bowl which curves gently up to the alpine mountains of the Hubsogol region on one side and the borders of China on the other.

It is still a vast region and although we drove for a week in a loop of around 800 kilometers we saw only a small part of the South Gobi aimak which in turn is only one of the Gobi provinces.

That day we were only a few miles outside the provincial centre when we came across a small temple. It consisted of a few *gers* and a square stupa of blinding white. A few people were attending a service and the lamas, when I had a chance to talk to them, told the usual story of the destruction of their monastery and the plans to build a new one.

In another *ger* nearby, locals sat in silence drinking tea. The people of the Gobi, as I had already found, were reticent at first, and generally in Mongolia it is considered impolite to show surprise or curiosity when meeting a stranger.

Conversation as we sat down with them followed the customary pattern with ritual greetings: '*Sain bai noo?*' Are you well?

'*Sain* – fine,' is the correct reply to give, regardless of the circumstances. Next comes: '*Ain Samda Sain Yao Noo?*' Is your road well? '*Sain.*'

Shepherds politely continue with, 'Are you wintering well?' or, 'Are you spending this spring in peace?'

The correct form if the hostess is milking a cow is to add in an unctuous tone, 'May your bucket be brimful of milk.'

Or if she is beating wool to say, 'May the wool be as soft as silk.'

After this exchange, which always takes place with much gravity, the guest is offered tea and a platter of *borzog* – crusts of wheat fried in oil – and pieces of cheese, sugar and biscuits.

The tea still comes from China in bricks and it is the cheapest stuff imaginable with bits of leaves and stems compounded together. A hammer is used to knock off a chunk which is boiled up with water and milk.

The result would be well-nigh tasteless were it not for the salt which is usually added in the Tibetan fashion. The tea – *chay* – must always be brewed in the presence of the guest and served with both hands outstretched.

The next step in the formalities is to exchange snuff boxes with a host and each party takes a sniff of the other's mixture. Cigarettes re-placed snuff with the coming of the Soviets but snuff is now in fashion again.

Further questions are invariably answered with one of two replies that I quickly memorised.

'*Medech gui*', meaning 'I don't know', and said in a sorrowful, apolo-getic way, or '*Baich Guo*', meaning 'don't have' and 'there is none'.

This probably had nothing to do with the notoriously tight-fisted people of the Gobi but with the perennial shortages under Com-munism. In China, the same answers, '*Bu zhidao*' and '*Mei you*' are as much a part of social intercourse as they were in the Soviet Union.

After the formalities, I found that conversation tends to limp a bit until it turns to the subject of the miraculous and fantastic, in which case everyone becomes animated. Stories of wonders witnessed are traded with great enthusiasm. Inevitably no one present has actually seen these things themselves but it was a cousin or a friend, or the cousin of a friend who had. The reliability of the source is, however, never held up for scrutiny because these tall tales serve the same social role as the weather does in Britain. Everyone's observations are equally valid and interesting and the more unexpected the events in question, the better.

Something about the shape of a *ger* makes it peculiarly conducive to swapping tales of the supernatural. The round space without any dark corners creates a comfortable womb-like feeling and when the floor is made of wood and laid with carpets, it is a cosy intimate place.

The wall consists of ten to fifteen wooden poles bound together in such a way that it is possible to fold and unfold the frame like an accordion. Pressed wool, that is, felt, is wrapped around the frame and then covered with canvas. At the top is the *tonoo* hole which lets light in and smoke out. The *tonoo* is propped up by two wooden posts which it is considered unlucky to lean against.

The *ger* has its own mythology and the posts symbolise the link with heaven and through them passes the past-present-future axis of the time. Mongols traditionally hang a purse of blue silk from the *tonoo* which holds a handful of grain as a totem of good fortune, a custom which had been forbidden under the Communists.

Legend has it that the first Mongol was born after a fair-haired man came through the *tonoo* and impregnated Alangua, the ancestral mother of the Mongols.

The hearth, now a stove, also has special significance connected with ancient fire worship and is always to be treated with respect.

Nowadays *gers* can be erected in a couple of hours and carried by two camels but when William Rubruk travelled through Mongolia they were built on wheeled platforms, thirty feet across requiring twenty-two oxen to pull them.

The best story that afternoon was of the local Party secretary, a Mr Enkbator, who in 1961 went out with his driver to a place where large poisonous snakes gathered every few years. He found hundreds of them, as thick as your arm and several metres long, which he destroyed, dousing them with petrol and throwing a match on to the writhing mass.

Shortly afterwards he died mysteriously of a heart attack and so did his driver. Later, local people asked two lamas to visit the spot to read prayers and appease the spirits of the snakes. The reptiles then returned and multiplied.

My contribution was the Loch Ness sea monster saga which was received with sympathetic attention and much nodding of knowing heads.

Andrews, arriving in Mongolia for the first time, had a rather similar time of it. He wrote that at first it was like entering an armed camp – full of secret police, inspections and interrogations. Finally he obtained an audience with the prime minister and various cabinet members in order to negotiate permission for the expedition.

The prime minister, suspicious to begin with, then asked him to capture on behalf of the Mongolian government a highly dangerous creature with the wonderful name of 'allegorhai-horhai'.

It is shaped like a sausage about two feet long, has no head or legs and is so poisonous that merely to touch it means instant death. It lives in the most desolate parts of the Mongolian desert. The Prime Minister said he had never seen it but he knew a man who had. A cabinet minister stated that 'the cousin of his late wife's sister' had also seen it. I promised to produce the allergorhai-horhai if we chanced to cross its path and explained how it could be seized by means of long steel collecting forceps: moreover I would even wear dark glasses so that the disastrous effects of even looking at so poisonous a creature would be neutralised. The meeting adjourned with the best of feeling: for we had a common interest in capturing the allergorhai-horhai.

Fashions change and seventy years on attention had switched from these lethal sausages to the pursuit of the Mongolian yeti.

The Russians had sent several expeditions to capture one. The Mongolian brand of this widespread genus roams the Altai mountains, both the forested north and rocky slopes of the south. Descriptions vary but in general, the Mongolian yeti can be distinguished from his Tibetan cousin by the alarming fact that the female has only one breast which is so large that she slings it over one shoulder when moving about.

'It cannot speak and smells most unpleasantly,' a retired school-teacher who had just published a book on them told me when I met him in Ulan Bator. He had spent twenty years on the trail of the yeti and produced some blurred and shaky photographs.

It is hard to get better ones, he explained, because all his sightings were in the early morning. The Mongolian yeti is a nocturnal animal and difficult to find in daylight hours. It slept curled up and once he had found the imprint of its body in the snow.

He reckoned it is a relative of Neanderthal man, sands about seven feet high and is covered in reddish hair like a camel. He collected some of the hairs which are now in a museum in Ulan Bator.

Once he found its footprints in the snow after giving chase. He showed me several of his sketches which illustrated how the creature sleeps or walks and among them was a picture of its foot, seen from the sole.

'I measured the foot exactly. The yeti takes shoe size number fifty-four,' he said with unshakeable certainty.

We left our hosts and to my surprise reached the Flaming Red Cliffs by the end of the day. The trail took us across the sprouting tennis courts past a drying salt lake and then disappeared up the red sand-stone cliffs to another plateau littered with grey-blue pebbles. In the distance a long jagged ridge of purple mountains shimmered in the heat.

We camped in a gulley where camels grazed. Above us kites and golden eagles rose lazily on invisible air currents.

It took Andrews weeks of arduous travel from Peking across the Gobi, fighting off armed bandits, desert storms and the heat. On one occasion wild dogs assumed they were corpses and attacked them in their sleeping bags.

He needed seventy-five camels to carry their equipment, in addition to Dodge automobiles from Detroit and trucks from Fulton, Long Island, and petrol from Standard Oil.

A fifteen-minute interview with the magnate, J. P. Morgan, and innumerable fund-raising speeches provided the funds totalling nearly a quarter of a million dollars.

Andrews must have camped in the same gulley because we found traces – a few scraps of paper and some rusting cans half buried in the soil – which bore witness to his sojourn here. Nothing seemed to have changed or been disturbed, which was hardly surprising given that from the point of view of the locals, it holds no special attractions.

It is though a visually stunning site and he does it justice in his book:

From our tents, we looked down into a vast pink basin, studded with giant buttes like strange beasts, carved from sandstone. There appeared to be medieval castles with spires and turrets, brick-red in the evening light. Caverns ran deep into the rock and a labyrinth of ravines and gorges studded with fossil bones makes a paradise for the palaeontologist.

In the 40 million years since the dinosaurs had vanished, the area had hardly been disturbed either by nature or man. Wind and weather had gradually and steadily stripped away the loose sand from the cliff face, adding to the loess soils of Shanxi, or carrying the finer particles all the way to the streets of Peking. I remembered how I had seen this same dust accumulating on the floor of my flat.

The whole Gobi plateau was once a stretch of forest and swamp which left the big coal deposits of Inner Mongolia. In the age of the dinosaurs, the cliffs might have formed the edge of a large swampy basin but even then the soil was probably dry enough for eggs to incubate.

On arrival Andrews' expedition had sat down for a feast of dried apple pie; we boiled a soup of potato, onions and dried meat over a fire. While it was cooking, I could not help clambering among the cliffs and starting the egg search. Almost immediately I was excited to find flattish and oval pieces of sandstone just the shape of the eggs seen in expedition photographs.

There were other lumps of the same hard material embedded in the soft crumbly soil and I began to dig them out. The expedition had found the first eggs grouped in clusters along with dinosaur bones somewhere in these very cliffs.

Others were found at their base so I looked too among the piles of rubble-like pieces of mud, washed by the rain and baked by the sun into curious shapes.

When the light faded into a purple twilight, I proudly returned to the fire with pockets full of likely specimens. My companions looked with undisguised scepticism at my collection which when spread out on the ground looked like so many brown potatoes.

None of them had the brittle coating of eggshell which would silence all doubts. The other two thought it was foolish even to try and the next day refused to join in as well.

As we sat eating, the last rays of the sinking sun caught the cliffs, turning their dull red into a flaming crimson.

It was only in the second year of the expedition that Andrews' expedition found the eggs but almost as soon as they crossed the frontier into Mongolia, the expedition's success was guaranteed by the discovery of bone fragments of the first dinosaurs ever found north of the Himalayas.

In fact, fossil bones had long been known in China as 'dragon bones', which were (and still are) powdered and then dissolved with acid in the belief that this compound is efficacious for everything from rheumatism to gunshot wounds.

The first eggs ever found were eight inches long and seven inches in circumference and flatter than modern reptile eggs. The pebbled surface of the eggs, Andrews wrote, was as perfect as if they had been laid the day before. The shells were about one sixteenth of an inch thick and fine sand had filtered through breaks. The interior had turned to sandstone. There were five of them, clustered together, and two were broken in half. Inside, the explorers could 'plainly detect the delicate bone of the embryonic dinosaurs'.

This was so remarkable, and is still so unique, that Andrews could with justifiable enthusiasm exclaim that 'never before in the history of science has it been possible to study palaeoembryology!'

In the next five weeks they discovered a complete developmental series of a dinosaur called *Protoceratops*. They found baby dinosaurs hatched only a few weeks before their death and adults nine feet long.

While they were carefully digging out the first cluster of eggs they discovered that the skeleton of a small dinosaur had been preserved in the soil underneath.

'It was a toothless species and we believe it may have been overtaken by a sandstorm in the very act of robbing the dinosaur nest. Professor Osborn has named it *Oviraptor* – meaning "the egg seizer" – *Philoceratops* – signifying "fondness for ceratopsian eggs",' Andrews wrote.

These two types of dinosaur – the *Protoceratops* and the *Oviraptor Philoceratops* – were rather enigmatic. They had no teeth but a small head with a beak like a parrot. Professor Osborn thought the beaks were suited to eating eggs, molluscs or oysters. Since then nothing has been learned to cast doubt on his theory although the beaks may also have been used for breaking off shoots or branches.

Eventually the expedition found eggs belonging to turtles, crocodiles, lizards and birds. Reptiles normally lay eggs in shallow depressions scooped out of the sand and bird eggs can be distinguished because they are usually round at one end to prevent them from rolling out of the nest.

Another type were like a 'loaf of French bread', around seven inches long and two and a half inches in diameter and laid two at a time by a fifteen-feet-long armoured dinosaur, an Ankylosaur.

By the end of the first trip they had discovered so many bones, they were reduced to tearing their clothes to make extra strips of cloth which were then soaked in flour paste and wrapped around the bones to preserve them. The specimens were packed in boxes and wrapped in wool pulled off the backs of the camels.

My own search was somewhat less successful. Next day I continued the search for dinosaur eggs and explored all sides of the canyon. In one exposed wall of a cliff face, the elements had exposed the outline of a mass of delicate bones (or so I thought). There were curiously shaped lumps of sandstone or rock but in such abundance that I began to suspect that the finds of the day before were, as my companions scoffed, nothing but worthless rocks made by chance.

It was disappointing. When Andrews' expedition returned the second year to what they boasted was 'the most important place in the world for palaeontology', they discovered dinosaurs and their eggs by the bucketful. One local Mongolian woman appeared daily with more eggs which she was happy to exchange for tin cans.

By then Andrews had all but abandoned the search for the 'missing link' but the expedition did discover traces of Stone Age 'dune dwellers' who 20,000 years ago had turned the eggshells into necklaces.

Flaming Red Cliffs had clearly been an ideal site for laying eggs for many millennia. The expedition members concluded that although part of the area was covered with lakes, the rest was not a swamp but semi-arid so that the hen dinosaurs covered their nests with sandy soil to keep them warm until they hatched.

In the end it was not the eggs which created the greatest excitement in New York but a tiny and obscure skull about an inch across. It belonged to one of the first mammals, a small shrew-like creature and it proved that mammals co-existed with the dinosaurs as far back as the middle Cretaceous period. Reptiles died out quite suddenly at the end of the Cretaceous period but by this time the small rat-like mammals were already flourishing.

Until then only one other mammalian skull from the age of reptiles had been discovered and this was in South Africa.

The conclusion was that this period must hold the explanation for the rise of the mammals and rapid decline of the dinosaurs. The research in the Gobi was later continued with Soviet and Polish expeditions which discovered other new dinosaur species and more specimens of early mammals.

Their finds were made in other parts of the Gobi and in hope of better luck there, I decided to abandon the Flaming Red Cliffs and try and find some of these other sites. The driver, who was called Basan, meaning Friday, had enjoyed sleeping out and had opened up a bit. He said he knew of a good place to go (if I really insisted on carrying on with this quest). The journey would take four or five days and take us round in a big circle and on the way I would have the chance to meet some of the people who lived in the desert. I would learn something of how they lived, which, I had the feeling, he considered to be a rather more sensible undertaking.

The next day we arrived at a small settlement called Bulgan, the headquarters of a commune, or as the Mongolians refer to them, a *negdel*. In a small and flyblown office Mr Nyandorjin sat at a desk piled high with documents and was scratching away with his pen at a report.

He was a tired-looking man of about sixty with greying hair and a seedy suit. He was the senior scientist in charge of the Institute for the Development of Animal Husbandry in the Desert.

I had not heard of it before but it had been set up in 1959 during the second round of collectivisation to promote the mechanisation and 'electrification' of stockbreeding in the desert.

Mr Nyandorjin had worked for fifteen years running breeding projects aimed at improving local strains of camels, goats and sheep. He had bred the young lambs which are killed at birth for their skins which are used to make costly Astrakhan hats.

'It was all a waste of time, all for nothing,' he admitted sadly. Everything had been a mistake, now they were trying to rediscover how it was done before the revolution when the old nomads had known how to make optimum use of pasture and water.

'Take our camels, they are dying out,' he said, wiping away the ash which had fallen from his cigarette.

Since the 1930s the numbers had fallen by 250,000 to 550,000 in Mongolia and their decline in the Soviet Union and China was even greater. Large numbers were simply slaughtered in 1932 when the first drive towards collectivisation was carried out on the instructions of Soviet advisers. There are now only 150,000 camels left in Inner Mongolia, Kazakhstan and the other Central Asian republics of the USSR.

Of the 700,000 Asian camels left in the world the majority are in the Gobi aimaks of Mongolia. This aimak had 900,000 animals of which 127,000 were camels and the rest cashmere goats, sheep and horses.

The Asian camel is more properly known as the Bactrian and has two humps. It is smaller than the dromedary, the Arabian camel, but is far more valuable because it alone produces a fine warm wool when it moults in the summer. It is wonderfully suited to the deserts of Central Asia and can graze on the sparse pasture and live for three months on nothing but water and in emergencies survive up to a fortnight without drinking. What is more it runs almost as fast as a horse.

In the past a local family would own over a thousand camels, a camel providing everything – transport, milk, cheese, meat, clothing and a source of income. Their milk tastes almost as good as cows' milk and the meat is tender too.

Pullovers are woven from the underbelly wool which is short and must be cut in mid-April before the desert bushes scratch it away.

The hairs on the back are left until mid-June when it is warm enough to moult, and are used for blankets. The long hairs from the neck can be sheared in March and turned into scarves.

The trouble was nobody wanted to breed them any more. 'You see, it takes a lot of time and trouble and the camel only gives birth every two or even three years,' the scientist said.

Since collectivisation the camel had only been valued for its meat as there was little demand in the Soviet Union for high-quality camelhair garments. The Soviet Union purchased Mongolian beef and mutton but since Russians have no taste for camel meat, it was used to supply the growing urban populations inside Mongolia.

'Few families wanted to breed camels after collectivisation because there was no incentive,' he explained. 'The wages of the camel breeders were not affected if there were fewer camels so they sold off the female camels for meat.'

Collectivisation also led to a concentration of people, as much as seventy per cent of the population, in cities or collective headquarters doing administrative jobs. Demand for meat to feed the even larger number of citydwellers increased as the demand for wool fell. Existing herds were just depleted.

'With so few people now looking after the animals, stockbreeders were even less inclined to waste their time on camels,' he said.

Collectivisation also brought extensive administrative controls which hindered the free movement of the herdsmen who used to move from place to place in search of pastures.

After the revolution the number of aimaks, the largest administrative area below that of the central government, was increased from four to eighteen. Herdsmen were not allowed to leave their native aimak without obtaining permission beforehand. The stockbreeders could no longer range freely from the desert south to the richer grasslands in the north as they used to. When there was a drought the animals often simply stayed put and died.

The restrictions on movement led to interbreeding among humans, he said. For instance if a man married a woman from another district in an aimak, known as a *somon* or arrow, it was not possible to transfer the animals belonging to the bride's family to the *somon* of her husband. People therefore tended to marry partners from among the relatives in the same *somon*, so as the population grew, idiocy increased.

'It is less common in a place like Hubsogol but it was very common here. Even before, people rarely married outside the region because only locals know how to live under these conditions,' Nyandorjin said.

The animals owned by the state were soon going to be auctioned off as part of the privatisation programme. Parliament was also preparing a law on camels designed to protect them so that stocks could be rebuilt. But, he said, it was going to take a long time to rebuild what had been lost.

'Yet now we are all asking ourselves how will we live without the state,' he said. His future and that of the institute looked uncertain. I said he would surely do well out of the changes since his expertise would be in great demand.

'You don't understand,' he said bitterly, 'when has knowledge ever been valued in our society?'

On another day we ran into the aimak's agricultural expert, Byamsuren, who explained why the experimental breeding projects had gone so wrong.

In a planned economy, quotas for wool production were set according to the quantity and not the quality of wool. It measured output of wool by weight and in the 1970s Soviet experts arrived with advice on how to increase production.

The wool of the Ukrainian goat is thicker and heavier than the fine wool of the cashmere mountain goats raised in the Gobi. Cashmere goats like the Bactrian camels are a rare mountain breed rarely found outside the remoter parts of Asia. They started a project and interbred the two types.

It worked, the new breed successfully produced hair that was seventeen microns thick, only now this wool was useless because the Japanese had invested in a textiles plant which required the finest wool – thirteen microns thick – to sell on the international market. The plant would accept nothing less.

'That's the difference between quantity and quality. Now we are trying to breed the old goats again,' Byamsuren said wryly.

He was optimistic that a market economy would bring great prosperity to the Gobi. The aimak could potentially support 10 million animals, ten times the current population even without large-scale investments.

With privatisation, people were returning from the towns to the empty countryside and the manpower was now becoming available. Families were getting together to co-operate and share some of the tasks.

The problem was how to abandon the Soviet practices and return to the old traditional ways. In a Soviet *kolkhoz*, or commune, centralisation and mechanisation were at a higher level than a Mongolian *negdel* but the principles were the same. They aimed to turn the nomadic shepherd into a factory worker with an eight-hour day and a fixed wage.

'During the collectivisation when all the animals were gathered together, people lost interest and became lazy. The state provided forage, transport and everything else,' he said.

The only benefit of the last thirty years was during a *zot*. Every twelve years or so, usually during the year of the monkey, a summer drought was followed by a sudden freeze in the spring so animals, already weak after the summer, were unable to dig through the snow to reach the grass below. In such times the state could provide forage.

In the past, families had been entirely self-reliant and self-sufficient. They moved with their herds four times a year to find fresh pastures. Now and again Chinese traders came to exchange tea or silk or sugar for hides and wool. Only a few families were entirely nomadic and those were responsible for driving animals to and from urban centres to sell as meat.

The poverty witnessed by Western travellers before and after the national revolution of 1911 was largely due to other factors. Most of the population was in debt to big Chinese trading houses and when the Chinese returned in 1919, they demanded the payment of all debts abrogated in 1911 plus interest and all taxes which had not been collected in the intervening period. Many herdsmen were reduced to beggary.

A large part of the herds were owned either by the monasteries or nobility and looked after by the ordinary herdsmen. The deeper the feudal nobility fell into debt, the harder they pressed the herdsmen; and the larger the lamaseries grew, the fewer men remained to look after the herds.

In theory the country could be as rich as Texas especially if the Gobi's underground oil resources were exploited. From time to time I tried to picture my hosts living in a ranch house with stone walls, fireplaces and trophy heads above.

There was so much land in the Gobi and so few animals that land ownership never figured in conversations. No one had any desire to own land. This had nothing to do with Communism and state ownership. There never was an intricate system of law or custom of pasture use. People just grazed their animals where they pleased and if there was someone there already they simply asked their permission.

Grazing practices are, of course, more complicated than this suggests. Mongols have over forty different terms for pasture, and herds are moved from one type to another according to specific principles.

It was only when Byamsuren introduced me to the rice farmers of the Gobi desert that its true potential dawned on me.

The rice seedlings had been brought from Japan, each carefully packaged in a neat bag of soil, and now made an unexpected and tiny patch of green in the desert.

The shoots in the paddy field were watered by an artesian well and formed part of a small experimental farm a few miles outside the aimak centre.

Under the Manchus, the Mongols had been forbidden to farm land and Western travellers had assumed they were culturally disinclined to till the soil or simply incapable of it. Under Soviet influence, in particular Khrushchev's virgin lands policy, they had grown wheat but overall this was no more successful than in the Soviet Union.

The rice project was the inspiration of a single Japanese tourist. By chance the chief of the Amouri prefecture in northern Japan had come to the Gobi on holiday last autumn and had thought to himself that this place, on the same latitude as his own village, presented a challenge for his rice-growing skills.

He was the chairman of the local rice-farmers' association in a region famous for its rice. He went backwards and forwards five times investigating the possibilities and discovered a suitable spot where the soil was not too clayey. Then he sent planters to look after the first seedlings.

This year they were going to send ten Mongolian youngsters to Japan to study rice farming and plant the first crop in Mongolia. In the first stage different types of rice were being planted to see which grew best. Next year they hoped to grow enough rice to export it to other parts of Mongolia.

At the little farm we met a Mongolian responsible for tending the small shoots. He said he liked farming and had a whole acre on which he grew a large variety of vegetables.

He pointed with pride to the garlic, onions and melons growing. He said conditions were good with plenty of sun and water and a fertile loess soil. When the farm was privatised, he intended to buy it and branch out into raising chickens as well. He already had a few eggs to sell.

The Gobi had vast amounts of subterranean water reserves. Last year he had successfully tried growing cotton and was planting five hectares this year. He was growing grapes too.

Château Gobi, best drunk chilled with camel meat, coming soon to a supermarket near you.

Every day we drove through the desert, the Gobi revealed more of its wildlife and hidden beauty. Once I went swimming amid the sand dunes in the clear waters of a pool fed by a spring trickling out of a rocky outcrop. Wild purple irises bloomed around the shore and bright yellow butterflies flitted among them. In a small patch of grass a small brown snake lay coiled in the sun and nearby a spider the size of my hand watched and waited.

The most common birds were sandgrouse which flew like a bullet. They had a fat body like a pigeon, a head like a grouse, feet padded like a camels' and long narrow wings.

On the clifftops were nests of golden eagles, lammergeiers and kites. Once I crept up to a nest from which tiny grey eagle chicks peered out, wide eyed.

The grasslands were infested with kangaroo rats that can jump six feet, marmots, hamsters and other small rodents I was unable to identify.

Occasionally we could see other lakes in the distance, surrounded by rushes and shimmering blue-green. Herds of horses grazed on the plains and awkward camels stood guarding their gawky offspring.

It was rare to meet another vehicle but on the horizon one occasionally glimpsed the silhouette of a rider hurrying on some unknown business. From time to time we passed an isolated white *ger* and snot-nosed children would run out to stare.

We raced herds of antelopes at fifty miles an hour on the open savannah, their white tails bobbing away as they effortlessly outpaced the machine.

Andrews saw herds of 6,000, so many that the whole horizon appeared to be a moving line of yellow bodies and curving necks. He shot them so often that they ate fried antelope for breakfast, stewed antelope for tiffin and roast antelope for dinner.

In the mountains he hunted wild argali sheep and ibex from the comfort of his car and from a distance photographed the shy wild asses.

American millionaires still come to the Gobi to hunt, and Basan, the driver, said he had taken part in the hunt for snow leopards. This American, who was so rich he brought his own cook and dogs, had paid 30,000 dollars for the one licence which the government issued every year. It had taken five days from dawn to dusk to kill the snow leopard.

The snow leopards live in the mountains, a part of which are set aside as a nature reserve. One day we had tea with its guardian who lived by himself in a grubby *ger* buzzing with flies. He had taken up photography to fill his time and showed us with pride blurry photographs in black and white of a snow leopard he had caught dozing on a rocky promontory in the sun. Its patterned fur was so like the rock that when I first looked, I could not see it.

'I almost stepped on it myself,' the warden said.

Inside the reserve, our route took us between high cliffs carved by a small stream. It was just wide enough for the jeep. We camped in this gorge where, hidden from the sun, the water had frozen four or five feet thick. It was blue like glacier ice. At night we made a fire out of dried horse manure and the flames threw huge shadows on the canyon walls.

Next morning we drove out of the canyon's mouth where the stream drained on to a secluded plain, and came across the ruins of a monastery. It was destroyed in the late 1930s and looked as if the soldiers had destroyed it with dynamite.

One could still recognise the high, thick and roofless walls of the main temple. Scattered on the ground lay broken tiles and pieces of the iron cauldrons used to boil tea.

Camels now grazed among the rest of the low mudbrick ruins. The monks must have been taken out and shot in the canyon but all I found was the dead carcass of a horse, its lips still wrinkled over its teeth.

The following night we camped on the savannah in the lee of an ancient volcano. Some forgotten Hun chieftain lay buried close by under a circular mound of black lava and pumice stone.

One could see for miles around. In the distance streaks of lightning flashed above the blue ramparts of the mountains and then a grey cloud of rain began moving swiftly towards us. Luckily the storm did not reach us but moved off in another direction.

Near our camp stood a shepherd's bothy and piles and piles of round, dried goat manure. We collected the balls of dung for a fire and they glowed like red lumps of coal. While gathering them a sandgrouse flew out, startled, from beneath my feet, more astonished than I to meet another being in this emptiness.

After the storm had moved off, there was no wind at all and once or twice only the distant hoot of a hunting owl broke the profound stillness. I had never been anywhere so quiet before and it must have made me feel uneasy.

My ears strained to detect some sound, some rustling somewhere however faint. Then, when not a sound emerged from the huge dark plain, I began to hear my blood pumping through my ears. Slowly, distantly, the peal of faraway bells came to my ears until I could picture them swinging in a belfry tower. A buried childhood memory surfaced and I was walking down a path in the high mountains filled with the rich smell of pine and fresh cut hay to an Alpine valley far below, where an onion-shaped steeple was calling.

Towards the end of the next day, the driver said we were now close to a good spot to search for the eggs. On the way, we stopped for some tea and came across Mr Cerenov sitting in his house dreaming of America.

'It must be wonderful in America to be able to make deals with anyone you want and to know they will stick,' he said wistfully, fingering the foxfur which hung beside him on the wall. 'Here we have only recently had such opportunities.'

He was a stocky middle-aged man with salt-and-pepper hair, who had formerly worked as the deputy administrator of various *negdels*. He was now an ardent believer in capitalism and related how his initiative had been punished under the old system.

He spent two years from 1985 to 1987 in a labour camp as a

punishment for building a garage at the *negdel* centre where he worked.

'There was this waste ash left over from burning coal and I had the idea of turning the ash into bricks. With the bricks I decided to build a garage to protect the *negdel*'s five vehicles during winter,' Cerenov said.

'There was an investigation and I was held in custody for seven months and charged with committing an economic crime. They said I had built the garage out of the budget and was therefore guilty of abusing my power.

'I had no personal interest in this. I just thought it was a good idea,' he said, still smarting at the memory of the injustice. He was forced to pay a large fine of 27,000 tugrik. The *negdel* chairman was put away too, and in the labour camp they were ordered to help construct a new dairy.

'It was built on the Soviet model for 2,000 cows. That's far too many and of course it was unprofitable but we planned to build twenty of these in Mongolia,' he said. 'The Soviets were obsessed with creating bigger and bigger units which like dinosaurs became less and less efficient.'

The prison, he explained, was full of people imprisoned for minor errors – a guard who had lost his gun or a nomad who had sold two camels. A judge could hand out sentences of up to seven years when it came to state property.

'There were lots of middle-ranking officials punished in the mid-eighties as they made one last attempt to make the Plan work,' he said.

He had thick strong forearms like a wrestler and now he picked up a little stool like the ones everyone sits on in a *ger*, and began to pull it around.

'You see this? It's collapsible and I invented it,' he said and folded it flat.

'It's ideal for nomads who move around a lot. I think I can sell a lot of these.' He planned to manufacture hundreds a year if there was a ready market. He was bursting with ideas and energy for the co-operative, a semi-private company, he had set up with four others using a state loan after leaving his job.

They had started last year growing vegetables – potatoes, tomatoes and cucumbers – and the profits were enough to repay the loan. To expand they needed equipment such as pumps to bring more water up from underground wells.

He had other plans too, big plans. Tourism, for instance, but they needed to change the psychology of the people first.

'When I first proposed setting up the company, people reacted as if they had seen a rabbit with horns,' he said. 'Now they can see the potential.'

Did I want to invest in any projects?

'We could sign a contract, do a deal,' he suggested happily.

At his house we met the camel breeder Bazcheck who was reputed to be the richest man around. He invited us to his camp a few miles away and which was on our way.

We raced for the safety of his *ger* before a duststorm caught us on the open road. We could see it moving swiftly across the stony plain towards us long before it arrived.

The wind, blackened by the particles of dust and sand, swirled around the camp making the guy ropes hum. Inside the *ger* we could hear the pitiful cry of the baby camels outside pegged in a circle like captured prisoners of war.

Sometimes the wind would twist around and carry the sound of the lambs penned in a small corral of rocks faintly bleating for their mothers. Just before, as we arrived, the lambs with thick curly black or white wool had jumped and wagged their fat tails when the herd was shepherded back into the camp.

The *ger* was furnished simply, with big pieces of misshapen black and red camel meat hung in rows along a rack set on one side. Along the other, his sons sat bare-chested and stared at us in silence.

The camel breeder stripped off his dark green *del* and beneath his white vest bulged the thick muscles of a champion wrestler. He was not just a wrestler but the local king of camel breaking.

A young camel was difficult to break in, he said, but afterwards they became quite obedient and meekly answered to their names. Every one – and he owned hundreds – had its own face and its own personality. He could recognise every one of them, he said. The camels were not stupid either. They knew how to find water, even if it lay a day's journey away, and made loyal and devoted mothers.

James Gilmour reported that a mother camel who lost its calf would always return to the spot where it had died. In fact Mongols used to slaughter a calf before the eyes of its mother when they buried a khan. Although the site was left unmarked the camel would always be able to lead relatives back to the spot to make offerings. When the camel died, the secret of the location was then lost.

We had *buuz* – steamed camel-meat dumplings – for dinner but I found the meat tasted old and tough. It had been slaughtered in the autumn as Mongolians never kill their animals in the spring, although they eat little else but meat the year round together with noodles, wild onions and occasionally potatoes.

Mongolians believe it is wrong to butcher young animals and recently a newspaper had carried an interview with the penitential butcher to the Tsedenbals. He was consumed with guilt because Filatova had demanded fresh lamb and veal and he was forced against his conscience to meet her wishes.

The camel breeder, the first to contract out camels from the collective, pulled out his documents to show us the details of his business. He contracted to breed a certain number of camels as well as horses, sheep and goats from the state and kept those born in addition to the fixed quota as his private property. After two years his profit was 25,000 tugrik, a small fortune where the average wage was 400 a month.

'What are you going to do with all this money?' I asked and everybody laughed.

Since the Japanese had built a woollens plant, camel wool was at a premium. Now he wanted his family to concentrate on breeding camels and split the connected work with the rest of the animals with other families in his district.

'Now the most important thing,' he said, 'is to teach young people how to work. This has been forgotten during these past years.' His sons listened without comment.

Next morning the family showed me how they cut and combed the camels. The beasts accepted the indignity stoically although they looked like plucked chickens afterwards. Then the calves were set free and ran off hopping and skipping like giant puppies.

Bazcheck then came with us to some nearby cliffs where Basan, the driver, said Mongolian, Polish and Russian scientists used to come each year to search for dinosaurs.

It was an impressive site. A huge table of land collapsed abruptly at the line of cliffs which overlooked an endless grey wasteland.

Bazcheck said you can tell the rocks from the fossils by tasting them. The stuff that sticks to your lips like glue is old bones so we spent the morning bone-tasting. Near the top of a gulley we found a white bone three feet long and a foot wide which had rotted away and crumbled at the touch.

On the south side of the Gobi palaeontologists have recently found the remains of Asia's largest dinosaur. When it lived 140 million years ago, it stretched ninety-eight feet from head to tail, weighed forty tons and probably lumbered along at an impressive maximum speed of ten mph.

This site was so rich that the Russians had used bulldozers to uncover bones when they worked here after the war. The most famous area though was the Nemegt valley, 500 miles to the west but in the same aimak. Hundreds of giant fossils were discovered at what was reputedly the richest dinosaur cemetery in the world. The corpses piled up when they lodged in a gulley which connected two large swampy lakes.

There is a peculiar excitement to hunting dinosaurs which breeds impatience.

'Without a doubt,' Andrews wrote, 'there were hundreds of bones lying just beneath the surface. But where? It is well-nigh hopeless to dig for fossils unless there are definite indications of their presence. There must be some clue, a piece of bone "running in" or something upon which to fasten hope. Otherwise one might dig and dig and miss the greatest treasures by a few feet or even a few inches.'

We wandered full of hope among the washed-out gulleys and lumps of mud carved by the wind and rain into strange twisted shapes like Zen sculptures, picking up odd pieces of rock or wood.

Somewhere here might just be another clue to the Marie Celeste of Darwinian science, the disappearance of the dinosaurs. After prospering for 140 million years until the close of the Cretaceous period 65 million years ago, they suddenly vanished. Why?

The question exerts a fascination on us not just as an intriguing mystery but because it undermines our beliefs in history as a record of evolutionary progress.

Darwin wrote in his book *On the Origin of Species* that 'the inhabitants of each successive period in the world's history have beaten their predecessors in the race for life, and are, insofar, higher in the scale of nature.'

Nineteenth-century thought, in particular Marxism, is imbued with the notion of history leading mankind in definable stages from one level of development – feudal to capitalist to Socialist - to the next higher form.

'Just as Darwin discovered the law of evolution in organic nature, so Marx discovered the law of evolution in human history,' Engels said when his friend was buried in 1883. Marx's followers held that evolution was progress and so, as the nineteenth-century naturalist Jean Baptiste Lamarck said, 'All life is evolving towards perfection.'

The development of dinosaurs put this in doubt. They are divided into two large classes, the carnivores and the herbivores, and a member of the expedition, Professor Osborn, conceived of dinosaur evolution as a smooth almost predictable linear development if not to better, at least to bigger animals.

'Defensive herbivorous types were of relatively small size and their defensive horns or armature were not very well developed. Similarly the offensive, flesh-eating types were of moderate size and power, capable of capturing all the small, herbivorous prey,' he wrote.

'Step by step, like the evolution of the modern armoured battleship and the long-range highpowered projectile, the herbivorous dinosaurs became larger and more stoutly defended, while their carnivorous enemies became more powerful and diversified.'

Stalin himself was influenced by such a philosophical outlook and he wrote in 1938 at the height of the terror that development must 'take place in gradual quantative change, leading to qualitative leaps'.

Yet evolution stopped for the dinosaurs, all at once, and most scientists drew the conclusion that nature had condemned them to extinction simply for becoming too large and stupid to survive.

More recent research suggests otherwise as they now appear to have had larger brains, modern mammalian binocular vision and behaved in a more complex way than was first assumed.

Andrews had first thought the primary significance of the expeditions' discoveries was to reveal that Central Asia was one of the two chief centres of dinosaur evolution, although strictly speaking Asia was then joined to Africa forming a vast continent geologists called Gondwana. The other centre was North America.

By tracing the development of fossils, it seemed clear that the species had crossed the Bering Straits back and forth so that many branches of American dinosaurs could be shown to have descended from Central Asian species.

When the Andrews expedition then discovered the eggs and eight-inch skull of a small herbivorous land reptile, the members chose to name it Protoceratops, signifying the 'first horned dinosaur'. In honour of the expedition's leader, it was given the full name of *Protoceratops Andrewsi*.

The discovery was hailed as an 'epoch-making event' because Protoceratops was proved to be related to Triceratops, a gigantic twenty-foot-long monster found in North America with three horns and a skull eight feet long.

After the 1920s dinosaur remains were discovered all over the globe thus destroying the theory of two centres of development. But the discovery of Protoceratops had in fact deepened the mystery of the dinosaurs because it demonstrated that the dinosaurs were continuing to evolve in the Cretaceous period and that not all the dinosaurs which developed in the final phase were giants.

The Andrews expedition's discovery of the Oviraptor Philoceratops with its parrot-like beak gave rise to another theory. The beak enabled it to crack open and eat the eggs of other dinosaurs which became larger and more nourishing as their parents grew in bulk. As the Cretaceous period also witnessed the appearance of small mammals, some propose that a lemming-like explosion of egg-eating dinosaurs and mammals was responsible for the end of the dinosaurs.

More recently the trend has been to look for evidence of a more random and (philosophically) meaningless event. Perhaps a gigantic catastrophe like a meteorite which suddenly and radically changed the earth's climate. On average, it is calculated that every 1.2 million years a comet with the impact of one million megatonnes of TNT hits the earth. Others have suggested a volcanic eruption or even that cosmic rays reached the earth in unusual quantities which caused excessive genetic changes and massive extinctions.

At the bottom of a small gulley a few hours later we found some larger bone fragments buried in the ground and a scattering of polished and fluted bones. One piece was large and curved just like a lower jawbone.

There were also rusting cans and bits of wooden packing cases left by the Russians or some other expedition. I scrambled further up hoping to find larger pieces of the skeleton but without success.

The driver was now anxious to leave and stood by the jeep impatiently when at the bottom of the cliffs, I found some purplish backbones. Several were fused together. For a while I didn't find anything more.

It was hot and I was getting tired and preparing to leave when I came across a cluster of more purplish bones sticking out of the ground.

At first they seemed like a jumble of weathered rocks but on closer examination they clearly formed a skull about eight inches long. The triangular jaw was clearly visible and looked large and powerful compared to the rest of the head.

I hurried to collect the others. Then slowly with mounting excitement we began to scrape away the soil around the skull with a small brush and a knife. The skull had to be left well alone. It was so weathered that if touched it crumbled.

Gradually more bones peeped out white and pale in the damp sandy soil. First the round collar bones, then the white ribs spread out like a fan and then the pelvic bone. Finally on either side the small limbs became clearly visible. The right leg was folded by the neck but the three others sprawled out lazily, each partly bent back to the body.

It was the skeleton of an animal none of us had ever seen before. The creature lay on its back, belly up like a dog waiting to have its tummy tickled. The tail was missing but perhaps I had found that already. Even without it the skeleton was a good two feet long.

When we had finished scraping away, it looked rather pathetic. The head was too big for the body and the limbs sprawled in an ungainly fashion. It looked just like a baby, a 75-million-year-old dinosaur baby. In London, months later, palaeontologists at the Natural History Museum identified it from photographs as a specimen of *Protoceratops Andrewsi*.

We carefully buried it again, this sad witness to random extinction and the unexpectedness of death. To have removed it would have been to destroy it. The bones would have crumbled away in our hands leaving nothing but a handful of dust.

Ten

Buryiatia

'Ah Pushkin! Do you know Pushkin? Such poetry. How I do love his poems,' declared Victoria in the most dramatic tones possible and swept forward to a waiting taxi driver.

The Ministry of Culture of the Republic of Buryiatia had despatched Victoria to be my guide but by profession she was a dancer and although in her early fifties still carried herself with the self-conscious poise of an artiste.

She wore a brightly coloured scarf wrapped around her head like a bandana, large round gypsy ear-rings, bright red lipstick, and she had blackened her eyebrows to the aggressive v-shapes of a stage Cleopatra. She was alarmingly theatrical for Siberia.

She specialised in performances of the Buryiat folk culture but was passionately and defiantly an admirer of Russian *Kulturny*, a notion which appeared to be loaded with as much significance in Russian as it is in German. It meant not only art but civilisation, and civilisation was what only advanced peoples could lay claim to.

Victoria loved Russian Kultur and was proud to share it. Great literature, she said lifting up both hands in worship, is a gift to all the world. Like your Shakespeare, she added graciously.

I didn't know much about Pushkin's verse, I confessed, but surely it is deeply and patriotically Russian and you are a Buryiat, a Mongol?

'Do you know,' she continued in a voice with the exaggerated precision of the stage, 'I was at a party the other day when a young man said it was time the Russians went home. I said to him if they were born here just as you were, they are as much natives of Buryiatia as you are. And do you know, he had no reply to that.'

The point made, she turned to the Russian taxi driver and ordered him to drive us to the Museum of National Culture. She insisted we go there because only there would I see real Buryiat culture. It had all been painstakingly collected, labelled and preserved in a park outside Ulan Ude.

This industrial city of half a million is the capital of the Republic within the Russian Federation set aside for the Mongol-Buryiats.

The museum was closed when we arrived and closed on the two subsequent occasions I tried to visit it. Inside the park we could see the Buryiat log cabins, a temple and a wooden church and a small enclosure of white-haired camels. The caretaker said we had better come back on a day which was not a public holiday.

The holiday was to allow the population to elect the first president of the Russian Federation. Victoria said she voted for Rhyzkov, the Party candidate and not for Boris Yeltsin. When the votes were counted later most of the Republic had voted against Yeltsin and had earlier voted against leaving the Soviet Union. Political power remained firmly in the hands of the Communist Party and a small Nationalist party established a few months earlier was still illegal.

After the museum Victoria was at a loss where to go next but finally suggested we visit a poet and former minister of culture, who had published thirty volumes of verse, in his country retreat.

The dacha was in a pretty corner of the countryside where other senior members of the cultural establishment were all obliged to own a dacha. The same system is repeated all over the Soviet Union.

Damba and his family were all out tending vegetables around a modest wooden house when we arrived. Even for ex-ministers growing vegetables was not a hobby but a time-consuming necessity to survive the winter.

He had started life as a border guard and had arrested a woman who later became his wife. While she prepared a meal, Damba talked enthusiastically about a Buryiat cultural revival.

For the first time since the 1930s, the traditional spring moon festival, the *tsagaalgan* or White Month, had been celebrated. There had been a beauty contest to select the White Month Princess who was judged not only for her looks but her replies to questions on national culture and her ability to sing folk songs.

The national King Gesar epic was being performed. Mongolian was being spoken and written again. Buddhist monasteries were being reopened and lost statues rediscovered, including one which he boasted dated from Buddha's lifetime, 2,500 years ago.

A neighbour from next door who edited a local magazine was organising a big ceremony to move the statue out of storage to its rightful place in a major temple.

Over the food and the vodka, the talk became more and more nationalistic and the claims for Buryiatia's historical significance wilder and wilder.

Damba had been cautious at first – Buryiatia had been closed for decades and even a year earlier a foreigner would never have been allowed to visit a private home without official permission – but with each fresh round of vodka, another veneer of lifelong loyalty to Soviet ideals fell away.

Buryiatia was the birthplace of Mongol nationalism, the centre of its art, religion, music ... Was not the mother of Genghis Khan a Buryiat? And was he not buried himself somewhere in Buryiatia? And was not Lake Baikal the centre of shamanism?

For sixty years the Party had done its best to bury Buryiatia and assimilate its population into the mass of 'Soviet' culture and failed. I watched Victoria's reaction to this. Damba had handsomely complimented her work to preserve Mongolian folklore but it was clear that everyone knew her dancing and singing were part of a pretence. Cultural troupes like hers put on performances for visitors to show traditions which ordinary Buryiats were not allowed to respect.

Victoria was quiet and awkward at first but then this chauvinistic fever began to infect her and when the conversation turned to shamanism and Lake Baikal she joined in.

To my astonishment, Victoria began to describe how each year she participated in the sacrifices on Alhon Island which lies on the western side of the inland sea and is the traditional site of ancient shamanistic sacrifices to the spirit of the lake and the ancestral deities of the Mongols. The ceremonies had been strictly outlawed since the 1930s but Victoria said senior Communist Party officials had continued them in secrecy.

She herself had cut open a black lamb and pulled its heart out. The spirits of the Lake, the guardians of the Mongol nation, demanded it, she said.

Through the fog of vodka, I tried to picture this lover of Pushkin, her arms red with the ritual blood of a pagan sacrifice. If she lived such a double life what happened to the rest of the Buryiats?

Nobody in London or even in Mongolia had been able to tell me very much about Buryiatia beforehand. All I knew when I boarded a trans-Siberian train to take me the 500 kilometers from Ulan Bator to Ulan

Ude was that the Mongols thought the Buryiats far too Russified. Some of them even dyed their hair blond, people told me, although they should be proud to be Mongols.

The area had been closed to the outside world since the late 1920s and much of its history had been purposely obscured. It took some time to piece together what had happened here, even after I arrived. So few people knew.

The very name Buryiat is a nineteenth-century Russian invention intended to create a belief that the Mongols inside Russia, especially those around Lake Baikal, are a different people from those which ended up as subjects of the Manchus. In 1689, the Treaty of Nerchinsk settled the boundary between the expanding empires of the Tsar and the Manchu Emperor and it still defines the boundary of the Soviet Union.

At first I had thought that the Buryiats had fared better than either the Mongols in China or the People's Republic of Mongolia but dreadful though all their histories are, the plight of the Buryiats seems if anything to have been still worse.

The Buryiats were colonised at a far earlier period. Ulan Ude dates back to 1666 when the Cossacks built a fort controlling the crossing where the Rivers Selenga and Uda meet some miles east of Lake Baikal. A town, Udinsk Zimoveyie, grew around it which after 1917 was renamed Ulan Ude. This means, depending on who you ask, either Red Gate, or the red River Uda after the partisans who died defending it against White Russians.

The Baikal region was the scene of fierce fighting during the civil war. Czech, Hungarian and Austrian prisoners of war, including Jaroslav Hašek, author of *The Good Soldier Schweik*, took part.

The early absorption of the Buryiat Mongols into the Russian Empire meant that they were better educated and informed than their cousins across the border. After the Communist victory many were sent to Mongolia with the Red Army and in fact held a majority of the politburo seats in the new Mongolian regime.

As the imperial government in St Petersburg collapsed other Buryiats seized the opportunity to launch a pan-Mongolian movement which set out to unite all Mongols in an independent, peaceful state which was to be as neutral as Switzerland. The opportuntiy was there. Other nationalities in the Baltic, the Balkans or in the Ukraine as well as the Turkic peoples led by Enver Pasha were taking similar steps.

Representatives from all the tribes met in 1919 at the border town of Khiatka (Chita) and organised a united Mongolian government headed by a lama from Inner Mongolia, Nidgi Toyen. The delegates proposed to unite all Mongol-speaking peoples and revive the old traditions and national culture.

It was backed by the Cossack White Guard leader Hetman Simenov (Baron Ungern-Sternberg's former superior) and the Japanese, who sent a representative of the Imperial army to the meeting.

Ambassadors of the new government were despatched to Paris, London and other European capitals but won scant recognition and returned empty handed. The Bogd Khan, struggling with an invasion by a Chinese general, Little Tsu, was unable to support the government. The Chinese general even justified his occupation of Mongolia by citing the threat from Buryiat Nationalists and bandits.

Further efforts foundered in the civil war and its leaders were accused of being no more than the tools of White or Japanese imperialists.

Stalin established the Buryiat Mongol Autonomous Republic in 1924, seven years after the Bolsheviks seized power. Its territory was then twice as large as the current republic and bigger than France. It included most of the region around Lake Baikal, the Irkutsk and Chita regions and controlled the vital Trans-Siberian railroad.

Despite its name, the establishment of the new republic inspired considerable fear among the Buryiats who fled with their animals across the unguarded border into Mongolia. Many continued their trek into Inner Mongolia and Manchuria where they settled around Harbin.

In 1923, the Buryiat population of this new Republic was 240,000 and accounted for fifty-two per cent of the total population. By 1928 when Stalin closed the borders of the Soviet Union, only 120,000 remained.

Stalin had once been in charge of the nationalities question and now used his unchallenged power to demand the return of all Buryiats who had escaped. He ordered Choibalsan to arrest all those not born in Mongolia and execute those over twenty-five. Choibalsan had no choice but to agree.

'In 1929–31 almost the entire male population of the Buryiats was executed or imprisoned and only freed after Stalin's death. All their relatives were victimised too,' one Mongolian Buryiat told me.

The exact details of the migration and this terrible punishment are now hard to determine. The entire event went unreported and unrecorded and has remained so – at least I have found no references to it anywhere.

On the other hand Beatrice and Sidney Webb, the British social reformers, reported in their book *Soviet Communism – a new civilisation*, published in 1935 that:

> Alongside this maintenance and strengthening of the minority culture there
> has been an unmistakable rise in the level of civilisation. Note, first and
> perhaps as most important, a marked increase, among national minorities,
> of their own self-respect. It is indeed the many backward populations,
> which had suffered so much under Tsarist repression that they had nothing
> which could be destroyed, which have gained most from the nationalities
> policy of the Soviet Government. [p. 120]

The terror continued with enforced collectivisation and the destruction
of the kulaks, the prosperous peasants. Then in 1937, Stalin split
Buryiatia into three parts, reducing the remaining Buryiats to an even
smaller minority inside their own Republic.

Many Buryiats, finding themselves isolated in other administrative
divisions, now attempted to leave their pastures and move to the Republic. The industrial development of the region during the war and
after, including the placement of other minorities such as ethnic
Germans, brought a rapid increase in the non-Buryiat population.
Much higher wages were paid to workers in the Republic than in surrounding areas specifically to encourage migration.

The Buryiats now account for less than a quarter of the Republic's
one million inhabitants. Buryiats claim that worldwide, there are about
half a million of them, including some in New Jersey.

In the late 1930s the purges saw the destruction of the entire Buryiat
intelligentsia and the Buddhist monasteries which were the traditional
repository of art and literature and to which every family sent one son.

By the mid-1950s, the history of the Buryiats was completely re-
written. The fiercely resisted colonial conquest of Buryiatia was
described as a demand from the Buryiats to seek the protection of the
Tsar. The absorption of the Buryiat Republic into the Soviet Union
was presented as a voluntary decision.

A professor of archaeology told me that it was specifically forbidden
to link Buryiat history with Mongolian and of course any mention of
Genghis Khan was taboo. In fact the history before the arrival of the
Russians was treated as though it did not exist.

A deliberate attempt was made to cut all links with Mongolia. I
found this particularly surprising since to all intents and purposes
Mongolia had for many years been as much a part of the Soviet Union
as Buryiatia. It took days to call Ulan Ude from Ulan Bator and the
connection had to go through Moscow. The two regions are even
separated by being placed in different time zones.

The progressive destruction of Buryiat identity continued in the 1950s and 1960s although demands for the restoration of the territory which Stalin had removed continued to be made. The language was no longer even taught. It was strange to meet young and angry Buryiat Nationalists demanding the expulsion of all Russians but having to say this in Russian because they no longer knew their own tongue.

'Every drunken Russian worker thinks himself superior to us because he speaks Russian better,' one Buryiat told me bitterly.

Even after six years of glasnost, any contacts between Buryiatia and Mongolia were rare. The memory of one evening remains in my mind. A delegation from Mongolia arrived on crutches and in wheelchairs in the restaurant of Ulan Ude's largest hotel. Among them was the ex-fireman who had lost three limbs and whom I had met in Ulan Bator the year before.

The Buryiat Association of the Handicapped had just been set up and I talked to one of the leaders, a girl paralysed from the waist down in a car accident. Although a Buryiat, she only spoke Russian and was as overwhelmed at meeting a stranger from England as a fellow Mongolian from across the border. She kept her hand on my arm as if to reassure herself that this was really happening.

'You don't understand how much has changed here,' she kept saying.

The visitors handed out badges and flags adorned with Genghis Khan's unsmiling portrait. The ex-fireman got up to make a speech, unsteady with the excitement of it all and everyone toasted each other with Genghis Khan brand vodka.

'Genghis Khan shows us how to be strong,' the girl beside me had said clutching my arm tightly.

The tale of this 2,500-year-old statue, the oldest Buddhist icon in the world, if Damba's friend was right, was intriguing.

Preparations were under way to celebrate the 250th anniversary of Buddhism in Russia which even the Dalai Lama was scheduled to attend and included an exhibition of Buddhist statues.

I went along to see the organiser. Ludmilla was a petite, part-Buryiat woman in her late fifties. She was nervous, abrasive and cynical.

'What do they know of democracy?' she had scoffed over lunch. 'What we need here is culture and science. Then we can talk about democracy.'

She held a doctorate in ethnography and was an expert on Buddhism in Buryiatia. Strange stories were told about her. She was said to have fallen in love with a lama who rejected her. Later she betrayed him, accusing him of taking part in tantric orgies and he died in prison.

It seemed an unlikely tale but there was something curiously defensive about her as if she did harbour some secret.

She explained that when in 1749 the Empress Elizabeth, daughter of Peter the Great, issued an edict of toleration for Buddhism, Buryiatia was chosen to be the centre of Buddhism for the Russian empire. Meanwhile another Buddhist and Mongol tribe, the Kalmycks, who had settled on the Volga, were oppressed.

The Buryiats had remained shamanists until the seventeenth century, and after the Russians arrived they at first protected the shamans and concentrated their attack against the lamas. As a less structured religion, the followers of shamans proved to be more open to Christian ideas.

The western Buryiats, who converted to Buddhism before the other Buryiats, were then forced to enter the Russian Orthodox Church. The eastern Buryiats, who were still largely shamanists, were left alone. After the recognition of Buddhism, the shamans came under attack both from the lamas and the Russian state.

And what about the famous statue? Ludmilla said it was called Damdenju and stolen from a temple in China in 1902 during the Boxer Rebellion and carried off in secret to Buryiatia. It was made of sandalwood and was old, very old but did not date from the Buddha's lifetime. I could go and see it in a storeroom.

After some telephone calls, we went to the former Cathedral of St Odigitri. It was the oldest stone building in the city and lay near the river among a handful of beautiful old Russian mansions built by rich traders.

The church had been turned into a storeroom. Plants flourished among the crumbling masonry and I had first mistaken it for a ruin. After a long wait a caretaker appeared and opened big steel locks on a side door.

Inside were rows of glass cases, preserving the costumes of shamans and Russian orthodox bishops, models of temple architecture and a large collection of statues and religious paraphernalia. In dark corners piles of Buddhist scriptures gathered dust. The objects were not entirely neglected but from time to time taken out for anti-religious exhibitions.

Up the last rickety flight of stairs, she brought us to the statue. It was about seven feet high and of a brownish colour except for the hair which was bright blue. The Buddha stood erect, and the long folds of his robes clinging to the outline of the torso were as carefully delineated as in a Greek sculpture. It suggested the influence of

Gandharan culture, where Alexander's army brought Greek ideas to a Central Asian Buddhist civilisation.

His right hand was raised in blessing and a white khadah scarf had recently been laid over it, placed by the Indian ambassador to Ulan Bator. Otherwise it had stood untouched since 1937. Scientists in Leningrad had shown it was made of limewood not sandalwood.

The caretaker did not know the age and since it was not carved in the Chinese style, Ludmilla suggested it could be over a thousand years old.

'It was never taken out for any exhibitions because the Party feared it would create too many emotions and feelings among the people,' the caretaker said.

'What are all these statues doing here anyway?' I asked. The caretaker was surprised by my question.

Didn't I know?

The League of the Militant Godless, a Stalinist organisation of the 1930s, had collected these treasures when they destroyed all the monasteries and churches. They kept them for anti-religious exhibitions.

It was Ludmilla's mother, a devoutly Christian schoolteacher who became a fervent Communist, who had led the League's local activities and saved the most important statues.

Language is probably the greatest and most mysterious creation of the human mind. No one is really certain how languages develop but they can become as extinct as any dinosaur. It is rare, though, to record how a powerful state sets out to drive a language and the culture that goes with it out of existence.

In Buryiatia the Communist Party attempted just that and came close to succeeding. It was national policy to assimilate all minorities to create a new race, the Soviets, with one language, Russian, so there was no point even preserving or tolerating the existence of others.

'Nobody ever found a document revealing a formal decision to abandon Mongolian,' Dr Valentin Rassadin, a philologist at the Buryiat Scientific Institute, said. 'In the 1970s it was just secretly condemned to extinction.'

The decision was taken by Modogoyef, the Party leader in Buryiatia, an appointee of Stalin who stayed in power for twenty years after Stalin's death.

'He did it because he wanted to be holier than the Pope,' Dr Rassadin said.

In 1976 Modogoyef announced that the wishes of the many herdsmen who had written letters to the Party demanding to have their children educated solely in Russian must be respected. Therefore, it was no longer necessary to teach the Buryiat-Mongol language in any schools. All teaching took place in Russian from the first day of primary school onwards.

'Beforehand the Party had sent letters to scientists here at the Buryiat Scientific Institute asking if it was necesssary to have more than one language in the Republic. Necessary? What does necessary mean?' Rassadin said. The Institute replied that yes, it was necessary, but Modogoyef ignored it.

As in Mongolia, the Mongolian-Uighur script had already been replaced by the Latin alphabet in the 1930s and this together with the destruction of the monastic libraries cut off the Buryiats from their own literature, history and culture.

The language fell into such utter disuse that by now almost no one under twenty-five could speak any Mongolian at all. The majority of the Buryiats spoke to each other in Russian. Rassadin was sending out questionnaires to find out exactly where it was still spoken but said that had things carried on in this way, no one would be capable of speaking it in a few more years. It would have become as much a museum piece as any fossil.

Dr Rassadin was now designing programmes to teach the language to adult Buryiats and Russians.

A tall man with blue eyes, Dr Rassadin was clearly not Buryiat but Russian. He had been raised near Leningrad by his grandmother who spoke Karelian, a Finnish dialect.

He held up a newspaper published in Karelian which had just been launched a year earlier as part of a similar campaign to resuscitate a dying tongue. The key to teaching Finnish or Mongolian, he said, was to remember that the structure of these languages is totally different from Russian. As they are not Indo-European languages, they cannot be taught by rote.

He was now trying to devise a textbook with which to teach both Buryiats and Russians at the same time because some villages had mixed populations. He clearly relished the challenge and as he talked I wondered why he of all the experts introduced to me at the Institute should be so concerned about preserving the language. He was almost the only Russian I met in Buryiatia who thought any culture existed before Russians arrived.

Dr Rassadin was not only an authority on Mongolian but above all an expert on Turkic languages. The two have a common root in a group called the Altaic languages which also include Manchu, Korean and ancient Japanese.

When even Mongolian was being forced out of existence, he had devoted himself to rescuing one of the most obscure languages in the world. He was a collector of languages, just as some people tried to save the panda or the white rhino.

He had invented an alphabet for a group of nomadic hunters who lived in the high taiga and called themselves the Tofalars. There were only 720 of them but they spoke a unique language which is a mixture of ancient Turkish and Mongolian. It was, he said, the oldest form of Turkish in existence.

They lived in mountains in the Irkutsk region, herded reindeer and built birch-bark tepees like American Indians. It was such a remote existence that when he first went there, it had taken him over a month to find them.

He pulled out black and white photographs of their wigwams in the forest and their shaman in cloak and feathers.

In the Middle Ages the Tofalars had paid tribute to Genghis Khan in gold and furs but had never taken part in his military campaigns. Until the Russians came, they continued to pay tribute to the western Buryiat khans. Then in 1648 came the first contact with the Russians. They were converted to orthodox Christianity and given Russian names and their own names became taboo. In 1930 even they were collectivised and settled in three villages although contact with the outside world was only once a year.

The men went into the mountains for two years at a time to look after the reindeer and when they returned, another group would go up. Every autumn, all the men went to the taiga to hunt and collect nuts and berries.

Dr Rassadin had spent months living among them, learning to hunt and to erect a tepee and studying the language. He now had a filing cabinet filled with index cards listing thousands of words and their Russian equivalents. When he first went there in the early 1970s, there were only 600 Tofalars, divided into five bloodlines.

The language had its own peculiarities. All the animals had their own names and there were ten words for, say, a bear, so that any particular bear, depending on its age, sex or colour had its own particular term. When the animal was actually being hunted, yet another term, or rather a euphemism, would be used.

'The hunter would not say, "I killed a wild deer," he would say "I killed a yellow animal,"' he said. A bear was 'a black animal' and a moose was 'a grey animal' as if this private hunting code could disguise what was really taking place.

The language was rich in verbs to express movement – the glimpses a hunter caught of an animal moving through the forests.

At first he had used Latin letters to express the sounds of the language but finally, the Tofalars had asked him to create a written language for them. In 1971, he had composed a textbook for them using a Latinised transcription. He had by then built up a dictionary of 50,000 words.

They then demanded from the state their own alphabet which more accurately reflected their pronunciation. Finally in 1986 their demand had been accepted and an order had come all the way from the Supreme Council of Ministers of the Soviet Union in Moscow. Dr Rassadin was asked to draw up an alphabet.

It had forty-two letters, thirty-two Cyrillic and nine Turkish letters. After it had been approved by other Turkic linguists, he went back to the Tofalar village and gathered everyone together in front of a big blackboard and explained what he proposed to do.

'It was a unique experiment,' he said. In 1989, he began instructing teachers how to use it in intensive courses. Teaching began at kindergarten level but now a dictionary and more textbooks were being published.

He showed me some of them. They were brightly coloured with illustrations showing reindeer, elk and wolf. There were pictures too of Lenin, spacemen and the Kremlin.

He was now married to a Tofalar girl but it so happened that she was one of the few who had become 'Sovietised' and had entirely forgotten the language which he had helped preserve.

The delicious smell of fried bacon and eggs wafted through the sparse little cottage and the old Russian peasant woman was brewing up the samovar for tea. All the while she grumbled that times were hard. Even after the Great Patriotic War there was more to buy than now.

Sasha the driver had stopped our car at a roadside village and knocked on the door of her cottage. He told me it was his grandfather's house, but it was just someone who shared his family name, Rubilov.

'It is a Semiskye name so we are all family,' he said. 'Semiskye' literally means family which is how this devout sect of Russian Christians are known in Buryiatia. They are more commonly known as Old Believers and are non-conformists and somewhat like the Amish in America. Time had stopped for them in the sixteenth century and I was told that here, in the midst of Siberia they had preserved the dress and customs of a vanished Russia, like a fly caught in amber.

The old woman looked quite ordinary to me and before we left she showed me how they lived, with a few pigs, a neat vegetable garden and an old Russian-style bath house.

As our car rattled its way along the banks of the River Selenga in the direction of Lake Baikal, it was, however, easy to tell which were the cottages built by Old Believers. They were painted in bold bright colours and had wooden gates and eaves carved in old peasant style.

It was my first trip out of Ulan Ude and I thought the countryside looked beautiful and prosperous in the summer sunshine. The wide, gently flowing river, the open pastures and the hills above clothed in larch and pine presented a picture of as rich a land as one could find anywhere. It was hard to imagine how one could want for anything here.

In the past Siberia was famous for its agricultural wealth. In 1907, N. S. Karzhansky, a delegate of the 5th Congress of the Russian Social Democratic Workers Party had recalled in his memoirs having breakfast with Lenin in London.

'I was delighted by the wonderfully fragrant butter and was just going to say something about how rich the British were when Vladimir Ilych remarked: "That must be Siberian butter."'

Lenin was right. Before the First World War and the Russian Revolution a quarter of the butter eaten in Britain came from the thousands of dairies in Siberia and arrived on special butter trains to the Baltic ports. The Thames was specially dredged to handle ships bringing the butter.

The story of why the Old Believers came to be here is curious. They were so called because they rejected the reformation of the Russian Orthodox Church by the Patriarch Nikon in the sixteenth century. He issued a new authorised translation of the Bible to replace the corrupted texts used in each village. Over time the Bible had been copied and recopied by hand so that the mistakes by careless clerks had multiplied and each differed from another.

The mass and other services were reformed. The faithful were taught to cross themselves with three fingers and not with two, symbolising the inclusion of the Holy Spirit in the Trinity.

Many deeply devout Russians were horrified and violently opposed to the reforms. It meant that their children had not been baptised, their marriages were unsanctified and their parents had not been properly buried. Patriarch Nikon, they raged, was the anti-Christ and priests ordained by him were not accepted. From that time on the Old Believers refused to accept change in any sphere at all.

Their rejection of the reforms amounted to an act of rebellion against the state and they were forced to flee, at first into the forests and remoter areas of Russia. Their leaders preached non-violence and they were ready to die rather than take up arms against their enemies.

Later they were expelled from Russia and settled in Poland. During the first Polish uprising against the Romanovs, Catherine the Great, fearing they would join the rebels, ordered them to leave. There are, though, still some left in modern-day Poland but the majority spread out to the boundaries of the Russian empire. As the empire grew, they kept moving in front, keeping out of the state's reach.

The first forty-six families arrived in the Baikal region in 1746 and the earliest settlement was a village called Bolshoi Tarbagatei to which we were now heading. At the time they were useful to the state because they supplied food for prisoners sent to work in the local mines.

The Old Believers took four years to walk here from Poland, driving their cattle along with them, stopping in the spring to plant crops and then, after the harvest, packing up again and plodding eastwards through the harsh Siberian winters. Many of them died on an epic trek which surpassed anything undertaken in America by pioneers in the West or by Boers in South Africa.

The part of this story which interested me most concerned a group which had first migrated to Murmansk in the Arctic Circle. Then, some time at the turn of this century, the group had heard rumours of a wonderful valley called Shambala which lay somewhere near a tall white mountain in Central Asia. The rumours were so convincing that they set off with all their children and goods to find this pure land and its snowcapped peak. The group was known as the Beloye Volge, the White Water community, after the White Sea which lies between Murmansk and Arkhangel'sk and from where they had set forth.

Before the Revolution there were 4 million Old Believers in the Russian empire and with their own patriarch in Moscow they formed a state within a state. Many were not only diligent farmers but successful traders, trusted and respected for their honesty. They refused to keep records or put contracts in writing but their word was their bond. After the late 1920s, they virtually disappeared from view.

When we arrived at the village, Andrei, the young Party secretary, met us. I had expected to find an old man with a long Rasputin beard, but he was blond, clean shaven with the big hands of a labourer.

Andrei was dashing around organising a village fête. A choir was coming from a neighbouring village and later on in the day sports were scheduled.

The village was a long straggle of neat log houses, a wooden meeting hall and a village shop which sold little more than tinned tomatoes.

Everyone seemed to be out working in the fields, but from time to time a motorcycle, jeep or tractor would roar down the street in a cloud of dust. Only an old woman in a shawl was outside on a ladder patting mud into the gaps between the timbers of her new house.

All the houses were neat and cared for, in contrast to most buildings in the Soviet Union. Behind the curtains were pots of bright flowers and above the windowframes, doves or flowers or other gay designs were carved.

I was disappointed though. Instead of shambling bullock carts driven by men and women dressed like the Pilgrim Fathers I had imagined, it all suggested a spirit of modern industry and enterprise.

Andrei rushed off to organise something else. 'Just wait for Biruta to come, then we can talk,' he said without further explanation and left us waiting on a bench in the sunshine. With me was Dimitri, a young Russian from the Buryiat Institute who had worked as a teacher in one of these villages before escaping to do research into folk songs. Another guide was Alexander, a former teacher of German, who was now running a business with his Buryiat wife, also a former teacher. Alexander and his wife had met studying in Leipzig and had now just launched themselves as a semi-private co-operative. They wanted to provide contacts and translation services to foreign businessmen but thought tourism was the future. Everybody I met seemed convinced that tourism was going to be a short cut to economic growth.

Then a minibus arrived with the choir from another village, Bolshoi Kunayeli, and a tall and slim German woman stepped out followed by the singers dressed in bright costumes. The men were in silk tunics, held by a sash at the waist, matching baggy trousers and high riding boots. The women wore richly embroidered peasant dresses of pink and green trimmed with lace. Around their necks were hung heavy necklaces of amber beads.

We all went into a small room in the village hall to have tea, with freshly baked plum cakes. Some of the locals joined us and soon a bottle of vodka was brought out. All the visitors had to down a glassful in one.

'It used to be strictly forbidden to drink or smoke but the war changed all that. The young men came back corrupted,' Andrei said with a smile. He smoked hungrily himself.

Then the locals began, almost without a signal, to sing. The women with their heads wrapped in scarves and their weather beaten cheeks, led the way. They all looked straight ahead, hands on their laps, con-centrating, and the unaccompanied tune wavered sadly in the air. The mournful notes were twisted and choked in the throat. The polyphonic tones were both medieval and Asiatic.

They sang 'Slain by your Brown Eyes' and the 'Black Raven' in which a girl waits for her fiancé to come back from the war until a black raven comes to tell her that he is dead.

'I had heard the choirs before but never like this. I thought I knew what it meant to be Russian,' Alexander said, surprised by the intensity of feeling the strange music evoked in an enclosed space.

Biruta sat next to me, drinking in the music. She was an architect in Paris but was raised in West Germany. Her father had been an Old Believer and a businessman who had left Leningrad before the Revolution. He had recorded 1,600 songs of the Old Believers and once in Germany had forced his daughter to memorise them. She managed to learn 400 by heart and all the Russian she knew was based on these songs. When she was older Biruta had organised her own choir in Germany to keep the tradition alive.

Along with every other institution which pre-dated the Revolution, the churches of the Old Believers had been destroyed in the 1930s. They were also forbidden to carry on any form of worship and it seemed as if all the traditions had died.

When Biruta came to Buryiatia for the first time last year, she found to her delight that it had all been secretly preserved. The visiting choir insisted on performing for us alone in the big empty meeting hall, accompanying themselves on balalaikas and washboards. The men sang the 'Island of the Hunters', stepping forward one after the other to mimic the actions of the hunters. They could not match the women though.

Then we had lunch, big bowls of bortsch and black bread. The choir sang all the time, getting on and off the bus, while they waited, just for the pleasure of singing this music that had been forbidden for so long.

The singing was not entirely banned. The Party had followed the motto 'national in style and Socialist in content', so a few choirs continued but could only sing Soviet songs. The children were also taught their history but only a distorted version.

They had carried on praying in secret with hidden copies of the Bible. In the library at Ulan Ude, I was shown a copy of such a prayer book which had been hidden in a cave and found damp from the rain. It was written by hand but in a curious way. To save paper, words had been abbreviated and red marks like hooks were written above many words to mark the absence of certain letters.

Biruta now wanted to rebuild the old wooden churches, made without a single nail, which had been destroyed. When her father had joined the Old Believers he had gone on a pilgrimage and kopek by kopek had collected the funds to build such a church. Biruta was now doing the same. We each dug into our pockets and gave her some kopeks which she carefully placed in an envelope.

The exuberance of the singing was not carried into their daily lives. The Old Believers lived austere disciplined lives. Women were not allowed to show their hair. They could only marry husbands chosen by their father. They observed frequent fasts which were adhered to right up until the war when there was so little to eat every day, they had to stop. They were also obsessed with hygiene and outsiders had to use paper plates. The intense desire to keep themselves separate was curiously reminiscent of the Hasidic Jews of old Poland.

They were intensely superstitious too, tying knots in belts to keep the devil from taking their soul and careful not to touch the threshold when they entered a house.

The women in the choir wore dresses which had been hidden since Stalin's time and although each village preserved slight variations, they were essentially identical to those worn when Peter the Great was alive. The lace was from Lyon, the silk from China, the amber from the Baltic, the woollen shawls from the sheep of Kazakhstan.

The sports were not very exciting but there were a handful of Buryiats who did some Mongolian wrestling and I asked about them. It seems that when the Old Believers first arrived here they found it hard to survive in the new and strange land. The Buryiats had helped them and given them land or traded horses for bread.

'Relations were very good then. There was plenty of room and we never tried to convert them,' Andrei said. Even the name of the village had a Mongolian origin from the word for marmot.

The village was now much smaller, he said. Like the Buryiats before them half the village had left after 1928 to escape collectivisation and had driven their animals and wagons eastwards towards the River Amur. Only the weak and old had stayed behind.

Those that remained had, in a way, adapted to collectivisation more easily than any other community in the Soviet Union since they were already a community which shared many things. Andrei said they were now quite wealthy. Every house had enough food stored in its cellar to last them three years.

Those that left carried on through China and from there sailed on to Mexico. From Mexico some groups began moving north again, up through California and Oregon.

Under the leadership of their Ustavtschik, or priests, stricter and stricter congregations tended to spring up, particularly whenever some of them feared that their way of life was being influenced from outside.

In America they objected to the teaching in schools which contradicted their convictions that the earth is flat and the history of the world began with the birth of Adam 7,499 years ago.

Biruta said recently she heard that some groups had migrated northwards to Alaska and were still heading north in search of a place to keep themselves untainted and pure. Neither she nor Andrei knew whether the White Water community had found Shambala or where their trek had brought them.

Tatanya was angry. As we walked through the old part of the city with its elegant and decaying mansions, her blue eyes looked about her with barely suppressed indignation.

'Look at these shops. Look what Communism has brought us. There's nothing to buy in any of them,' she said bitterly, brushing aside the brown hair overhanging her face.

The former marketplace with its columned shop fronts still looked graceful, but dispirited shop attendants lounged inside guarding empty shelves. Even the store reserved for army veterans had only a few pathetic tins of sour cabbage in stock.

We had just been discussing ideology. Tatanya, who was showing me around, thought there was little to choose between Communists and Fascists. Her parents and grandparents had been persecuted in the 1920s and 1930s but she was relatively well off and worked for an established trading co-operative which was branching out into tourism.

Her bitterness astonished me. Life before the Revolution seemed a distant historical epoch to me but to her it was the recent past. She recounted with enthusiasm the history of the merchants who had built these fine houses. Ulan Ude had grown prosperous and rich out of the trade in tea, timber and furs. Goods from China came across Mongolia and Russia's trade branched off to Vladivostok or Peking.

When I thought of Russia, I thought of Communism. The two seemed twinned as if it were the natural order of things, the destiny of the Russians, but Mongolia always had other associations and so when I went there, Communism seemed more apparently a system imposed and temporary.

Tatanya, however, delighted in referring to the October Revolution as the 'October Coup d'Etat' to show that there was nothing inevitable about it. In her eyes Russia need never have gone down this path.

The conversation had started when I began comparing the Communists to the Old Believers. I argued that they shared a similar mentality. Both groups of people had an absolute belief that they alone knew what was right, what constituted the truth, and were determined at all costs to create or find a paradise on earth.

'How can you say that?' she cried, angry at me now. 'The Old Believers had let themselves be slaughtered rather than lift a finger in anger against anyone, even to save themselves.' She shook her head furiously, to dismiss the idea.

There were other similarities, I pressed on. Before the reforms of Patriarch Nikon, the Russian Church had begun to regard itself as the chosen vehicle of a mission to revive the Christian faith in the West. After the fall of Constantinople in 1453, the centre of the Orthodox faith was lost and Moscow began to consider itself as the 'Third Rome', the last true centre of Christianity on earth.

Nikon's reforms were bitterly resisted because they were an assault on this vision of a Russia with a special calling. A Russia which, despite its backwardness on the periphery of Europe, had a moral leadership over the corrupted West.

We were now approaching the central square with its gigantic sculpture of Lenin's head.

'Look at this.' She stopped abruptly. 'Do you call this culture? The sculpture was inspired by the bust of Marx in Highgate cemetery and they wanted to copy it so they made it a hundred times bigger! It's grotesque, a mockery!'

The bust was surreally big, almost as big as a house and its exaggerated size seemed to proclaim the overwrought loyalty of a distant vassal.

Lenin resembled the Old Believers because he too believed Russia had a unique civilising mission. He thought so especially after the expected failure of Communist revolutions in Europe after 1918. In his eyes the new Russia the Bolsheviks were creating, would be a beacon for a new morality and Russia was destined to save the West from its decadence.

I joked that perhaps one day we would find small communities of Russian Communists farming the land in Buryiatia and clinging to their beliefs long after everyone else had abandoned them.

Tatanya thought I was mocking her and when we reached our destination, we dropped the topic. At the municipal library the weekly meeting of the Russian Cultural Society was taking place. It had been set up less than a year ago to celebrate Russian culture and history and I was now its dinner guest.

Food was laid out on a table with bottles of vodka. There were wild mushrooms, vegetables, potatoes, salami and fish, all unavailable in any of the restaurants I had been to. The mushrooms were particularly good.

Around the table were about a dozen people including a painter, an archaeologist, an engineer, a retired journalist and others whose profession I did not catch. The atmosphere was self-conscious and refined and the talk inevitably turned to Gorbachev, Yeltsin and the return of capitalism.

Then they wanted to know about England. About the fog, the double-decker buses, Baker Street, Sherlock Holmes, Dickens. It was as if after seventy years they could wake up and find England just as it had been. And as if they too hoped it was possible that Russia could begin anew just where things had been left in 1917.

I tried to steer the conversation back to the Buryiats but there was little interest, only a certain unease.

'Let them celebrate their heritage, and we ours,' one of them said. I looked uncomfortably at a lady with an obviously Oriental face who sat at one end of the table. She did not look put out and perhaps she was one of those Buryiats who had converted and now considered herself a Russian.

'Relations have always been good here,' another said and added that no one wanted to see another Azerbaijan or Lithuania developing.

'My brother was in Kizil when they brought the dead bodies into the square,' the painter said, referring to neighbouring Tuva where the locals had forced thousands of Russians to flee in an unprecedented outburst of violence. The Tuvans had called the Russians 'colonialists' and wanted them out.

Nobody wanted to think much about the future. Talk turned to the past again. The archaeologist said the bones of the Hungarian poet, Sandor Petofi, had been found here and sent to the Pentagon for identification. The great nationalist had disappeared in the battle of Segesvar in July 1849 and may have been sent to Siberia as a prisoner. The Pentagon was using the expertise developed by examining the bones of MIAs handed over by Vietnam in order to establish their identities.

A heated argument broke out over the fate of an icebreaker ship built in Newcastle and sunk during the fighting between the Whites and the Reds. Two ships were commissioned, built, disassembled and transported across Siberia to the Baikal where they ferried trains across the lake. Some said the icebreaker lay full of treasure and in the deepest part of the lake, others at the table disputed this and claimed it was broken up and sold for scrap.

And did I know too that English missionaries were buried here? There was still a stone monument erected by one of them, Robert Yuille, in memory of his wife, Martha, and a hill called the

Anglachanka – the English woman.

It is an odd story. They made the first attempt to convert the Mongols under the mistaken impression this would provide a bridgehead to China, ruled by another 'tartar' tribe, the Manchus. In 1814, the London Missionary Society despatched an Englishman, Edward Stallybrass, two Scotsmen William Swan and Robert Yuille and a Swede, Cornelius Rahm, to the Baikal region. They set up a mission at Selenginsk, not far from Ulan Ude. Twenty years later the mission was abandoned as a failure. Few Buryiats were converted and not another British attempt to convert the heathen in Central Asia was made until James Gilmour arrived in Kalgan.

William Swan strikes a note of absolutism which Lenin might have been proud of when he described the objectives and challenge of a missionary in his reports home: Missionaries

> aim at nothing less than changing the moral face of the world. When they establish themselves in a heathen country, they set themselves to subvert the established belief of the people on the most important subjects – they give the lie to the gods the people worship and to their sages who taught them to do so – they lay the axe to their most deeply rooted prejudices, oppose their favourite dogmas and ancient customs – they say and do that which is equivalent to pouring contempt on their most venerated institutions, and draw down infamy on their priesthood, and ruin their craft – all to introduce a new, a foreign religion.

The mission's greatest achievement was the translation of the Bible into Mongolian. Although it required a prodigious intellectual effort, few copies survived and its existence was almost forgotten.

'We have a copy, just wait,' the librarian said suddenly and to my surprise went out and returned with a heavily bound volume. It was a copy of their translation of the Old Testament, approved in St Petersburg and printed in 1833.

Tatanya said she now took English tourists to see the monument in Selenginsk. The evening ended with toasts to the history of relations between England and Siberia.

The Buryiat poet had been trying to make conversation in French all over lunch but each sentence ended in a fit of embarrassed giggles. I found him rather peculiar especially after hearing that though a praised Buryiat poet, he wrote in Russian. I began to think him even more eccentric when he started talking enthusiastically about Zen Buddhism.

He insisted on taking me to meet the founder of the Buryiat

Buddhists' Association, started up nine months earlier by an academic at the Buryiat Institute. I followed the poet down the corridors of the Institute where every door opened up, like the cells of a prison, to reveal a small office.

In one of them sat Dr Abayev, a contemplative and middle-aged man, who was more than willing to explain his ideas.

His Association was founded 'with the acknowledgement of the vast spiritual, moral and intellectual potential, which the Buddha's teachings contained, its humanism, high efficiency in moral psychic development of a personality and self-fulfilment of the creative faculty of a person.'

Dr Abayev had translated from English the book *Zen and Creative Management* and was fascinated by the vast benefits the introduction of Zen philosophy could have on the thinking of the bureaucratic minds which ran Buryiatia.

'We Buryiats do not live in a genuine Oriental culture. Our mentality is now Western,' he said sadly. 'We have to find our way back.'

After years of study, he had reached the conclusion that of all the Buddhist branches of philosophy, the Zen school was closest to the Western Judeo-Christian mentality. Zen originated in China where it was called Chaan and stressed that the truth was not to be found in the scriptures but in man's own heart.

Much could be achieved, he said, by using the techniques of meditation and self-study developed by Chinese masters.

'Zen Buddhism is,' he declared, drawing deeply on a cigarette, 'one of the greatest achievements in human history.'

He came from a family of Christian converts and had spent many years translating Chinese texts from the Tang Dynasty into Russian. He had studied Chinese in Vladivostock but had later moved to the Institute of Oriental Studies in Moscow where he could access the resources of the Central Library. It had been difficult to obtain permission from the authorities to pursue his studies, he admitted.

'I argued that it was part of a great cultural tradition which we should study and preserve, irrespective of ideology,' he said.

The great Zen teachers had shown the oneness of everything, the path between extremes and the road to enlightenment, he said. He proposed that Party officials should be made to study Zen in order to change their thinking, to alter the patterns of a lifetime, otherwise he feared the system could not succeed.

I tried to imagine them in their suits sitting in their offices learning to do nothing and emptying their minds in meditation. Perhaps it would not be too hard for them.

'Yet the difficulty for us is that without a Zen master it is difficult to apply the teachings preserved in these works,' he said. 'But Zen is a technology of knowledge.'

He liked that phrase and repeated it.

'It is a method of transmitting not the letter of knowledge but the essence. It is an intellectual training system,' he continued.

The technique of riddles and dialogues enabled the teacher to impress upon his pupil the correct way of thought. It freed him from his traditional way of regarding the world so that he might take a sudden leap in understanding.

The problem, though, was how to apply these methods in the Soviet Union where there are no Zen masters. It was here that he had had his own burst of inspiration – computers.

The personal computer, he said, is a tool for the creative analysis of data but could it not be programmed along Zen Buddhist lines to serve as a substitute for a master?

He pulled out a lengthy typewritten document he had written and partially translated into English.

It was a proposal for a computerised training system for the solving of mental problems.

'We have to get people to think again after all these years of mental and psychic death. Otherwise there will be no perestroika,' he said tapping his head. 'In a dialogue with the computer, the user will rediscover his psychological possibilities.'

He sat back at his desk and lit another cigarette and said, 'What do you think?'

I was not sure if he was serious or joking and the poet who had listened to our talk giggled at my silence.

During my last days in Ulan Ude, I spent a lot of time meeting nationalistic Buryiats who were determined to shake their countrymen out of their political apathy. They wanted to force the Russians out, first of all by cutting all the financial incentives, then by privatising the land and returning to traditional agricultural and pastoral practices, and if need be, by violence. They feared that if nothing was done, the Buryiats would disappear.

'We have a right to fight for our future,' one said bluntly.

All of them wanted to declare independence and some wanted to join Mongolia. Opinions varied but the overall intention was to pick up where things had been left at the end of the First World War.

One day a professor came along to one of these meetings with a very different view of the past. In his own way Professor Chagdurov, an expert in philology at the Buryiat Pedagogical Institute, had his own eccentric view of the role the Baikal region played in world affairs.

He was an enthusiastic follower of a theory developed by a brilliant young Russian philologist Vladislav Ilyitch-Svitich, who had tragically died in a car accident before fully expounding his belief that all the 2,800 languages known to exist derive from six families which share roots in 1,200 common words.

Professor Chagdurov was convinced that the Baikal region holds the key to understanding the origins of languages. Some evidence has been found to suggest that modern man first appeared in Siberia. The climate, especially in the Gobi, was once far warmer and wetter than it is now.

The professor claimed that the Buryiats could trace their origins as far back as the Sumerians. In fact he thought that the Sumerians might well have originated from Baikal.

There was, or so he said, a well-known theory that the Sumerians had come to Mesopotamia from the Far East. Indeed some Japanese scholars suspected the Sumerians were originally Japanese. It was something to do with the shape of their heads, he said vaguely.

It was hard to see what any of this had to do with politics and besides it seemed rather far-fetched. I suggested we continue over dinner and we went to one of the few restaurants in the city. It was inside a hotel and the large dining-room had a band and a dance floor. Everyone there was drinking too much vodka too quickly and the din was awesome.

Despite the noise, the professor began to talk quickly and fluently, displaying an impressive erudition.

He asserted that there are strong linguistic and cultural connections between the Sumerians and Mongols or rather their predecessors, the Turkic-Mongol Hunnish tribes of Central Asia.

The Sumerians prayed to the God Uta and worshipped fire, the sun and light. A day in Sumerian language was *udu* and in Mongolian, it is *uder* and the word for sunrise in Mongolian is *ur*.

'Or take another word, *Denger* which means God in Sumerian, in Mongolian the word is *Tenger*,' he said with a triumphant air. He also maintained that some of the letters found on 3,000-year-old clay tablets written by the Sumerians are strikingly similar to the early Turkic alphabet created in the fifth century AD in Central Asia.

As Professor Chagdurov continued his story above the loud music, I wondered how the nomadic and pastoral Huns could possibly be connected with the Sumerians who invented urban civilisation.

The link was Zoroastrianism, the fire-worshipping religion which was widespread all over Asia. Zoroastrianism was the religion first of the ancient Persians and then of the Assyrians whose empires succeeded the Sumerian civilisation in Mesopotamia. It now only survives in Persia and among the Parsees in India.

The prophet Zarathustra (also written Zoroaster) after whom it is called was not its founder but a later reformer. Professor Chagdurov said that Zarathustra was born near the shores of Lake Baikal and a relief of the winged god of the Zoroastrians had been found carved on a cliff face near the lake.

Even today *zora* means to prophesy in Mongolian. Traces of zorastic practices are evident in Mongolian custom, particularly rituals of purification by fire which William Rubruk observed in the thirteenth century. Visitors like Rubruk were, for instance, obliged to walk between two fires to cleanse themselves.

The Mongolians and Tibetans were also influenced by the zorastic practice of exposing the dead on 'towers of silence' where the corpses were eaten by vultures.

According to Zarathustra, the world was involved in a Manichean struggle between good and evil, light and darkness. There were seven gods but evil was represented by Akriman and goodness by Hormusta who also represented the sky and light.

Zarathustra was the prophet of the king of the Medes, a group of six tribes whose realm extended across much of Central Asia from the frontiers of China to the Caspian. They had fought a long war with the ancient Assyrians, the regional superpower, and under King Huvashashtra, defeated them in 602 BC.

Huvashashtra was a historic figure who, the professor said, was half Turkic-Mongol on his mother's side. He was known to be a just king and had in the long and bloody war with the Assyrians championed the side of poor ordinary people.

He became a legend and through the centuries his name had somehow become corrupted to its present form Gesar, a legendary king, whose struggle against evil was the stuff of an oral epic tale which exists in dozens of versions all over Central Asia. It is still recounted in Mongolia, Inner Mongolia, Tibet and Kazakhstan by professional storytellers and can take over a week to recite.

The connection between Huvashashtra and Gesar seemed rather weak to me but the professor was now warming to his main theme.

Before the Second World War Stalin had provided funds for research into the epic, and preparations were made to celebrate the 600th anniversary of its composition although in fact no one had the faintest idea of its age.

Then in 1949 Stalin unleashed a new wave of repression directed against folk religion. Shamans were arrested and killed and the recorders of the epic, now condemned as reactionaries, were dismissed from their posts. The full text of the Gesar epic has never been published but it was written down in 1948.

At great personal risk a copy of the recorded text was rescued and the professor said it was soon to be published. He was organising an international conference on the King Gesar epic in 1995.

It is still immensely popular among the Buryiats. The epic recounts how Tenger, the god of light, sent his beloved son to the earth because a fierce war between East and West had begun. This, the professor said, was a memory of the long war with the Assyrians.

The land was devastated. The rivers had run dry, the grass had withered, the cattle had died and the people were starving. Tenger sent his son to rescue humanity and set them free.

Gesar descended not as a god but as a human being who was born in a tepee, swimming in his own urine and shit.

In the epic Gesar takes up the struggles against the demons and monsters who were causing these calamities but refuses to use violence. He is against killing and blood. Although the instruments of war are sent to him from heaven, he is unable to use them. Instead he achieves his goal by other means.

On one occasion, he fights the monsters with the sort of stick nomads use to beat felt. His enemies are never killed but tied up and publicly humiliated.

The epic was constantly changed and embroidered to reflect whatever new oppressions were suffered by ordinary people.

The earliest form of the epic he had been able to identify dated back to the seventh century AD when tantric Buddhism from India was imposed on the Tibetans by military force.

In this version King Gesar becomes an ass, a beast of burden for the monsters who represent the new religion. King Gesar defends the traditional, peaceful ways of the shamans.

Subsequently the lamas tried to suppress the cult of King Gesar and destroyed all manuscripts of the epic.

When the Russians forced the conversion of the western Buryiats to Russian Orthodox Christianity, another version evolved out of the resistance to this change.

And when both Buddhism and shamanism were being persecuted by the Communists, yet another version was composed. In this King Gesar is introduced to a girl by the Chinese but refuses to marry her.

Yet he spends a night with her on the steppes and then sends her away. Later she has two children – the Dalai Lama and the Bogd Khan. New variations of the tale are still being composed.

'All other national epics are about great warriors, feudal chiefs and their conquests and battles. In the Buryiat epic, King Gesar is a hero of the simple people. He always appears when the people are oppressed, when they sought a way out, some hope, a dream ...' he said.

'That is why Gesar cannot resort to superhuman force but only the articles used in daily life,' he said. 'The epics are a protest against force and violence.'

The restaurant was emptying now. The professor cast his eye around the room where a waitress was trying to shove some shouting and drunken youths out.

'And now you will know why I do not believe that violence can save the Buryiats. It is not our way,' he said with a shy smile.

If you looked carefully Markizova Angelsina Cheshkova still bore traces of her former beauty but an air of nervous vagueness has replaced the confident smile of the little girl in the photographs.

She lived in a well-furnished but ordinary apartment on the top of one of the innumerable high-rise blocks on the outskirts of Moscow. She brought out old pictures of herself and a few recent newspaper cuttings. One showed a petite and radiant Oriental girl in a silk cocktail dress shaking hands at a reception.

When she was small, she was 'Gelje', the smiling little Buryiat girl who gave Stalin a bouquet of flowers. It was the most famous propaganda photograph of the 1930s and hung in every classroom. It showed the love of little children everywhere for Uncle Stalin and his kindness and humanity.

She had not kept any of these photographs and had agreed to meet me with obvious reluctance. Two years ago she had returned to Buryiatia to set up a branch of the Memorial organisation which keeps alive the fate of the millions who perished in Stalin's prisons and camps. Now, I suppose, as another kind of symbol she felt obliged to talk about herself.

Her efforts in Ulan Ude had been far from successful. She published an advertisement in the local paper calling for the survivors of the camps or the relatives of the missing to come forward.

Those who came to the meeting received a signed copy of the Gulag Archipelago but only eighteen survivors turned up and a few relatives of the dead, but no one from the countryside where most Buryiats live.

'The Party's influence is so immense there, I feel ashamed to call myself a Buryiat,' she said. She spoke disparagingly about the place – the lack of culture, the corruption and rottenness of the youth – with a touch of a Muscovite's contempt for a rural backwater.

'In the presidential elections they just gave people two bottles of vodka and told them how to vote,' she said. 'Hardly any voted for Yeltsin. The young don't have pride or dignity any more.'

She now thought of herself more as a Russian than a Mongol and showed little interest in the prospects of independence from Russia.

'I especially dislike the snobbery of the Buryiats,' she said wrinkling her small nose. 'It is there from top to bottom especially among the Party leadership. When they come to Moscow they change entirely and become so obsequious.'

Yet the horrors inflicted on Buryiatia were as awful as any suffered under Stalin.

'Recently, I went to a small village with only a hundred inhabitants. They had a quota, so many people from each village arrested for such and such a crime. So in this place they imprisoned twenty peasants and accused them of being followers of Trotsky,' she said.

'They were just herdsmen, shepherds. Most of them had never heard of Trotsky but were forced to confess or accuse their neighbours of being Trotskyists. The authorities just had orders to arrest twenty people. Sometimes a whole family would be arrested so that no 'roots' would remain.'

She paused and prepared small cups of fresh coffee for us. She borrowed a cigarette and smoked it hungrily. She must herself have been of these 'roots' that had not been pulled out.

'I don't usually smoke,' she said, 'but when I talk about these things . . .'

She paused again.

'It is very hard for people in the West to comprehend what it was like then and what kind of fear people here lived with,' I suggested.

'Yes, it is beyond human understanding,' she said abruptly. I waited for her to say something more but instead she hesitantly began to talk about her life.

'When I was about seven, a delegation from Buryiatia came to Moscow to celebrate a festival of Buryiat culture. There were in all sixty-seven prominent people as well as model workers, peasants from a collective farm which had achieved great results and so on.

'My father was second secretary of the regional Party committee. I remember it quite well. I was living with my mother who was studying at a medical college in Moscow. My father came up in the delegation and lived in a hotel.

'It happened by accident. I was playing in a corner of the room and I overheard that Father was going to the Kremlin to see Stalin. Of course, I wanted to go with him. My father said it was impossible. I had no pass and was not a member of the delegation.

'I remember my mother supported me and decided to buy a bouquet of flowers for me to take. It was the 27th of January 1936,' she said and drank some coffee her daughter had made for us.

'Once I went back to the Kremlin and tried to find the banquet hall again but I couldn't. It had been refurbished but I even went and looked at the archive films to refresh my memory. The sight made me feel so bad I couldn't watch them.

'I was in the banquet listening to speeches and then had to go up to the podium and give the bouquet to someone. Stalin and other leaders and ministers were on the podium together with some famous Buryiats. I came from the back and someone led me to Stalin. He turned his head and took the flowers and put me on the table. Lots of cameras clicked and flashed.

'I think Stalin made a speech about these flowers from the children of the Buryiat-Mongol Republic. I don't remember what happened next. I just remember being anxious to see if I was going to get a present.

'Stalin called me Gelje – from Angelsina – and gave me a wrist-watch. He said that I would not be able to carry a record player because it was in a big box. I replied that I would call my father to help me.' She stopped there, reached for another cigarette and began again more defensively.

'It was not something that had been planned at all. It was spontaneous, yet there was a lot of talk among the delegates afterwards. Some of them said it should have been their son or their daughter who was chosen. It was all rubbish.

'The next day I was famous all over the world. The photograph appeared in all the newspapers. It symbolised the happy childhood of Soviet children. It showed that Stalin was a close friend of all children.

'The symbol took on a life of its own for the next sixty years that was quite different from my own. The sculptor Georgi Lavrov made a statue of the meeting. There were 3 million copies made of Stalin holding me in his arms. One was nine metres (twenty-seven feet) high and made of white stone and it stood in the metro station in Moscow called Stalin. They only removed it and changed the station's name after his death.

'Until two years ago nobody knew that Stalin had both parents killed and the girl was sent to live in exile.' She stopped again.

'In 1939 Stalin had Lavrov arrested and he stayed in a labour camp for seventeen years. I have met him and he is now ninety-six years old. He had been in France at the Academy of Art and only returned in 1935. After his arrest, his French wife starved to death.'

She was speaking almost as if she was confessing. As if she was responsible for what had happened and had tried to put the blame on her other self but the past had now come back to claim her.

She resumed again. 'After the meeting, we went back to Ulan Ude. My father was arrested in 1938 and my mother was exiled. My uncle wrote a letter to Stalin saying that my father was a hero during the civil war who fought against Admiral Kolchak and a founder of the Republic's Communist Party so how could he be an enemy of the people?

'My father had attended the University of the Toilers of the East in Moscow. He was an original Bolshevik revolutionary who joined in December 1919. He had been an interpreter and worked on the newspaper called *Sunrise – Ur* in Buryiat – which was edited in Irkutsk by Jaroslav Hašek, the author of *The Good Soldier Schweik*.

'There was one episode many years later when I was in Buryiatia for the sixtieth anniversary of the republic when an old man asked me if I was Gelje. When I said yes, he broke down and started crying. During the civil war, the old man and five others were arrested by Kolchak's men and were going to be shot. My father led a guerilla detachment which freed them. He took an oath to remember Markizov and all his children.

'He was living in Buryiatia when he was arrested. I was at school so I did not see him being arrested. When I came home all his books were on the floor and everything was upside down. My mother witnessed his arrest. He told her not to worry because he was innocent. They would soon find out their mistake and set him free. No one would believe he was a traitor to Stalin.

'Last year I saw the papers of the interrogation and the confession he had signed. It said: "I was a Japanese spy and was preparing a terrorist attack on Stalin."

'From the signature I could tell he had been tortured because of the big "m" and the small "a".

'I know how he was tortured. Someone told me, who had come out alive. At the start it was fairly gentle, like being forced to sit on the edge of the chair for seventeen hours. Then for three days he was dressed in winter clothes and kept near an oven. When they brought him back to the prison cell, his feet were so swollen he was unable to pull off his boots. They had to be cut off.

'The most elaborate torture was to tie him between two chairs and hang him upside down. When he lost consciousness, they woke him up and gave him a paper to sign. The rest of the tortures were those used against prisoners everywhere. After he signed, he was taken out and executed. The date was the 2nd of July 1938.

'He was rehabilitated in 1955. The document admitted there was no evidence he was responsible for any crimes. There was a brief apology.

'At that time few people knew how to apply for rehabilitation but fortunately my aunt and her husband knew the procedures.

'After his execution my mother, brother and myself were sent to Turkestan, a city in southern Kazakhstan near the Syr Darya River. It's a beautiful town. We lived in a small village and there were lots of orchards. I remember how warm it was after the Siberian cold. I read in papers recently that now they have opened a Muslim university there.

'My mother, Dominika Federovna, worked as a doctor and we stayed there for two years.

'She had to report every day to the NKVD so they could keep an eye on her. She tried to find out what had happened to her husband. They told her he had been given a ten-year sentence with no right of correspondence. This is what they said when someone had been executed but we did not know that then.

'In November 1940, she was found dead in her hospital with her throat cut. She was thirty-two when she died and I have never found her grave. My brother and I were just kids then but even so I don't believe she committed suicide. They told us she killed herself with a broken bottleneck. It does not make any sense because the wound was very thin and in the hospital she had access to sharp knives.

'There are lots of reasons why she would not have committed suicide. She was needed at home. I was twelve and my brother was fourteen years old. If she was planning this, she would have sent us to my aunt in Moscow or made other plans.

'It is clear to me that she was assassinated. Perhaps something happened the day before. A sick child was brought to the hospital and died. Probably the parents blamed her because she was an enemy of the people.

'I think it was the NKVD. It was nothing for them to kill a person like that. Of course, I cannot be sure . . . yet such an organisation . . . such a ruler . . .' She hesitated, overcome with the emotion.

'But why didn't they assassinate me?' she resumed. 'It was normal for the NKVD to do that to the children of enemies of the people when they reached fourteen and sixteen. I knew of such cases. Or at least they would imprison the children.

'Afterwards we wrote a letter to my aunt in Moscow and she replied, asking us to join her. In January 1941 we travelled by ourselves to Moscow. After the war started we returned to Ulan Ude with my aunt's family. Her husband was at the front.

'In Moscow there were a lot of people and no one knew my background. Perhaps the portrait somehow defended me, maybe NKVD officers knew who I was, but they could not be sure what Stalin's attitude to me was. If they repressed me, then they might be repressed too.

'When I had finished school I applied for a university place and changed my name from Arolan to Sergei so that Stalin didn't find me.

I changed the details about my mother too. Yet no one noticed that I was born when my mother was only eleven years old. No one scrutinised my papers.

'At university I studied Chinese and wrote my thesis about the women's movement in China. Stalin's daughter, Svetlana, was in the university. She was one year older and we met in the history faculty.'

It sounded more and more unbelievable. That she should gain admittance to a university reserved for only the most privileged by a transparent lie – and there meet the daughter of the man responsible for her parents' death.

'Oh, yes, she knew who I was and I met her in classrooms,' Angelsina continued. 'But I never cared to be on friendly terms because our fathers were enemies. When she presented her thesis, she read it out in public. She declared at the beginning that the basis of her diploma study was the works of Comrade Stalin, so we knew she would pass.

'I graduated from Moscow State University in 1951. Two years later Stalin died. When I heard the news, I stood by the loudspeaker weeping, thinking only that my daughter never had a chance to see the leader, the Vozhd, alive.'

When her daughter was eight months old, her first husband became cultural attaché in the New Delhi Embassy. In India she met Nehru and the Dalai Lama and taught Russian.

'When people started being released from the camps, only then did I begin to think differently. Only then I suddenly understood the scale of the agony of our state,' Angelsina said and began to talk about her second husband.

She worked in the Soviet Institute of Oriental Studies. The Institute refused to publish her doctoral thesis on relations between Cambodia and Vietnam before the arrival of the French. It revealed a pattern of Vietnamese aggression against Cambodia which was politically inconvenient to acknowledge.

Her future second husband was in a labour camp but there he somehow also wrote a candidate doctoral thesis on Vietnam which he sent to the Institute. It disappeared but later he found his ideas used in academic papers published by others.

After his release he wrote another thesis about India but became involved with the dissident movement. He organised discussion groups on the future of Socialism, wrote leaflets and distributed them in postboxes. All the leaflets were returned to the KGB in 1957 and he was arrested as a state criminal and given an eight-year sentence.

'People were not ready to accept his ideas then,' she said. 'He understood that our kind of Socialism was not the real one.'

After six years he was released and they fell in love. In 1967 she remarried.

'I was very interested in talking to him and he thought I was very pretty,' she said simply. 'With him I started to understand about Stalin.

'I think Stalin knew exactly what happened to my family. He signed the lists of prisoners given to him and Markizov was well known to him. With him they also arrested the Republic's first secretary.'

'Why did it happen?' I asked, curious to see what she, of all people, would say.

'Stalin was a criminal, a pathological criminal. Look at how he was always behind the curtain during Bukharin's trial, how he organised it. I don't consider him to be human,' she said.

After Stalin's death, the ubiquitous pictures were removed. 'I felt distanced from the portrait. It lived its own life, I lived mine. I didn't imagine a time when it would be of interest again,' she said.

In 1988 *New World* magazine published an article about 'Gelje', describing the fate of her parents and adding that afterwards she lived 'unknown and in poverty'.

After Memorial started up two years ago, she went to Ulan Ude. A man from the regional party committee telephoned her in her hotel and demanded a meeting.

'He was anxious to meet me because they wanted to create the appearance that all such informal movements were initiated by the Party,' she said.

'The officials quickly prepared documents to rehabilitate my father as a Communist. They held a ceremony to give me documents posthumously rehabilitating him as a Party member,' she said.

'I said that I appreciated these efforts but I didn't think my father would be delighted. Why? Because the Party to which he gave his life had betrayed him. The officials were shocked,' she said.

She received the documents renewing his Party membership on January 25th, 1989, thirty-five years after his rehabilitation when the criminal charges against him were erased. She also received an envelope with his last two months' pay.

'It was as if my life was specially designed to illustrate Stalin's crimes,' she finished.

Eleven

Tuva – Among the People of the Far Forest

Tuva is the lost world of Central Asia. A vast basin of impenetrable forest and swamp hidden behind a rampart of high mountain ranges which the first Europeans reached little more than a century ago.

The mighty Yenisey River, the Amazon of Siberia, rises in Tuva and forces its way north through a narrow valley. When it reaches the Arctic Ocean 4,000 miles later, the river's mouth is a hundred miles wide. Only after the ice melts in late April does the Yenisey become navigable and offer an easy route into this hidden country.

A small passenger plane from Ulan Ude takes the visitor west and up over a jagged rim of snowcapped peaks before descending and crossing a limitless expanse of jungle green. This is the taiga. A word which in its original sense means the wild, the unknown, the incomprehensible.

'The utter loneliness of its waiting lands appalled us,' confessed the explorer Douglas Carruthers who in 1910 was the first Englishman to reach Tuva.

He travelled on foot and raft, exhausted and depressed through a 'vast sea of choking vegetation, dwarfed by the giant world of forest.' It was the worst struggle with nature the veteran explorer of Africa and Asia ever experienced. On the first day, it took his party two hours to cross two hundred yards.

Much of it was still unmapped and unexplored when he arrived on the eve of the Chinese revolution. Tuva lay nominally under the control of the Manchu empire but the first Russian colonialists had begun filtering in twenty or thirty years before, living in scattered farms, growing a few crops or trading furs but keeping to the banks of its winding rivers and mosquito-infested lakes.

Within a few years the turmoil of the Russian Revolution had closed it to the rest of the world. When I boarded the plane, it was unclear whether Tuva was even now open to foreigners. Tuva was reported to be on the verge of civil war. A few months earlier the special crack army unit, the Black Berets, had been sent in to keep the peace. Since then few reports had filtered out even in the Soviet press.

Carruthers had called it *Unknown Mongolia* when he wrote a two-volume account of his journey from Minusinsk on the Yenisey, south through Tuva, across the Altai Mountains and into the Dzungarian Basin to the Mountains of Heaven in Chinese Turkestan.

Geographically and culturally, Tuva is part of Mongolia. The Sayansk mountain range which is nearly as high as the Alps curves in a circle around the western limits of Mongolia and marks the watershed between eastern and western Siberia.

The inhabitants are not Mongolians though but a forgotten Turkic-speaking race whom the Mongols called the Uriankhai and Chinese called 'People of the Far Forest'.

In 1921 these forest-dwellers became, of all people, the founders of the world's third-oldest Socialist state which they called 'Tannu Tuva' meaning the 'Country of the High Mountains'.

Carruthers, after struggling through the dense thickets of virgin forest and the evil-smelling swamps into which his horse sank up to his saddle, recorded his pleasure in coming across the 'silent, shy, forest lovers, the reindeer-keeping Uriankhai'.

> It was strange to come suddenly upon these quaint and interesting people, living their retiring, self-centred lives away in the depths of this remote part of the world.
>
> Such a sight was well worth coming so long a way to see, and it will remain vividly impressed on my mind. In the evening the slanting rays of the sun caught the rich sepia and white of the birch-bark coverings of the tepees and showed them up against the dark forest behind, the curling smoke of the 'wigwams' rose in blue films, and the reindeer trooped home-wards for the night, herded by small boys and old women; then the silent night – broken only by the grunt of the herds – settled down upon the quiet valley in this far removed and remote corner of the world, and hid from view the quaint encampment.

The Uriankhai, cut off in their inaccessible basin, wanted nothing from the outside world, he reported. They obtained everything they needed from their reindeer.

However in 1914 they wrote to St Petersburg and asked Nicholas II, the White Tsar, as they called him, to be taken under his protection.

'We are a small country left with no one to protect us. As we are few, how will we defend ourselves?' the highest lama wrote. It may be though that they did so involuntarily under pressure from army officers ever anxious to extend the Tsar's dominions.

In 1911 the Tuvans declared themselves independent but rejected an invitation by the Bogd Khan to join the new Mongolian Republic. After the Russian Revolution, they fought off an attack by Chinese troops who had marched in and occupied Mongolia.

With the outbreak of the civil war, the quietude of their existence was shattered for good. The Communist partisans seized power from Tsarist officers and the name of the tiny capital was changed from Town of the White Tsar, to Kizil, meaning red.

About this time the Polish-born geologist Dr Ossendowski, the author of *Beasts, Men and Gods*, escaped across the Sayansk mountains from Krasnoyarsk, crossed over the Tannu Ola mountains which separate Tuva from Mongolia and reached Ulan Bator where he met the Baron Ungern-Sternberg.

In 1920 he fled his home and certain arrest to spend the winter alone in the taiga. Then with the coming of spring, he followed the Yenisey south and witnessed the annual spectacle of the thaw.

Amid the huge blocks of ice grinding and splashing against each other, he saw to his horror the bodies of executed counter-revolutionaries, the soldiers of the retreating Admiral Kolchak.

> Hundreds of these bodies with heads and hands cut off, with mutilated faces and bodies half burned, with broken skulls, floated and mingled with the blocks of ice, looking for their graves; or, turning in the furious whirlpools among the jagged blocks, they were ground and torn to pieces into shapeless masses . . .

As he continued his journey, he found corpses and evidence of executions everywhere. At last he bribed a border guard with a pair of trousers and crossed into Uriankhai country.

There he linked up with fleeing White officers, fought off Red partisans and met the Uriankhai – Soyots as the Russians call them – who helped him across the border.

'They are the eternal enemies of war and of the shedding of blood,' the Polish geologist said.

Away back in the thirteenth century they preferred to move out of their native land and take refuge in the North rather than fight or become part of the empire of the bloody conqueror Genghis Khan, who wanted to add to his forces these wonderful horsemen and skilled archers. Three times in their history they have thus trekked northward to avoid struggle and now no one can say that on the hands of the Soyots there has ever been seen human blood.

They behaved the same way, he said, when the Russian Communists, 'mad with blood and crime brought this infection into their land'.

The Uriankhai avoided all meetings and encounters with the Red troops or partisans and again trekked with their families and cattle far into remote mountains and forests.

Either Dr Ossendowski had not been telling the truth or something very unusual was now taking place in Tuva. Since 1990 the Tuvans had taken up arms against the Russians, shooting several, burning their houses or attacking their vehicles. Others received death threats and thousands had fled to Krasnoyarsk. A violent anti-Russian and Nationalist movement had suddenly blown up.

From the air the high-rise apartment blocks of Kizil stuck up like white pegs out of a reddish wasteland. On the ground it looked even less inspiring. A taxi took me to the only guesthouse in the city, a low, charmless, two-storey building hidden amongst the trees by the river.

The streets were empty but there were no signs of violent unrest, merely a somnolent lethargy. The weather was hot and humid and the white blossom drifting from the trees stuck to my sweating skin.

For several hours the receptionist refused to open up a room for me and when he did, I found myself in a suite where the bathroom taps dripped and the water pipes wheezed and coughed all night.

The place had no restaurant. Although there was another hotel next door it was closed and there was nowhere else to eat. Finally someone led me through the kitchen into a closed restaurant which was full of flies and stank of stale mutton fat and found me some cold food.

It was depressing. I knew no one in Kizil and had just a few phone numbers that the Tuvan teachers I had met in Tsaghan Nor near Lake Hubsogol had given me. There was no answer at any of them.

The night was hot and oppressive and I slept badly, dreaming of a river of corpses.

Next morning I tracked down a teacher whom the Tuvan girls had suggested I meet and who worked at a teachers' training college. Rolanda was a tall and bespectacled Tuvan who spoke English in calm, cultivated tones.

She introduced me to her class of eighteen- or nineteen-year-old girls starting their first year of English. They were mostly from the country and revealed a curious mixture of racial characteristics. Some had high cheekbones but the reddish hair and freckles of a European, others the finer bones and pallor of the Chinese and the rest had the round and deep-brown cheeks of Mongolian country girls. Some Tuvans even have Nordic features, blue eyes and fair hair as if this place lay across some genetic borderland between East and West.

When Rolanda could get away she showed me around Kizil. When Carruthers passed this way there were no towns at all in Tuva and no buildings other than Buddhist temples. Even fifty years ago Kizil was little more than a village of log houses with 300 or so inhabitants.

Most of the town centre was now given over to a huge concrete piazza bounded on one side by the Party and government headquarters and on the other an odd-looking cultural centre with wooden carvings on its walls. A statue of Lenin stood between them as well as an elaborate fountain with concrete reindeer in which little naked children were splashing around.

Behind the cultural centre was a park with railings and a fading placard advertising *Gone with the Wind*. A statue of Stalin had once stood there. A bit further on we stopped before a black bust of a man I did not recognise.

'This is Toka, our Stalin,' Rolanda said with an air of civilised disdain. Toka, she said, ruled Tuva for forty-four years and continued even after Stalin's death to stay in power until only his own death in 1973 removed him.

He was installed as General Secretary of the Tuvan Communist Party in 1929 when Stalin made himself unchallenged ruler of the Soviet Union. Toka was a Tuvan who was sent to be educated at the University of the Toilers of the East following the civil war.

Like Choibalsan, he was set up as a 'Little Stalin'. After the Second World War lots more of these Little Stalins would appear all over Eastern Europe.

Everything that Stalin did in Moscow, Toka had to duplicate in Kizil. Between 1937 and 1939, Toka had all the leading members of the Party, including the entire politburo, executed or imprisoned on trumped-up charges. The monasteries were closed and the lamas liquidated. The alphabet – the same Uighur letters used in Mongolia – and in fact the entire culture of the Tuvans was systematically suppressed. Leading Party members were ordered to marry Russian women selected by the NKVD, even if this entailed divorcing their existing wives.

Tuva was nominally an independent country but recognised as such only by Moscow and Ulan Bator. In practice the Soviets ran everything as a copy of Moscow and in 1944 Toka brought Tuva 'voluntarily' into the Soviet Union. It became the last part of the Soviet Union to be annexed. Rolanda did not know why the fiction of Tuva's independence was maintained for so long and for what reason it was then terminated.

Nobody I asked later seemed to know but it was probably because China under Stalin's ally, Chiang Kai-shek, had claims on both Mongolia and Tuva since they had both been part of the Manchu empire. Granting both states independence was a way of postponing a decision on their future.

'No, no, we don't hate him, Toka,' Rolanda continued, raising her slender eyebrows at the thought. 'What for? He was a victim like everyone else. He was really one of us.'

The rest of the world had never heard of Tuva let alone Toka but here in this most obscure corner of the world, the pattern had been repeated. But why? What point did it serve? It was the mass production of Stalinism on industrial lines and it conjured up in my mind an image of infinite repetition, of Stalins repeating themselves on ever smaller scales like the trick of computer graphics or a mystifying pattern of symmetry in natural structures. Perhaps if one tried, one could discover a similar pattern with little copies of Toka reproduced down every level and sublevel of the bureaucracy in Tuva.

We walked on towards the river and the hotel.

'This is called the Cottage,' she said, pointing to my guesthouse. 'It was Toka's residence where he lived with his family. It is now run as a private guesthouse.'

As a dictator's residence, it looked rather modestly suburban, the only luxury being an outsized billiard table downstairs. It occurred to me that I might be sleeping in the bedroom of a mass murderer.

Rolanda pointed across the street to a much larger building with a forest of aerials on the roof, 'And that is the house of Soviet power in Tuva. It is the headquarters of the NKVD.

'So you see, he was just a puppet of the secret police,' she said. Over the next few days I watched the building to see who came or went but it showed few signs of any activity. Occasionally a man with a briefcase entered through the door and passed under the eye of a video camera or a Lada drove up to the side gate which slid open silently.

We walked back along the banks of the River Yenisey. Even here it is several hundred yards wide and was flowing strongly.

'A big battle took place here during the civil war when White armies were prevented from crossing it,' Rolanda said. We stopped to look at a memorial obelisk topped by a red star. On either side the names of the Red partisans who had given their lives were listed. She was not quite sure about the details but thought it was the Baron Ungern-Sternberg who was defeated here in 1921.

'What do we know of our history? Everything is secret here,' she said bluntly. 'All I care about now is my daughter. I want her life to be better than mine.' She was separated from her husband and struggling to raise her daughter by herself.

'I am not involved in these politics,' she went on as we strolled along the river bank and looked at the children fishing or swimming in the grey-green waters.

'I am neutral. I don't trust these Nationalists who are now saying we must kick out all the Russians. They just want the power themselves. What do people here understand about democracy? It's a joke. The Russians are not bad people. Why should we blame them for all these bad things? We should examine ourselves.' She stopped and then her thoughts went off in another direction.

'We are now poorer than ever. I earn only 350 roubles a month, how can anyone live on this? People like me do all the work but the officials have everything. Did you know there are 2.3 bureaucrats to every worker in Tuva?'

She stopped for a while, embarrassed at having revealed so much to a foreigner. 'I once went to England, you know. I remember Windsor Castle, the Houses of Parliament. I think of myself not as a Tuvan or a Russian but as a cosmopolitan. I speak German too, I know Goethe, Schiller, Dickens, Shakespeare, Byron.'

She recited the names as though they were a charm that could ward off the barbarity around her.

We stopped in front of another obelisk with a large concrete globe stuck in the middle. Underneath it said in English and Russian: The Exact Centre of Asia.

Several Tuvan youths in T-shirts and jeans who were sitting by the monument lurched over to us. They were slightly menacing and wanted to know who I was but then looked with unconcealed astonishment after Rolanda explained. One of them put his arm through mine and tried to drag us away for a drink, mumbling in broken English. He said he was a student of agronomy. We shook him off.

'You know, gangs of youths began stopping people in the street or on the bus and testing them to see if they spoke Tuvan. If they couldn't, they would beat them up. I speak Tuvan although I hardly use it but many people, especially the young in the cities, never learned it. It was not taught in the schools. They told us it was primitive and if you wanted a job, you had to speak Russian,' Rolanda said.

'This is what has happened to our youth. They have lost their culture, their dignity. Now it's just violence and drink,' she said, wrinkling her elegant features in disgust. 'And now they talk of democracy!

'In the summer the streets used to be full of people, sitting around playing guitars,' she said, 'but since last year's violence people were afraid to go out and stayed at home.' We strolled back through the town and she went home herself.

I went to eat in a restaurant near the park. Loud music was coming out of the building which had a grand entrance supported by two pillars. Outside, a tall and fat militiaman in black, perhaps one of the famous Black Berets, was being taunted by several Tuvan youths who looked like pigmies beside his bulk.

Inside it was a mixture of bizarre contrasts. An elegant staircase divided in two up to the eating-hall like in a ducal mansion. The restaurant was equally pretentious with high ceilings raised by more pillars and below were a few sparse rows of vacant tables. On a small stage in the corner four Russians with long hair, beards and T-shirts played drums and electric guitars half-heartedly.

A hefty blonde waitress appeared infrequently out of a side door as if she had a bit part in some stage drama. Several groups of Russians were sitting together drinking heavily. From time to time, one would stagger across to the other table shouting.

A group of Tuvans came in, small and nut-brown like Amazonian Indians. The waitress bustled forward and declared loudly there was no more vodka being served and the restaurant was closing. The Tuvans, who were wearing suits and seemed to be from out of town, stared at the Russians.

The atmosphere became tense but the waitress, taller than the Tuvans, began to push them towards the door impatiently insisting they leave. They began protesting and gesticulating and the Russians watched with amusement to see who would win.

'This is discrimination. Go back to Russia!' one of the Tuvans yelled shaking his fist. 'This is our land, you can't tell us what to do.'

'Go back to your country and leave us alone!' another joined in and they began talking to each other in Tuvan. The others in the restaurant got up to leave and I joined them; if a fight broke out, no one would know I was not a Russian. As I left the militiaman was coming up the stairs talking into a hand-held radio.

Two Russians controlled the Democratic Movement in Tuva and I went to see them in the local parliament building. Yenrich and Juri were both followers of Yeltsin but said that few people outside of Kizil had voted for him.

A Tuvan Democratic Movement which was set up in February 1990 had died away after its leader, Kadyr-col Bicheldei, a philologist had moved to Moscow after being elected to the Supreme Soviet.

'The anti-Russian feeling was just connected to last year's elections,' Yenrich said, passing a hand over his balding head. 'People just played on the nationalist feeling of the population to get elected. You see the cultural level is not very high here.'

He was a lawyer born in Siberia who moved to Tuva twelve years earlier, attracted by the fishing and the rafting.

He admitted that so far 10,000 Russians had fled Tuva over the previous ten months. It was a significant part of the Russian population which was about 120,000 strong. Tuva's total population was some 300,000, leaving the ethnic Tuvans unlike the Buryiats still a majority in their own land.

'They were afraid for their lives and for their children,' Yenrich said. He blamed the violence on provocateurs employed by the Communist Party. It was a policy of divide and rule. The Party, especially the Tuvan members, wanted to keep their power and the only way they could do so was to appeal to the nationalist feelings among the Tuvans. That was why, he said, the culprits were never caught and over 760 legal cases were pending trial.

There had been dozens of murders, Russian houses burnt and Russian cars shot at. Many who had lived in Russian-only villages received anonymous letters warning them to leave or be killed.

Yet curiously, the region – it was now a republic – had voted over-whelmingly to stay in the Soviet Union.

'It is like this. The Communist Party is very strong in the country-side. People are frightened of them, not just because of the repressions in the past but because they have so much power. If the First Secretary in the village comes to them and tells them where to put their cross on the ballot, they obey.' He shrugged his shoulders. It was, I suppose, the same reason why the rural populations of Mongolia, Albania or Romania had continued to vote for the Communist Party.

Juri was an engineer and a teacher at the local polytechnic and had lived in Kizil about the same length of time. He had moved from Kazakhstan after a dispute at his factory. It was a typical Soviet problem. He had refused to sign a paper with inflated production figures and had been dismissed.

He liked Tuva and said it would be disloyal to run away at this point.

'If all the Russian specialists leave, the economy would collapse. There would be no coal, no electricity, no light. How would anyone survive the winter?' he said. The Tuvans, he explained, were just not properly trained in these technical fields.

He thought the idea of independence for Tuva was laughable.

'They would never survive without the subsidies from the centre. Perhaps one day in the future ... Who knows?' he said.

Tuva's economy was set up on the same colonial principles applied in Buryiatia, Mongolia or by the Chinese in Tibet. The Russians were brought in with higher salaries and given special access to food and housing. They built factories and the rest of the infrastructure necessary to develop an industrial economy but none of it was economically viable. It existed purely on subsidies from the central government. Although minerals and other natural resources were exploited, economics was secondary to the real objective, which was to bring in a large influx of Russians to consolidate control over the territory and assimilate the native population.

Until 1944, most of the population consisted of the families of landless Russian peasant migrants who together with the Old Believers pushed down the river valleys to escape the jurisdiction of the Tsarist empire.

Then after the annexation, the population of Kizil jumped from a few thousand to nearly 80,000 with a huge influx of Russians. Almost a third of the population now lived in the capital. The rest of the territory – 130,000 square kilometres – was barely touched.

The Russians had the best housing, the best jobs, the best education while the Tuvans, especially the young, suffered from high unemployment.

Now the subsidies were being stopped and the access to better food and housing went with them. Tuva was barely connected by road with the outside world and sooner or later the plants, nearly 4,000 miles from Russia's industrial centre, would have to close.

I thought many Russians would want to leave anyway. It was, I pointed out, the end of empire. Juri disputed the charges of Russian colonialism.

'You have to look at it dialectically. Put together the positive elements. We taught these people how to wash, how to plant vegetables, how to live in villages. The Russians brought civilisation!' he said, spreading out his hands and fixing me with his blue eyes. 'They were dying of TB and living as nomads before we came. It is not like your India. They could not survive without us.'

Yenrich concurred. 'People may hate the Party but no one wants the Russians to leave.'

It was hard to make contact with the Tuvan Nationalist Movement but one Saturday a Tuvan ethnographer invited me to his dacha for a special barbecue. Natasha, an ethnic Russian who taught English asked to come with me to practise her English and interpret. She was a youthful-looking grandmother and as we waited for our host to collect us, we sat outside talking. Last year she had left Russia for the first time in her life to join a peace delegation to America.

'Oh, it was only a few days but I could never believe what I saw in those schools. Such equipment! In Kansas I met a teacher who had brought up six children by herself. None of them were her own. She just adopted them. Imagine that, bringing up six children without a husband. I can hardly cope bringing up two children with a husband. We write to each other now. In her last letter, she wrote and asked what kind of computer I used? Imagine her thinking I had a computer! It will take generations before our schools are like those over there.' She talked quickly, unable to stop her astonishment at the outside world. She had lived all her life in Kizil and her parents had come just after the Revolution.

Finally, the small car arrived and took us a few miles outside the town to a little village composed entirely of small summerhouses.

Along the way, Natasha fretted about missing a day at her own dacha. 'If we don't grow enough vegetables in the summer then there is nothing to eat in the winter. We have to spend every weekend working in the vegetable garden. Our government thinks of so many ways to keep us busy and stop us from thinking. I suppose in England people grow flowers not vegetables in their gardens but for us it is an obligation.'

I had foolishly conjured up an idea of a suburban barbecue with sausages and pieces of lamb sizzling on a charcoal fire by a riverside gardenhouse.

Instead when Alexander's Lada swung into the gateway, there was a small patch of dusty ground and a tiny garden shed. A much bigger dacha was in the process of being built.

Alexander worked at the Institute of Tuvan Studies and had three children, a little boy and two girls. The two lanky girls were around ten or eleven and looked almost English in their shorts. Their skin was pale and the hair reddish brown.

His wife and mother were there with an older man with a white mass of hair who had founded a society to revive Buddhism in Tuva. Like the rest of Mongolia, the Tuvans had converted from shamanism to Buddhism and he was now planning to rebuild all temples and monasteries destroyed in the 1930s.

The barbecue was Tuvan style. A live sheep was pulled quietly into the half-built house to be slaughtered. The men asked me to watch. They laid it on its back, gripped its feet and then the Buddhist took a sharp knife and cut open the stomach. Through the slim line of blood, he plunged his hand into the living animal and squeezed its heart. The sheep struggled briefly and after a brief spasm, it was dead. The two men carefully skinned it and slowly pulled out the internal organs full of blood. They were put in a pot and left to boil into a soup.

It was late afternoon by the time we all sat around a ramshackle table. Natasha was ill at ease as pieces of heart and intestine were ladled into her bowl. She ate the meat with even less enthusiasm than I did and I began to suspect that it was the first time she had ever really done anything on their terms.

She grew increasingly disturbed as I began to ask the Tuvans about the Nationalist Movement. It became clear that however much they talked about the importance of introducing democracy their aim was to force all the Russians to leave, and establish an independent state. The strategy, unstated in public, was to use the democratic Russians to break the power of the Communist Party, then to establish Tuva as a fully autonomous Republic and finally to leave the Russian Federation altogether.

'But what about me?' she said, quite appalled after she realised what was intended. 'I have lived here all my life. Surely this is not what you want. I have many Tuvan friends who understand the nationality question properly. What about the friendship between the two peoples?' she said plaintively, shocked to find that even these privileged and apparently assimilated Tuvans could say these things.

'Do you know what happened after 1944?' Alexander's mother broke in. She was a broad, handsome woman with thick black hair and a curved Turkish nose.

'We were an independent country. Then the Russians forced us to join the Soviet Union. Then they passed a law – it was law number 58 – making it a crime for any Tuvan to call a Russian a Russian. You Russians could call us Tuvans a Tuvan. After this law many people disappeared all because they had said, "there's a Russian," just as you would say, "there's a tree." Somebody would inform and next day they would be gone. You were supposed to call the Russians citizens. After 1944, every second family lost someone. And this came after all those people died during the 1930s. Even now old people are too frightened to use the word Russians, they still say citizen. We don't blame Toka for all this. He wanted us to join Mongolia,' she said.

'Well, we don't want to be your citizens any more. We want to go back to our old way of life. We had everything we needed. Life was better before the Russians came.' She stopped abruptly. In the silence, flies settled over the half-eaten meat in front of her.

Natasha was shocked. She looked at the faces around the table with her mouth slightly opened and her eyebrows creased in concern as if for the first time she noticed they were different, not really Russian at all, despite the familiar way they spoke her language. All her life, these people she had patronised and helped were not grateful but in fact hated her.

I don't think she had ever suspected that the Tuvans could be anything but what they seemed, what they had pretended to be.

In her astonishment she took in little of what Alexander's mother said about the repressions after 1944 although I was sure she had never heard about it before. It was quite possible that it had all gone on without her knowing about it.

Afterwards when we were driving back to Kizil, her bewilderment turned to resentment.

'They were helpless savages before we came,' she said. 'My parents lived in a village with them. My parents taught them how to make clothes, how to sew, how to look after children. We taught them how to read and write. They had no alphabet, they had nothing before we came.'

In fact the ancient Tuvans had invented a script to express their proto-Turkish language in the fifth century AD, some five hundred years before a Greek missionary, St Cyrill, put forward an alphabet to suit the Slavic peoples in southern Russia when they converted to Christianity.

The ancient script is found on the mysterious stone pillars and statues which were once scattered in their thousands all over the Yenisey basin. Carruthers was fascinated by 'these images standing solitary, waist deep in the dry, dusty soil ... like the effigy of some Crusader in an English Cathedral.'

Carruthers thought their heads were carved to resemble the real features of the dead person.

'We often saw the strong features of the warrior – a type we amused ourselves by likening to a Colonel of the British Army by reason of his well-groomed moustache and general military appearance.'

Rubruck noticed that before the arrival of the Mongols, the ancient Turks 'raise a tumulus over the dead, and set up a statue to him, its face to the East, holding a cup in its hand at the height of a navel.'

Some were clearly female but it was not obvious what the figures were holding. Carruthers thought it was a snuff bottle but it is now believed they are holding a victory cup of kumiss.

The slabs, he reported, were placed 'in every conceivable combination of numbers yet they were always alike in one respect, namely in the orientation of the stones. All the slabs, without exception, faced north and south, with their narrow edges east and west.'

They are evidence that Tuva and the Yenisey basin were once the centre of a significant civilisation and indeed Soviet archaeological discoveries reveal irrigated agriculture and metal-working on a high level 1,500 years ago.

Carruthers had said the figures were venerated by the Uriankhai although they refused to tell him more about their significance or history.

> Nevertheless, they treat them as sacred and in most cases venerate them by hanging them with bits of cloth and ribbon, and even old clothes . . . We have seen these monuments presenting a most ridiculous appearance as they stood alone on the wide, open steppe, dressed up in old clothes like some scarecrow on an English plough. The Uriankhai sometimes undress and bow before these idols, beating their foreheads with the palms of their hands. All are not considered equally worthy of a sacrifice, namely, those that are recognised as being able to bring good or evil to the natives.

His description reminded me strongly of 'Old Mother Rock', outside Ulan Bator that I had visited in the snow.

I planned to go out into the countryside to see these mysterious effigies but I was told they had almost all been destroyed except in a few isolated or inaccessible spots.

Instead I went to the little national museum where a few had been preserved. They stood buried in the grass at the back of the small wooden building like mysterious messengers from another time.

They were different sizes. Some taller than a man, others no more than a foot high with blurred features of archaic art. The heads on even the best sculptures were as wide as the torsos which stood with their gowns touching the ground. The garment was still recognisable as a *del*, girded by a belt from which hung a sword and a small bag like those in which Mongols kept their tinderflints.

Alongside the statues were the erect stone slabs with runic writing scratched on to them, just visible underneath the lichen.

The curator of the museum was an elderly man with white hair, a smooth skin and bluish eyes called Mongush. He said the script had remained in use until the Mongol invasion of the twelfth century. It was first deciphered a century ago by a Danish scholar Professor Vilhelm Thomsen of Copenhagen University and simultaneously by a Russian scholar, Professor Wilhelm Radlof of Petrograd who had visited Tuva in 1866. He said that in 1993, Tuva was planning to host an anniversary to celebrate his scholarship.

The inscriptions had been most numerous in Tuva, he said, and excavations of the tumuli revealed that the skeletons of the dead had the same slender bones as contemporary Tuvans.

Mongush said all the other slabs and effigies were pulled up by tractors or used as building materials on the orders of the Russians after 1944.

'They wanted to destroy our past,' he said bluntly, 'and they almost succeeded.'

The Tuvan language was a direct descendant of the Turkish spoken in the fifth century by the ruling tribes of Central Asia. It is probably directly related to the language of the Huns, although their script, if they had one, remains to be discovered. Baikal and Hubsogol Lakes are both Turkic names, the former means lake with blue water and the latter, rich lake.

Some forty nationalities in the USSR speak a Turkic tongue including the Azerbaijanis, the Kirghiz, the Kazakhs, the Hakkas and the Tartars.

The Tuvans are, he thought, descendants of the Tubas, one of the tribes which moved from Shansi province after the fourth century AD. These Tubas were almost certainly the builders of the vast rock Buddhas outside Datong in China.

The Tuvans are now the most eastward branch of the Turkic-speaking tribes.

Mongush, I found out, was the only person in Kizil who had tried to preserve the history of Tuva but it took some persuasion for him to sacrifice some of his time and explain it.

'I am only doing it because you are the countryman of Carruthers. He was a great humanist and scientist,' Mongush said. The first volume of his obscure book *Unknown Mongolia* had been translated into Russian and was now a precious record of a lost past. He was proof, perhaps the only proof, of what life was really like before the Russians came.

'We don't know our own culture or history any more,' Mongush said. 'After 1930 all our legends, myths, festivals and songs were forbidden. The script was abandoned and we were made to believe everything we had was a gift of the Russians.'

The lengths taken to distort the past were extraordinarily petty. Even the foundation of the republic was not celebrated, only the anniversary of the entry into the Soviet Union. Only Russian names were listed on the obelisk erected in 1954 for the martyrs of the civil war. Tuvans who lay buried alongside the Russians were forgotten.

We sat outside under a birch tree in the courtyard surrounded by the watching stone warriors, and Mongush's eyes began to close. After a while I began to think the interview was over.

Then he started to tell stories about himself in a sing-song voice which with its rising and falling tones might have been Finnish.

'The summary of my story is the history of all Tuvans. I was born in a yurt and my father was a hunter and storyteller. The road to Mongolia and China went through our district. A camel caravan took thirty-five days to Ulan Bator and another thirty-five from there to Peking. Many people stayed in our yurt: lamas, tramps, the emperor's messengers. My father knew Tibetan and had followed the caravans even as far as Urga. He knew all the medicinal herbs and where to find them. One day men came with two rifles and arrested him. They said he was breaking the law by treating sick people without a proper licence or authority.

'I never saw him again but he was the first victim of the repressions. In the winter of 1934, I was nine and one day a woman came to our house. She was tied to her horse and was so frozen that she could not dismount. We lifted her off with great difficulty and gave her tea and food. Only after a long time was she able to speak. Her husband had been arrested and she was left with eight children, the youngest was a month old. She did not know why but he had been arrested and sent off to a prison. She went there but was not allowed to speak to him. Afterwards she was forced to live as an outcast. The children were forbidden to attend school or go to any public gathering.

'Near my home, there was a great shaman who had a son whom he tried to educate as a shaman. But the authorities sent the boy to Moscow to study at the Toilers of the East University and then sent him to Mongolia as our ambassador. When he returned he was imprisoned as a Japanese spy. He was tried in 1938 by a tribunal of nine judges and shot on October 16th, 1939. He was only thirty years old.

'It was the most horrible day in the history of Tuva. Nine others were shot: the prime minister Sat Churmit, the foreign minister, the minister of Trade and Industry, the state president of Tuva . . .'

Here he stopped and consulted a collection of index cards. He said seven were shot and two given sentences of eight years, and then resumed.

'The shaman was also seized and disappeared. After Tuva joined the Soviet Union, the shaman's wife was arrested and given a ten-year sentence. She was seventy and the police took her across the mountains on horseback to a labour camp. It was called the Black Mountain Camp and is near Krasnoyarsk.

'They say shamans can foresee their death. One night she dreamt of a brilliant sunny day. Suddenly a strong wind came with dark clouds, thunder and lightning and all the birds flew away in fright. Then she dreamed that the sky began to rain down milk and raisins.

'She said that the meaning of her dream was clear: a great event was about to take place. The rain of white milk meant that it would be a good event because white is a good colour.

'Three days later Stalin was dead and all the shamans and lamas in the camp were set free. She was released too and travelled back to her home but there was no one left, even the widow of her son had re-married and moved away. When she came to our yurt, she begged to stay, saying she was very old and had nowhere else to go. When we woke next morning, she was dead, sleeping her great dream.'

A breeze rustled through the tree above us and in the silence that followed the end of his story his eyes seemed to fill with tears. I felt a kind of despair too. How many of these stories had I now heard from almost everyone in China, Mongolia or Buryiatia?

But I felt admiration even awe for the courage of those rare individuals who like Mongush had struggled to rescue something amidst the seventy-year-long era of destruction which had swept through even this forgotten isolated corner of the world.

Mongush had spent most of his life collecting and preserving shamanistic lore ever since a prescient teacher at Leningrad University where he studied, encouraged him to record as much about them as he could.

I suspected he was a shaman himself. Once during our talks he had suddenly fixed me with his blue eyes and said unnervingly, 'I can read your thoughts.'

When he returned to Tuva he decided to write his thesis on 'The Poetry of Shamans in Tuva' and wandered through the taiga collecting their hymns and songs. The Party had tried to stop him and when he submitted his work to academics for supervision – his original professor having been arrested – they refused even to read his thesis once they saw the title.

For thirty years the Party blocked every attempt to publish his work here or abroad. The honours that should have accrued to him as a popular writer of fiction and children's stories were never given.

Even fate seemed to be against him. A Hungarian professor who had invited him to Budapest to defend his thesis died suddenly of a heart attack before he could go. Last year he had finally tried again and had sent a Russian translation to Leningrad for publication; there was no reply. He waited and waited until finally a letter came admitting that the text had been lost.

'The shamans are all dead now but their hymns are still here, just waiting to be published,' he said and put his hand on a dusty folder thick with typewritten sheets.

The only way of reaching the reindeer keepers was to hire a helicopter or spend several weeks travelling by boat and on horse up into the roadless mountains and forests. After lengthy negotiations with Aeroflot, I took off one morning heading for the Sayansk Mountains in the north with a group intent on buying reindeer horns.

As the machine followed the river's winding course through the lush green forest, I searched eagerly for signs of human habitation. They existed and after an hour the helicopter dropped into a state farm where the nomadic Tuvans had been settled in the 1950s.

A crowd of women and children stampeded into the helicopter dressed in shabby European clothes. Seeing them off was a small brown-skinned man somewhat more elegantly turned out in a brown suit with a brash green tie over a red shirt. He was Alexander, chairman of the Association of Reindeer State Farms, and I invited him along. He was delighted and brought his wife who had never seen a reindeer in her life.

His position was somewhat less grandiose than his title suggested since only a handful of state farms still bred reindeer.

The trouble was, he said, the Russians were not interested in reindeer. The animals were never part of the official economy and reindeer production was excluded from the plan. Reindeer breeding was nomadic and the Russians wanted to settle the herdsmen so they could reach a higher stage of development. The reindeer numbers had steadily decreased. In the Toja district which we were now in, there were only 10,000 reindeer, less than half the number in the 1960s. Altogether no more than one hundred families now herded reindeer in the whole republic.

When Carruthers had met the very same people from the Toja clan he had found it hard to tempt them to sell even a single reindeer which he wanted for his collection.

'All our trade goods too, were spread out in a tempting array, with the object of ensnaring the fancies of some passing Uriankhai herdsman; but although knives, needles, soap, musical instruments, coloured beads and automatic pipelighters amused them, yet they did not seem to think them worth a reindeer.

'All the Uriankhai really want is to be left alone,' Carruthers wrote thoughtfully.

Alexander had been trained in Moscow as an agricultural specialist and now ran the state farm we had just left while his wife taught sewing and knitting. Most of the tribe lived there and instead of hunting and herding now depended on farming vegetables.

The remaining herdsmen sent their children to the school all year and now they were going back for the summer holidays. The children, some as young as seven or eight, sat silently each clutching a small bag with their belongings.

Half an hour later the helicopter deposited some of them in a small clearing in the taiga. I could see no sign of any human habitation but they walked away into the forest, their faces blank with bewilderment and apprehension.

Finally the helicopter landed on a small ridge high in the mountains near three flimsy white canvas tents and a herd of reindeer. It was above the treeline and the ground was carpeted with yellow flowers and rich grass. In the clear air 10,000 feet up, the colours were dazzlingly bright. From the ridge, one could see across to a panorama of peaks, tipped with snow.

By the side of a small pool, newly born reindeer calves were tied to stakes and looked pitifully at their mothers grazing nearby. Many of the reindeer were covered in white fur and had large velvety antlers. For all their noble appearance, they grunted as grossly as pigs.

For the first six months of their life, the calves are tethered and the mothers roam free. Then the mothers are tied for six months.

Alexander's wife wandered over to touch them with amazement.

Outside one of the tents, the reindeer keepers silently offered us fresh reindeer milk and brewed some tea in a pot which hung over the fire on a stick. The milk was rich and creamy.

'I would love to live here in the taiga again,' Alexander said with genuine emotion. Until then he had been relentlessly cheerful but now a touch of wistfulness entered his voice. I looked with disappointment at the pathetically few possessions of the families that lived here. The old and flimsy tents were bare inside apart from a worn sleeping bag with holes in it. The people wore old pullovers and trousers that were equally ragged. I wondered what had become of the embroidered buckskin and handsome *del*s which they had once worn.

Were these really the shy, contented, forest dwellers that Carruthers had met? I had expected a more romantic encounter.

Alexander had recovered his optimism.

'It was all my idea,' he said happily, pointing to the men who were now preparing to saw off the horns of the reindeer. He had been to an All Soviet Conference of Reindeer Breeders and there he had met some eskimos who told him there was a new way of making money from reindeer. People from Sweden and Alaska were willing to help build a plant to process the horns into medicine and sell them in the Far East where the stuff could fetch a high price.

'These horns are worth thousands of dollars,' he said. 'And to think we have been throwing them away all these years!'

In fact Carruthers noted that Chinese traders bought the horns for the same purpose before the revolution and preferred the young horns filled with blood. The horns are powdered and Chinese buy it as a sexual tonic.

Competition between different companies anxious to buy the horns was putting up the price and Alexander already had plans about how to spend the money.

'I want to buy a video camera, tents and some rifles,' he explained. 'Can you buy this for them? We can't buy anything here.'

He wanted to improve the life of the herdsmen. Their old guns had ben confiscated and were needed to fight off bears.

'After they mate, the bears are very wild and dangerous. They often rip open the tents and kill people,' he said. We entered into a long discussion on the best place to buy the equipment. I suggested he come to London or Hong Kong but his enthusiasm faded from his face as he contemplated the sheer hopelessness of travelling alone to such obscure and distant places.

We set off a while later to another encampment where three other families were waiting for us. This time I watched closely when the men seized the struggling animals and saw how after the blade had severed the delicate horns, a rich red fountain of arterial blood spurted out. Some struggled violently, their doey eyes opening in alarm. Afterwards the Russian vet fastened a rubber band on the stump to stop the blood flow and sprayed on antiseptic.

The reindeer looked a pitiful sight staggering in shock with blood dripping down but the vet said it did them little harm. The horns grow very quickly each spring but in any case fall off in the autumn. These discarded horns are still valuable but those containing fresh blood and growth hormones are even more prized for their alleged medicinal potency.

The deer were wonderfully docile and trusting. It was easy to touch or ride them. Anyone could simply place a crude bridle over the head, jump on and ride anywhere he fancied.

When they finished, everyone – the Russian pilots, the vet and the Tuvans – sat around a fire and cooked reindeer meat and freshly caught fish. They had brought the herdsmen a few sacks of potatoes as a gift.

'No one supplies them with anything unless we come – except of course during an election,' one of the pilots said. He liked to come up here hunting. The herdsmen lacked even a radio and if they fell sick the nearest doctor was many days' journey away. Otherwise they came down in the winter and stayed with relatives.

I said they were the poorest people I had ever seen, poorer than the nomads in Mongolia. They had lost everything – their culture, their animals, their clothes, even their houses, and the Russians had given them nothing in return.

'You say it was the Russians who did this – no, no, it was not us, it was the Soviets,' he replied with a cynical smile.

Only one of the families still lived in a tepee, half covered in plastic sheets and I asked Alexander what had happened to the way of life which Carruthers had observed.

He hesitated and stared down the empty green valley to where a distant river caught the sun.

'We are a very quiet and obedient people. We followed the Russians in everything. We thought they would help us,' he said slowly.

'I don't even know what it was like before. We were taught there was just feudalism, and rich and poor people. I can't say what kind of justice there was before but my father was a herdsman who could not read or write. Some time after 1944, they arrested him and said he was a counter-revolutionary plotting to overthrow Soviet power. Even now I don't really know what they accused him of but he was sent to prison for ten years. He came back as an invalid after six years, his ribs broken by a tree which fell on him.' His voice trailed off again. He picked up a handful of the blue forget-me-nots which grew in profusion on the grass around us.

'Now we even don't trust each other. How can the young respect the old? In the old days no one under thirty was even allowed to drink or smoke. A young man was not allowed to pass in front of an older man out of respect. Or if a young man wanted to join us, he would sit further away and wait to be invited. People venerated the old. Nowadays there is no morality – that is why there is this violence now,' he said and for an instant looked into my eyes with an expression of infinite sadness.

Twelve

Leningrad

Professor Lev Gumilev was nearly eighty and in ill health after many years spent in Stalin's labour camps when I went to meet him in his Leningrad home.

The Mongolians regarded him as a national hero although he had never been to their country. In Russia opinion was sharply divided between those who dismissed him as a crank and those who had hailed him as an intellectual giant.

He had devoted much of his life to investigating the history of Central Asia and arrived at some spectacular conclusions which overturned all accepted theories. More than this he had gone on to develop a universal theory of world history which had earned him decades of ridicule and persecution from the Soviet establishment. He was in short a typical Russian genius.

With the collapse of the Soviet regime, visitors were now almost beseiging the once disgraced historian. Every week nationalities all over the Soviet Union, that prison of forgotten peoples, sent delegations asking him to provide a new history for them, stripped of the distortions and lies imposed by their former imperial Russian masters and Communist successors.

Gumilev was especially venerated in Mongolia after asserting that the Mongolian conquests were not the fruits of unbridled aggression but defensive wars. Genghis Khan was not a feudal imperialist aggressor but a peace-loving statesman. The Mongols had been attacked by their neighbours so often that they had had no choice but to hit back and happened to be so successful they ended up with an empire. The avenging hordes were, thus, not culprits but victims. An explanatory guide for tourists newly published in Ulan Bator had quoted him approvingly on this score and when I saw it, I became curious to meet him.

Above all, Gumilev is virtually unknown in the West and I wanted to hear his theory which not only explained the secret rhythms of Central Asian history but the rise and fall of every great empire.

It was difficult for him to find time to see me and while waiting, I walked around Leningrad. Even in summer, the city built by Peter the Great in the marshes on the shores of the Baltic had an autumnal feel. Away from the main sights, the crumbling palaces brooding beside their cold and empty canals had a *Death in Venice* feeling.

Leningrad was a fitting terminus for a journey across the empty spaces of Asia. The huge imperial ambition which underlies its monumental architecture corresponded to the megalomania of the Great Wall. The first emperor of all China, Qin Shi Huang, built it with the same wasteful use of uncounted prisoners of war as Peter the Great spent on his city.

The Great Wall aimed to separate the Chinese from the nomadic barbarians to the north, and St Petersburg is also the symbol of a deliberate effort to turn away from Asia's interior and all memories of the Tartar yoke. St Petersburg was a new capital designed to open Russia to the West as a sea-faring and trading nation. The Mongol empire flourished before the rise of naval power and when trade with Asia went overland. The new Russia wanted nothing more to do with these traditions.

The city's profusion of Greek gods and Roman emperors who adorn its Italianate palaces seem to be placed half-naked in the thin sunshine as a bid to ask the West for recognition.

Peter the Great transferred the capital northward in 1712, a mere forty years after the Tartars had, for the final time, sacked Moscow.

Even the word for the citadel in which the terrified Muscovites sought refuge, the Kremlin, is taken from the Mongolian word for a fortress. Outside it stands the Cathedral of St Basil, built by Ivan the Terrible to celebrate his victory in 1552 over the Tartars in Kazan.

'Against the wrath of the Tartars, O Lord Deliver us!' the Russians prayed. Some Russian cities were sacked over a dozen times by the Tartars between 1270 and 1300.

'There was nothing to be seen but earth and dust, sand, ashes, many dead bodies lying around and the sacred churches, devastated, orphaned, widowed. The churches mourn for their brethren, most of whom were slain, as a mother mourns for her children,' said a Russian account of the capture of Ryzan in 1237.

There were seven invasions alone between 1439 and 1459.

The centuries of Tartar subjection were blamed for Russia's back-wardness when Peter the Great compared his country with the West. As the Great Soviet Encyclopaedia asserts: 'The Mongol-Tartar yoke lasting some 240 years was one of the main reasons why Ru's lagged behind some West European countries.'

Perhaps it is no coincidence that when Stalin moved the capital back to Moscow and moved into its fortress, the Kremlin, his rule marked the end of Russia's opening to the West. Similarly, the Nazi invasion was regularly given in the press as the reason why the Soviet Union suffered material shortages even until Mikhail Gorbachev came to power, forty years later.

The Mongols crossed the Volga and arrived in 1276 with a lightning attack led by Batu, the grandson of Genghis Khan. He returned a year later and laid waste the tiny principality of Muscovy.

When the Mongol empire was divided on the death of Genghis Khan among his four sons into *ulu*s or parts, the sixty-four Russian states formed part of the territory of the Golden Horde. The word horde comes from the Mongolian word, *ordu*, for a camp. The Golden Horde survived intact for longer than Kublai Khan's empire in China or the Ilkhan Dynasty in Persia.

The Russians became tributaries of the Khans of the Golden Horde and every court had its Mongol adviser or political agent. The Russian princes became tax collectors for their Mongol overlords who estab-lished their capital by the Caspian Sea at Sarai on the Volga.

The Pax Tartarica which extended from China to the Mediter-ranean encouraged trade to flow overland across the continent. The Genoese and Venetians shipped goods to the Black Sea ports and then through the territory of the Golden Horde, or across a Middle East controlled by the Ilkhans.

Russia played a negligible role in this trade until the terrible des-truction wrought by Tamurlaine interrupted the southern routes and accelerated the long decline of the Golden Horde.

The Muscovy Princes developed particularly close relations with the khans who in turn appointed them Grand Dukes in preference to their rivals.

The internecine wars weakened the Mongol khans and gradually the centre of power shifted northwards. By the turn of the sixteenth century, Muscovy was the largest state in Europe. It continued ex-panding, absorbing all the territories once subject to the Golden Horde and their khans.

St Petersburg symbolised a complete break with this past. It lies on the misty Bay of Finland amid the bleak woodlands of the north as far away as possible from the steppes where the Mongol khans had built their capitals.

For all its architectural glory the city was now a dismal place. Its inhabitants seemed to be awakening from some catastrophe, as if indeed the Tartars had just left and a fresh invasion was so imminent that nothing was worth repairing. There was a listless, hopeless feel to . e empty shops, the closed cafés and the half deserted streets.

I had dinner one night in a modern hotel, a tall pile of concrete manned by waiters in black jackets. To get in I had to pay fifty roubles to a big thickset man who stood outside the entrance with one of the waiters. Once inside a band was playing on stage in front of a hundred tables decked with white tablecloths and champagne glasses. They were all empty.

Yet slowly memories were being revived and a change was in the air. Once, looking for Dostoievsky's former residence, I stopped an old lady to ask the way. She took me through the side streets and the courtyards of decaying tenement blocks talking about the old St Petersburg she had known.

'You know,' she said as we parted, 'I was born in the room where Pushkin died.'

There was no memorial to Gumilev's aristocratic father, the symbolist poet and former Tsarist officer, Nicholas Gumilev, who was shot in 1921 in the wake of the Kronstadt rebellion not for taking part but as a lesson to others. Yet the tiny room where Lev Gumilev's mother, the poet Anna Akhmatova, had lived in poverty had just been turned into a museum in her memory.

One morning, I went to look for the Buddhist temple where Nicholas Roerich had hoped to hang his father's paintings and which his father may even have helped build.

Few people knew of its existence. It lay away from the city centre beside a busy road centre like the embassy of a hostile foreign power, hidden by tall trees and high gates. The architecture is a curious mixture of Tibetan sloping walls and irregular rhomboid windows and an art nouveau gaiety that belonged more to Hollywood than the classical simplicities of Leningrad.

It was finished in 1915 and operated until 1937 when its twenty monks were arrested and shot. Until the end of 1990, it had functioned as a medical laboratory.

Now its overgrown garden, crumbling portals and leaking roof added to an air of mystery. In the bare prayer hall, a handful of pale and long-haired Russian youths prayed in a corner. By the side of a small table selling Buddhist pamphlets, I fell into conversation with a young man with Mongol features. He was a Kalmyck, a Mongol from the Volga basin who had left a course in mechanical engineering to study Buddhism. He said it was a way back to his past.

The Kalmycks were a part of the Mongol nation who had migrated from Zhungaria in 1630. Now there were some 20,000 in an autonomous region around Astrakhan, north of the Caspian Sea. Zhungaria – which is now in the Chinese autonomous region of Xinjiang - means 'on the left hand', because it formed the left wing of Genghis Khan's Army. They are also called the western Mongols or the Oirats and established a confederation under the last great Mongol khan, Galdan, when they sought to revive the old empire. Although they won little support from the eastern Mongol tribes, they posed a serious challenge to the might of the Manchus, reaching within a hundred miles of Peking before being defeated.

The Manchus employed superior technology, cannons and muskets against their bows and arrows and finally pursued them to their homeland. Some historians claim the Manchus massacred nine tenths of the 600,000 Oirats. The details are obscure but the remainder trekked westwards to the Volga in search of a land of good fortune called 'Bumba', defeating the Khazakh tribes on the way.

At first the Russians welcomed them. Peter the Great even visited them. The Russians supplied them with cannons, lead and gunpowder and in return they furnished cavalry deployed against the Turks of the Ottoman Empire. Later Catherine the Great tried to force them to settle down and encircled their territory with a ring of fortresses.

They secretly decided to return to Zhungaria. First they asked the Dalai Lama – whom as Buddhists they regarded as their spiritual leader – to propose a propitious date. Then in the winter of 1771, the entire tribe set off with their wagons and cattle to fight their way home. Of the 400,000 who left, only 120,000 returned. Their epic trek made front-page news in Paris and De Quincey, the English prose writer and opium addict, was inspired to write an account, *The Revolt of the Tartars*, of what he called 'an exploit without parallel'.

Some were caught on the west bank of the Volga, which melted on the day of departure. Their name stems from a Turkish word meaning 'those left behind', or that is at least one of the explanations for their origin.

Kalmyck cavalry officers were still being used by the Imperial Russian Army as late as the Napoleonic Wars when the French mistook their lasso poles for something to do with cooking.

Although Lenin's grandmother was a Kalmyck, they were barely assimilated by the time of the Revolution.

Their fate under Stalin makes an equally extraordinary and brutal saga.

The Germans occupied the Kalmyck territories during the Second World War in what was to be a carefully conceived operation. Otto Doll, an intelligence officer from the Sudetenland who spoke Mongolian, was designated to be the T. E. Lawrence of the steppes. The Kalmycks, of which there were just over 100.000, were promised a free state and the Dalai Lama was to be invited to support it. Doll set up a Kalmyck Cavalry Corps which then fought on the side of the Wehrmacht.

In fact when the German 16th Motorised Infantry Division arrived, it carried out the usual brutal policies and won little support. The Kalmyck cavalry ended up in Lublin, Poland, where they behaved so brutally the unit was disbanded and the remnants evacuated to Bavaria.

When the Red Army drove the Germans out in 1943, Stalin ordered massive reprisals. In four days, the entire population was shipped to Siberia.

'The trucks arrived at three a.m. and my family was given fifteen minutes to get ready to leave,' the young Kalmyck in the temple said. He talked all the while in a low, almost casual voice.

'My mother left with the pot still on the stove. A kindly soldier told her to take some warm clothes, otherwise she would have died. They were locked in closed cattle wagons with little water or food on a journey which took over a month. Many people died on the way and when the train stopped, the dead were thrown on to the snow. Only a third of the 200,000 arrested from the territory ever came back. They were dumped in the Siberian tundra forest, north of Lake Baikal, to survive as best they could,' he said.

'After Stalin died, they were returned in 1957 and we lived in a dug-out. The local authorities refused to allow us to build a home, or give our animals and land back. Russians occupied all official positions. My father was called up in 1939 and fought against the Germans. He was wounded three times, once in the seige of Stalingrad and then in Poland. He was still in a hospital on the front when his family was arrested, and returned with a paralysed arm. When he was demobilised, he was told his family had betrayed the motherland and that he was an enemy of the people. He was inevitably arrested and spent many years trying to find his family.

'There was no betrayal of the motherland. Only eight per cent of the

Kalmyck Cavalry Corps were Kalmycks, the rest were Cossacks or Ukrainians or Russians. It merely operated on Kalmyck territory,' he said.

When he had finished he took me upstairs to see the abbot of the monastery who sat in a small office. Tenzin was a plump boisterous monk, born on the border between Tuva and Buryiatia, who liked to tell stories. He did not seem in the least surprised that I had arrived so unexpectedly.

'Look at this!' Tenzin said soon after I sat down, and he pulled out a large poster advertisement from behind his desk.

'The Tibetan School of Eternal Life! A ten-day course at the Soviet Union's first university for Tibetan medicine, only 700 roubles!' he said, becoming angry. 'Who are these charlatans promising miracle cures?'

Tenzin said there was great vogue for Oriental philosophy among young people who were turning up at the temple in large numbers. He found it alarming because they often had mistaken ideas.

'This is dangerous, very dangerous,' he said looking gravely at me. These charlatans, he went on, were spreading a particularly damaging and corrupt form of philosophy based on Zen Buddhism. They argued that everything is only an illusion, nothing was real, so the difference between good and bad did not matter.

'This is very, very wrong. Buddhism is a very moral philosophy,' Tenzin said emphatically. It was only proper that Buddhism filled the void left by the rejection of Communist-inspired ethics – he had once been a Communist himself – but he was furious that its message was now being distorted.

Morality, he stressed, could not depend on one's point of view. Buddhism should not be subverted to become like Marxist-Leninism – a philosophy in which there was no absolute right or wrong.

The current fashion for Tibetan Buddhism was not entirely new, he said, since it had been the rage in St Petersburg just before the Revolution. The last Tsar, Nicholas II, and especially his wife, had strong leanings towards mysticism.

Tenzin then began to relate some curious stories concerning the origin of his temple which – if he is correct – puts some important historical events in a new light.

An important figure at the court was a Buryiat doctor of Tibetan medicine, Badmaev. His flourishing practice in St Petersburg was popular among the aristocracy and he became an influential adviser on Central Asian matters to Tsar Alexander III. He was full of schemes to extend the empire. In 1893, he sent a memorandum proposing that the Trans-Siberian railway should branch southwards from Lake Baikal and be extended to Tibet through the Chinese province of Gansu.

He even offered to engineer the annexation of Tibet to Russia with the help of Buryiat lamas studying in Lhasa. Count Witte, the finance minister, examined his ideas carefully as they suited his policies of extending the Russian empire southwards.

Badmaev was then given 5 million roubles to stir up a rebellion in Lhasa. It is quite likely that he appropriated the money himself because no rebellion took place but instead an anonymous donor contributed most of the funds used to build this temple, the only lama temple in St Petersburg and indeed in Russia proper.

Badmaev's contact in Lhasa was probably Agvan Dorjiev who was a member of Drepung monastery and tutor to the thirteenth Dalai Lama. He instructed him in the techniques for debating Buddhist dialectics, a necessary part of the education of any lama.

In 1898 Dorjiev arrived in St Petersburg as an emissary of the Dalai Lama and on subsequent visits began to negotiate an agreement between Tibet and Russia. Tibet was then nominally under the influence of Peking but anxious about the threat from the British who were busily bringing all the Himalayan kingdoms under their control.

At the first meeting in Yalta, he was received by Nicholas II and the rest of the court. A year later on his second visit, the Tsar gave him a gold watch studded with diamonds as a gift to the Dalai Lama.

British suspicions were deeply aroused. When challenged by the British ambassador, the Russian foreign minister Lamsdorff said the very idea of diplomatic negotiations was 'ridiculous and utterly unfounded'.

Then the British heard through their secret agent, Chandra Das, that the Tibetans were being armed with Russian weapons. This was the final straw and in 1904 the British invaded Tibet determined to forestall further Russian expansion which might threaten the British hold over India.

The Younghusband expedition was the last and one of the most controversial adventures of the British Empire. With the loss of a handful of men, the force succeeded in reaching the heart of the mysterious kingdom, the holy grail for so many nineteenth-century explorers. By the time the army arrived, the Dalai Lama had fled to Ulan Bator to stay with the Bogd Khan, still accompanied by Dorjiev.

Tenzin maintained that it was all a misunderstanding. There were no Russian weapons in Lhasa and instead the British 'pundit' had intentionally or deliberately misreported a Buddhist ceremony in which weapons are consecrated and stored in temple stupas.

Tenzin also said that what the British did not know was that the Tsar Nicholas II was anxious to obtain the Dalai Lama's help to obtain the son and heir he despaired of gaining after his wife had given birth to four daughters. This was the reason for the contacts with the Dalai Lama. Whether or not the Dalai Lama provided any 'alternative medicine' or not, the Tsarina Alexandra gave birth to Alexis, a boy suffering from haemophilia, in 1904.

The idea that the Tsarina would seek the help of the Dalai Lama in such a matter is not entirely unsupported by the known facts. Badmaev was certainly a friend of Rasputin and frequently prescribed pills and other medicaments for both the boy and his parents.

Badmaev supplied pills thought to contain hashish to the Tsar in 1916 on the instructions of Alexandra. Like Rasputin, he was certainly part of her entourage, encouraged her interest in mysticism and aided the search for a cure for her son's incurable disease.

On the other hand, Dorjiev, as the rest of his remarkable career shows, was more notable as a political operator than a purveyor of alternative medicine. After the collapse of the Manchu Empire in 1911, he actively sought recognition for the independence of Mongolia and Tibet in his travels to France, Germany and Italy. With the clouds of the impending war hanging over Europe, the chanceries of Europe had little attention to give to such obscure and distant matters.

He did though represent the Tsar in Mongolia and was instrumental in the 1913 treaty between Mongolia and Tibet in which each mutually recognised the other. Mongolia was in fact the only country ever to grant Tibet full diplomatic recognition, not that too many countries recognised Mongolia's independence either.

Dorjiev was intent on promoting a pan-Mongolian and pan-Buddhist unity. He wanted the Tsar to be the patron of the regrowth of Buddhism in Asia and he managed to persuade the Dalai Lama of the Tsar's good intentions and gave currency to the beliefs that Shambala was none other than Russia itself. He was able to sell this idea to the credulous Tibetans whose ideas of geography were somewhat hazy.

The most remarkable part of his career began after the Revolution when, according to Tenzin, he managed to become a confidant of Lenin. He was arrested after the Revolution but later released from prison when the Bolsheviks found him useful. After revolutions in western Europe failed to materialise, Lenin switched his hopes of exporting revolution from Europe to Asia.

The millenarian Shambala movement was already widespread in

Central Asia. Many there were easily convinced that the 1917 revolution and ensuing civil war marked the start of the fore-ordained War of Shambala.

Tolstoy too had embraced many Buddhist ideas and had propagated them among the Russian intelligentsia so there was fertile ground for convergence of Communist and Buddhist ideas.

The Soviet Communist Party organised national Buddhist conferences in 1923 and 1926. Dorjiev declared that Buddhism was actually a religion of atheism and there was no different between the Buddhist ideas on the emancipation of mankind and those of Marx or Lenin.

He further argued that Buddhism was actually a forerunner of dialectical materialism and wrote a book called *Socialism and Buddhism*. Other lamas went even further and claimed that Buddha, not Lenin, was the founder of bolshevism.

Dorjiev organised a Buddhist reform movement to bring about a return to the vows of poverty taken by the first disciples of Buddha. He wanted to do away with the monasteries and all the wealth and corruption that went with them.

This convergence between Buddhism and Marxism is not quite as absurd as it sounds because Buddhism is primarily about philosophy and not the worship of a divine being. There are also striking similarities between the Hegelian dialectic philosophy which Marx and Engels adopted and those ideas put forward by the early Buddhist schools of philosophy in India.

Both Buddhists and Communists approached the fundamental question of understanding reality in similar ways. It was as Engels said the 'great basic question of all philosophy, that concerning the relation of thinking and being'.

Hegel's dialectical philosophy defines reality as a sequence of events because all parts of the world as we experience it are interdependent and in a state of flux.

He argued that the whole is by itself not completely real, and nor are the parts because they partake of reality only in proportion to their relation to the whole. The word 'dialectic' describes this interdependence and sequence of events. He also thought the whole cosmic process was directed by a rational principle embodied by what he called the World Spirit.

Marx largely abandoned this mystical world spirit notion and concentrated on the position that the material world is the fundamental reality. This means that our sensory perceptions give us accurate 'copies' of external reality.

The addition of the word 'materialism' signifies that all spiritual values derive from matter which can be objectively perceived by our senses. 'The subjective creates the objective,' as Mao put it in one of his 'thoughts'.

Engels explained this Hegelian dialectical philosophy in his book *Anti-Duhring*.

'Everything is and also is not: for everything is in flux, is constantly changing, constantly coming into being and passing away.'

Further on he says that 'every organic being is at all times itself and yet something other than itself. Closer investigation also shows us that the two poles of antithesis, like positive and negative, are just as inseparable from each other as they are opposed, and that despite all their opposition they materially penetrate each other.'

He then borrows from Hegel the example of a grain of barley to illustrate dialectical development at work in the world: the grain sprouting into a plant is 'the negation of the grain' and when its seeds produce more plants this is the 'negation of the negation'.

In the fourteenth century Tsong Kapa, the founder of the Yellow Hat sect of Tibetan Buddhism, considered the same issue and used the same image.

'Consider a sprout. It cannot exist truly, for it is interdependent,' Tsong Kapa said. His view was closer to Hegel's and rejected the 'materialism' of Marx.

Tsong Kapa was deliberating on the arguments of the four great schools of thought ancient India produced on the question of what is reality. They split into two main camps and Tsong Kapa took the middle way between those who argued that things do not exist at all so that everything is an illusion; and those who said things only exist as we perceive them and the appearance of things is thus the unchanging reality.

Tsong Kapa wrote in his verses, 'The Three Principal Paths':

> You've yet to realise the thought of the able
> As long as two ideas seem to you disparate:
> The appearance of things – infallible interdependence;
> And emptiness – beyond taking any position.

Tsong Kapa put forward the same notions of the dialectical process. The sprout only exists as part of a changing process, a development out of a chain of cause and effect.

> A person has entered the path that pleases the Buddhas

When for all objects in the cycle or beyond
He sees that cause and effect can never fail,
And when for him they lose all solid experience.

Of course while Marx accepted the world of matter as the sole existent reality, Buddhism asserts that a state of being exists which transcends the world of matter and the goal of human existence is the liberation from matter.

Whatever the similarities between Hegel and Tsong Kapa, there were none between Stalinism and Buddhism. Dorjiev's renewal movement collapsed after 1928 when Stalin clamped down on economic and religious freedoms and concentrated on building Socialism in one country. Dorjiev returned to Buryiatia in 1937 and a year later died in prison.

Dorjiev's influences on Roerich were crucial. When the mystical poet and painter helped build the temple, he became fascinated by Dorjiev's tales of Shambala.

Tenzin said that Roerich actually went to search for the Shambala mountain, not in Tibet or Mongolia but in a region I had never heard of. This is the Gorno Altaysk autonomous oblast. Tenzin looked around his office and finally found a map on which he pointed it out. The oblast is next door to Tuva, where the long chain of Atlai mountains peters out in the great Siberian plain, just to the north of Mongolia.

The inhabitants are similar to the Tuvans and are Buddhists, he said. In 1904 while the Dalai Lama was in Mongolia they became inspired by his millenarian ideas. They gathered on top of the highest mountain, the 13,500-foot-high Gora Belukha, to greet the new era, the age of Shambala.

This took place during the Russo-Japanese War and local Russian officials sent in Cossack troops to beat the worshippers whom they suspected of being Japanese agents or sympathisers. They misunderstood several words of the local language including the phrase *Ligden Japo* which had nothing to do with the Japanese but is the name for the King of Shambala.

So it must have been these stories which attracted the attention of the Old Believers living around the White Sea, north of St Petersburg.

To my surprise Tenzin had heard of them. Yes, he said, that same year the White Waters Sect began their long trek to Gora Belukha and settled there. What has since become of them, Tenzin did not, however, know.

Yet remarkably, the legend of a Shangri-La in the Altai mountains continued to spread even after the Revolution and seized the imagination of the prisoners in Solzhenitsyn's Gulag Archipelago:

> For some reason, a legend about the Altai region in particular flourished in the cells. Those rare persons who had been there at one time or another, but especially those who had never been there, wove melodious dreams about the wonderful country of the Altai for their cellmates! It had the vast expanses of Siberia and a mild climate. Rivers of honey flowing between banks of wheat. The steppe and mountains. Herds of sheep, flocks of wildfowl, shoals of fish ... Oh, if only we could find a hiding place in that quiet!

Perhaps some of the Old Believers who were arrested had spread the stories. More interestingly, it is possible that if Roerich's writings on his search for Shambala did inspire *Lost Horizon*, then the original, perhaps the real, Shangri-La is located in the valley beneath Gora Belukha where the Old Believers settled.

I felt a twinge of sadness that it was now too late to go back and find this mountain. Its Russian name means the 'White Mountain' but its Mongolian name is *Uch Sumer* which in turn means 'The Centre'.

It plays a central role in the mythology of Central Asia. A Kalmyck myth relates how the gods used Mount Sumer as a stick to stir the ocean, creating the sun, moon and stars.

Local people, Tenzin said, consider it not merely the highest peak in the world but the actual centre of the world, the cosmic axis of both Buddhist and shamanist legend which links heaven and earth.

In his study of shamanism, Mirceau Eliade noted that the Mesopotamians also believed a central mountain joins heaven and earth and the Sumerians built their ziggurats to represent this Cosmic Mountain. The language and origins of the Sumerians are to this day a mystery but perhaps the name of this mysterious peak in the Altai, Mount Sumer, is more than a mere coincidence. Could it be that just as Professor Chagdurov said, there is some link between the Sumerians and Mongolia?

One afternoon, I turned off the bustle of Alexander Nevsky Prospekt into a small street for my appointment with Lev Gumilev.

His apartment was in an old town house with generous wide stairs leading to it and was filled with comfortable old-fashioned furniture. He sat at a big wooden dining-table and as he talked, he smoked the cheapest cigarettes, the *papirosi* with a twist of cardboard at the end instead of a filter, called Belomor Canal.

'When I was a boy,' he began, 'I read all the stories of James Fenimore Cooper like *The Last of the Mohicans*. I was very interested in the fate of the American Indians but when I grew up, it was impossible to go to America. Instead I became interested in the "indians" of my own continent. I discovered there was no proper scientific work done on the history of these peoples – the Huns, the Turks, the Mongols, the Khazakhs – so I decided to investigate the history of these early peoples myself.'

He stopped and his pale blue eyes fixed on me in a kindly way.

'As I did so, I became interested in finding out why nations appear and disappear. Where are the Philistines now? What happened to the ancient Greeks? Or the Romans?'

By the time he had finished school, Stalin was firmly in power and for four years he was refused admission to university. Not only were both parents members of the aristocracy but the regime had executed his father and banned his mother's poetry.

'I suppose we cannot live without tragedy in Russia,' he said with a ghost of a smile and, refusing to talk more about these events, continued his story. In 1934 when he was nineteen, he was arrested for the first time.

'The accusation was simply that I loved my father,' he said. In 1938, he was sentenced to be shot but at that moment Nikolai Yezhov, the secret police chief, was himself arrested and executed. Instead Gumilev was given another five-year sentence.

'I helped build this Belomor Canal,' he said holding up the cigarette packet. On the back it showed the waterway's route linking the White Sea to Onega Lake. About 120,000 died building it with picks and wheelbarrows. He smiled again as if recalling some pleasant memory.

'Do you know when Maxim Gorky came to inspect it, they gave us some new green uniforms?'

In 1944, he was released to serve in the Red Army and took part in the liberation of Berlin. After demobilisation, he went back to university but was soon in prison again. His mother's work was briefly tolerated after the war but in 1946, the Leningrad Party secretary Zhdanov launched a ferocious attack against her.

In 1949, he was arrested again and not released until 1956.

'The exact words of the prosecutor was that I knew too much and so I was dangerous,' he said abruptly. His wife, a large matronly woman who sat watching the interview anxiously, got up and began pulling out some old photographs of him. They were taken in camp at the beginning and end of his sentence and despite all the suffering, he looked then much as he did now.

His number, B739, was visible on all of them and like Solzhenitsyn, he was in Spezlags, reserved for political and not criminal prisoners.

In the camps he continued his research and from the fellow prisoners learned the Turkic languages of the Kazakhs and Kirgiz. A former teacher sent him two volumes of Chinese histories translated into Russian and he was able to write his first thesis on the history of the Turks between the sixth and ninth centuries.

He fell ill in camp and used the opportunity to study. When he recovered, friends in the camp, in particular a Georgian doctor, arranged to prolong his stay in the infirmary by conducting an unnecessary operation on his intestines. At one stage they even put a false plastercast on his leg.

'Maybe that's how I survived. I didn't lose interest in life because my research kept me going,' Gumilev said.

All the while he said he continued to ponder the cause and effect behind the fate of nations throughout history.

'My ideas were close to Toynbee's but he never found the key. The answer came to me in prison one day. I was in a terrible condition and starving. I couldn't sit up any more and was lying under my bunk when the answer came to me,' he said.

'Suddenly I knew why Alexander the Great led his 40,000 men in a campaign of conquest which took him all the way to India. And why it was that they followed him even though they asked, "Why are you risking so much when you have everything – food, wine, palaces?" Some energy pushed him. People who are filled with this energy make history. I called this force 'passionaris' – from the word passion – and it enters them and fills them with drive.

'I was in the Christy Prison in Leningrad when I noticed a shaft of light coming through the cell window and I understood that this was the energy,' he said and stopped, remembering the illumination with another modest smile.

'It was not until 1965 when I read a book by the scientist Vernadsky called *The Chemical Component of the Earth's Biosphere and its Surroundings* that I completed my theory,' he went on.

Vernadsky had been a biologist who had studied the relationships between animals and their environment. He eventually fell foul of Lysenko and his false theories of genetics and died in prison.

'Vernadsky once saw a huge cloud of grasshoppers moving across the desert in Africa and decided to calculate its mass. He worked out that it was larger than that of all the copper in the earth. And then he wondered what possessed them to fly to their death in the desert. Vernadsky developed a theory about the energy of living tissue and said there is some force which propels creatures to do unnecessary things.

'Now Vernadsky did not know history very well. He could not see the link between the flight of the locusts and emigration, say of Anglo-Saxons to America. But I knew history well and used his ideas to describe historical processes.' He leaned back for a moment with satisfaction and pulled out another Belomor Canal.

'A kind of energy exists which propels us to do unnecessary things. When this energy is transmitted to a group of people it inspires them to perform feats which are superfluous to their daily survival,' he said leaning forward with excitement.

'And what is this energy? It is spread over the world but does not come from below the earth's surface or it would be constant. No, this energy appears only occasionally so the answer must lie in astrophysics. No other science can explain it. The energy arrives as solar radiation brought by solar winds which strike the earth's atmosphere with the rotation of the earth. These cosmic rays have affected certain parts of the earth – and certain nations – at different periods in history,' Gumilev said. I looked at him slightly bemused and even disappointed.

Cosmic rays sounded cranky, eccentric rather than scholarly. I had been fascinated by this story when, bereft of all energy and when anyone else would have been in despair, he had been excited by this burst of understanding about the nature of energy.

It reminded me of Soeren the shamaness working herself up and receiving spiritual visitations in a mental flash, and the lama astrologer with his technique of achieving enlightenment by exhausting himself through months of fasting and chanting.

Yet I suppose the cosmic rays were just a 'factor x', a convenient explanation for something that was as yet inexplicable. It was no more absurd that the various scientific theories – which indeed include cosmic rays and asteroids from outer space – put forward to explain why the dinosaurs disappeared.

Gumilev said that he considered next the question of what constitutes the nature of a nation. A nation cannot necessarily be defined by a single language or race. The British, he pointed out, are a linguistic and ethnic mixture of Celts, Angles, Saxons, Normans, Scandinavians and Picts.

He decided to reject the word nation and use a concept he called 'ethnos'. They rise and fall according to distinct pattern and within a timescale of between 1,200 and 1,500 years. He took the example of the Mongols, an ethnos formed out of a group of tribes without a common language or religion in the tenth century and now at the end of their life.

The influence of cosmic rays is preserved in the myths surrounding the birth of the nation, he said. According to the legend the first Mongol was conceived after a man descended on a shaft of light which entered through the *tonoo*, the hole in the top of a *ger*, and impregnated a woman.

Armed with these two ideas, Gumilev said, he went back and looked at the history of the world to identify the separate bursts of cosmic energy which had passed like a whip across different parts of the world in various centuries. He had found eleven such bursts and drew them as lines on a map.

He took a copy of his book out and pointed to a map showing the lines crisscrossing the globe in different directions.

'For instance, there was a burst in the eighth century BC which touched the ancient Greeks, the Latins, the Celts, went through the Syrian deserts, touched Persia and ended in the Indian Ocean,' he said.

In the peoples which absorbed this energy, a transformation took place which he christened 'a mutation'. Those who absorbed the energy became filled with drive, with what he called 'passionaris' and passed it on to their children. Or when they conquered other peoples, they left traces of the energy in the children they fathered. Britain was a case which had inherited its 'energy' from the migration of dynamic people from places already touched by the cosmic wind.

Over the lifespan of an ethnos, the cosmic energy gradually dissipated but as it did so a distinctive pattern of behaviour was demonstrated by all these ethnoses. To show the rise and fall of the energy, he had plotted a graph.

He found the page in the book and I looked at it. It showed a fairly steep rise in the initial phase of an ethnos until at the peak, the ethnos 'overheats' and an 'energy breakdown' occurs when people within an ethnos start to fight amongst each other in a civil war.

Then there is a long slow decline, interrupted by occasional peaks of energy but at ever lower levels, before an ethnos declines into complete inertia and the energy levels disappear. Then the ethnos lingers on in obscurity, ruled by people with low levels of energy. The Mongols had now reached this stage.

A breakdown had taken place in Britain during the English Civil War, another during the French Revolution and a third in the Russian Revolution. This was, he said, because the British are an older ethnos than the French who, in turn, are older than the Russians.

'We were born 500 years later than the British and are now in a dangerous and hazardous period as you were during the time of

Cromwell,' he asserted. The British were also fortunate because the 'energy-possessing people' went abroad and kept the level reasonably comfortable.

With the Chinese, the energy level had collapsed entirely since the Tang Dynasty and now its culture was virtually extinguished, he said.

Gumilev argued that individuals – such as Genghis Khan or Stalin – play only a small role. However, he pointed out that Genghis Khan's place on the graph was on the initial upsurge of energy while Stalin came at a point where the Russian ethnos was in a steep decline.

Naturally, all these theories had won him little public recognition despite the considerable number of books he published. They ran counter to Marxist theories of history as class struggle and a series of continuous economic development through certain stages.

He continued to face persecution and discrimination under Stalin's successors. His fellow academics had declined to grant him the honours which would normally have been his and it was only now, with glasnost, that the Russian Academy of Sciences had elected him one of its members.

Most of his official career had been as a geographer and while his straightforward historical research had been published, these ideas had only recently been published in a book *Ethnogenesis and the Biosphere*, written fifteen years earlier.

Gumilev thought little of these belated honours but regretted that he had never had the chance to present his ideas abroad.

All those wasted years and now there was so little time left, I thought, looking at his face which had become visibly tired as we talked. His wife had warned me to stay no more than three hours.

Yet Gumilev also had a contented air about him while so many others along the way, like the deranged professor of ancient history in Ulan Bator whose books were burnt, had been bitter.

For all those years in prison, Gumilev evinced the calm assurance of someone who had made sense of his time, who knew how it fitted in with the past and the future.

Next day Gumilev promised to illustrate his theory with examples from history. When I arrived he was waiting with one of his students but looked weaker than the day before.

He started by explaining the history of Central Asia, from 300 BC when he claimed the region was touched by a burst of cosmic energy. Two empires formed. In China Qin Shi Huangdi forged the competing states into one empire for the first time and built the Great Wall. North of the Wall, the Huns were united by the Emperor Mode, who after killing both his father and stepfather, used his army to sub-jugate other nomadic tribal confederations of the Sarmat and Xianbi. These were the Huns.

The Huns' key military invention was that of whistling arrows (later used by the Mongols) which enabled a commander to issue signals on a battlefield and quickly direct his troops.

The two empires, one based on the steppes and nomadic animal husbandry and other in the south, highly organised around the irri-gated fields of China's industrious peasantry, confronted each other. But Gumilev said the issue between them was not culture or even territory, but lice.

'The Huns wanted the silk which the Chinese alone made because silk is the only material in which lice cannot lay their eggs and breed,' Gumilev said.

'Silk made life bearable. Anyone who has lived with lice bites – and I lived with lice for many years in the camps – knows the misery they inflict,' he said and reminded me of the Abbé Huc's complaining to the same effect during his journey through Tartary.

'For that reason, everyone wanted silk,' Gumilev said. It was that simple. An international trade in silk had therefore dominated the politics of Central Asia down to Columbus.

In their new and centrally organised state, the Chinese turned the silk industry into a state monopoly, raising the price so high that the Huns could no longer afford to buy even the cheapest. The Huns had also relied on the silk to trade with the Sarmats and Sogdians to the east, who in turn sold it to the nations of the Mediterranean. This, he said, was the origin of the silk route.

'After the empire was established the Chinese sold only such small amounts of silk that it became a kind of commodity – and its price was soon as high as gold's,' he said.

'The Wall prevented the Chinese from escaping the empire or breaching the monopoly. So the Huns started a war and the Chinese were defeated. Later the two sides agreed on a peace treaty under which the Huns bought high-quality silk and sold the Chinese low-quality horses.

'The Chinese – now ruled by the Han Dynasty – realised that the Wall had not provided an adequate defence against the fierce and sud-den attacks of the Huns and decided they must organise cavalry detachments to match the Huns. They lacked good horses and there-fore mounted two attacks on Ferghana to capture the best horses,' he continued.

Ferghana is now in Soviet Asia and a Chinese army set off

westwards across what is now Xinjiang to capture the famous breed of horses in the Ferghana Valley.

'The Chinese already had horses but those from Ferghana were particularly superior because they did not need to be fed with opium to keep them quiet before an attack,' he said.

While Chinese diplomats tried to foment dissent among the tribes, the nomads employed Roman foot soldiers to defeat the Chinese troops.

Gumilev recited the Chinese sources verbatim: 'A strange people appeared out of a fortress with square shields. The Chinese laughed and used their crossbows, killing the soldiers who ran back into their fortress.'

These troops, he said, were prisoners captured during the disastrous invasion of Parthia (Persia) by Crassius, one of the triumvirate which together with Julius Caesar had ruled Rome. The Parthians had traded the Roman prisoners with the Huns.

With this new breed of horse the Chinese were able to defeat the Huns and eventually succeeded in dividing and pitting the tribes against each other.

The Chinese were able to do so because the ethnos of the Huns had reached boiling point. It was what Gumilev called the Akmatic phase, borrowing a Greek word to mean the 'blossoming'.

The Hun state broke up. A part went to the north of China and became the Toba who later built the vast Buddhist statues in Datong which I had visited. Another group moved westwards to the Volga and finally, under Attila the Hun, invaded Europe.

'It triggered a great movement of the peoples. The Hun migration pushed other tribes like the Vandals further westwards and they finally reached Spain and North Africa. The Goths invaded Italy and sacked Rome and the Huns followed them,' he said.

The Hun invasion resulted in the addition of the word 'Hurrah' to our vocabulary. It was the battlecry of the Hun armies and they shouted it when attacking. It originally meant 'forward!'. Attila became the wicked Etzel in the Germanic saga, the Nibelungenlied, which in turn inspired Wagner's Ring Cycle.

When Attila died suddenly in AD 451, the Huns retreated. A part remained in Hungary but others returned across the steppes to the Yenisey valley where Tuvans now live.

Another burst of energy in the fifth and sixth centuries AD traversed Asia touching the Huns as well as the Arabs, Rajputs and Tibetans. The Huns mixed with the Turkish tribes in the region and together they established a khanate in Central Asia which controlled the silk trade to the Byzantine Empire. The Turks financed their wars against the Persians from the tax revenues gathered from the silk trade.

In the tenth century another burst, number eight, energised the Mongols.

'The Mongols were like the American Indians, constantly subject to attacks by the Jurchen rulers of northern China, and other more powerful tribes like the Tartars or Naimans,' Gumilev said.

Under Genghis Khan's leadership, the Mongols defeated their oppressors one by one. After their defeat the Naiman tribe ended up in Asia Minor as the Seljuk Turks.

He went on to describe how Genghis Khan's empire grew. Genghis Khan set about organising the silk trade. He sent tradesmen to the Khwarzim Empire which ruled Hither Asia, the stretch of land between the Caspian Sea and the current frontiers of China.

'The Khwarzim killed the 400 merchants sent by the Mongols and when Genghis Khan sent ambassadors, they were executed too. Genghis Khan had not intended to conquer that empire but he had to take action or lose face as the Mongols had a strong code of honour. Although the Khwarzim Shah, Mohammed, had 400,000 troops, double the forces of the Mongols, he was defeated because the drive of the Mongols was too high,' Gumilev explained.

The execution of Mongol ambassadors, followed by invasion and victory, set the pattern for the next century. The ambassadors, whether they were sent to Sung China or Japan, Hungary or Russia, were almost invariably executed.

Most contemporary accounts point out that the Mongolian ambassadors met their fate because they accompanied demands for instant submission with threats. Thus the issue of the ambassadors was merely a pretext for aggression.

Gumilev, all too aware of how propaganda distorts history, said this explanation was 'pure anti-Mongolian propaganda'.

'Remember that the contemporary histories, including that by Rashid al-Din, were written by their enemies,' he said.

Such injunctions demanding submission were not unique to the Mongols but are found in all diplomatic missives of the time. Even the eighteenth-century Manchu emperors of China refused any dealings with English monarchs unless they recognised a vassal status.

'In fact all the Mongols wanted was to establish reliable frontiers,' he said. 'Their wars were defensive.'

The King of Armenia Cilicia, a small state on the Mediterranean coast north of Cyprus was almost the only potentate not to slaughter the visiting Mongolian ambassador and successfully survived the

Mongolian whirlwind.

Until the thirteenth century, it was customary all over Europe and Asia to have the ambassadors of unfriendly nations executed.

It was, Gumilev argued, Genghis Khan who first established the concept of diplomatic immunity that is now almost universally accepted.

'His law, the Yasa, outlawed the murder of ambassadors for the first time in history. Diplomats everywhere should build a monument to his memory,' Gumilev said.

It was only when Peter the Great moved the court to St Petersburg that the Russians dropped the diplomatic etiquette they had inherited from the Mongols. Western ambassadors, much to their irritation, had until then been obliged to remove their swords when entering the Tsar's residence and accept his hospitality which was so encompassing that many felt they were prisoners rather than guests.

Russian diplomats were surprised and insulted when they travelled abroad and found they were not considered the personal guest of the ruler but required to pay for their board and lodgings.

Furthermore, Gumilev argued that all the reports of Mongol atrocities were either grossly exaggerated or attributable to their mercenaries.

The number of real Mongols in the forces was never more than 110,000 although the overall strength was swollen by mercenaries to 500,000. When Batu, Genghis Khan's grandson, led the first Mongol invasion of Russia, his army included only 4,000 Mongols.

Most of the troops who defeated Sung China were drawn from tribes in Vietnam, Yunnan, Burma and the rest of its southern borders, who bore a traditional enmity against their overbearing neighbours. Gumilev thought they were responsible for the worst atrocities. He also dismissed the idea put forward by some scholars that the Mongols had carried the black death to China and were therefore responsible for the death of many millions of Chinese.

'We talk about 300 years of the Tartar yoke but how despotic were they? Look what the British did to the Australian aborigines. Or what happened to the American Indians. The khan was elected by the army and the people. The Mongols taught the Russians to obey the law, the Yasa,' he said and we stopped there. Gumilev was in pain from his stomach.

'Something he acquired in the camps,' his wife said as she showed us out of the door.

In the eighteenth century the French had coined an epigram, *'Grattez le Russe et vous trouverez le tartare*' (scratch a Russian and you find a tartar) and I hoped to ask Gumilev more about the influence of the Mongols on the Russians.

Some historians such as Michael Prawdin consider that the Russians are the successors of the Mongols. It was 'not by throwing off the "Tartar yoke" but by the deliberate adoption of the Tartar heritage with all which it entails that Moscow became great and powerful,' he wrote.

The Bolsheviks were often compared to the Mongols by their opponents. Rosa Luxembourg said, for instance, that the Bolsheviks ruled with 'Tartar-Mongolian savagery'.

When Stalin was appointed chairman of the Nationalities Commission, Leo Tolstoi commented that he would be like 'Genghis Khan with a telephone'.

It was true, after all, that Lenin, who looks vaguely Asiatic with his high cheekbones, had Mongol blood through his paternal grandfather Nikolai, a serf who had married a Kalmyck woman, Anna.

Some claim Stalin had Mongol blood although this has never been proven. It was said that his forefathers were Crimean Tartars but it was also put about that he was the illegitimate son of the explorer Prejevalsky. There is, in fact, a black statue of Prejevalsky in Leningrad which I found surprising as he emerges in his writings as a classic nineteenth-century imperialist.

For all Tolstoi's comparison, the difference between Stalin and Genghis Khan is considerable.

Stalin confided to his secret police chief, Dzerzhinsky, that 'to choose one's victims, to prepare one's plans minutely, to slake an implacable vengeance, and then to go to bed ... there is nothing sweeter in this world.'

Genghis Khan said something that at first sight appears similar: 'The greatest joy a man can know is to conquer his enemies and to drive them before him. To ride their horses and take away their possessions; to see the faces of those who were dear to them bedewed with tears and to sleep on the white bellies of their wives and daughters.'

It is the difference between the open frankness of Genghis Khan and the deceitful pretence of Stalin who murdered his own colleagues and supporters in spiteful severy.

The next afternoon Gumilev looked tired and drawn but sat smoking his *papirosi* and ready to talk. This field was his latest focus of interest and he took up the story with enthusiasm.

After the Mongol invasion, he explained, the Muscovites under the great Russian hero, Alexander Nevsky, turned away from the West. The Pope had offered to send Teutonic knights to help him against the Mongols but Nevsky rejected it because it was made on condition that the Russians transfer their allegiance to the Roman Catholic Church.

Nevsky persuaded other Russian states to follow the same path. Some of them thought his successor, Grand Prince Vasili, was going too far. They asked in a letter: 'Why did you bring the Tartars on to Russian soil, assign them towns and country districts which are taxed to provide means of support? Why are you so excessively fond of the Tartars and their language? And why are you so immoderately harsh and oppressive to the peasants, though you give gold and silver and all good things to the Tartars?'

In the fourteenth century the northern Russians were threatened from two sides. To the west were the Lithuanians, then a powerful and expansionist power which included Poland and who had converted from paganism to Catholicism.

In the south the Golden Horde was breaking up into different khanates and one part in the Volga basin accepted Islam. A warrior called Uzbek seized power in what Gumilev described as a *coup d'état* backed by merchants in the Volga cities.

Uzbek ordered his men to convert to Islam and tried to force all the Mongols to do the same. Many refused and in a civil war lasting three years, many Mongols moved to the northern Russian towns like Moscow, Rzan, Tver and Suzdal and in particular Rostov.

There they married Russian wives and some converted into the Russian Orthodox Church. The Grand Dukes of Russia absorbed increasing numbers of Mongols, creating a Mongol officialdom and army. Many of the most famous Russians have Mongol blood, from Boris Godunov down to nineteenth-century writers like Gogol or Saltikov and Russian generals like Suvorov, or Kutuzov who defeated Napoleon.

'Instead of suppressing the Russians, the Mongols protected them from the aggressive intentions of the Lithuanians on the one side and the Muslim world on the other,' Gumilev said. 'Without the protection of the Mongols, the Russian Orthodox Church could never have survived.'

At some point the real history of Russia was replaced by a different version – and one that was actively propagated by Soviet historians. This version holds that – as the *Great Soviet Encyclopaedia* puts it – after 'centuries of heroic resistance', the Russian people threw off the Tartar yoke.

According to this mythology the famous battle of 1380 when the Grand Prince Dimitri of Moscow, later known as Dimitri Donskoi, defeated a southern Mongol force on the Upper Don, is celebrated as the first defeat of the Tartar hordes by the Russians.

In fact, said Gumilev, the battle was part of the conflict between the Islamic Mongols in the south and the northern Mongols known as the White Horde. The real issue at stake for the Russians was taxes. The Russians knew that they would have to pay their Mongol overlords higher taxes if the Uzbeks won.

At the close of the fourteenth century Tamerlaine defeated the northern Mongols led by Tokhtamysh but in the process, he permanently weakened the wealth of the Golden Horde. His armies devastated Astrakhan, Sarai, and the Crimea and wrecked the patterns of trade between Europe and the Orient. Northern Russia began to grow in importance.

Gumilev also demolished another myth. In 1480 the Russians supposedly threw off the Tartar yoke in a heroic stand at the River Ugra when a Muscovite army outfaced the forces of Khan Akhmad leading southern Mongols.

In fact, he said, the Russians were merely the allies of one Tartar group against another. Nor for that matter was there ever a battle because Khan Akhmad waited for a Polish-Lithuanian army and when it failed to arrive, he withdrew.

Even in the fifteenth century, Russia still acknowledged the power of the Crimean Khans and paid them tribute. Gradually the balance of power shifted in favour of the north and in the sixteenth century Moscow expanded southwards taking Kazan in 1552, Astrakhan in 1556 and eventually occupying the whole of the Volga basin.

On the Russian coat of arms, the three crowns of Moscow, Kazan and Astrakhan – the principalities of the Golden Horde – are placed above the Byzantine double-headed eagle.

Ivan the Terrible (1533–84) assumed the role vacated by the Khan of the Golden Horde, recognising only the Sultan of Turkey and the Khan of the Crimea as his equals.

The Crimean Tartars retook Moscow in 1571 and Russia continued paying them tribute until Peter the Great's time. Crimea was only absorbed into the empire in 1783 under Catherine the Great.

'The Russian state was really the successor to the empire of Genghis Khan,' Gumilev said.

When Peter the Great opened Russia up to the West in the eighteenth century and the Russian nobility began to wear European clothes, they sent their children to study in France. According to

Gumilev's researches, there they read a false version of history written by a scholar called Detui.

Detui read documents drawn up in fifteenth-century Lithuania. At the time the joint King of Lithuania and Poland wanted to conquer the Russian state and was looking for support to further his plans.

Detui based his views on documents drawn up by a Lithuanian minister called Gebbonstein who portrayed the Russians not as the partners of the Mongols but as their oppressed subjects. The Polish-Lithuanian King could therefore justify an invasion of Russia by representing it as an attack on barbarians who threatened to destroy Europe instead of an unprovoked aggression against fellow Christians.

'Russian nobles forgot their own history and accepted a new role as the frontline state on the defence of Europe against the Mongol invaders from the East,' Gumilev explained.

His stomach was giving him pain and his wife insisted we stopped there. I wondered as we prepared to leave whether his positive view of the Mongols, the stress he laid on their tolerance and humanity, was not a reflection of his own times. It had the effect of casting Stalin's brutality into even greater relief because Gumilev seemed to be saying that compared to Genghis Khan or his successors, Stalin had butchered more Russians and destroyed more of Russian culture.

As we stood up, I tried to ask Gumilev more about his prison life but he refused. Then I asked if, during this time of shortages, there was anything I could bring or send him; he looked tired and when he smiled I caught for the first time a look of bitterness in his blue eyes.

'When I was in prison no one in the West cared about me. I never once received a Red Cross parcel. No one bothered then, why should you care now?' he said.

The next day, my last day before flying back to London, I had lunch in a large deserted restaurant on Alexander Nevsky Prospekt. I met two Azerbaijanis who had heard what I was doing and were anxious to meet me. They were both large, voluble and vaguely Turkish-looking ladies. One worked in the Culture Ministry and the other was an ethnographer at the Institute of Oriental History.

They were deeply involved in the nationalist movement and deluged me with information about the history of Azerbaijan and the conflict with the Armenians. They urged me to go to Azerbaijan and write a book introducing their people to the rest of the world.

I had no idea, they said, how rich and important their contribution to world history and civilisation was ... Did I know about the Sumerians ... the ancient epics ... Alexander the Great ... Bach's music ...

'Bach's music?' I asked with a start.

'Oh yes,' they said and they both began humming Bach's Toccata and Fugue for organ.

'Do you recognise it? Now listen to this!' And they launched into a rendering of an Azerbaijani folk song.

'It's the same tune, isn't it? He borrowed it from us,' the fatter one said triumphantly.

'And do you know Jimi Hendrix? Well . . .' The not so fat one began.

'Don't tell me.' I started to laugh. 'He was from Azerbaijan too.'

It only struck me, after we parted, what the two women wanted to convey by making such curious claims about Azerbaijani music.

It was not just an expression of heady national pride after a century of Soviet domination. The point was not whether Jimi Hendrix or Bach were really influenced by their music. The truth of these claims was almost irrelevant. They wanted to show that Azerbaijan too was linked to the great whole, was part of the ebb and flow, the cause and effect of all human history.

So that one could take any thread in history and follow it through and one connection would lead to another and another, until the most unlikely parts could be seen as linked and in some way interconnected and interdependent.

And so to be isolated like Gumilev, forgotten and starving alone in his cell, must be the worst, the most terrifying experience of all. Tsong Kapa had said that not even a sprout could truly exist alone. And that we can only recognise something exists when we see it for what it is and what it will become. Only when a thing is seen in the whole, can we give it a proper name and recognise its true identity.

Otherwise I suppose that a country too could, like a prisoner in a cell, simply disappear.

Bibliography

Alioshin, Dimitri *Asian Odyssey*, 1941

Andrews *Across Mongolian Plains; On the Trail of Ancient Man*, New York, 1921

Arlington, L.C. and Lewisohn, William *In Search of Old Peking*, Oxford University Press, 1987

Bawden, Charles *The Modern History of Mongolia*, Kegal Paul International, 1989

Behr, Edward *The Last Emperor*, Bantam Books, 1987

Bell, Sir Charles *People of Tibet*, 1928

Brent, Peter *The Mongol Empire*, London, Weidenfeld & Nicolson, 1976

Bulstrode, Beatrix *A Tour in Mongolia*, London, 1920 [visited 1913]

Carruthers, D. *Unknown Mongolia*, Hutchinson, 1913

Conquest, Robert *Harvest of Sorrow, The Great Terror, Lenin*

Eliade, Mircea *Shamanism – archaic techniques of ecstasy*, Arkana, 1964

Fleming, Peter *Bayonets to Lhasa*, 1961

Great Soviet Encyclopaedia

Grousset, Rene *Conqueror of the World: the life of Genghis Khan*, Viking Press, 1972

 L'Empire des Steppes, Payot, Paris, 1939

 The Rise and Splendour of the Chinese Empire

Gumilev, Lev *Searches for an Imaginary Kingdom: Ethnogenesis and Biosphere*, 1987

Heissig, W. *A Lost Civilisation: the Mongols Rediscovered*, 1966

 The Religions of Mongolia, London, Routledge & Kegan Paul, 1970

Henning, Haslund *Tents in Mongolia*, London, 1935

Hoang, Michel *Genghis Khan*, Librairie Artheme Fayard, 1988

Hopkirk, Peter *Setting the East Ablaze – Lenin's dream of an empire in Asia*,

Oxford University Press, 1986

Huc, Regus (translated by W. Hazlitt) *Travels in Tartary*, Alfred Knopf, 1927

Jagchid, Sechin and Hyer, Paul *Mongolia's Culture and Society*, Westview Press, 1979

Karnow, Stanley *Mao and China*, Viking Press, 1972

Lamb, Harold *Genghis Khan: Emperor of all Men*, Robert McBride & Co., 1927

Lattimore, Owen *Inner Asian Frontiers of China*, Oxford University Press, 1940

Lattimore, Owen *Nomads and Commissars*, Oxford University Press, 1962

Lovett, Richard *James Gilmour of Mongolia*, Religious Tract Society, 1892

Maclean, Fitzroy *To the Back of Beyond, An illustrated companion to Central Asia and Mongolia*, 1974

Ma Ho-tien *Chinese Agent in Mongolia*, Baltimore, 1949

Malqinhu *On the Horqin Grasslands*, Panda Books, 1988

Manz, Beatrice Forbes *The Rise and Rule of Tamerlaine*, Cambridge University Press, 1989

Mehnert, Klaus *Peking and Moscow*, London, Weidenfeld & Nicolson Ltd., 1963

Mongat, A.L. *Archaeology in the USSR*, Pelican Books, 1961

Montagu, Ivor *Land of the Blue Sky*, Dobson Books Ltd., 1956

Morgan, David *The Mongols*, Basil Blackwell, 1987

Onon, Professor Urgunge *The History and the Life of Chinggis Khan (The Secret History of the Mongols)*, E.J. Brill, 1990

Ossendowski, Ferdinand *Beasts Men and Gods*, New York, 1922

Phillips, E.D. *The Mongols*, London, Thames & Hudson, 1969

Polo, Marco *The Travels*, London, Penguin Books, 1958

Prawdin, Michel *The Mongol Empire; Its Rise and Legacy*, London, Allen & Unwin, 1940

Prejevalsky, Lt.-Col. *Mongolia*, London, 1870

Rossabi, Morris *Khubilai Khan: His Life and Times*, University of California Press, 1988

Rubruk, *Travels*, Huklyat edition

Rupen, Robert A. *How Mongolia is Really Ruled; a Political History of the MPR 1900-1978*, Stanford Hoover Institution Press

Sanders, Alan J.K. *Mongolia – Politics, Economics and Society*, Pinter Reinner, 1987

Schram, Stuart *The Thoughts of Mao Tse-Tung*, Cambridge University Press, 1989

Short, Philip *The Dragon and the Bear*, London, Hodder & Stoughton, 1982

Sinar, Denis, *Inner Asia*, Indiana University, 1969

Solzhenitsyn, A., *Gulag Archipelago*, Collins Harvill

Spuler, Bertold *Die Goldene Horde; Die Mongolen in Russland 1223-1502*

The Tibetan Book of the Dead (translated by Francesca Fremantle and

Choygyam Trungpa), Shambala Dragon Editions

Tsong Kapa (translated by Geshe Lobsang Tharchin with Michael Roach) *The Principle Teachings of Buddhism* Classics of Middle Asia, Mahayana Sutra and Tantra Press, 1988

Vasel, Georg *My Russian Jailers in China*, Hurst & Blackett Ltd., 1937

Waddell, L. A., *The Buddhism of Tibet*

Waley, Arthur *The Secret History of the Mongols and Other Pieces*, London, Allen & Unwin, 1963

Webb, Beatrice and Sidney *Soviet Communism – a new civilisation*, *Mid 1930s*

Wheeler, Geoffrey *The Modern History of Soviet Central Asia*, London, Weidenfeld & Nicolson, 1964

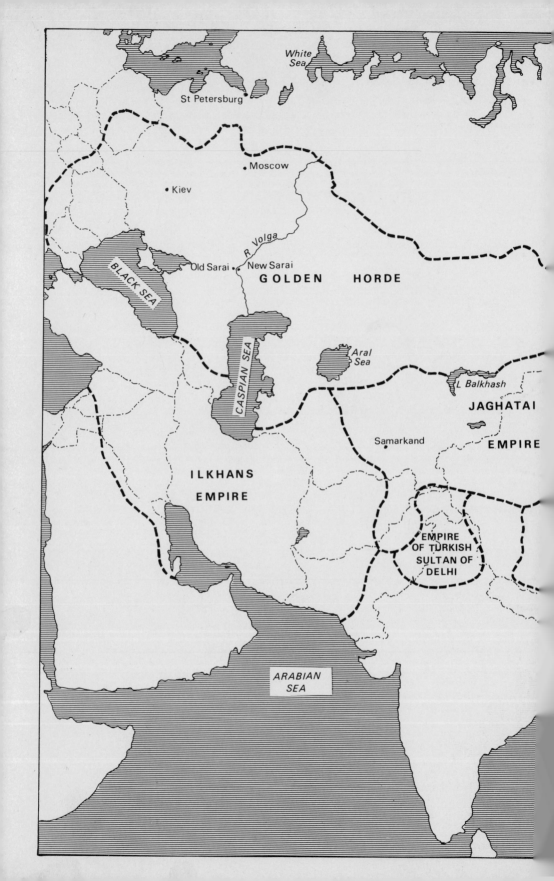